Texas Land Grants,
1750–1900

# Texas Land Grants, 1750–1900

## *A Documentary History*

JOHN MARTIN DAVIS, JR.

*Foreword by* Light Townsend Cummins

McFarland & Company, Inc., Publishers
*Jefferson, North Carolina*

**Also of Interest**

*Parole, Pardon, Pass and Amnesty Documents of the Civil War: An Illustrated History*
John Martin Davis, Jr., *and* George B. Tremmel
(McFarland, 2014)

Library of Congress Cataloguing-in-Publication Data

Names: Davis, John Martin, Jr., 1944– author.
Title: Texas land grants, 1750–1900 : a documentary history /
John Martin Davis, Jr. ; foreword by Light Townsend Cummins.
Description: Jefferson, North Carolina : McFarland & Company, Inc.,
Publishers, 2016. | Includes bibliographical references and index.
Identifiers: LCCN 2016031480 | ISBN 9781476665498 (softcover : alkaline paper) ♾
Subjects: LCSH: Land grants—Texas—History—18th century—Sources. |
Land grants—Texas—History—19th century—Sources. |
Public lands—Texas—History—18th century—Sources. |
Public lands—Texas—History—19th century—Sources. |
Frontier and pioneer life—Texas—Sources. | Ranches—Texas—History—Sources. |
Land speculation—Texas—History—Sources. |
Texas—Colonization—History—Sources.
Classification: LCC HD211.T4 D38 2016 | DDC 333.1/6—dc23
LC record available at https://lccn.loc.gov/2016031480

British Library cataloguing data are available

**ISBN (print) 978-1-4766-6549-8**
**ISBN (ebook) 978-1-4766-2530-0**



Front cover images: Mexican graphic from the letterhead of G. A. Walters, Abstracter, San Saba, Texas, *Lands, the Texas-Bridal Gift of a Separate Estate in the Republic's Marriage to the United States*, ca. 1930 (Author); painting of Sam Houston by William Henry Huddle; hand-colored stone lithograph of a West Lipan Apache warrior by A. Schott from Emory's U.S. and Mexican Boundary Survey, Washington, 1857; Map of Polk County, Texas from Texas General Land Office, 1879 (Library of Congress)

Printed in the United States of America

*McFarland & Company, Inc., Publishers*
*Box 611, Jefferson, North Carolina 28640*
*www.mcfarlandpub.com*

# Table of Contents

# Acknowledgments

During the decade-long production of this history, countless friends and associates encouraged and enlightened me. My trusted dealer, John Rowe, deserves my greatest gratitude. His gentle guidance toward significant Texana was something I only appreciated years later. He made available jewels from the personal collections of Amon Carter, Thomas Streeter and Bob Medlar. Unnamed dealers at paper shows, antiquarian book fairs and book stores enhanced this growing collection. Special mention is due the helpful staff of the Texas General Land Office, who dutifully protect the priceless State archives. The Special Collections of Southern Methodist University's DeGoyler Library and the Garrett Collection at the University of Texas at Arlington yielded details necessary to properly tell the story. Russell Martin and Ben Huseman of these respective institutions were unselfish in their time. To the "picker" supreme of West Texas, Martin Stringer, I am indebted for many unique documents filling gaps in the manuscript. Many of these roach-infested papers and pamphlets were previously unknown in the field of study. Mary Bones of the Museum of the Big Bend, Sul Ross State University, Alpine, Texas, has again deciphered and transcribed my notes, thoughts and ramblings with thoroughness. A special debt of gratitude is due Professor Stephen Alton, Texas A&M Law School, Fort Worth, and Professor Gerald Saxon, University of Texas at Arlington for their suggestions and corrections of an early draft. Historian, friend and neighbor Lonn Taylor was also encouraging. Most appreciated is the learned reading of the manuscript by Professor Light Townsend Cummins of Austin College. His subtle comments better focused this complicated history. Without the loving support of my wife, Yana, the project would have ended with my collection of Texas land documents and gone no further.

# Foreword by Light Townsend Cummins

The history of Texas rests part and parcel on the history of land ownership and the grants upon which it is based. From the time of the first European arrivals in the region to the present day, land has attracted a continuing succession of residents from many diverse places to settle today's Lone Star state. For whatever other reasons they came, ownership of land was a prime motivation for the steady stream of people who have come to live their lives in Texas. Each successive legal system in the history of Texas has left its mark on the physical array of land ownership in the state because, progressively, what came before provided a foundation for subsequent rules of law. And, to a remarkable extent, the history of Texas land since statehood is exceptional in our nation because of the criteria by which the Republic of Texas joined the union. The terms of the 1845 annexation to the United States permitted the State of Texas to retain ownership of its public domain instead of ceding it to the national government.

In spite of the historical importance of land tenure, Texas historians have been slow to provide a comprehensive exposition of the land grants upon which the state's history rests. This has been the case due to the multifaceted, subtle, and complicated legal intricacies of Spanish, Mexican, Republic, and State of Texas legal jurisdictions across time. These present profound historical complexities for historians to master. It has therefore been a difficult and daunting task for historians to sort through them. To date, few, if any, historians of land grants in Texas have had the essential combination of patience, research ability, and legal training to ferret out and integrate this complicated historical body of law into a synthetic study easily accessible by the general reader. John Martin Davis, Jr., does exactly that in this work.

This study of Texas land grants breaks new ground in expanding the historical understanding of land ownership as an integral component of the larger history of Texas. Earlier studies of the subject have mostly considered only part of the complexity embodied in the evolution of land grants, focusing respectively on Spanish, Mexican, Republic, or state laws.

Those studies dealing with the arrival and dominance of the Common Law, as well, mostly consider the activities of the General Land Office. Although an important governmental authority necessary to understanding land law, this state agency is not the only influence and determinant significant to the subject. Davis embraces a much larger and integrated approach by offering a detailed narrative that clearly emphasizes the evolution of land grants across the centuries, from the beginnings of Spanish settlement to more recent times.

Additionally, the narrative that follows in these pages also relates the development of Texas land grants to the governmental, political, economic, and social milieu of the times in which they occurred. One of the essential lessons to be learned in reading this book is that land grants, and their history, are inexorably linked to the social and political values of the eras in which they were made. Land ownership, and the way in which a succession of governmental sovereignties across the centuries implemented it, cannot be considered in isolation from the temper of its times and the larger society surrounding it. As such, land grants mirror the hopes for success of the state's citizens as defined by the various authorities that created the legal underpinnings for land ownership in Texas. The numerous illustrations in this volume further enhance the narrative discussion by driving home this point while, as graphics, they also permit the reader to cross-reference the interrelationships of the various land grants made across time in Texas. In short, this volume presents a concise and very accessible understanding of land grants in Texas history as part of a holistic approach to appreciating the story of Texas within a larger historical context.

*Light Townsend Cummins is the Bryan Professor of History at Austin College and a former State Historian of Texas.*

# Introduction

Land lured Europeans to Texas. Later, free land excited Anglo-American colonists. Land speculators helped spark the Texas revolution in 1836. Land scrip financed the new Republic. Endowed lands funded education. The symbioses between Texans and their land is legendary. To waste or trespass land are crimes of the highest order. This heritage is displayed in the hallmark of a San Saba County Title Company. An abstract for bounty land was decorated with General Sam Houston and a Mexican gentleman with a sombrero. The message read, "When Texas intermarried with Uncle Sam she reserved her own lands as her bridal gift. This constitutes her own separate estate!" (Fig. 1) This letterhead captured the inherited traditions still present today.

Cheap land was sought by Anglo-Americans who risked all for a freehold estate. *Seisin*, ownership of an estate, was reserved for only the privileged in the Old World. In the eighteenth century, the Spanish Crown used land to accomplish all manner of objectives. Native tribes were baptized on mission lands in the name of the Church. Soldiers of Spain volunteered for frontier service in return for rancheros. The Mexican government offered grants to colonial contractors for establishing new settlements. After the Texas Revolution, the Republic rewarded veterans and loyal families with land. The State of Texas would give away homesteads to populate its frontier. Far more land was granted than titled by the General Land Office. A land certificate was only the right to locate, survey and request a patent if the land was unappropriated. Only after proving loyalty and paying government dues could a settler be vested with a patented deed.

The United States initially disposed of its public domain to source national revenue. It next adopted a land policy encouraging settlement and economic development. By the midpoint of the nineteenth century it had acquired by conquest one and a third billion acres of public domain lands. At its inception the Republic of Texas came into possession of almost two hundred and fifty million acres of public lands. It too soon abandoned the sale of this valuable source of state revenue in favor of policies directed toward settlement and internal improvements. In addition to the vast acreage each granted to the railroad companies, both sovereigns granted land for roads, canals and river improvements. The federal government's internal improvement land grants only continued from 1823 to 1869. Texas programs lasted longer. The United States never owned the public domain land in Texas.

Spanish land laws are vital to Texas real estate titles. The Republic of Texas, in 1840, layered Spanish on traditional elements of English common law, creating a uniquely Texas set of rules. Land laws for the New World, compiled in 1567 under the authority of Phillip II in the *Recopilación de Castilla*, was codified in 1661 as the *Recopilación de las Indias*. Spanish rules were unfamiliar to American immigrants, but free land made the laws understandable. Until the financial Panic of 1819, American homesteads (measuring 640 acres) from the United States General Land Office cost two dollars an acre. After the Panic, prices dropped to $1.25 an acre, but parcels were only 80 acres. In contrast, Stephen F. Austin's first colonists could claim over four thousand acres at a tenth of the United States price. By midcentury the United States was rewarding veterans with eighty acres of bounty land, while Texas veterans received eight times that for similar military service. (Fig. 2)

Individuals received land grants based on their worthiness to the colony. Loyalty to the sovereign was absolute. The politically connected received special recognition. The third preferred class were military and veterans, followed by colonists. Public works contractors providing essentials such as military supplies, roads and rails were always granted priority. Specifically excluded from grant requests were Indians, blacks, disloyal individuals and aliens, except under special circumstances. Speculators, banks and foreigners were suspect unless circumstances forced the government to recognize them.

Possessing land was not legally owning land. Only through patented deeds was permanent ownership assured. The most readily available land was always located in untamed territory. Even "civilized sections" were hazardous, as noted by the English traveler Nicholas Doran Maillard in *A History of the Republic of Texas*. He described frontier Texas as full of "habitual liars, drunkards, blasphemers, and slanderers, sanguinary gamesters and cold blooded assassins." After the Civil War, the State was more welcoming. Indian hostilities were being subdued. Railroads connected most parts of the State by the 1880s. The Constitution assured a small farm to every homesteader willing to relocate, cultivate and become a permanent resident. That constitutional guarantee ended when the public domain was depleted prior to the end of the century. The United States Bureau of the Census also announced in 1890 that no open frontier remained. The century of free land was concluded, except across the Red River in the Indian Territory then opened to white settlement. Oklahoma welcomed "would-be" Texans after the State's public domain was exhausted.

During the fifty years of state-sponsored immigration, the population grew. Between Austin's first colony and the year Texas declared its land depleted, prices increased sixteen times, according to the government minimum price schedule. Market values overall were much higher because this schedule was only a minimum for unimproved, unappropriated land:

| *Year* | *Approximate Population* | *Price* |
|---|---|---|
| 1825 | 5,000 | $.125 per acre |
| 1830 | 20,000 | $.15 per acre |
| 1835 | 50,000 | $.50 per acre |
| 1840 | 100,000 | $.50 per acre |
| 1845 | 150,000 | $1.00 per acre |
| 1850 | 200,000 | $2.00 per acre |
| 1860 | 600,000 | $1.00 per acre |
| 1865 | 700,000 | $2.00 per acre |
| 1870 | 800,000 | $1.00 per acre |
| 1880 | 1,600,000 | $.50 per acre |
| 1890 | 2,200,000 | $2.00 per acre |

Several historians and researchers have described parts of the Texas land story. Three State Land Commissioners, Bascom Giles, Bill Alcorn and Gary Mauro, were responsible for pamphlets from the General Land Office. Bascom Giles contributed his personal notes to Curtis Bishop, who wrote the informative work *Lots of Land* (1949). Reuben McKitrick's century-old *The Public Land System of Texas, 1823–1910* was diligently researched. Aldan Socrates Lang's *Financial History of the Public Lands in Texas* concentrates on the revenue side of Texas land. To date, no one has compiled a documentary history of the subject. This study fills that void with grants issued to people and companies responding to government programs. Bascom Giles stated, "Land without population is wilderness." Texas was populated because immigrants were eager to fill that vacancy.

| *Disposition of Public Lands in Texas* | *Approximate Acres* |
|---|---|
| By Spanish Crown | 10,000,000 |
| By Mexican Government | 16,000,000 |
| To Texas Creditors | 3,000,000 |
| To Texas Military and Veterans | 3,000,000 |
| To Headrights Claimants | 37,000,000 |
| To Colonization Companies | 5,000,000 |
| To Homesteaders | 5,000,000 |
| To United States Upon Annexation | 67,000,000 |
| For Education | 52,000,000 |
| For Internal Improvements | 39,000,000 |
| Total Acres Disposed | 237,000,000 |

Source: Commission of the General Land Office Reports, 1889; 1902; 1910. Appendix II, McKitrick, Reuben. *The Public Land System of Texas, 1823–1910*, 158.

Mention should be made of the methodology used to construct this legal and fiscal history of Texas land grants. Illustrations were selected from the author's collection accumulated over more than three decades. The cartographic section of that collection is housed at the Museum of the Big Bend, Sul Ross State University, Alpine, Texas. The central theme of both collections is Texas land. Land documents are more obtuse in use and purpose than maps. Executions of claims and issuance of deeds often contained as many breaches in regulations as compliance; only through type grouping along a timeline do patterns reveal themselves. An almost endless variety of formats and printers, plus the manuscript documents themselves, confuse both collectors and historians. Others such as Thomas W. Streeter in his *Bibliography of Texas 1795–1845* previously detailed most printed land documents issued during the Republic and Mexican periods. His work, in multiple volumes, allowed me to concentrate on the purpose and means employed by the sovereigns of Texas to dispose of the vast Texas public domain. That legal process and financial saga has long eluded simple explanation for students, collectors and historians alike. Unlike Streeter, I did not strictly adhere to a timeline within and across chapters. Chapters are organized by the purpose for which the grants were awarded, e.g., homesteads, internal improvements, etc. Each chapter, although a vital part of the total story, is a stand-alone piece, as a strict chronology would be confusing and shed less light upon the subject.

# Chapter I

# Spanish Grants, 1750–1820

European claims to American soil were accomplished through "acts of discovery." A Christian sovereign could possess newly discovered lands after conducting a symbolic ceremony, known as "acto de posesión," that included a public display of marker boundaries and usage. This exercise formalized, in some form, Mexican and Texan claims. An example is recorded for Antonio Rivas of San Juan Bautista de Rio Grande in March of 1765. His 88,000 acres in present day Maverick, Dimmit and Webb counties, Texas, was cited in later title searches. Before three officials, Rivas "pulled weeds, threw stones, sprinkled water from the river, and made other motions of true possession." His walk across the lands was not disturbed by any person, so the possession was granted. The procedure was outlined in the "Leyes de los Reinos de las Indias." Occupation of the land by non–Christians did not defeat royal claims. Grantees had three months to mark boundaries and prove exclusive possession. Affirmative evidence such as monuments marking boundaries, planting trees and occupation demonstrated possession. Often the ceremony was postponed due to hostile natives or weather. The survey usually stated the size of the claim, but not always. Spanish grants were measured in the following[1]:

1 vara = 33⅓ inches
1 acre = 5,645.4 square varas
1 Caballería = 105.7 acres
1 Labor = 177.1 acres = 1,000,000 square varas
1 League (Sitio) = 25 Labors = 4,428.4 acres
1 Hacienda = 5 Leagues = 22,142 acres

Spain's claim to Texas dates to 1519 after Álvarez de Pineda landed and mapped the coast from Espíritu Santo (Mississippi) to Las Palmas (Rio Grande) Rivers. The Royal Governor claimed the Gulf Coast for the crown under acts of discovery. Pope Alexander VI had promised King Ferdinand and Queen Isabella all discoveries made by Christopher Columbus during his voyage to the New World. That dispensation included the privilege of granting titles to individuals. A condition of the Treaty of Tordesillas (1494) was that the crown would oversee religious instruction for native peoples. Pope Julian II in 1508 added a requirement that churches and missions be built to spread Christianity to the natives. The grant from the Pope applied to both discovered and unknown lands. All formed the basis of the Spanish system of missions, presidios and pueblos.[2]

Until Frenchman René-Robert Cavelier, Sieur de La Salle, landed at Matagorda Bay in 1685, Spain did not pay attention to lands east of the Rio Grande. Afterwards expeditions explored the land of the Tejas. Father Damian Massanet of the Holy Cross of Querétaro founded the mission of San Francisco de los Tejas (1690) and Santisimo Nombre de María (1691) along the Neches River in what is now East Texas. Attacks by natives forced abandonment in 1693, and the region remained quiet until 1715.[3]

Spanish occupation of the upper Rio Grande followed the revolt of New Mexico in 1680. Native and European refugees relocated to present day far West Texas. The Mission Nuestra Señora de Guadalupe, next to the Presidio El Paso del Norte, was protected by only four dozen soldiers most of the time. The pueblos of San Lorenzo, San Pedro, Señor José and Isleta were founded. Near present day Ojinaga, Mexico, at the junction of the Rio Grande and Concho Rivers, the Misión La Junta de los Ríos was organized in 1715. Attacks by natives forced the site to be abandoned. Not until 1773 did a European settlement return to the "La Junta." Land grants were not forthcoming for a century.[4]

French adventurer Louis Juchereau de St. Denis in 1713 traveled from Louisiana to Mexico to open trade. The Spanish Viceroy in Mexico was alarmed at the ease with which he moved from Natchitoches, Louisiana to San Juan Bautista, on the western bank of the Rio Grande. St. Denis did possess a passport. Spanish officials reacted and began to occupy the region. Between 1716 and 1721 the Spanish established the missions San Miguel de Linares de los Adaes (1717) near Natchitoches, and San José de los Nazonis (1716) and Nuestra Señora de la Purísima Concepción (1716) along the Neches River in East Texas to convert the Sis and Tejas Indians and establish trade. Less than a hundred soldiers, missionaries and civilians managed the settlements. In 1719 the Spanish settlers in East Texas were forced to retreat by the French in what is now known as the "Chicken War." The Spanish refugees relocated along the San Antonio River in Mission San Antonio de Valero (1718). Later, Missions San José (1720), San Francisco de la Espada (1731), San Juan Capistrano (1731), Nuestra Señora de la Purísima Concepción de Acuña (1731) were established. Franciscan priests founded a mission on the Rio San Antonio de Padua. The College of Guadalupe de Zacatecas controlled these missions. The Mission Fathers of Concepción, San Juan Capistrano and San Francisco de la Espada were given land grants in 1731 by the Spanish Viceroy. In 1758 Andrés Hernández received a private royal grant for four leagues and five labors. Luis Menchaca was personally granted eleven leagues and two labors in the same vicinity.[5]

Land grants to individuals since 1682 were governed by the "Recopilación of the Laws of the Kingdom of the Indies," and subsequent compilations, orders, decrees and royal resolutions between 1775 and 1804. Beginning in the last half of the eighteenth century, individuals worthy of special recognition could request large tracts for ranching in northern Mexico. For almost a century, the King had awarded tracts to colonial contractors in the New World for settling between ten and thirty families in unpopulated territories, referred to as "wastelands." If the colony was formed within the prescribed time period, a royal grant was transferred. The land was divided with one-quarter to the contractor and his family, and the balance set aside for the town, common pasture and individual lots, farms and grazing lands. Settlements were encouraged along the King's Highway. All had to contribute to public buildings such as the church, mill and town hall. Settlers had to construct a dwelling and fulfill public service and a residency requirement. New colonies could not infringe on native corn fields or hunting lands. If tribal lands were damaged, settlers were subject to removal. Each settler was entitled to only one colonial grant. The Spanish, through the efforts of José de Escandón, established colonies within the Lower Rio Grande Valley. Only one settlement north of the Rio Grande remains, Laredo, founded by Tomás Sánchez in 1755. An official inspection of this so-called "barbarous" region began in 1747. By 1750 sixty-five families resided at Camargo with another forty-six in Reynosa. The economy was ranching. José Vásquez Borrego was granted permission to cross the Rio Grande to ranch at Hacienda Dolores. The ranching community of Mier was founded two years later. In 1755 Captain Tomás Sanchez was granted fifteen leagues of ranchland along the eastern side of the Rio Grande between Jacinto and Garza. These ranchers received no government subsidies or protection. The normal stipend was 200 pesos annually for families living west of the river. All settlers were promised deeded land at a later time. The missions overseen by the College of Zacatecas had only sub-missions, or "visitas," near the ranches.[6]

Another city tracing its roots to the efforts of José de Escandón was La Bahía (1749) on the San Antonio River. There the Franciscan Fathers had established Mission Nuestra Señora del Rosario for the benefit of the Karankawa, Xaranamer and Tamique Indians. Most ranched. In 1788 Carlos Martínez, for his sixteen years of military service, was granted fifteen leagues by the Captain of the Presidio Bahía del Espíritu Santo, Luis Cazorla. Commandant General Juan Ugalde, head of the Interior Provinces, confirmed Martínez' grant. The Medina and Nueces Rivers were the border between Nuevo Santander and the Province of Coahuila and Texas. West Texas and the Big Bend were part of the District of Chihuahua, and the Pecos River served as the natural boundary. Although Trans-Pecos land grants were awarded, none were recognized by Texas until after the Peace of Guadalupe Hildalgo between the United States and Mexico in 1848.[7]

Royal Commissioners inspected the Lower Rio Grande settlements in 1757. Residents were questioned, lands inspected and a census made for the villas of Reynosa, Camargo, Mier, Reynosa (Guerrero) and Dolores on the Texas side of the Rio Grande. At the conclusion, the inspector recommended no delay in deeding lands to worthy citizens, based on their merit and seniority. Protection to Indian ancestral rights was assured. Ten years later, the Royal Commission for the Colonies of Nueva Santander confirmed the grants. "Acts of Possession" had already been performed. Engineers recommended the size and shape of parcels. After setting aside public lands, family parcels were assigned. Access to water was assured by rectangular parcels touching the stream, known as "porción."[8]

The Royal Commission delegated to chief magistrates of the villas responsibility for performing the Acts of Possession. The grant document, "protocol," was the official record. The grantee received a "testimonio" copy. A third was placed in the official repository. City dwellers received lots on condition of constructing a dwelling within two years. Residents for six or more years, known as "primitives," were entitled to two leagues of land for pasture and twelve caballerías for a farm. "Old" settlers, those present between two to six years, were entitled to two leagues with six caballerías for agriculture. "Agregados," those arriving within the last two years, only received two leagues of pasture land. Commanders of presidios received an allotment similar to "primitive" settlers, or 17,712 acres for pasturage plus a farm. Some in Rio Grande City and Laredo can trace their acreage to Royal grants from King Charles IV's Viceroy.[9]

All Spanish possessions in the "Kingdom of the Indies," were governed by a vice royalty. By treaty with the English in 1670, New Spain extended from the Pacific to the Atlantic Coast. Texas and California by the nineteenth century were administratively governed by an "audiencia" in Guadalajara responsible to the Mexico City vice royalty. A governor and commandant of the "Las Provincias Internas" oversaw revenue, judicial, military and general administrative matters. Affairs for villas and municipalities were managed by town councils (ayuntamientos), councilmen (regidores), and municipal judges (alcaldes ordinares). Local decisions were reviewed by the "audiencia" at Guadalajara if for the Internal Provinces. For a short time, Texas and New Mexico were governed from

Chihuahua. Texas and Coahuila were later placed under the "Provincias Internas del Oreinte," in Monterrey.

Not until the Treaty of Paris (1763) did Spain gain control of the Gulf of Mexico. The residents of French New Orleans learned of the shift to the Spanish Crown in 1769. The King's General for Public Finance José de Gálvez appointed Marques de Rubí to examine the territory between California and Louisiana and make recommendations regarding defense. Rubí's report of April 10, 1768, called for fewer presidios and expressed concern for the settlements' exposure to attacks by the natives. The Texas government at San Antonio was enlarged. Spanish in Los Adaes, San Saba and East Texas were relocated to San Antonio. Hundreds were affected. Refugees from East Texas petitioned officials for permission to remain. A small group under Gil Ybarbo, the largest landowner in East Texas, returned. By 1779 the refugees founded the community of Nacogdoches between the Neches, Sabine and Angelina Rivers.[10]

Rubí's plan only provided presidios at San Antonio and La Bahía. La Bahía, founded in 1749, protected the Missions Espíritu Santo de Zúñiga and Loretto on the lower San Antonio River, near Goliad. By September of 1772 all other presidios had been abandoned. "New Regulations for Presidios" assured the growth of San Antonio. Governor Domingo Cabello's census of 1783 showed the population at Presidio San Antonio de Bexar to be 2,800. Over six hundred married couples lived in the five San Antonio communities. The population was divided between Spaniards and natives, plus mestizos, mulattos and slaves. The census counted only 450 in La Bahía and 350 at Nacogdoches.[11]

Officials appointed priests to be the fiduciaries for the native peoples in the mission complexes. Once the Indians were converted to Christianity and settled, the plan was to grant them land and disband the missions. Individual grants of town lots and farms formed the pueblo. Small contingents of soldiers in presidios were spaced to assist travelers along the royal highway.[12]

Fiscal support of the missions, presidios and pueblos was constrained by limited funds in the royal treasury. The churches built were rude basílicas, sparsely adorned with religious objects often brought by the priests from Europe. The presidios were simple stockades with "torreones" or defensive towers. The soldiers often married natives, forming ties with the indigenous peoples and increasing the yearning for homesteads. As the missions became secure, civilian artisans and traders were invited to join the community. Afterwards, priests and soldiers no longer dominated the European presence in the land of the Tejas. Texas was a frontier where persons of different cultures and backgrounds contested for position and advantage.

The Jesuit missions were placed under the control of the Franciscans and College of Zacatecas after 1767. The Texas governor first confirmed Franciscan ownership of the mission lands at San José . In 1794 the San Antonio missions were notified to prepare for secularization of mission lands, as originally intended under the Royal plan of colonization. The San Antonio missions were not deeded to individuals until much later.[13]

The individual farms and lots intended for Mission Indians occurred over a period of years, often delayed by civil and church officials. Detailed inventories of church property and census of occupants in San Antonio and Bahía preceded the transfer. Irrigated parcels were surveyed in fan shapes along the networks of acequias. By the time the process was completed in 1814, the city had transformed from a villa to a municipality, but few Indians retained land ownership. Mission Valero was the last to be secularized. During the era of Republic of Texas, the General Land Office affirmed the legitimacy of these transfers to Indians. The mission lands in Chihuahua District were not secularized during the Spanish or Mexican eras. These pueblos continued to be protected by garrisons funded by the central government. (Fig. 3) Not until the last half of the nineteenth century were Pueblo Revolt natives living in the Trans-Pecos deeded land. Non-Pueblo Indians were even less successful in securing homelands.[14]

Second to be deeded after the mission grants was the four-league tract "El Rincón," located between the San Antonio River and Cibolo Creek. The 1758 deed to Andrés Hernández, who had served at a Spanish outpost, was for sixteen leagues located west of Bexar. Pioneer or "antiquos" settlers were always threatened by Indian raiding parties. (Fig.4) The soldiers at Cibolo Creek withdrew to the safety of San Antonio in 1782 resulting in the abandonment of the Hernández Grant. Not until 1830 did Canary Islander José Luis Carvajal reestablish ranching at Cibolo Crossing. Grants of land in the Trans-Nueces were recorded in Ciudad Victoria rather than in the Bexar Spanish Archives at San Antonio. Few royal grants were recorded in Texas. More common were town lots and ranches granted and recorded in Santa Fe in New Mexico. Worthy applicants would petition the governor for land. The local *alcalde* and two witnesses would verify the boundaries and absence of conflicting claims. If the location was deemed open, the public ceremony of demonstrating exclusive possession would follow. Only after a four-year residency was fulfilled would the deed be recorded in the register. Often hostile attacks by native tribes would force the homesteader to withdraw from his hand for the security of a presidio. Breaches in residency or abandonment could lead to forfeiture of the claimed estate.[15]

Enormous ranches in the Trans-Nueces region were granted to influential Spanish families. These royal grants were not patented until after passage of the Texas Validation Act of Spanish and Mexican Grants (1852) following the Treaty of Guadalupe Hidalgo in 1848. Patents were issued in the 1870s.

Some of the notable grants were the "Llano Ranch" 25-league grant (1790) to Juan José Hinojosa; the "La Feria" 12-league grant to José Mari Belli; the "Las Mesteñas" 35-league grant (1794) to Vicente Hinojosa and Dona Rosa Balli; the "Ojo de Agua" 12-league grant (1798) to Rosa María H. de Balli; the "San Salvador del Tule" 72-league grant (1798) to Juan José Belli; the "Santa Anita" 15-league grant (1798) to Manuel Gómez; the "Espíritu Santo" grant (1781) to José Salvador de la Garza; the "Concepción de Cerrictos" grant (1789) to Bartolomé de la Garza; and the "San Juan de Carricitos" grant to José Narciso Cavazos. Many smaller ranches were not validated because of abandonment, incomplete records or inadequate legal representation.[16]

Ranching settlements along the eastern bank of the lower Rio Grande did not become municipalities until after the Treaty of Guadalupe Hidalgo in 1848. Periodic attacks by Apaches, Lipans, and Comanches threatened the communities. Settlers lived in simple dwellings, "jacales," made of adobe. The royal inspector on a visit to the five "villas del norte" in 1795 described the inhabitants as "vagabonds and malefactors," and although dressed in luxury, were lazy, dissipated and "sarcastic mourners." This description was in stark contrast to the river dwellers described by Cabeza de Vaca two hundred and fifty years earlier when he reported them to be "the best formed people we have seen, the liveliest and most capable." Many original Spanish grants in this region lapsed back to the public domain after abandonment.[17]

After Spain gained control of Louisiana, settlers returned to East Texas in 1779. The Mission Nuestra de los Dolores established for the tribe of Hasinai Indians living along the Ayish Bayou had twice failed. Anglo settlers usually entered Texas though Louisiana. Lieutenant Governor Antonio Gil Ybarro was given authority to record land grants. Juan Cortés, Commandant of the military outpost, in 1792 confirmed possessory lands tenancies to worthy residents. Twenty years later Governor Manuel de Salcido traveled from Bexar to Nacogdoches to validate titles, including those acquired by assignment or through inheritance. Many grants were never deeded because the owners had abandoned the properties. Some claims were located east of the Sabine River, in Louisiana rather than Texas.[18]

During the Napoleonic War, King Ferdinand VII of Spain was replaced by Napoleon's brother, King Joseph. Mexican officials in San Antonio watched for French agents from Louisiana. Ports strictly enforced passport controls. After King Ferdinand was returned to power in Spain, civil rebellions broke out in Mexico. Father Miguel Hidalgo, a creole priest sympathetic to the principles of the French Revolution, was a leader, until he was captured and executed. Unrest followed. By 1820 a coalition of conservative clergy, politicians and property owners installed creole General Agustín Iturbide to form a limited monarchy, the "Plan of Iguala." The coalition tried to assure the supremacy of the Catholic Church and equality for creoles. Colonization was mostly dormant during this period.[19]

By decree, on September 5, 1813, the Province of Texas was transferred to Chihuahua. In November, Texas became part of the Eastern Interior Provinces along with Coahuila and Nuevo Santander. The provincial capital was moved from Monterrey to Satillo. An Englishman, Richard R. Keene, proposed to the Spanish government to settle Irish Catholics in Texas, preferably near Matagorda Bay. Less than 7,000 Europeans resided in Texas at the time. Keene suggested to the Spanish government that a colony of Europeans would discourage Americans from entering from Louisiana. Keene offered to oversee the project in return for land grants in Texas. Nothing materialized, but it opened the government to subsequent proposals. The approach had to overcome the distrust imbued by land schemes such as the "Mississippi Bubble," which had been orchestrated by John Law in France in 1720.[20]

Spanish officials, due to the weakened condition of their central government, opened settlements in Texas. In 1811 Bernardo Maximiliano Gutiérrez, from the Rio Grande villa Revilla in Nuevo Santander, attacked San Antonio and La Bahía. He was joined by Captain Augustus William Magee, U.S. Army, from Fort Jesup in Natchitoches. A counteroffensive was successful in 1813. Captain Magee died of natural causes after his capture and imprisonment. Gutiérrez survived the revolt, and later became a provincial governor. All who supported the rebellion lost their Spanish land grants.[21]

The United States and Spain formalized the border between Texas and Louisiana with the Adams-Onís Treaty of February 22, 1819. The following year a company of colonists petitioned King Ferdinand VII for permission to establish a commercial settlement of Swiss and German immigrants somewhere in Texas. Company representatives were encouraged by Spanish diplomat Luis de Onís, while in the United States negotiating the border treaty. The Swiss immigration project never materialized. A major problem was the company's insistence that immigrants be assured religious freedom because the German and Swiss families were Protestants.[22]

The Adams-Onís Treaty boundary alarmed those already settled in Texas. Most preferred an American border at the Rio Grande. Another filibuster company entered Texas from Louisiana in June 1819. Dr. James Long, of Nacogdoches, along with 300 volunteers, declared Texas independence. Volunteers were promised lands. The American rebels were defeated at La Bahía by Spanish Colonel Ignacio Pérez. After escaping to Natchez, Long reorganized, and joined forces with liberal revolutionary José Félix Tres Palacios. Long was captured and died in prison in Mexico City. Long's expedition included Benjamin Rush Milam and New Orleans merchant William H. Christy, who would later play vital roles in the Texas Revolution. These two were also captured. A prior

United States Envoy to Chile, Joel R. Poinsett, secured Milam's and Christy's safe passage back to the United States.[23]

During the Spanish period massive tracts of land were ceded to the church and individuals, but not deeded. The number of recipients was relatively small, but the acreage was large. The majority would never be patented. Most were simply abandoned. Records lost or of questionable authenticity threatened many deed applications. Grants located in the Trans-Nueces section were open to patents after the Treaty of Guadalupe Hidalgo, 1848. The common reason for a deed denial was vagueness and incomplete surveys. Even with such frustrations, over ten million acres of Hispanic grants were eventually patented by the General Land Office.[24] (Fig. 5)

Least successful in obtaining deeds were native tribes. The Lipan Apaches dominated land settled by Anglo-Americans. By the end of the eighteenth century, both Mexico and Texas failed to recognize claims for tribal homelands. The United States relocated the Tonkawas to the Indian Territory and the Mescalero Apaches to New Mexico. Despite a long presence in the four corners of Texas, Louisiana, Oklahoma and Arkansas, the Caddos endured similar frustrations in securing land. Long masters of the horse and buffalo, the Comanches remained the largest tribe in Texas, without a permanent reservation. Few tribes ever had permanent lands in Texas to which they held title. The Comanches too were expelled.

# Chapter II

# Mexican Empresario Grants, 1821–1829

The Adams-Onís Treaty disappointed many when the eastern border was set short of the Rio Grande. Economic conditions still drew Anglo-Americans to Texas. The Panic of 1819 had bankrupted American farmers and businesses. Many lost homes and the means of providing for their families. Thousands searched for a fresh start in virgin country. Lands in the western section of the United States were priced at $1.25 an acre by the General Land Office. Homesteader tracts measured eighty acres. Economic prospects in Texas at that time were not good, as described November 20, 1820, at the opening session of the "Diputación Provincial" convened in Monterrey. Agriculture was ruined. There was no local industry and state funds failed to provide for hapless inhabitants living in "deserted stretches." Towns had survived only at San Antonio, Nacogdoches and La Bahía. Outside the security of these presidios the people were subject to "the furor de los Indios bárbaros." The Mexican Commission on Foreign Relations reported in 1821 that European and American colonizers coveted the fertile lands of the Province of Texas. For security reasons, the Commission recommended that it would be good policy to encourage Irish and German emigrants recruited in New Orleans to settle in Texas. If not protected, that body feared that in the near future the United States would attempt to annex Texas, Coahuila, Saltillo and Nuevo León "like the Goths, Visisgoths and the other tribes that assailed the Roman Empire." Tadeo Ortiz, Diego Barry and Felipe O'Reilly petitioned the government for 6,000 leagues to establish an Irish and Canary Islander Colony in Texas. Nothing materialized. This was the state of affairs in Texas at the time Moses Austin received permission to bring a group of colonists to the Province.[1]

Moses Austin of Missouri was already familiar with Spanish law and language. He was permitted by contract to settle three hundred colonists on about 200,000 acres in a land concession dated January 17, 1821. After Mexican Independence and the Plan of Iguala of July 3, 1821, the royalist Arrendondo was forced to retire to Cuba and Austin's contract was suspended. The National Congress managed to pass the National Colonization Law of January 4, 1823. Although the Austin contract was approved by decree on February 18, 1823, initiation was held in abeyance. Austin's contract was confirmed April 14, 1823, after Moses Austin died. His son, Stephen F. Austin prosecuted the land claim and won the new government's approval.[2]

The National Colonization Law as well as the Law of Colonization for the State of Coahuila and Texas allowed contractors to colonize if all declared residence, promised loyalty, observed the State religion (Catholicism) and registered. None could settle within either the coastal reserve or close to the boundary with the United States. Mexican natives under Article 24 could purchase up to eleven leagues of land for about $100 plus government dues and fees. Despite the cheap price, only the most adventuresome with adequate means were willing to move to the frontier. Most new residents were simply squatters without the benefit of deeds or citizenship. Naturalization and allegiance was preceded by evidence of a colonist's good character. The pledge was solemnized by placing the right hand on the cross of "Our Lord Jesus Christ." The colonist promised to defend the government and give allegiance to only Mexico after denouncing such other potentates and not to hold correspondence with any foreign power.[3]

Austin was the only person ever qualifying as an empresario under the Colonization Act of 1823. As a result of its more generous terms, settlers received an additional labor of land (177.1 acres). Significant to Austin individually was the additional premium lands available if his colony was successful. The Imperial Act of 1823 offered the empresario three haciendas plus two labors of land for every 200 families introduced. Under the National Colonization Act of August 18, 1824, and the March 24, 1825, Act for Coahuila and Texas, premium lands were reduced to one hacienda plus five labors of land. Austin had twelve years to fulfill his contract. One-third of the premium lands could be retained, but the balance had to be sold within twenty years. Colonists had two years to cultivate their land.[4]

The preamble to the national Colonization Act of 1824 stated that the purpose of the law was "to augment the settlement of its territory, to advance the raising and increase of stock and the progress of the arts and commerce…" in regions east of the Rio Grande. Military and native Mexicans were preferred colonists. Only foreigners of good moral character need apply. Artisans were encouraged with promises of free town lots. Austin could "found one or more towns at such points as he may deem most proper." He might select a limited number of lots for himself and family. Lots not reserved for church or municipal purposes were sold at prices agreeable to the government officials. Proceeds were held for church and public purposes. Austin had trouble meeting his required numbers in order to qualify for premium lands. The unmarried men always outnumbered families. Austin devised a scheme to satisfy his quota. Unmarried men were encouraged to "unite in pairs," with one declaring as the "head of the family" in order to qualify as a family. Some "coupled up."[5]

The five-league town of San Felipe de Austin was surveyed by Seth Ingram in 1824. The community located above the Brazos River grew to a population of 1,400 whites with 400 slaves. This became for a short time the center of American culture within Mexican Territory. The Governor of Texas appointed a former *ayuntamiento*, Baron de Bastrop, to be Austin's first land commissioner. Within two years, Bastrop issued 300 titles, thereby entitling Austin to premium lands. Sylenus Castleman received the first deed. Gaspar Flores replaced Bastrop as land commissioner in 1827. Joseph White was appointed sheriff. The town on August 14, 1828, paid Sheriff White 71.4 pesos for imprisoning a murderer. (Fig. 6) The captured felon was bound to a tree and guarded by the sheriff because there was no jail.[6]

Instructions implementing the colonization plan allowed "empresarios" to recover costs incurred from the settlers such as travel, provisions and surveys. The government always expected the empresario to collect the government dues. Stephen Austin initially charged 12½ cents per acre which amounted to about $500 for a league. This charge, payable over time, was often settled by barter rather than money. (Fig. 7) The charge never covered Austin's out-of-pocket expenses. After resistance, Austin reduced his charges to only $127.50. Government dues included $60 to the contractor; $30 to the state treasurer; $15 to the land commissioners; $10 to the clerk/translator; plus a charge for the certificate of good character. Surveys cost varied: $15 for a league; for an irrigated labor, $2.50; and for a standard labor, $2.00. Additional costs were due when titles were issued.[7]

Austin's land commissioner issued titles to colonists after their property was located, surveyed and the required documents completed. Oaths of loyalty, certificates of good character, and an assurance they would adhere to the State religion were prerequisites. (Fig. 8) The deed was known as a "protocol," and was formally executed before an official and witnesses after a full recitation of the grant, boundaries and laws. Simultaneously executed was a second copy, the "Testimonio," for the settler. A third copy was deposited with the custodian for the provincial government. The process was detailed in Article 18 of the Colonization Law of March 24, 1825. Until February 9, 1828, all had to be completed on pre-taxed "stamped" government paper and prepared in Spanish. On March 19, 1827, land commissioners were instructed by the Governor of Coahuila and Texas, to preserve deeds, together with all government decrees and surveys in an official "Register." This was the beginning of the Texas General Land Office records.[8]

The second empresario, Martín De León, was a Mexican national. His permit to colonize also had several unique features. The geographic location, along the Lavaca River, was within the normally excluded coastal reserve. De León's April 13, 1824, grant had no specific boundary, expiration date or required number of colonists. De León's second grant in 1829 had both a border and a minimum requirement of 150 families. Because De León's first grant was not defined, a number of title disputes erupted. De León laid off the traditional four-league town, named Nuestra Señora de Guadalupe de Jesús Victoria. Although the majority of settlers were Mexican, some were from Ireland. Individual grants as well as the town of Victoria were surveyed by José M. J. Carbajal. Carbajal married De León's daughter, Refugia. The land commissioner issued 41 titles, automatically qualifying De León for his premium lands.[9]

The Mexican Colonization Laws grew more inviting to Americans still suffering through the Panic of 1819. Cheap farmland, tax waivers and protection from creditors were strong inducements. On March 10, 1822, a group of Tennessee investors sent D. Andres Erwin and Robert Leftwich to apply for a land concession. The representatives met Stephen F. Austin in Mexico City. But as Austin had experienced with his own grant, an unstable government delayed the Tennessee empresarios. Their petition was resubmitted in October 1824 to the Legislature of the State of Coahuila and Texas. This time the request was made only by Leftwich in the name of the "Texas Association." The grant, approved April 15, 1825, was along the Guadalupe River, ten leagues above the coastal reserve next to Austin's colony. (Fig. 9) The Leftwich boundary against De León's grant was vague.[10]

The number of families required in the Texas Association grant was 800. Within a year, Leftwich became ill and died, but before his passing he transferred ownership to the "Nashville Company," and named Hosea H. League as the agent. Settlement was delayed for years, not to resume until Sterling Robertson gained control of the Texas Association. Austin obtained a second contract, June 4, 1825, north of the coastal reserve. Land Commissioner Miguel Arciniega issued 460 titles, again qualifying Austin for premium lands. In appreciation of his second success, the Mexican government granted Austin a third contract for one hundred families, November 1827, in the so-called "Little Colony" located east of the Colorado River and north of the San Antonio Road. The four-league town of Mina (Bastrop) grew. Land Commissioner Arciniega issued fifty-nine titles to settlers in the "Little Colony." More premium lands were earned.[11]

Austin received permission in 1827 to organize the town of Matagorda. The town became the site of the Mexican custom house in 1830. The Governor of Coahuila and Texas declared, on March 6, 1834, the town of Matagorda to be a municipality. (Fig. 10) Sales of town lots were made by public auction. Speculators bought up many blocks, encouraged by liberal payment terms of two annual payments, interest free. Title did not transfer until fully paid. (Fig. 11)

Missouri colonizer Green DeWitt's 1822 empresario petition was initially rejected. He, along with several others, was successful on April 15, 1825. DeWitt could bring 400 colonists to a site between the Lavaca, San Marcos and Guadalupe Rivers, below Austin's first colony. (Fig. 12) DeWitt's settlers conflicted with De León's because of the indefinite boundaries. The town, Gonzáles, was laid out by Major James Kerr and located at the confluence of the San Marcos and Guadalupe Rivers. Due to lack of local money, the Gonzáles council issued scrip to cover operating expenses. The private currency read that it was to be "received as cash payment for $_____ [amount] on account of fees from land in DeWitt's colony, located on the River Guadalupe, District of Gonzáles, October 15, 1835." Land Commissioner José Antonio Navarro issued 189 titles to settlers after receiving the necessary surveys, certificates and registration once the residency was established. DeWitt, like Austin, earned premium lands from the government.[12]

Haden Edwards of Virginia, with his son-in-law Frost Thorn, from New York, were the third contracts awarded April 15, 1825. (Fig. 13) Their authority was for 800 families in the Nacogdoches Department of eastern Texas. Families were already "squatting" on some of the land, but without the benefit of title. The government, in deference to these claims, provided that Edwards had to recognize their rights if later proven legitimate. Hoping to clear any potential cloud on future titles, Edwards announced all had to request titles from him or risk having their rights forfeited. This agitated the community of squatters. To aggravate the situation further, Haden, his brother Benjamin, along with a representative of the "red people," Richard Fuller, declared independence from Mexico on December 21, 1826, and formed the Republic of Fredonia. Their rebellion failed and most left the district. Haden Edwards lost his empresario contract. Frost Thorn later joined DeWitt and Benjamin R. Milam in other land projects. Early squatters eventually obtained titles with the help of land commissioners José Chirino and John Durst.[13]

The Fredonia revolt was defeated with the assistance of soldiers from Stephen F. Austin's San Felipe militia. The "Republic" lasted only two months, ending on January 31, 1827. Although the Cherokees, under "Chief" Richard Fields, allied with the rebels, the union did not last long. An aftermath of the ill-fated Cherokee alliance was distrust and delay of their claims to tribal lands. Peter Ellis Bean, the Indian agent for the Nacogdoches Department, supported the rebellion and lost all of his land grants. The *alcalde* of Nacogdoches seized Bean's land and voided documents under the order from the Governor at Bexar. The United States during this period of unrest dispatched American Minister Joel R. Poinsett to Mexico in hopes of shifting the international border from the Sabine River to the Rio Grande. Mexico declined. Two years later, Poinsett presented a United States offer to purchase Texas for a million dollars up to the Rio Grande or a half million if to the Colorado River. Both offers were rejected.[14]

Richard Fields, representative of the Cherokees, on November 8, 1822, was allowed to settle Cherokees in Texas. On September 1, 1824, Fields negotiated a peace agreement with most coastal tribes. In 1826 Fields became the Principal Chief of the Cherokees. Mexico also approved 5,000 Shawnees to settle in the Nacogdoches Department. Tribal reservations were promised but no deeds were issued.[15]

The government preferred Mexican and European Catholic settlers over Protestants from the United States. Irishmen James Power and James Hewetson were given a coastal grant between the Lavaca and Guadalupe Rivers on September 29, 1826. The boundary was moved to the Nueces River on June 11, 1828, and the time period extended to April 12, 1829. The site included the old Misión Nuestra Señora del Refugio. The minimum number of families was 200, but was waived by the Legislature of Coahuila and Texas after only 174 titles were issued, and they were granted the premium lands. The empresarios had both become Mexican citizens. Homesteads were surveyed by James Bray. Land Commissioner Jon Jesús de Viduani issued deeds. In appreciation of the Irish success, the legislature granted them a three-year extension to their original six-year contract. Refugio became their seat of government, and was declared a municipality in 1834.[16]

The year after the Fredonia Rebellion, the Governor of Coahuila and Texas instructed Texas land commissioners that only colonists of good Christian character and willing to swear loyalty to Mexico would be permitted to immigrate. All oaths and land documents had to be prepared on government stamped paper, in Spanish and attested to before officials. The new towns were to be preapproved and provide for a church, town hall, market square, jail, school and cemetery, and have sixty-foot-wide streets. Lots were to be distributed only by auction. Remaining lots were opened to the public. Bridge and ferry tolls would be determined by the council. Public facilities contractors were to be selected only if qualified.[17]

A second Irish colony was awarded John McMullen and James McGloin for 200 families. On August 17, 1828, the two Irishmen were reissued a grant that had originally gone to John G. Purnell and Benjamin D. Lovell on October 22, 1825, but had been forfeited for nonperformance. The location, west of the Nueces River, was above the ten-league coastal reserve. The four-league town was named San Patricio de Hibernia in honor of the Patron Saint of Ireland. The second "Irish Colony" had a port at Powderhorn (Indianola) on Matagorda Bay. Only 85 titles had been issued by land commissioners José Antonio Saucedo and José María Balmaceda when the grant expired, even with a four-year extension. They failed to earn premium lands. Unlike the first Irishmen, officials this time did not waive the premium lands minimum colonist requirement.[18]

Englishman General Arthur Goodall Wavell assisted Stephen F. Austin while trying to resurrect his father's grant. Wavell had become a Mexican citizen after service during the Mexican Revolution. Wavell joined with Benjamin Rush Milam, from Kentucky, for an empresario award dated March 9, 1826. (Fig. 14) Milam, too, became a Mexican citizen, after the revolution. The concession was in East Texas adjacent to the border reserve along the Red River. The grant of 400 families was speculative in purpose and financed by British capitalists. Milam was resident agent and land commissioner. Although Milam issued 140 titles, the number fell short of the minimum to qualify for premium lands. The contract was not renewed after its expiration date.[19]

Ben Milam also secured a contract of six leagues. It was for three hundred families and situated between the Colorado and Guadalupe Rivers. Milam sold a quarter of this grant to Frost Thorn, Haden Edward's son-in-law, whose contract was for 400 families and dated April 15, 1825. The balance of the Milam Colorado River grant was assigned to the British capitalists. The company offered shares to the public. They claimed to have made an investment of fifty thousand pounds to transport, sustain and settle up to 600 European families. The promotional brochure "Observations Upon the Mexican Province of Texas" touted Milam's and Austin's success. Milam's land commissioner, Talbot Chambers, only issued fifty-three titles before the time ran out. The government reissued the grant to another and Milam earned no premium acreage.[20]

Ben Milam next invested in silver mine claims located within the interior of Mexico. On July 1, 1829, Milam partnered with David G. Burnet of Cincinnati to form the "Western Colonization and Mining Company." Milam tapped foreign markets for $50,000 to build a Texas sawmill and schooner to transport Texas lumber to Mexico. The promotional literature noted that the venture might also undertake a colonization project. After potential investors realized that the Company would not actually own any real estate, pending subscribers withdrew and the enterprise dissolved.[21]

David G. Burnet, prior to his arrival in Texas, had suffered several commercial failures. He received an empesario contract for 300 colonists on December 22, 1826, located in East Texas. His territory was northwest of Nacogdoches, twenty leagues from the border. Before his contract expired it was extended for two years. In 1830 Burnet joined with Joseph Vehlein and Lorenzo de Zavala to market land in the United States. Burnet's land commissioner recorded 251 titles, thereby qualifying him for premium lands. His land commissioner, George Anthony Nixon, worked out of Nacogdoches and San Augustine.[22]

Two Germans from Mexico were awarded three Texas colonization contracts. Joseph Vehlein and John Lucius Woodbury received a concession on November 14, 1826, for the settlement of 200 families between the San Jacinto and Sabine Rivers above the ten-league coastal reserve. On December 21 their quota was increased to 300 colonists. On November 17, 1828, the two businessmen were awarded an adjoining Gulf Coast reserve. Twice their grants were extended. Woodbury simultaneously participated in a twenty-three year Mexican iron and coal monopoly with fellow American John Cameron. Woodbury served as his own agent and earned premium lands. Land Commissioner George Anthony Nixon signed 358 titles. Woodbury and Vehlein assigned their contracts to the Galveston Bay and Texas Land Company in 1830.[23]

Native Mexican Lorenzo De Zavala, from Merida, became active in politics after the revolution. On March 12, 1829, he was granted lands in Southeast Texas that extended from the Louisiana border to the Neches River. The grant included the "Villa de la Santísima Trinidad de la Libertad," now simply Liberty, Texas. Within his concession lived many squatters. Land Commissioner José Francisco Madero was directed by the legislature of Coahuila and Texas to give titles to qualifying squatters even if living within the prohibited coastal zone. The land office opened in Libertad in 1831. Titles to those living west of the Sabine River were effective for residences after October 22, 1828, and those residing between the Trinity and San Jacinto Rivers were after November 11, 1828. Madero granted seventy-eight deeds. Zavala had not introduced any new settlers when he transferred his rights to the Galveston Bay and Texas Land Company on October 16, 1830. Afterwards, Zavala traveled to Europe to recruit colonists for the New York venture. Eventually Land Commissioner Nixon issued 464 titles.[24] (Fig. 15)

Austin also received a coastal grant. On April 22, 1828, he was awarded a concession for 300 families, below his original site, located between the Lavaca and San Jacinto Rivers. His kinsman John Austin laid out that colony's seat of government along Clear Creek at its junction with the Brazos River. Appropriately named Brazoria, the Mexican municipality was surveyed in the normal four-league grid. The low country contributed to seasonal diseases. Within six years officials relocated to Columbus. Stephen F. Austin served as his own land commissioner. Seventy-five titles were issued.[25]

As the "Coastal Colony" was organized, Austin published a "notice" from his San Felipe press, dated November 20, 1829, in which he detailed the steps necessary for a colonist to qualify for a deed. The emigrant had first to petition for entry to

Texas. Proof of good character, substantiated by witnesses, was a prerequisite. If acceptable, the newcomer would receive a certificate of entry. After located, the emigrant would verify if the land selected was open. If free of claims, the settler could apply for title, assuming residence and certifications were in order. The land commissioner after receiving the proper documents would accept a survey and verify that there were no property disputes. If all were satisfactory, a deed, in triplicate, would be executed before witnesses, on government tax-stamped paper. Fees and government dues had to be satisfied prior to the title being conveyed. Most colonists signed promissory notes for charges and dues. These obligations most commonly were paid with bartered goods or promissory notes. Normally, Austin's agent, Samuel M. Williams, handled the paper work. Once all was in order, the settler received a deed and one was sent to the seat of the provincial government in Bexar with the original, or "protocol," bound in the official land register.[26]

After the Fredonia Rebellion, Mexican officials were nervous with the growing number of unauthorized Americans living within the coastal and border reserves. The Texas Association or Leftwich Grant went dormant. The Texas Political Chief, José Antonio Saucedo, requested guidance from Governor José Ignacio de Arizpe regarding the Anglo trespassers. The next Political Chief, Juan Martín de Veramendi, in 1828 appointed General Juan Antonio Padilla special commissioner to examine and make recommendations regarding land occupied by interlopers. A few of these settlers were deemed legitimate because of their loyalty and contributions. Nacogdoches *alcalde* E. Chirino issued title for a three-league ranch on Loco Creek to Manuel de los Santos Coy. A four-league ranch went to the widow Helena Kimball in the name of her deceased husband James Dill for property along the Angelina River. Both clearly established their loyalty. Francisco Guerrero was denied his eight-league ranch because it was within the littoral reserve and he had been warned not to settle there.[27]

Commissioner Juan Antonio Padilla joined with Thomas Jefferson Chambers for a grant dated February 12, 1830, for lands located in North Texas allowing 800 families. Padilla once served as Martín De León's land commissioner. Padilla's service in Nacogdoches was cut short after accusations of murder. Thomas Chambers, a nationalized Mexican attorney from Alabama, served as the Surveyor General for the State of Coahuila and Texas. In appreciation for this service, Chambers was awarded over a hundred thousand acres of land. The 1830 empresario contract earned no premium lands for Padilla and Chambers because it was never developed.[28]

North Carolinian Stephen Wilson, after becoming a Mexican citizen, was awarded a contract to settle 200 families in the Panhandle of Texas on May 27, 1826. British merchant Richard Exter later purchased half that contract. The two received a second concession dated September 23, 1828, for 100 colonists that was below the Arkansas River. Exter died at sea late in 1829. Wilson sold his interest to James C. Van Dype of New Jersey. Exter's widow married Dr. John Charles Beales of New York, who hoped to fulfill the Exter contract. The utopian socialist Robert Owen made contact with Milam regarding a "New Harmony" like community in the Trans-Nueces region. Owen had been the Mexican house guest of Richard Exter during a February 1829 visit. Owen, while pressing for his colony, made overtures to the American diplomat Joel Roberts Poinsett, Plenipotentiary to Mexico. Poinsett was a business associate of Mexican Secretary of the Treasury Lorenzo de Zavala. Despite such acquaintances, Owen was unsuccessful in securing land for his Texas utopian community. David G. Burnett, after meeting the reformer in Cincinnati in 1829, described him as an honest but "misguided and infatuated visionary."[29]

Cuban Juan Domínguez y Valdez, after also becoming a Mexican citizen following the revolution, received a 200 family colonization contract dated February 6, 1829. The forty by twenty leagues in the Texas Panhandle was next to the Wilson and Exter grant. Sales agents promoted the property in New York. A former Governor of Coahuila and Texas served as Domínguez's agent. The agency published a "Map of Domínguez Grant in Texas" locating most of the land in present day Oklahoma. The New York scrip certificates were marketed by H.A. Green, A.O. Dayton and C.V.S. Kane. Scrip was denominated in leagues or labors of land. The certificates entitled owners to locate claims within the grant but were not fee-simple real estate deeds. No titles were issued.[30] (Fig. 16)

Most empresario contracts were abandoned, revoked or reverted back to the government after the contractor failed. Austin was the most successful empresario. Several contractors died before taking action, such as John G. Purnell, who received a grant on October 22, 1825, for 200 families. Colonel Reuben Ross died with two unfulfilled contracts dated May 21, 1827, and February 19, 1828. Although expired, a group of Nashville speculators tried to revive the Ross grant, naming their venture "The Ross Company." Shares gave subscribers a right to locate 3,833 acres. The validity was always questionable, and no titles resulted. Even the Governor of Coahuila and Texas, Manuel R. Arizpe, held a contract in his own name dated November 12, 1828, for 200 families, nothing developed. Later empresarios were always hindered by the Fredonia Rebellion after which Mexican immigration policies changed.[31]

Mexican officials between 1830 and 1835 continued to make large grants to favored citizens in parts of the Province of Texas already promised to empresarios. Within the Bexar and Goliad Districts, sixty-one such deeds were issued by officials including land to José Navarro, Juan Seguín, James

Patrick and Andrew Ponton. James Bowie received an eleven-league special grant November 10, 1831, for the benefit of Antonio María Enaurizar, part of which was located on the San Antonio Road and Guadalupe River. Land Commissioner José Miguel de Arciniega ceded twenty-one special grants for parcels within Austin's colonies. José Madero, land commissioner, recognized seventy-eight citizens worthy of deeded lands located between the Sabine, Trinity and San Jacinto Rivers.

# Chapter III

# Other Mexican Grants, 1830–1835

Soon after the failed Fredonia Revolution, civil government in Mexico deteriorated. A split between centralists and federalists divided the republic. After President Vicente Guerrero, a federalist, assumed his second term in 1829, Spain attempted to retake Mexico, but failed. General Manuel de Mier y Terán had completed his tour of Texas, for the State of Coahuila and Texas, in 1828. As Commandant General of the eastern "Provincias Internas," he interviewed citizens and reported on conditions. He was alarmed by the prominence of American culture in the colonies. He was satisfied with some empresarios such as De León, Austin and DeWitt. More native Mexicans immigrated to Texas. After his report, the legislators of Coahuila and Texas took action. Texas was closed to Americans and grants opened more to Mexicans.[1] (Fig. 17)

After Joel Roberts Poinsett, of South Carolina, failed to conclude the purchase of Texas from Mexico, American interest waned. The suggested purchase excluded the valuable Santa Fe Trail territory. This region was governed from Chihuahua City in northern Mexico. Land grants and governance was always separate from central Mexico. Colonization by empresarios was never adopted in this region.[2]

States beside Coahuila and Texas also encouraged American immigration. The State of Tamaulipas' Colonization Law of December 15, 1826, included Texas land west of the Nueces River. On October 28, 1830, that legislature offered to underwrite costs for towns established along the Nueces River, "the most fertile in the state." Colonists in 1833 were promised unmolested freedom in the exercise of religion and politics. Laredo was the only Texas town represented in that state's legislature, having six of the 176 electors. Land titles were authorized for Laredo residents by Decree No. 24, October 19, 1833. Governor Francisco Vital Fernández on November 23, 1834 (Decree No. 63), confirmed titles to the barrier islands located at the mouth of the Rio Grande. Few empresarios were interested in Tamaulipas land, unlike the State of Coahuila and Texas estates.[3]

One individual from the United States expressing interest in Tamaulipas was abolitionist Benjamin Lundy. Between 1832 and 1835, Lundy traveled to Texas three times. He was promoting a colony of free Negro immigrants who would cultivate sugar, cotton and rice. On March 10, 1835, the Governor awarded Lundy a contract located near the Nueces River. Civil unrest constrained Lundy from initiating the colony. Hans Wilder and Baron von Racknitz, a Danish Consul, also planned a settlement along the Nueces River. Prospective sites on the Colorado River were also examined. Disease and the Texas Revolution thwarted most of these efforts. The land records of Tamaulipas for grants made in the Trans-Nueces region during the Mexican era were archived in Ciudad Victoria, founded in 1825 as Villa de Santa María de Aguayo by José de Escandón. Some land records were held in the Mexican towns of Mier, Reynosa, Camargo and Guerrero.[4]

Even less active than empresarios in the lower Rio Grande valley were those in the Trans-Pecos region of the State of Chihuahua. The Indian lands held in trust after the Pueblo Revolt were not deeded until after the Mexican War. The San Antonio Indians always fared better than the New Mexican tribes in securing lands. The *alcalde* of Bexar began to issue Indian titles in the 1830s. Natives were entitled to homesteads under the Coahuila and Texas Decree No. 177 of May 2, 1831. Unclaimed or "extinguished" mission lands within the towns of San Antonio, Goliad, Nacogdoches and Victoria were auctioned off to the public at large. As early as 1826 the Cherokee representative, John Dunn Hunter, tried to formalize Indian titles, but was unsuccessful.[5]

Before mission lands were secularized in the 1790s, church officials were allowed to withdraw essential church property. Residents of San Antonio became land owners beginning in 1834. That same year the government divided the Province of Texas into three land divisions. San Antonio was the headquarters for the Department of Bexar. Stephen F. Austin's colony at San Felipe de Austin was responsible for the Department of Brazos. Nacogdoches was in charge of the Department for eastern Texas. Both the Spanish and English languages were administratively acceptable for matters of commerce. Only the Castilian dialect was acceptable for religious and legal affairs. Each department had a sheriff and was entitled to legislative representation.[6]

Members of the so-called "friendly" tribes from the United States suffered delays in their requests for land. The Political Chief of the Department of Bexar in 1830 forwarded requests from the Coushatta and Cherokees to Governor José Maria Letona. The Governor appointed José de las Piedras as a special land commissioner to accomplish Indian transfers from Nacogdoches beginning in March 1832. Two years later Chief Richard Fields was still waiting. The Indian Agent, Peter Ellis Bean, assured Cherokees their patience would be rewarded. Coahuila and Texas authorized lands for friendly tribes on May 12, 1835. The reservations were to serve as buffers between the white settlers and hostile Indians. Events precluded these grants from being deeded.[7]

The *alcaldes* for the Ayish and Teneha Districts, Elisha Roberts and J. Harrision, lobbied for the removal of the Texas Choctaws to Arkansas. The tribe members had to exit before petitioning to reenter. The Governor left it up to the local settlers to force the Choctaws to leave. The Caddos and Coushatta had settled near Libertad in eastern Texas. Commander General Perfecto de Cos tried to protect them from white settlers. Although the Spanish Archives of the General Land Office contains a December 24, 1824, contract for a square mile of land for each member to be located west of the Colorado River, none was deeded.[8]

The Congress of Coahuila and Texas, on April 6, 1830, modified its colonization law. Significant to empresarios was Article 11, which declared available for Mexican settlement lands previously granted to contractors if not occupied by immigrants who qualified for Mexican citizenship. The provision effectively suspended most empresario contracts. Excluded was Stephen F. Austin because of his prior loyalty to the government. The decree encouraged future Texas immigration only by Mexicans and Europeans. Mexican citizens with twenty-year residence were allowed to purchase a league and a labor of Texas land at half the posted price. For Texas residents of forty years, the land was free. The awards were in appreciation for those Mexicans defending settlers from "savage tribes." Proof of residency had to be certified by local officials. Land commissioners would issue title only if the Governor was convinced each was loyal and worthy. The land could not be sold for four years.[9]

Governor José Mari Viesca of Coahuila and Texas, on April 25, 1830, gave detailed instructions to Texas land commissioners after passage of the Colonization Law of April 6, 1830 (Decree No. 128). All officials were advised to be vigilant before admitting foreign colonists, especially any from the United States. Proof of good character and loyalty to Mexico were essential for entry, plus oaths of allegiance. The "Instructions" reminded commissioners of all the requirements under the Colonization law of March 24, 1825, regarding land titles. Colonists again had to use stamped paper for both original and attested copies of land documents. Repeated were rules concerning surveys, streets, squares and public structures. Artisans could only receive a free lot if they constructed a home. Town maps had to be charted and forwarded to the seat of government. Ferries at vital crossings were required to be publicly funded and tolls regulated.[10]

Article II of the National Colonization law of April 6, 1830, virtually revoked any executory colonization contracts, except those held by Mexican or European empresarios. Italian General Vicente Filísola, a commander for Agustín de Iturbide, became a naturalized Mexican citizen. He was awarded, on October 15, 1831, an East Texas grant that allowed 600 Mexican and European families. The site was adjacent to the Cherokee reserve along the Trinity River. After General Mier y Terán's death in 1832, General Filísola was appointed Commandant General for the Provincias Internas. His official duties diverted him and no titles were issued for his grant. The Cherokees were granted lands September 1, 1831, and the Shawnees on April 16, 1825, but neither were deeded.[11]

Several Americans received grants after changes in the Colonization Law of 1830 because of special circumstances. James Bowie, a former slave trader and land speculator from Tennessee, also took Mexican citizenship, became a Catholic and married the daughter of the first *alcalde* of Bexar, Juan Martín de Veramendi. Bowie's father-in-law made connections in the Department of Monclova, enabling Bowie to build a cotton and woolen mill in Saltillo. His company was chartered three days before his citizenship was approved by the Legislature of Coahuila and Texas. Bowie's wife died in 1833. After a return to the United States, Bowie purchased eleven leagues of land along the Guadalupe River, north of the San Antonio Road. He also served as land agent for several speculative land companies. Saltillo physician Dr. James Grant of New York also was nationalized. He was given a ten-year license to manufacture cotton and wool goods in 1834. Both his franchises included three leagues of land as incentives for economic development.[12]

The National Congress, on April 28, 1832, amended the Colonization Law of Coahuila and Texas (Decree No. 16) dated March 24, 1825. Afterwards, only Mexican citizens could acquire lands in Texas. No American empresarios need apply. Mexicans contractors could settle ninety families at a time if done at their own expense. Contract terms were reduced from six to four years. Upon the establishment of thirty families, the contractor could request a town site of four leagues. Wealthy Mexicans individually could also purchase eleven leagues in Texas for ranching or speculation. Purchasers were charged for grazing land, at a rate of $200 along the coast. Inland ranches cost $100 per league, unless irrigated, which was $150. In the frontier, a league of land was only valued at $15. None could purchase land if precluded by the law of April 6, 1830, such as an American. Although the law excluded sale of the eleven-league tracts to Anglos, some Mexicans purchased land and resold for a profit to Anglo-Americans. Samuel Williams served as land agent for many of these speculators.[13]

Another method used to populate Texas at this time were grants to landless Mexican ranchers. The Legislature of Coahuila and Texas on April 28, 1832, authorized the *alcaldes* of Goliad and San Antonio to donate veteran lands to "republican citizens." The directive resulted in sixty-one titles. Included among the recipients were such familiar Texas names as José Antonio Navarro, Juan Seguín and Andrew Ponton. Under Article 26 of that decree, the Mexican secretary of state accepted applications detailing the veteran's service record worthy of recognition. If the Secretary deemed the veteran of "special merit and services rendered the country," the *alcalde* could issue a title. Credible witnesses were essential to securing donation grants.[14]

More Mexican troops were sent to Texas after suspension of American immigration. Other changes followed. Land sales were a vital source of state revenue for Coahuila and Texas. Mexican contracts under the National Colonization Law of April 28, 1832, then became speculative in nature. "Beales and Grant," "Soto and Egarton," and "The Mexican Company" took advantage of this speculative opportunity. In the fall of 1833, Tadeo Ortiz was appointed Director of Colonization in Texas and charged with enlisting in New York City incoming German, Swiss and Polish emigrants to settle in Texas, to offset the influx of Anglo-Americans entering from Louisiana and Arkansas. His plan was to recruit two hundred families for grants located along the coastline and islands between Corpus Christi and Matagorda. After receiving his 5,000 pesos stipend and travel expenses, Ortiz died en route to New York, October 18, 1833. The plan was abandoned.[15]

The suspension of immigration was repealed by the Mexican Congress on November 21, 1833, and the Legislature of Coahuila and Texas on December 7, 1833. Unexpired empresario contracts again could qualify for premium lands, if contracts were fulfilled. The State Legislature revised its immigration law through Decree No. 272 of March 26, 1834, by offering a labor of land for a minimum bid of ten dollars. Squatters living east of Austin's colonies could now request deeds if deemed loyal. Suspended empresarios applying for premium lands had to prove that any delay in colonization was through no fault of their own and they had invested at least $10,000. No new colonization contracts were granted. Foreigners had to be nationalized and domiciled for a year before title applications were accepted. Land Commissioners Carlos S. Taylor and George W. Smyth issued 336 titles under these acts.[16]

The most active developer during the post-suspension period was Dr. John Charles Beales of New York, who had moved to Mexico to practice medicine before marrying the widow of Richard Exter, María Dolores Soto. Dolores had inherited half of the Exter-Wilson 1826 grant. Dolores owned another eleven leagues in central Texas in her own name. After the marriage, Beales joined with Manuel Royuela and received a March 14, 1832, contract for 200 families to be settled between the Guadalupe and Colorado Rivers, on ground previously awarded to Benjamin Milam. Beales and his brother-in-law, Captain Fortunato Soto, formed the "Mexican Company" on May 1, 1832, and acquired parts of the old DeWitt grant, which they combined with the contract dated October 9, 1832, owned by Dr. James Grant. This included the expired Vehlein-Woodbury property. Another grant lay between the Rio Grande and Nueces Rivers. The settlement called for 800 families. Beales' final enterprise was with fellow New Yorker William Henry Egerton, a naturalized citizen in Matamoros. The two partnered with Captain Soto for a January 1, 1834, contract for 800 more families.[17]

Beales, along with his associates, marketed thousands of Texas acres in New York. The Exter-Wilson grant of 5,600 leagues was extended and combined with the "Twenty League Boundary Strip" before assignment to the Arkansas and Texas Land Company. The property had been broadly surveyed by Alexander Le Grand, after which it was unsuccessfully promoted to English investors. (Fig. 18) Royuela released his interest in this contract on October 11, 1832. As the time of expiration of the Wilson grant approached, Beales, on April 29, 1833, transferred rights to the "New Arkansas and Texas Land Company." Investors in the Arkansas and Texas Land Company were permitted to exchange their shares for "New" company securities. The New York officers were Daniel Jackson, Thomas Ludlow Ogden, Edward Curtis and attorney John Woodward. Woodward received four million acres in scrip for arranging the complex series of transactions.[18] (Fig. 19)

Beales, Fortunato Soto, Mariano Domínguez and Juan Mila de la Rosa organized, on May 1, 1832, "The Mexican Company" for settlement of 800 families. Their agent was Juan Vicente Campos. Beales and Grant combined this contract, on October 9, 1832, with the old DeWitt and Milam grants to form the New York "Rio Grande and Texas Land Company." The merged association owned rights between San Antonio and Laredo, from the Nueces to the Rio Grande. The 800 shares of the August 21, 1834, chartered company represented 10,000 acres in the form of "rights to locate." Original shareholders included Beales (300); Thomas E. Davis (93⅝); Charles Edwards (31¼); Samuel Swartwout (unknown); J. Watson Webb (unknown); and five other New Yorkers. Dolores Exter Beales added her eleven leagues to this venture. The 1834 colony was laid out on Los Moras Creek near present day Eagle Pass on the Rio Grande. Although over fifty English settlers tried to form a town, drought and Indians defeated their efforts and a year later the venture was abandoned. Land Commissioner Soto never issued any titles.[19] (Fig. 20)

The "New Arkansas and Texas Land Company," successor to the Beales and Royuelo Grant of March 14, 1832, became the "Colorado and Red River Land Company," located on the Colorado and Guadalupe Rivers and west of there. The least valuable of their holdings was the vast stretch surveyed by Le Grand. This "bulked up" offering enhanced their promotional efforts. It was commonly referred to as "Beales Colorado Grant." Stock certificates were signed by Beales as "Empresario," along with two trustees, Ebenezer Joseph and S.R. Childs, and Secretary L. B. Woodruff. Shares only represented a "right to locate." (Fig. 21) No titles were issued, although the shares were actively traded. Beales received no premium lands from any of his ventures. He claimed to have invested over $100,000, but failed to convince authorities he was entitled to any premium award. Attorney John Woodward received compensation for his legal efforts. All benefited from the securities sales to the public.[20]

Beales advertised his colonies in New York newspapers. Promotions for "The Rio Grande and Texas Land Company" reported an expedition would depart New York in January 1835 to Texas where Dr. Beales and his family awaited in their new residence. All tracts were "guaranteed" healthy and rich, with assurance of titles after establishing residency. Land was valued at ten cents an acre in the marketing brochures. Steerage passage for couples was $25 and $5 for a child and $15 for a single adult. Emigrants had to provide provisions for a half year. Most of the emigrants were English. Dr. Beales appointed his brother-in-law, Captain Soto, surveyor for the colony. Travel was arranged through Charles Edwards or Dr. Beales located at 57 Broadway, New York.

The genesis of what became "the animating pursuit of speculation" originated with the 1830 chartered "Galveston Bay and Texas Land Company." The venture was a consolidation by three contractors. After the Mexican suspension law, three empresarios transferred their colonization contracts to the New York company in hopes of salvaging some value. Without approval of the Mexican government, the desperate empresarios vested power in a board of trustees: George Curtis and Anthony Day of New York, and Bostonian William Summer. The venture sold Texas scrip to the public. Their inventory included over three million acres of unsold land. Agents were John Prentiss and Samuel Swartwout. The one thousand certificates entitled owners to locate unclaimed land, then survey and pay fees and government dues to receive a title. The land certificates were denominated in either labors or leagues.[21] (Fig. 22)

Although not prohibited by Mexican law, land scrip issued by companies was never mentioned in the Mexican Colonization Laws. The settlers had to pay normal charges, plus the cost of a share in the Galveston Bay and Texas Land Company. Scrip was sold to other speculative companies. The "Union Land Company" in 1831 acquired twenty-eight leagues of Galveston Bay and Texas Land Company scrip. The four-partner venture was headed by Henry Bowdoin Prentiss. A small group of settlers from New York tried unsuccessfully to establish a colony halfway up the Trinity River. The scrip passed on to "The Trinity Land Company" of New York in 1834; it eventually held 142 leagues. That venture tried to place over a hundred settlers but the revolution cut short the colony in 1835. Scrip was initially valued at a nickel, but advanced to a dime an acre. José Antonio Mexía sold scrip in Europe. Later, the Republic of Texas refused to recognize the Company's rights to do business as a foreign land company. Equitable titles were eventually patented to actual settlers and 251 titles were issued.[22]

The resident agent of the Galveston Bay and Texas Land Company, Archibald Hotchkins, conducted negotiations with agents for acquisition of the Filísola land grant. Benjamin Hawkins, agent for the Creek Nation, wanted to purchase tribal lands. Earlier the Indian agent at Nacogdoches, Colonel Peter E. Bean, complained to the United States, that the Creeks were unlawfully entering Texas just as the Choctaws had done years before. By 1835 it was alleged that 5,000 Creeks from Alabama were in Texas. Hotchkins was unable to strike a deal for the dormant Filísola contract and the grant was never fulfilled and no titles were issued. Others, such as South Carolina diplomat Joel Roberts Poinsett, invested in the Galveston Bay and Texas Land Company scrip. Litigation associated with the Galveston Bay and Texas Land Company continued for years. Lawyers involved in the long enduring case included James Pinckney Henderson, Sam Houston and John C. Watrous.[23]

While Beales and the Galveston Bay Company sold scrip, Austin continued in his colonization efforts and his colonists received deeds. Sterling Robertson and Alexander Thompson revitalized the Leftwich-Nashville Company grant located between the Navasota, Brazos and Colorado Rivers. Complicating their application was suspension of the Mexican emigration law. Austin was substituted as agent and joined with Samuel Williams to secure an extension for Sterling Robertson's Nashville company. The so called "Upper Colony" grant was issued to Austin and Williams on February 25, 1831, for 800 settlers. It included parts of the revoked De Zavala and Vehlein contracts. Only Mexican and European colonists could qualify as colonists. (Fig. 23) Williams sold one million acres carved out of the grant to speculators. Austin was frustrated by his partner's speculation and sold his interest to John Austin, Jr. Years of litigation followed. Land Commissioner Richard Rodgers Peebles ultimately issued 152 titles.[24]

Sterling Robertson, as empresario of the "Texas Association," was angered by Austin's and Williams' apparent deception. The open land was sold to speculators for about $50 a league. (Fig. 24) After efforts by agents in Mexico, Robertson was confirmed as the legitimate empresario. The legal case went back and forth through the courts and statehouse in Coahuila and Texas. Land Commissioner William H. Steele ultimately issued 279 titles from the town of Viesca. By decree, on May 18, 1835, the governor recognized Sterling Robertson's contract dated April 29, 1834. Judge Thomas Jefferson Chambers served as the translator for the "Robertson Colony" and "Nashville Company." Attorney Archibald Wynns of Houston represented the companies through 1843. Robertson, after years of lawsuits, finally received thirty leagues of premium land for the benefit of the Texas Association.[25]

Mexico endured a decade of unrest after Vice President Anatasio Bustamante deposed President Vicente Guerrero in 1831. Santa Anna and Gómez Farias became president and vice president. Farias installed the "Reforms of 1833," affecting the church and public education. Santa Anna in 1835 dissolved Congress and replaced officials and states with departments. Governors were appointed rather than being elected. Many protested the seizure of power and centralized government. Land grants by governors were ordered to be discontinued. Although several northern states revolted, only Texas would be successful. Texas land deeds and transfers were suspended by order of Mexican officials.

The State of Coahuila and Texas donated over 1,700,000 acres to individuals. Another 7,500,000 acres were sold to wealthy Mexicans. This accounted for half the land disposed of during the Mexican period. About a hundred individuals received eleven leagues or more, representing a third of all sales. Most transfers occurred during the suspension of Anglo colonization. On April 19, 1834, Governor Agustín Viesca announced that 400 leagues of Texas land was to be sold. Proceeds were needed for the militia. The lobbyist for the Galveston Bay and Texas Land Company, John Thomson Mason, a native of Virginia, was active for the speculators. Mason purchased 300 leagues in his own name under Decree No. 278, dated June 19, 1834. James Bowie served as Mason's land commissioner.[26]

Before John Mason could prefect his leagues, he was forced to pay an additional $26,000 to the government. The legislature refused to recognize the sale to Mason under the militia act of 1834 because the decree was intended only to benefit those who had defended towns from the "perfidy, rage, and barbarity" of hostile Indians. Governor Viesca, short of funds, issued emergency Decree No. 293 on March 14, 1835, granting 400 leagues to any who would provide volunteer militia. Samuel W. Johnson, Samuel M. Williams, Francis W. Johnson and Richard Peebles took up his offer in return for several leagues of land. The Governor appointed Radford Berry, the *alcalde* of Nacogdoches, to title these lands between August and December 1835. Included among the forty buyers of these leagues were Gail Borden, Jr., and Thomas F. McKinney. Most land was located between the Sabine and Trinity Rivers. Such dispositions were noted as "sold" in the official register. Later most of the league grants, such as ones to John A. Roberts and David Wade, were deemed invalid and reverted back to the government.[27]

Samuel May Williams and John Durst purchased fifteen-league parcels scattered along the Sabine, Trinity, Brazos and Angelina rivers. John Durst for years had traded with the Indians, accompanied by his brother, Joseph, *alcalde* of Nacogdoches. Land Commissioner Carlos S. Taylor issued titles for the Williams and Durst leagues. The Mexican National Congress annulled Viesca's sale to Williams and Durst on April 25, 1835, because it was considered contrary to the Colonization Law of August 18, 1824. The Government of Texas would respect this revocation, declaring void all titles flowing from Williams and Durst. Samuel Williams and John Durst were well-situated to speculate. They both represented Texas in the state congress in 1835. In 1836 the two were accused of fraud stemming from their acquisition of their eleven-league grants.[28]

As troops of General Martín Perfecto de Cos, Santa Anna's brother-in-law, marched to the capital of Coahuila and Texas, the state legislature authorized Governor Viesca "to take of himself whatever measures he may think proper for securing the public tranquility in the state." Decree No. 297 of April 17, 1835, allowed the governor to use land and rents on public property to pay for troops in defense of the city. On April 20, the governor sold land to legislators including James Grant and David J. Toler. These were resold to speculators. John Cameron, as land commissioner, issued a dozen titles. Most land was located near the Red River. All deeds were deemed invalid by the Government of Texas. Thomas Jefferson Green's "The Texas Land Company" was also an eleven-league grant grab prior to the revolution.[29]

As a consequence of the political unrest in Coahuila and Texas, Mexican lawmakers appealed for support from Texas squatters. On May 2, 1835, Decree No. 309 allowed East Texas squatters to file requests for deeds along with proof they were loyal and resided on the property before April 21, 1832. No longer was permission from an empresario required. More recent squatters were allowed to purchase their land for $60 a league. Old-timers received the property gratis except for government dues.[30]

As the Mexican rebellion spread into Texas, officials resorted to other tactics to win over allies. War Minister José María Tornel assured Indians that if the Texans were subdued and rebels expelled, their promised homeland would become a reality. Slaves were offered freedom. Mexican soldiers fighting the rebels were promised confiscated lands. Although Mexico had outlawed slavery in 1829, as proclaimed in the "Guerrero Decree," Texas slaveholders were exempted from the Mexican law. Other than a few abolitionists, the late-date proposal benefitting Indians and African Americans went unheeded. Mexican officials threatened the rebels with tariffs, dismissal of empresarios, expulsion of Anglo immigrants and emancipation of slaves.[31]

The last land decree affecting Texas was passed May 18, 1835, by the Legislature of Coahuila and Texas. The lawmakers set aside ten leagues of grazing land west of the Rio Grande for the citizens of Guerrero, located on the west bank of the Rio Grande. In establishing the municipality normal provisions for water, as required by Decree No. 266 of March 8, 1834, were waived. The towns of Giyedo, Nova, Allende and Morelos were surtaxed 5 percent annually to provide water for the municipality of Guerrero. The new town was abandoned as uninhabitable due to drought and raids soon after its founding. During this period Texas municipalities were forced to issue scrip to pay governmental expenses. The Municipality of Gonzáles, Green DeWitt's colony, issued Scrip No. 2 for $18 to reimburse delegates to the provincial assembly to discuss actions necessary during those unsettled times.[32] (Fig. 25)

# Chapter IV

# Loan Scrip Certificates, 1836–1863

The Coahuila and Texas legislature closed their session as members fled, ahead of General Martín Perfecto de Cos's arrival in Monclova on May 21, 1835. Between the disbanding of the legislature and declaration of Santa Anna's "Seven Laws," the State of Zacatecas revolted. Subsequently Coahuila and Texas was divided into three departments: North Coahuila (Monclova), South Coahuila-Rio Grande (Saltillo) and Texas (Bexar). Governor Viesca, escaping from Monclova, was captured en route to San Antonio. The Centralist government of General Santa Anna was in control by October 1835.

General Perfecto de Cos declared null and void all land sales by the Governor of Coahuila and Texas under his Decree No. 293 of March 14, 1835. Land commissioners in Nacogdoches were instructed to close their offices until the political situation calmed. Government dues continued to be remitted to officials in San Felipe. (Fig. 26) In San Augustine and Nacogdoches, the Texas Committee of Safety confiscated dues and custom funds. J.L. Hood, Jacob Garrett and Pierre J. Menard were appointed by the provisional government to be custodians for San Augustine and Nacogdoches. J.H.G. Borden and R.R. Royal became custodians of the other two departments, under provisional government orders.

Mexican troops withdrew from the Texas garrisons at Anáhuac, Velasco, Nacogdoches and Tenoxititlan. The garrison at Gonzáles was taken by the Texans. General Santa Anna's troops were attacked by Texans at Bexar Municipality. Santa Anna's brother-in-law surrendered the town on December 9. Benjamin Milam died in the battle. Santa Anna arrived in late February to defeat the Texans at the Battle of the Alamo. Another empresario, Dr. James Grant, fell during a skirmish at Agua Dulce Creek. On November 7, 1835, the Texas Provincial Government in its "Organic Laws" debated many grievances concerning land. The Texas assembly declared null and void "fraudulent" "Eleven League" grants. Delegates also took actions to protect pending titles. Texas volunteers were promised land for their military service.[1]

Some individuals helped finance the revolution. Donations were crucial because the provisional government had few resources and no credit. Thomas Jefferson Chambers recruited troops for the Texas Army throughout the south and paid enlistment bonuses with personal funds. Chambers spent over $9,000. As "Commandant General of the Army of Reserve for the protection of the Liberties of Texas" he was authorized "to pledge the faith of the Republic, for the means to raise equipment, possession, and transport." Chambers issued 6 percent promissory notes receivable "in discharge of debts due the Republic for lands." A few were redeemed, but most were discounted to brokers who used them to pay dues on land purchases. Congress later thanked Chambers after approving his claims for reimbursement in 1838.[2] (Fig. 27)

The Mexican legislature of Coahuila and Texas had appointed three land commissioners "to take charge of the examination of land titles that may be in dispute in what was formerly called the Province of Texas." The "Commissioner General" was to be paid $1,500 annually. The two-year appointments for commissioner and secretary were open only to Mexican natives. The jurisdiction included the Departments of Bexar, Brazos and Nacogdoches. Land commissioner Carlos S. Taylor continued to operate in Nacogdoches despite the Texas closure order. Article XIV of the November 13, 1835, Plan for the Provisional Government of Texas declared all land commissioners, empresarios and surveyors suspended until "a properly systematized land office" was established. Disregarding that order, several offices remained open and continued to issue deeds. Especially troublesome were titles to late-date "Eleven League" grant holders.[3]

The Anglo-Americans were upset with Mexican land commissioners. The Commissioner of the Texas General Land Office would eventually record sixteen million acres from the Mexican period. A number of these late grants and sales were voided. The Republic of Texas began its existence with over two hundred million acres of public land. Mexican dues and taxes were confiscated by the Texas provisional government. The new government considered itself the legitimate successor to all Mexican property within its border.[4]

Texas took control of government funds due on unpaid land sales and other deposits. The Provincial Government, on December 28, 1835, informed all with outstanding balances such as taxes and fees to pay these to the newly appointed Texas collectors. The practice continued in the Republic. Some debts dated back to Stephen F. Austin's first colony. The collector for the Department of the Brazos, Gail Borden, was the most active. Receipts evidencing full payments of dues and fees were necessary to secure land patents.[5] (Fig. 28)

Texans never forgot the late Eleven League "land grab" by speculators. These bargain sales to a few speculators devalued all other grants. The Texas Constitution and Supreme Court declared null many of these transfers. Among those voided and reverting back to the Texas public domain were:

| *Name* | *Titles* | *Leagues* | *Acres* |
|---|---|---|---|
| Austin and Williams Colony | 74 | 61 | |
| Burnet's " | 3 | 3 | |
| Vehlein's " | 13 | 9 | |
| Zavala's " | 24 | 24 | |
| Robertson's " | 3 | 3 | |
| C. A. Taylor, Commissioner | 92 | 88 | |
| G. W. Smythe " | 55 | 66 | |
| Berry, Alcalde of Nagocdoches | 6 | 40 | |
| Williams et al. "League" Grants | 24 | 237 | |
| Other "League" Grants | | 10 | 100 |
| J. Zekainki | 1 | | 1,107 |
| J. Hibbens | 1 | | 4,428 |
| James Power | 1 | | 97,416 |
| Howard Robleau | 1 | | 4,428 |
| J. Haynie | 1 | | 4,428 |
| Smith and de la Garza | 2 | | 17, 712 |
| Total | 301 | 629 | 170,148 |

Just under three million acres were recovered and added back to the vacant lands of Texas. A large number of these were titled by George Anthony Nixon as land commissioner. He ante-dated hundreds of deeds after the suspension order of November 13, 1835. Grantees received titles prior to the closure date because of Nixon's fraudulent actions. Some transfers managed to pass as legitimate.[6]

The Texas General Council, during November 1835, held secret sessions to consider finances. The Committee on Finance declared that "money is the sinew of War." After considering possible sources of revenue, the report concluded that the only available means was the Republic's public domain. The Committee had at its disposal almost 250,000 square miles. The Committee hoped to raise $250,000 annually from land sales. The critical concern was an uncertain market. Until victory, the government had to rely on tariffs and duties.[7]

The logic of the Finance Committee was theoretically sound, but practically difficult. Customs and taxes required regulations, assessors and collectors. The Provisional Government had no tax machinery or personnel. The General Council appointed Stephen F. Austin, Branch T. Archer and William H. Wharton to be "public agents" to secure a million dollars in loans from the United States. The offering of ten bonds of $100,000 each, at 10 percent interest, were to be five to ten year terms. The Convention allowed public land to be pledged, if the bonds could not be "advantageously negotiated." Two New Orleans banking houses served as the Government depositories.[8]

In the interim, for cash needs, Thomas F. McKinney of McKinney & Williams of Velasco was authorized to borrow "as speedily as possible" $100,000 through short term loans with interest at 10 percent. Although authorized January 8, 1836, the bonds were part of the general funding act of December 4, 1835. McKinney & Williams became the purchasing agent and were reimbursed for advances. Not until statehood did the firm finally receive settlement. Land scrip was occasionally used to satisfy portions of government debt. Manuscript "Certificates of Title" for 640 acres were issued in 1836 from the seat of government at Harrisburg in return for such advances.[9] (Fig. 29)

The Texas loan commissioners entered the United States to "solicit loans and volunteers, arrange credits for munitions and equipment, fit out warships, and do whatever they could to commit the Government of the United States to recognition and eventual annexation of Texas should [it] declare independence." Others assisted the commissioners. William Bryan was appointed purchasing agent for North America, effective January 14, 1836. Edward Hall served in a general capacity. Toby and Brothers of New Orleans became the Government's chief financial agent. Thomas Toby was a successful New Orleans merchant and doctor. After independence, the Republic established several consul offices. The most active were New Orleans, New York and Mobile. David White of Mobile was the primary broker for bonds after his appointment December 10, 1836. He received a 5 percent commission on revenue collected and half that rate for disbursements made on behalf of the government.[10]

With the assistance of these fiscal agents, loan commissioners Austin, Wharton and Archer had secured subscriptions for $200,000 by January 11, 1836. The subscribers were a consortium represented by Robert Triplett and William Fairfax Gray of Virginia. A long-time supporter of Texas independence and survivor of the failed James Long Expedition of 1821, William H. Christy, of New Orleans, served as their trustee. Business was conducted in Christy's New Orleans office. Subscriptions were taken in New Orleans by Triplett and agent Thomas Toby. A subscriber was given an option for Texas land by depositing 10 percent down on the bond purchased. The remaining 90 percent "may or may not" be paid at the buyers discretion. Land scrip was the incentive used to entice buyers to purchase junk bonds issued by a rebel government.[11] (Fig. 30)

Land scrip is similar to a real estate option. Scrip permitted the owner to identify acreage, survey and file for a patent. Scrip holders had no residency or cultivation requirements as was traditional under empresario land grants. Even during the revolution, Americans still desired Texas land. Benjamin Reynolds and ten associates contributed $2,000 each to form the Mississippi Texas Land Company, January 10, 1836, for the purpose of speculating in Texas lands. Three partners travelled to Texas "to make the investments contemplated by this agreement." They arrived during the middle of the war.[12]

Remarkably, the Texas Loan Commissioners received a second commitment. It was for $50,000 from another group of New Orleans subscribers, led by James Erwin. Their January 20, 1836, contract also required a 10 percent deposit for an option to purchase land at fifty cents an acre. The scrip came in lots of 640 and 320 acres. The Erwin consortium paid $45,802 in cash for their commitment of $50,000. The Triplett contract had only yielded cash of $20,000. Scrip holders were promised priority in locating their lands. This preference was later revoked after many complaints. No land could be located on salt springs or precious metal lands. These were reserved by the government, as was the custom under Spanish law. No one could locate specific land until the land offices opened.[13]

Although the two "Texas Loans" provided preference in locating land, officials refused to recognize it, and modifications were negotiated. The "First Loan" subscribers, represented by Trustee William H. Christy and Robert Triplett, released their privilege in return for bonus acreage and were subsequently patented beginning in 1838. (Fig. 31) The "Second Loan" subscribers, represented by James Erwin, first declined six months interest at 12½ percent. Finally, all subscribers were given the same status as all others in locating and patenting lands after the General Land Office opened.[14]

The Texas victory at San Jacinto on April 21, 1836, was followed by the Treaty of Velasco, May 14, 1836, wherein Santa Anna agreed to withdraw Mexican troops from Texas in return for his safe passage home, but Texas was not recognized as a free and sovereign state. The Constitution of the Republic of Texas was unanimously passed at Washington-on-the-Brazos, March 17, 1836, a month before the victory. During the first Congress on November 18, 1836, President Sam Houston was authorized to borrow up to five million dollars in thirty-year bonds at rates not exceeding 10 percent. Two new loan commissioners were dispatched to New York and Philadelphia with thousands in bonds to sell. As collateral, the debentures were backed by a pledge of proceeds from public lands and tax receipts collected after 1838. The commissioners could borrow two million dollars in short-term loans. Again, lenders were given the option of converting the debt to land by bidding in a public auction and satisfying the obligation with the $1,000 bond certificates. (Fig. 32) Bankers showed little interest.[15]

Financier Thomas Toby, on May 24, 1836, became the "exclusive agent" authorized "to raise money for the Government of Texas." The land scrip, in parcels of 640 acres, was priced at fifty cents an acre. Toby received 500,000 acres of scrip from President Sam Houston under his authorization of December 10, 1836. Toby and Brothers, General Agent from June 10, 1836, had subagents in Baltimore and New York. There was no minimum price for the land certificates and the market widely fluctuated. Sales declined as the quantity of certificates issued increased. Results disappointed the government. Some scrip was reassigned to Almanzon Huston, Quartermaster General, who used it to pay off contractors. Toby's land agency was closed December 15, 1837. (Fig. 33) The market had dried up after June 9, 1837, when Congress authorized another half million acres in order to redeem outstanding promissory notes. Toby and Brothers returned the unsold certificates and was due $75,000, which was not settled for decades. Eastern speculators made the market for Texas scrip after the price fell to pennies on the dollar. As far north as Vermont, land trusts were organized to take advantage of the speculative interest. The "Vermont Texas Land Company" of Bethel was established September 13, 1836, as a joint venture to purchase real and personal estates in Texas. Investors had several years to pay for their subscription, which was represented by a $100 share certificate. Although shares circulated in Vermont for almost a decade, no evidence exists that any Texas land was ever patented through the efforts of this or other foreign speculative companies formed during the early days of the Republic.[16]

After closing the New Orleans Agency, Texas attempted to market land scrip directly. The need to resupply arms and military stores prompted this action. The plan was to use $20,000 to buy foreign arms. To no one's surprise, there were few buyers of the surplus land scrip. Government purchasing agents could not pay army suppliers. The certificates were discounted and depressed the market further. Scrip prices fell to only twenty cents an acre. The decorative certificates designed by a New Orleans printer always appeared more valuable than they were. They circulated no better than broken bank notes.[17] (Fig. 34)

Beginning May 16, 1838, President Houston began negotiations with possible lenders for a five million dollar loan. Lenders were again offered scrip. The securities were printed in several languages for the benefit of European investors. After initial resistance, the Congress, on January 29, 1839, added a bond sinking fund along with a pledge of future tax revenue to cover the semi-annual interest obligation. James Hamilton, from South Carolina, contacted his banking relations in New York and Philadelphia. The Pennsylvania Bank of the United States bought several hundred thousand dollars, but at deep discounts.[18]

A contributing factor to the soft market for Texas bonds

was the severe depression known as the "Panic of 1837." This financial chill continued for years. Hopes ran high that France would take some of the Texas bonds. A scheme was proposed and pushed through congress by the French Charge d' Affaires. It involved a million acre colonization scheme, but failed to win congressional approval. French interest in Texas revived in 1840.[19]

Conditions forced Texas to consider many schemes. An Act of February 5, 1841, allowed creditors to exchange outstanding debts for land scrip, priced at $2.00 per acre. Few agreed to accept the scrip at that inflated price. Another attempt thirteen years later was only slightly more successful. Creditors were offered 160 acres of land at a dollar an acre for past due debts.[20]

Another interesting and desperate measure to entice lenders to accept land scrip occurred during the Civil War. Crafted after the Gettysburg and Vicksburg defeats of Confederate forces, a December 16, 1863, act authorized two million dollars in twelve-year bonds, at 7 percent interest to fund a "New" Military Board to purchase cotton. Bond holders had the option to convert principle and interest into scrip valued at fifty cents an acre. (Fig. 35) With wartime inflation, the half-dollar price was truly a bargain, but there was no real estate market during the war. A thousand dollars bond could purchase two thousand acres for only fifty cents while the posted price was two dollars. Almost two hundred thousand dollars were issued. No records exist as evidence that any of the land options were ever exercised, but it is probable some land was deeded under this authority.[21]

Several Texas suppliers to the military bonds also qualified for wartime land scrip. One, the cotton factory doing business as Waco Manufacturing Company, survived the war. By 1878, the Confederate supply company successfully patented a number of sections received as scrip. The company located and received title to sections in Blanco, Palo Pinto, Burnet, Dimmit and Kendall counties. If deed land was dispersed by the General Land Office, and the patent signed by the Governor as a result of the company redeeming its war date scrip, the titles were voidable. Section 4 of the Fourteenth Amendment of the United States Constitution disclaimed any debt or obligation incurred in aid of insurrection or rebellion.

When the Republic merged with the United States, Texas public debt was only a million dollars, consisting of audited drafts, treasury notes and warrants. The nation had no bonded debt. Banks and financial houses were reluctant to loan the Republic money. Land was the coin of the realm by necessity. During its ten years, the Republic disposed of over 1,300,000 acres of land scrip. The most accomplished agent was Toby and Brothers of New Orleans, who accounted for 80 percent of all such transactions. Quartermaster General Huston received scrip to settle claims of military contractors. The Erwin syndicate of New Orleans earned over 120,000 bonus acres through scrip. The "First Texian Loan" consortium of Triplett, et al., held over 50,000 acres in certificates for a deposit of only $20,000. McKinney and Williams and William Bryan, purchasing agents, accounted for another 200,000 acres. The various programs of land scrip were crucial to the new Republic, which had few financial alternatives. Even the United States took advantage of cheap land through scrip redemptions. The federal government patented ten acres with scrip in Cameron County May 9, 1877, for Fort Brown.

# Chapter V

# Military and Emigrant Headrights, 1836–1887

The Provisional Government of Texas announced its intention of rewarding soldiers and loyal citizens with headrights after independence. Any Texan supporting the enemy or leaving the Republic to avoid military service during the revolution would forfeit any lands owned. Commissioners, on November 6, 1835, urged all in support of the cause to join their struggle. A notice read "Any who embark in our course, in the army and navy, shall be liberally rewarded in land and money, and in the blessings of a grateful and redeemed people." Mexico also promised land to those remaining loyal to Mexico.[1]

On November 13, 1835, the Provisional Government of Texas began to form a government. The Texas General Council, on November 24, provided for an army of 1,100 men to be augmented with "all able bodied men over sixteen, and [below] fifty years of age." Each regular soldier was promised bounty land after the war. A full section was the standard bounty for a full term of service. Three months earned volunteers a half section of land. Death entitled heirs to an additional 640 acres. Regular bounties were increased by an additional 160 acres. To keep patent claimants on equal footing, land offices remained closed. Citizens were again reminded that anyone who refused to fight or left the country would have their land confiscated. Because of the outrage at foreign land speculators, the Convention declared null and void all purchases from the State of Coahuila and Mexico made within the last two years, such as the "Eleven League" grants.[2]

On March 14, 1836, the delegates increased the military bounty to 1,280 aces if military service continued to the end of the war. Less service earned less acres: three months, 320 acres; six months, 640 acres and nine months, 960 acres. So many changes were made in the bounty system that confusion followed. To clarify matters, bounty laws were combined into a single act effective December 4, 1837. All those honorably discharged would be entitled to 320 acres for every three months of service, up to a maximum of 1,280 acres per enlistment. (Fig. 36) Within ten days of that change the program was modified. Any honorable veteran arriving in the Republic before August 1, 1836, and not already entitled to a full grant, was assured a league and labor of land. Military grants eventually numbered 7,469, amounting to over a million acres. Technically the war was never concluded by treaty and enlistments continued as if "during the war." Bounties were awarded to veterans enlisting after the war.[3] (Fig. 37)

Texas always expressed its appreciation to its soldiers. Almost 2,000 land titles were issued to veterans of the battles at San Jacinto, the Siege of Bexar, the Alamo, and Goliad as well as those securing baggage at Harrisburg. These sectional bounties were termed "Battle Donations." These could not be sold or mortgaged during the life of the soldier, as provided in the Act of December 21, 1837. Over a million acres were patented as Battle Donations. The transfer prohibition was repealed on March 2, 1848.[4]

Veterans had to apply to the Secretary of War for documents in support of bounty and battle donation claims. To prove qualifying service, an affidavit from the War Office proving honorable service was the best evidence. For volunteers, enlistments, musters and discharges were not always available. Sworn statements from fellow servicemen were acceptable if verifiable by credible witnesses. Unpatented bounties expired if not approved by the Court of Claims prior to a December 31, 1861. The application complications forced many veterans to sell their warrants for as low as a dime per acre. Battle donations initially could not be sold, rendering them worthless until Congress changed the law in 1848. Medical discharges were considered honorable completion of the enlistment term.[5] (Fig. 38)

Texas never had secure borders with Mexico during the Republic era. To protect that frontier, on December 21, 1838, Congress granted homesteads to soldiers willing to settle in the northern part of the territory. The act called for a frontier regiment of fifteen companies with fifty men each. In addition to an enlistment bonus and a private's pay, the soldier was entitled to 160 acres near the outpost. Actual grants were delayed until December 10, 1841. Congress at that time raised the bounty to 240 acres and allowed open locations rather than being restricted to the vicinity of the post. Like Battle Donations, frontier grants were initially not transferrable. The program lasted only three years.[6]

During Reconstruction, the loyalist legislature wanted to reward those who fought to preserve the Union. Bounty land was offered to Union Army veterans then residing in Texas.

The bounty was based on actual service: 80 acres for three months; 160 acres for six months; and 320 for a full year. There is currently no record of a "Union" veteran receiving a grant as provided in the April 21, 1868, Act. After Reconstruction, the legislature authorized land for Confederate veterans.[7]

Veteran programs continued after the war. During the financial panic of 1879, the Texas Treasury was again depleted. To economize, the legislature repealed pensions for veterans and signers of the Texas Declaration of Independence. A month later, lawmakers voted to donate a section of land to any survivor as a substitute measure. To qualify, applicants had to prove they were impoverished, with less than $500 in assets. The lawmakers, on March 15, 1881, doubled the grant to 1,280 acres and removed the poverty requirement. Applicants had to document three months service and prove they qualified for a bounty grant under earlier acts. Lawmakers soon realized they had promised more land than they could deliver. On February 15, 1887, the veterans' law was repealed. During its existence, almost 1,400,000 acres were granted. Sadly, most were forced to sell the bounties for an average price of about $1.34 per acre rather than patent the land.[8]

Later, Texas would support its aging population of Confederate soldiers. Impoverished and disabled veterans, with net worths of less than $1,000, were entitled to "Confederate Scrip" of 1,280 acres. The veteran had to survey an equal amount of school land before qualifying. After issuing over two thousand scrip certificates for 2,600,000 acres, the public domain was depleted. Unappropriated land was reduced to only two million acres. The pension act of April 5, 1881, was repealed February 16, 1883, with 342 certificates unsurveyed and unredeemed.[9]

Texas veterans were always a favored class. Disability and poverty were special conditions when the State was low on funds. Grants ranged in size from a quarter section to two sections (1,280 acres). Usually, the benefit was stair-stepped depending on the term of service. Two regrettable aspects plagued all veteran land programs: fraud and speculation. An investigating committee in 1856 found evidence that a hundred thousand acres had been patented to unqualified applicants. One of the few prosecutions for land fraud or forgery of bounty grants involved a clerk of the General Land Office. John T. Shanks, familiar with the formalities of documents and handwriting in general, according to testimony, forged signatures and execution oaths on an 1857 six hundred and forty acre bounty grant for veteran Hugh Henderson. In 1860 the State appropriated $500.00 for a reward that led to his arrest in Cass County. He was tried in Travis County and found guilty, for which he was sentenced to three years in the penitentiary. Most veterans sold bounty certificates to speculators rather than settling. Quick money was more valuable than a homestead. Despite problems, over three million acres were patented under the veteran programs.[10]

Like eighteenth-century Spain, the Republic favored its first families. The Spanish termed such settlers as "primitives," and second generation homesteaders as "old" families. Newcomers were less favored. Texas incorporated most Spanish customs concerning headrights. Congress had four classes of headrights plus the first family category similar to the Mexican Colonization Act. (Fig. 39) For a Texas headright, a resident had to swear he had not refused to participate in the war or given aid to the enemy. The affidavit was verified by two credible witnesses. As in the Mexican period, the colonist had to pledge loyalty, pay dues and survey costs before applying for title. Since money was always scarce, public dues could be satisfied with claims or drafts drawn against the Republic or Provisional Government. Mexican Colonization grants were termed "Constitutional" grants as distinguished from new colonist's headrights and were good for a league and a labor.[11]

The Texas Republic's Constitution contained three sections devoted to land matters. The March 17, 1836, charter provided that all white persons, other than Indians, residing in Texas on March 2, 1836, (Independence Day) were citizens, entitled to benefits, except any who had aided the enemy, left the country to evade service or refused to participate. Disloyals were subject to forfeiture of estates. All married citizens were entitled to a league and a labor of land, similar to original colonists, if a six months residency was established. Single citizens that were at least seventeen years old could claim a reduced allotment. Citizens were not required to reside to qualify. Aliens could only be issued titles under special circumstances such as widowhood. New York speculator John T. Mason and foreigners acquiring "Eleven Leagues" from the Government of Coahuila just prior to the revolution held *prima facie* null and void claims.[12]

Headrights classified as "Constitutional Grants" were for a league and a labor, or 4,605 acres. Later colonists were entitled to only a league (4,428.4 acres), and an unmarried man was due a reduced amount. Pioneers could claim additional acreage to make up any deficiency if their holdings were less than the grant. No residency or cultivation applied to "Constitutional" grantees. Widows and orphans could claim a colonial headright even if not living in Texas. Many grants were assigned to others. (Fig. 40) Relief was also allowed for aliens inheriting headrights. Although title could not be transferred, foreigners were given time to dispose of inherited acres. The General Land Office classified "Constitutional Grants" as "First Class" headrights. The purpose of all these land donations was to recognize, as stated in Section 10 of the 1836 Constitution, those supporting independence. All were expected to give loyalty oaths.[13] (Fig. 41)

On December 14, 1837, the Congress adopted a second headright program to encourage more immigration. Unlike the first awards in appreciation for supporters of the revolution, this second series was economic and had conditions.

The head of a family arriving in Texas after March 2, 1836, and before October 1, 1837, could claim two sections (1,280 acres) and an unmarried person half that, if residing three years and proving all duties of citizenship had been performed. (Fig. 42) The residency oath was required. (Fig. 43) The "conditional" or "second class" grant program was successful as an inducement to immigrants. The population grew. The Commissioner of the General Land Office was instructed to survey a large quantity of land, divide it into full and half section parcels in order to satisfy outstanding requests. Sectionalizing was never carried out because of budgetary constraints.[14]

The General Land Office finally opened in February 1838. "First class" claimants, veterans, "Constitutional" grantees and land scrip holders were first in line. Others applied six months later. Eleven regional offices provided assistance to "second class" headright claimants after passage of the inducement to immigration act. County Land Commissioners issued certificates to board approved "second class" applicants. A surveyor was necessary to locate lands, prepare field notes and provide a certificate for patent application to the General Land Office. The county land offices were:

1. Red River
2. San Augustine
3. Liberty
4. Nacogdoches
5. Matagorda
6. Washington
7. Milam
8. Mina (Bastrop)
9. Gonzáles
10. San Antonio
11. Victoria

Those claiming Spanish or Mexican grants had to provide the Land Office evidence of the original conveyance, official signatures and receipts for dues paid. Within two years of opening, over 30,000 applications were presented to the General Land Office requesting fifty million acres. All were not patented.[15]

The Panic of 1837 increased immigration into Texas. The lure of free homesteads attracted the bankrupt and homeless. The success of the second program prompted Congress, on January 4, 1839, to enact another immigration act. (Fig. 44) This third act reduced headrights to only a section for family men and a half section for the unmarried. Emigrants took advantage and their numbers exceeded prior applications. The qualifying dates were from October 1, 1837, to January 1, 1840. The "third class" program continued the minimum age requirement of seventeen years. The third-class oath was shorter. (Fig. 45) When the act expired, Congress took measures to reduce fraudulent warrants and counterfeit land documents. Two traveling boards examined records east and west of the Brazos River. Land cheats were most prevalent in Jasper County. County commissioners were often parties to spurious certificates. Many bogus claims were indistinguishable from the genuine because of authentic signatures, fraudulently obtained. The fraudulent document law of January 3, 1840, discouraged some creators of phony documents.[16]

The fourth class and final headright program applied to immigrants arriving between January 1, 1840, and January 1, 1842. The January 4, 1841, "fourth class" headright retained the same allotments for married and single men but changed qualifying conditions. The lawmakers revived the Mexican rule that at least ten acres of the land needed to be in cultivation. Oath, good citizenship and the three year residency requirements continued. (Fig. 46) The law was repealed February 4, 1842. Over thirty million acres were distributed by the Republic through all its headright programs.[17]

# Chapter VI

# Lot and Island Sales, 1836–1907

The Texas population was as impecunious as their Republic. Trade was most often conducted through barter because the currency was almost worthless and specie rare. Some contributed the "coin of the realm," land, to help pay for the war. The San Felipe de Austin weekly, *Telegraph and Texas Register*, on March 25, 1836, reported that five men had offered land to the treasury. The merchants McKinney & Williams also donated a league. James Kerr, DeWitt's surveyor, gave a quarter section to help the treasury. All were responding to a plea from the government that considered all "necessary to make the machine of government go on sleekly." The editor's appeal for land was made to all capable of giving.[1]

Land was third on the Republic's legislative agenda, after defense and the depleted treasury. By the time Congress opened, land issues had been widely discussed and positions were well known, but there was no consensus. The first land acts were passed over President Sam Houston's veto. An act in December 1837, provided that the county surveyor and land commissioner were to be elected rather than appointed, as supported by Houston. Also, the President vetoed the December 1837 law providing no more full "headrights" to new immigrants.[2]

Lacking money for a full survey of the state, private surveyors were essential to the titling process. Arthur Henrice of New Orleans was one such surveyor. The Galveston Bay and Texas Land Company hired Henrice to plot the Zavala's, Vehlein's and Burnet's grants. His field notes were integral in mapping most of East Texas. Henrice also operated as a real estate agency and charged commissions of 20 percent for sales under $5,000; 15 percent between $5,000 and $10,000; and 10 percent on property exceeding $10,000 plus $100 per certificate. Owners of land scrip, bounty certificates and headrights often paid the surveyor with land. A half of the grant was common to early surveyors.[3] (Fig. 47)

Texas used land for political purposes. The Republic land sales were not productive. The largest transfer was to the United States in conjunction with the annexation of Texas. The second most significant conveyance was to build a new capitol building after a fire.[4]

Texas' first customs station was Espíritu Santo Bay at the mouth of the San Antonio River, twenty-five miles south of Lavaca Bay. Goliad, near San Barnard Bay, from the inception of Austin's Colony was a "duty free" port. Galveston Island was reserved to the Crown under Spanish law. Only with special dispensation could colonists settle within the littoral reserve. On December 9, 1836, Texas recognized a questionable coastal grant on Galveston Island held by Michel B. Menard and others. The venture agreed to pay the Republic $50,000 to settle the land claim. For years, the press questioned the propriety of the transaction. Menard and his associates Samuel M. Williams, Thomas F. McKinney and John K. Allen did business as the "Galveston City Company."[5]

The island tract had been granted to Juan N. Seguín in 1832. Menard joined with Robert Triplett and William F. Gray of Richmond, Virginia, to consolidate their island holdings. The Galveston property was placed in trust, of which Menard held 40 percent. The ownership units were marketed at $1,500. The venture, the Galveston City Company, held its first directors meeting April 13, 1838. Shareholders were allowed to redeem shares for lots in the City of Galveston. Share prices reached a high of $2,300. By 1841 the company had sold 1,543 lots for $1,218,911. Of that sum, shareholders had redeemed over $900,000 in shares for land. That year Galveston had grown to six hundred buildings with a population of 3,000. The company's resident manager was Gail Borden, Jr.[6]

The Congress also sold portions of Galveston Island to the public. The President was authorized to survey the island's western end in preparation for sale. Excluded were fifteen acres reserved for a fort and custom house. The property was posted for auction June 12, 1837. Notices ran in newspapers in New Orleans, Mobile, Nashville and Louisville. The auction began on November 15, 1837, in Houston. Successful bidders had a couple of methods to purchase land. Cash was the least popular. Speculative purchasers could settle up in nine months for gold, silver or audited drafts of the Republic. Individual buyers normally made a 25 percent down payment and signed a note due in quarterly installments. (Fig. 48) Delinquent buyers risked foreclosure. A similar but less successful auction took place for Matagorda Island on January 21, 1839. Pelican Island was donated to the City of Galveston in 1856. Other barrier islands with less market appeal were sold over the next seventy years.[7]

Another Texas land sale was associated with the move of the new seat of government to Austin. When the site was selected as the permanent seat, the government was leasing property in Houston. In 1838, Edward Burleson founded Waterloo, and it was incorporated January 15, 1839. After the Republic purchased the site, the lawmakers surveyed and subdivided the parcel into lots that ranged in size between five and forty acres. The auction began August 1, 1839. Bidding resulted in 309 purchases. "In Town" parcels were spread among 166 blocks, which normally consisted of eight or twelve lots. Successful bidders could pay 20 percent down and finance the balance over eighteen months, with no interest. (Fig. 49) The town was surveyed by L. J. Pilie and Charles Schoolfield. The "Lithographer to the Republic," Green Co. of New Orleans, published the first city map, priced at $200.[8]

Lawmakers in 1848 provided that each organized county, except San Patricio and Nueces, hire a surveyor and produce a map for public record and filing in the General Land Office. Thirty-one years later, Governor O. M. Roberts warned the elected officials at a joint session on March 26, 1879, that this requirement as published in the Civil Code Article 3956 had long been ignored. This dereliction, if continued, in his opinion would place the GLO in danger of having all patents suspended should the statute be strictly enforced. Soon thereafter, the GLO was charged with the creation and dissemination of county maps. In 1873 the GLO had already begun replacing manuscript surveys with mechanically reproduced copies. In 1879 the office contracted for lithographed copyrighted county maps, for sale to the public for either 50¢ or $1.00, depending on size. The cost per copy of the sparsely populated counties could run as high as $35.00. The official GLO state maps that were directed to be displayed in the county clerk's office were by Pressler, 1856 edition, and the Pressler and Langerman of 1891.

Some buyers of the Austin lots were speculators. Installment payments were not always timely, and a number went into default. The government did not want the land back or the bad publicity from foreclosures. Congress, on January 12, 1841, extended the time for payments and waived any defaults. (Fig. 50) On January 1, 1842, further sales were suspended. By 1850 construction was active and property values appreciated. Auctions resumed. The second round required buyers to pay in full. After slow sales, installment terms were reinstated. The final Austin auction occurred March 6, 1865, at the end of the Civil War. The Treasury realized almost two hundred thousand dollars from the Austin sales. Most were during the first two years. A portion of the proceeds was dedicated to the construction of the Governor's Mansion, as directed by an Act of February 11, 1854. Forty percent of the capital costs were covered by allocated auction proceeds.[9]

Some Texas towns became commercial centers, but most did not. San Antonio, the provincial capital during the Mexican period, was the mercantile center. San Felipe de Austin, although the seat of government for a time, had little commercial success. The Washington townsite, known as "Washington-on-the-Brazos," was home to delegates at the time of the Texas Declaration of Independence. (Fig. 51) The town was promoted by John W. Hall. Another provisional seat of government, Velasco, was first a customs station. Velasco was home to McKinney & Williams, purchasing agents of the Republic. After destruction from a 1875 hurricane, Velasco rebuilt and became a resort advertising itself as "the Liverpool of the Texas-Mississippi." Developers claimed Velasco was immune to malaria and pneumonia because of favorable winds, but the "Great Hurricane" destroyed the town.[10]

Congress allowed Mexican chartered municipalities to auction "useless" town lots to raise revenue for public projects like jails and courthouses. Towns began to incorporate and conduct affairs in the charter form. The pueblos of Nacogdoches and San Antonio were chartered in 1836 and 1837, respectively. The chartered municipalities of Tenehow (Shelby) and San Augustine were carved out of Nacogdoches in 1837. San Felipe de Austin, after receiving its charter, issued land scrip, backed by a pledge of municipal real estate, to pay civic expenses. (Fig. 52) The old towns of Matagorda and Brazoria were also chartered. Later towns were often real estate developments promoted by speculators.

Sterling C. Robertson's Sarahville de Viesea became the town of Milam. After the Civil War the community was reborn as Marlin, but it never prospered. Martín de León's seat of government, Victoria, was more successful. The influx of Irish immigrants to that primarily Mexican community assured commercial success after its incorporation in 1839. That town sold excess town lots for civic projects. (Fig. 53) The old capital and transportation hub of Harrisburg did the same. That 1835 municipality merged with its sister city, Hamilton, located on the opposite bank of the Buffalo Bayou. Harrisburg Town Company sold commercial parcels and prospered, but was later destroyed by fire. (Fig. 54) It was absorbed by Houston.[11]

The Texas Envoy to France, General James Hamilton, sold 100,000 acres for $1.50 an acre, to found the 1842 French colony by Antonio Snider-Pellegrini named "Sniderton." The initial group landed at Matagorda in 1842. All brought six months' provisions. Snider-Pellegrini purchased land from the Harrisburg Town Company, hoping to start a bank, commercial house and railroad. He eventually held 15,000 acres in Harris County before admitting failure and leaving Texas in 1847.[12]

Land sales by the General Land Office were negligible during the Civil War. The State, in 1862, lowered the minimum price for vacant land to fifty cents an acre. After Confederate inflation, the 1863 legislature raised the posted price for land to ten dollars an acre. No matter the price, sales were few during the war. The Government was overwhelmed with tax foreclosed land after the war.[13]

Texas retained ownership of the barrier islands for years. Robert Mercer ranched at "El Mar" on the north end of Mustang Island, Nueces County. The United States maintained a quarantine and lifeguard station on the island. The General Land Office announced, on August 15, 1910, 2,900 acres of beach property for sale, at ten dollars per acre. Terms were 50 percent down with the balance due in a year, at 5 percent interest. Commissioner J. T. Robison offered a patent for an additional five dollars. To promote sales, the GLO issued maps printed by Von Boeckmann-Jones Co., Austin. After the sale, the United States government continued as the primary resident. (Fig. 55)

Although Texas always used land to fund the government, seldom was the market receptive to the amount of land being offered. Tax receipts and custom dues were always ten times greater than land sales as a source of revenue. Circulating government-issued land certificates depressed the real estate markets. Land prices regularly fell back to fifty cents an acre. The Legislature attempted to charge $2.00 an acre but was unsuccessful. Not until the public domain was depleted did vacant land increase in value.[14]

# Chapter VII

# Republic Empresario Grants, 1841–1844

President Sam Houston's first term was challenged by problems encountered by all new nations. The situation worsened with the Panic of 1837 in the United States. A permanent peace with Mexico was not achievable. Accordingly, defense consumed much of his budget. The need for outside capital was crucial to the survival of Texas. Houston dispatched bond agents to American and European financial centers to secure loans. Great Britain and France considered an independent Texas consistent with their own interests. The Republic stood in the way of westward expansion of the United States. Texas's security was a strong reason to be annexed by the United States. European immigration could spur closer ties to the Continent and lessen the Republic's reliance on America.[1]

Texas was never free of intruders, squatters or rustlers. Frontier outposts were widely spaced. Mexican troops threatened Laredo regularly. Equally exposed were settlements near Indian Territory. President Houston resorted to the empresario system to populate the frontier. Eleven land concessions were offered along the Rio Grande from the mouth of the river up to Laredo. That region remained part of the States of Tamaulipas and Coahuila as far as Mexico was concerned. All northern Mexico was politically fluid. Despite the risk, Houston hoped to colonize the border.[2]

The Texas Revolution encouraged other rebelling Mexican States to resist General Santa Anna's dictatorial rule. Tamaulipas, Nuevo León and Coahuila had close contact with Texas that continued after its independence. Mexican rebels in Guerrero, Laredo and Victoria formed a confederation, "The Republic of the Rio Grande," and claimed territory west to the Nueces River. No Texas headrights were being patented in this region at the time. The Rio Grande Confederation was defeated by General Mariano Arista on March 25, 1840, at Morales. Mexican rebels regrouped in Victoria, Texas. Some Texans joined their revolt. The Republic of the Rio Grande came to an end November 6, 1840. The Texas meddling angered the Mexican government.[3]

The next year an expedition left San Antonio to establish trade with Santa Fe. The Texas party expected to be welcomed by American merchants in that city. The caravan of merchants, reporters and rangers became lost in the Llano Estacado. The party was forced to surrender to Mexican forces in September 1841. Survivors were marched to Santa Fe before being moved south where they were imprisoned until April 1842. Their release was accomplished through the efforts of American envoy Francis M. Dimond. In 1852, his family received a donated league of land in appreciation while he was "Late Consul at Vera Cruz." That same day, Texas lawmakers donated a league to the heirs of William S. Henry for his help to the Santa Fe captives. Major Henry had supplied the Santa Fe Expedition, and was reprimanded by the U.S. Army for that support. Texas donated a league to Ramón Ortez of El Paso for his kindness to the Santa Fe captives during their imprisonment. There were few outright donations of land other than for military service.[4]

Five months after the Santa Fe prisoners were released, Texas Ranger, Colonel Matthew Caldwell, with two hundred volunteers, met invading Mexican troops at Salado Creek. That month, three dozen Texans lost their lives to Mexican forces during the Dawson Massacre. In retaliation, Texas volunteers, led by customs official Alexander Somervell, crossed into Mexico. The Texans captured Laredo and Guerrero in December 1842, but were captured at Cuidad Mier and imprisoned at Matamoros and Monterrey. The survivors remained jailed until September 1844. All these invasions from Mexico made apparent the Republic's vulnerability. The Rio Grande border was unprotected. Settlements along the east bank of the Rio Grande seemed to be a practical solution.

The Texas Congress had suspended emigrant headrights on January 4, 1839. European interest in Texas homelands remained high. Emigrant travel guides and books touted the benefits of Texas emigration. Most popular were Mary Austin Holley's *Texas* (1836), William Kennedy's *Texas* (1841) and Artur Ikin's *Texas* (1841). For German audiences Prince Carl of Solms-Braunfels' *Texas* (1846) and Viktor Bracht's *Texas Im Jahre* (1848) provided maps with detailed instructions on the selection of lands. On February 15, 1842, Texas passed a law similar to the Mexican Colonization Act. Applications from empresarios soon followed. The act continued only for a short time. Although repealed on January 30, 1844, foreign interest was high. James Hamilton successfully negotiated trade treaties with England, Holland, France and Belgium, partially based on the possibility of greater immigration. Cheap land for European settlers was popular.[5]

The forerunner of Rio Grande colonization was Dr. Beales efforts at "Dolores" on Mora Creek near present-day Eagle Pass. The triple threats of disease, Indians and revolutionaries defeated his effort. Abolitionist Benjamin Lundy hoped for a freedmen settlement west of the Nueces River. A German colony in the same vicinity was seriously discussed. Both proposals were tabled after Texas independence. The "Franco Texian" colony never had sufficient political support to sway the legislature. Arthur Ikin's "Texas Trading, Mining and Emigrating Company," chartered January 30, 1841, was allowed to settle "hardy Americans" and "easily contented Germans" along the Rio Grande. He tried to buy 40,000 acres from John Woodward and form a 300-man militia. The venture languished after Ikin discovered the $50,000 land scrip from Woodward was worthless.[6]

Mexico launched its own program to settle the Rio Grande Valley. Santa Anna, on October 25, 1842, granted to General Francisco Garay a twenty-five-year colonization concession for all lands feeding into the Rio Grande. Garay also held the river steamboat franchise. That privilege allowed him to form a bank. Garay could only populate his colony with Mexicans, Europeans and Canary Islanders. The venture never materialized.[7]

Texas needed to populate the Rio Grande Valley before Mexico. Grants were made to contractors such as Frenchman Henri Castro and his silent partner Jean Jassoud of the financial firm J. Laffitte & Company. They received two tracts. A few homesteaders survived, but insufficient to qualify for premium lands. Other empresarios with diplomatic credentials received contracts. Belgian diplomat Victor Pirson received, on March 9, 1842, two parcels. Texas hoped his government would invest in Texas bonds. No colonists were introduced and few bonds were purchased.[8]

The grant considered most valuable at the mouth of the Rio Grande was awarded to Alexander Bourgeois D'Orvvanne and Armand Ducos of France on June 6, 1842. The empresarios organized the "Compagnie de Colonisation de Générale." After promotion in Europe, the businessmen, on April 7, 1844, sold one of the contracts to Prince Carl of Solms-Braunfels of Germany. The contract expiration date lapsed and reverted back to the Republic.[9]

After Texas independence, Mexican bond holders in Europe were uneasy. To calm British concerns, Mexico assured creditors that 100 million acres of land was available to hypothecate the loan. A quarter of the land was in the north and suitable for Anglo colonization. Concerns continued but the prospect of land was inviting. By 1841, hopes of any Mexican recapture of Texas had passed. After a treaty between Great Britain and Texas recognized independence, William Kennedy was dispatched from the British foreign office to report on conditions in the Republic. Kennedy and his attorney William Pringle received two empresario grants from Texas, one along the Rio Grande and another west of San Antonio on the Frio and Nueces Rivers. After Mexican forces occupied Victoria, Goliad, Refugio and San Antonio, President Houston declared a national emergency. In 1842 Kennedy was appointed British Consul to Texas, forcing him to transfer his contracts to James Grave to avoid a conflict of interest. The empresario grants expired with no titles issued.[10]

The Mexican military presence deterred settlement of the lower Rio Grande Valley. Texas attention turned to the Indian lands of North Texas. The new empresario law offered a section of land to settlers, conditional upon their building a dwelling, cultivating a fenced plot of land and residing for three years. Single men qualified for half the family allotment. If the contractor paid for the colonist's travel, seeds, tools or provisions, he was permitted to keep half the settler's land as reimbursement. Contractors, if they fulfilled the terms within the statutory time frame, earned premium lands of ten sections (6,400 acres) for every hundred families settled.[11]

The region between the Nueces River and Rio Grande, along the border, would remain vulnerable until after the war with Mexico. North Texas was more suited for settlement, being closer to the United States. Nineteen American and English speculators, led by W.S. Peters, received a February 4, 1841, empresario contract. Intrigue, double dealing and litigation characterized this venture from inception. Company headquarters were in Louisville, Kentucky. Their first contract for 200 families measured twenty by sixty miles and was located south of the Red River. Their second grant of November 9, 1841, was forty miles southward, and allowed 800 families. The third grant extended the first contract for six months, and added another twenty miles of land. The final authorization extended westward and moved the termination date out to January 20, 1843. The so-called "Peters Colony" was organized with 2,000 shares of stock with a value of $250 per share. The company soon underwent reorganizations and changes in ownership.[12]

Effective November 20, 1841, the Peters Colony owners reorganized the venture, becoming the "Texas Agricultural, Commercial and Manufacturing Company." The minority faction, led by Charles Fenton Mercer, struck out on their own. By December 1843, the Louisville investors had gained control from the English. The Mercer faction and original English owners withdrew. The venture then became the "Trinity and Red River Colony, Texas." Mercer's group received their own contract on January 29, 1844. The Peters Colony again reorganized on October 15, 1844, becoming the half-million-dollar "Texas Emigration and Land Company," successor to the "Texas Agricultural, Commercial and Manufacturing Company." Agents in charge of Texas colonization were Ralph H. Barksdale (1842–1845); Charles Hensley (1845–1846); and Henry O. Hedgcoxe (1846). The Peters Colony grant expired June 30, 1848.[13]

The Peters Colony in the fertile Trinity River Valley was twenty two miles wide, extending from the Red River for a hundred miles. The investors needed to fulfill the quota of families by July 1, 1843, to earn premium lands. Mercer simultaneously was promoting his contract when he sold the Peters Colony in July 1843. In 1848, the "Texas Emigration and Land Company," successor to the Peters Colony, began to wind down. Titles had not been given to colonists; however, Agent Hedgcoxe, in 1846, issued "deed-like" certificates to disgruntled colonists. He subtracted half their promised land (320 acres), to reimburse the company for costs incurred. Colonists were angered, making allegations of fraud. The "Hedgcoxe War" erupted. A special land commissioner, Thomas William Ward, was appointed to clean up the mess. "Ward Certificates" were issued to settlers if they could prove residency before July 1, 1848. With such certificates, settlers applied for land patents from the GLO. (Fig. 56) The Company's premium lands were earned and ultimately were scattered across much of North Texas including over 200 sections in the southern half of Clay County. That massive tract ran along the Red River below Indian Territory. The Texas Emigration and Land Company patented multiple half section tracts in Young County between 1857 and 1859, totaling two leagues.[14]

The Hedgcoxe "faux" titles were even recorded in Denton County. The document resembled Texas land patents issued by the GLO. By the summer of 1848, the County Clerk had certified 168 Hedgcoxe deeds. In 1869 Edwin A. Graham, from Kentucky, acquired controlling interest in the Trinity and Red River Colony. The primary asset was the premium lands located in the former Brazos Indian Land Reservation. As company agent, Graham sold parcels for about a dollar an acre. The price dropped to fifty cents and to encourage sales he took promissory notes, bearing 10 percent interest. The deeds noted the land was from the "Texan Emigration and Land Company."[15] (Fig. 57)

Charles Fenton Mercer was in the United States Congress with Sam Houston of Tennessee. Mercer was an Andrew Jackson supporter like Houston. He moved to Florida after the Panic of 1837 to speculate in real estate. Mercer's empresario contract of January 25, 1844, was issued one day before the Texas Congress repealed the president's authority to sign such agreements. Mercer's 8,000-square-mile colony, between the Brazos and Trinity Rivers, required one hundred families within a year to qualify for premium lands. He met his quota, but Mercer's conflict with the Peters Colony created hard feelings. The Mercer Colony operated as a joint stock company, the Texas Association of Kentucky. Most investors were from Florida and Virginia. Mercer retained two-thirds control of the company.[16] (Fig. 58)

Many of the squatters already living within the Mercer Colony created problems for surveyors and the Land Office. By May of 1845 two hundred of Mercer's families had settled. Colonists could purchase a half section of land before March 20, 1845, by simply providing a survey and paying filing fees. After July 1, 1846, settlers could buy only 200-acre tracts. Residency, a cabin and cultivating fifteen acres preceded their application for title. Daniel Rowlett, a Texas investor in the Colony, was the company's resident agent. (Fig. 59) The company's surveyor was P. J. Pillows. Nacogdoches County Surveyor C. C. Taylor continued to issue certificates within Mercer's colony after the contract date. Squatters were warned by General Land Commissioner Thomas W. Ward not to interfere with Mercer's settlers. Notice of Mercer's contract was posted September 5, 1844. (Fig. 60) If squatters applied for titles before that date, Taylor still issued them certificates.[17]

Because of the competing surveys, Mercer's titles were contested, delayed and litigated for years. A Texas court first ruled that Mercer's contract was void because it was not in accordance with the enabling statute, but that decision was overturned by the Texas Supreme Court. Litigation continued for thirty years. The United States Supreme Court ultimately held that the Texas Association claims were valid but the contractor was not entitled to premium lands. Mercer was not affected because he had sold his shares February 27, 1852, to George Hancock of Louisville, Kentucky. Colonists in Mercer's colony who met the conditions of residency prior to October 25, 1848, received patents from the GLO.[18]

The four Rio Grande empresarios, Castro, Pirson, Kennedy, and Bourgeois D'Orrvvane failed. Unlike the Europeans, the American empresarios, Mercer and Peters, successfully introduced colonists to Texas. The Texas contractors did business as a company rather than individually because the law precluded foreign ownership of land. Promoters formed partnerships to apply for empresario contracts. The short time period hindered their earning premium lands. Two European empresarios were successful in colonizing east of the Nueces River.[19]

Frenchman Henri Castro, in February 1842, a year after Dubois de Soligny's "Franco Texian Commercial and Colonization Company" failed, applied for another contract for settlement of 600 families from Alsace, France. Castro's Rio Grande contract had already lapsed. His second tract, located between the Frio and Medina Rivers, proved more successful than his first. French colonists enrolled at Castro's office, located at Rue Lafitte, No. 18, Paris. Castro provided expenses to farm. In return, the settlers assigned half their promised land back to the contractor. Castro considered his colonists "cultivators" rather than settlers. The first group arrived in Texas in November 1842.[20] (Fig. 61)

Castro incurred more expenses than either Peters or Mercer because of overseas travel, provisions and livestock. Castro had a line of credit from D'Hanis and Associates totaling $70,000 to finance his venture. The joint stock company was capitalized with 350 shares of $200 common stock. Several thousand dollars were drawn by Castro against his line of credit. A lawsuit for breach of the financing agreement concluded in a settlement that allowed Castro to retain control. Castro purchased John McMullen's military certificate in order to have more land. By 1844, the town of Castroville had two thousand "cultivators." John M. Carolen was the colony's land commissioner. By February 15, 1847, over five hundred colonists had patented 250,000 acres. Three quarters of those acres were assigned to others. The project financially depleted Castro's personal wealth. He only earned half the premium lands, because he failed to meet the number of required colonists.[21]

The final empresario effort in Texas was the most complex. It attracted many German settlers to Texas. Others had tried before to lure German immigrants. Dr. Beales, Joseph Vehlein and John Lucius Woodbury all failed in their effort. Henry Francis Fisher and Burchand Miller, on June 7, 1842, received a contract allowing one thousand German and Scandinavian families destined for the "Hill Country" between the Llano and Colorado Rivers above Austin's Colony. (Fig. 62) The enterprise, known as the "San Saba Colonization Company," contained over three million acres in the Indian wilderness. Fisher subsequently was appointed Texas Consul to Breman, Germany. He sold the Hill Country contract to a group of German nobles who formed the "German Emigration and Railroad Company," which consisted of forty $2,000 share certificates. The company also held a charter for the Lavaca, Guadalupe and San Saba Railroad, dated May 8, 1846, with authority for a line from Indianola. This venture was commonly known as the "German Emigration Company." (Fig. 63) The railroad charter lapsed.[22]

On January 17, 1844, Texas restored the president's authority to secure foreign loans. Congress considered its public domain more valuable to secure foreign loans rather than premiums to empresarios. Three days after the act, Congress cancelled all empresario contracts if not perfected and in compliance with the terms and conditions of the law. On March 25, 1844, the German purchasers of the Fisher-Miller Grant organized the "Adelsverein" Society for the protection of German immigrants in Texas. The Society bought private land and founded the towns of Indianola, New Braunfels and Fredericksburg. The German commissioners were Prince Carl of Solms-Braunfels, John O. Meusebach and Louis Bene. As provided in its charter of April 9, 1844, the Society wanted to direct German immigrants to favorable locations in Texas, assist with their travel and assure them homes in the frontier. Each adult male was granted 160 acres and families twice that allotment. The first 150 colonists also received half-acre home sites in one of the towns in addition to their farms. The German Society raised, through subscription, several hundred thousand *gulden* to underwrite the project. The San Saba Colonization Company, in 1848, merged into the "German Emigration Company." In 1853 creditors gained control of the German Emigration Company, including the old Fisher-Miller Grant.[23] (Fig. 64)

The creditor trustees transferred the assets of the German Emigration Company on September 15, 1853, to the "Texas and German Emigration Company," a joint stock association of $100 per stock. Company offices were in San Antonio with banking offices in Galveston. The 1,200,000 acres held by the old Fisher-Miller grant along with the unsold lots in the towns of New Braunfels, Fredericksburg and Indianola were part of the bankrupt estate. Most Germans settled in towns rather than the hostile Indian lands of the Fisher-Miller grant. On May 1, 1848, the Texas land commissioner began to issue titles.[24]

In 1853 the "Adelsverein" withdrew from Texas, leaving Fisher and Miller unpaid. The Colony essentially claimed premium lands based on the successful settlement of 1,600 German families and 1,000 unmarried men within the grant. The claim for one hundred thousand acres was rejected because most settled on purchased land. The Land Commissioner and the Texas House of Representatives in 1852 rejected the claim. According to a November 1855 report from the General Land Office, Republic era empresario claims remaining outstanding were considered restriction on the public domain until resolved[25]:

| *Empresario* | *Acres Originally Claimed* |
|---|---|
| Peters Colony | 872,920 |
| Texas Emigration and Land Company | 1,088,000 |
| Mercer Colony | 691,840 |
| Castro's Colony | 299,846 |
| Fisher-Miller Colony | 1,735,200 |

# Chapter VIII

# Trans-Nueces and Trans-Pecos Grants, 1840–1858

During its opening session the Texas Congress defined its international boundary. The border ran from the Rio Grande to the Sabine River and north to the forty-second degree north latitude, as set by the Adams-Onís Treaty of 1819. Despite that sovereignty claim, the Republic was incapable of defending itself west of the Nueces River or within the "stovepipe" of upper Texas. Both Mexico and Spain placed the border of the Province at the Nueces. The Mexican State of Tamaulipas governed the lower Rio Grande Valley from Laredo to the Nueces. The Trans-Pecos region was the jurisdiction of the State of Chihuahua. On occasion Texas showed the flag within the disputed territories, but the failed Santa Fe Expedition revealed the Republic's weakness. Texas colonization of the Rio Grande Valley was only aspirational. Land grants in New Mexico until the mid-nineteenth century were officiated by the State of Chihuahua. Typical acts of possession and oaths of loyalty were prerequisite to title. The pueblos of Acoma and Laguna received seventeenth-century royal grants that contained about four square miles. Town and private grants followed in the eighteenth century. Because of no organized empresario system for contractors, distance and threats of natives, the number of private grants were small. In the mid-century, the United States Surveyor General began to receive requests for permanent titles confirming old Spanish and Mexican land grants. Hubert Howe Bancroft in his *History of New Mexico* (1889) compiled from the U.S. Land Office several hundred confirmed grants comprising almost thirteen million acres. Texas confirmed none in New Mexico.[1]

The Republic of Texas originally claimed over two hundred million acres. Immediately the Republic recognized some grants bestowed by Spain and Mexico, unless the recipient was disloyal to Texas during the revolution. The Texas treaty of annexation with the United States allowed it to retain its public domain as existed December 29, 1845. By agreement, five years later, Texas transferred 67 million acres of the "stovepipe" to the United States, in return for five million dollars in United States bonds, yielding 5 percent interest plus funds in escrow to liquidate the debts of the "Late Republic." The per-acre price for parts of New Mexico, Colorado, Wyoming, Oklahoma and Kansas was seventeen cents an acre, a third of the half dollar posted price.

The annexation of Texas was followed by a war with Mexico (1846–1848). President James Knox Polk had earlier instructed diplomats to settle the long standing border question. War erupted in May 1846. American forces overwhelmed the Mexicans and entered their capital September 13, 1847. The Treaty of Guadalupe Hidalgo of February 2, 1848, declared the Rio Grande as the international border. All lands from El Paso to the Pacific above the Gila River were ceded to the United States. Mexico was compensated under the treaty with $15,000,000 plus a release of claims by Americans against the Mexican government.

Texas retained the right to divide itself into more than one state under the terms of its annexation to the United States. Virginia was so divided during the Civil War. Citizens of the upper valley of the Rio Grande in 1850 submitted a "Memorial" to the United States Congress requesting a government for the Trans-Pecos and southern New Mexico. The petitioners requested the retention of Mexican law until a territorial government was formed. The Texas loyalty requirement during the revolution was a deep concern. The "Memorial" was tabled. (Fig. 65) During the constitutional convention of 1868 another proposal was made for a separate West Texas. The western region of Texas was bounded by the Rio Grande, Colorado and Pecos Rivers. The "People of West Texas with the grace of God" presented their proposal in 1868 which contained a Constitution and Bill of Rights similar to the Texas Constitution. Immigration was to be encouraged by offers of a quarter section to newcomers. Outlawed were banks and systems of peonage or use of "coolies." A curious provision clearly voided any outstanding Civil War land scrip issued during the rebellion to Military Board contractors and cotton bond holders. This too failed. Texas was readmitted to the Union on March 30, 1870, as a single entity. Whenever distraught with national policies, Texas habitually reconsiders division.[2]

The legality of Mexican grants was assured by Articles VIII

and IX of the Treaty of Guadalupe Hidalgo. The United States Senate established a protocol for Americans to submit claims for damages against the Mexican government. American courts had exclusive jurisdiction under the July 26, 1848, protocol for reparation. Mexican land issues were delegated to Texas. The topic was also a subject of the Gadsden Purchase agreement. Article VI of that agreement made "obligatory" all titles recorded in Mexican archives. Texas had possession of some Mexican archives, but the records were incomplete. The Texas Legislature created a commission to investigate land claims for those living in the Trans-Nueces and Trans-Pecos regions. Governor P. H. Bell appointed William H. Bourland and James B. Miller as commissioners of the Rio Grande Commission to investigate the Trans-Nueces claims. Commissioners began taking evidence in Laredo on July 15, 1850.[3]

First considered were residents of the Lower Rio Grande Valley. After hearings in Laredo, testimony was taken in Rio Grande City, Eagle Pass, Brownsville and Corpus Christi. Most valuable in establishing grant validity were continued occupancy and legal documentation. Only the largest landowners normally participated in the process. Language barriers, costs and absence of legal representation hampered most claimants. A second board, the "Rio Grande Commission," was established February 11, 1854, to consider claims in the Trans-Pecos, formerly a part of the State of Chihuahua. The majority of the lands were initially held in common for the pueblo communities. At the conclusion of both the two Commissions, evidence was compiled and reports prepared for the Legislature along with specific recommendations. Lawmakers determined the merits of each grant claimed. The Legislature confirmed the majority submitted by the Rio Grande Commissioners. Subsequently legislative acts, between 1860 and 1901, confirmed most other claims.[4]

The uncertainty for smaller property owners in the Trans-Nueces continued for years. On February 11, 1858, the Texas legislature passed the Texas Relinquishment Act. This relief allowed the Commissioner of the General Land Office to issue patents to worthy claimants. Lost grants, destroyed archives and questionable documents continued to hinder most. Titles patented as a result of the Commissions numbered over 350. Deeds to Mexican claimants were authorized by the legislature in 1852, and subsequently in 1860, 1870 and 1901. The Texas Land Commissioner reported on November 1, 1853, that 3,746,244 acres had been deeded according to the treaty.[5]

One Texas-Mexico barrier island not considered by the Bourland-Miller Commission came to national attention during the Civil War. The port of Bagdad was safe from seizure by Union blockading squadrons because of its strategic location at the mouth of the Rio Grande. Bagdad was within the territorial boundary of Mexico. The village population grew during the war by the addition of cotton dealers, profiteers and government purchasing agents. Town lots sold at inflated prices. By 1865 La Villa de Bagdad was a vibrant port. After the war, the Municipal Syndicate of the Villa through the Political Prefect of the Department conducted land sales. Although mainly populated by Texans, the island remained Mexican. The village was washed away during the 1889 hurricane. (Fig. 66)

The Trans-Pecos land claims involved over a century of grants. The oldest Texas Indian settlement, Socorro, dated back to the New Mexican Pueblo revolt. The pueblo mission received a royal land grant from King Ferdinand II in 1751 that was similar to other New Mexico pueblo grants. Most Socorro residents date their property rights to a second grant in 1832. The Socorro community and San Elizario long existed without titled lands. Not until the Texas Relinquishment Act of 1858 did the Socorro residents submit claims. The town was patented in 1889. Affidavits, surveys and fees accompanied requests. Individual deeds followed. In 1871 the pueblos of Ysleta and San Elizario were chartered by the Texas Legislature. Through the 1850s residents in the Trans-Pecos were still executing Mexican deeds for property in Mexico on government tax stamped paper. The "Testimonio" protocol continued in El Paso to the end of the century.[6]

The residents of Ysleta claimed a royal land grant. In 1854 the legislature recognized two leagues and surveys were ordered for this grant. Land deeds in Spanish and English followed. Applications for titles began in 1858. In 1873 the county seat moved from San Elizario to Ysleta after the Rio Grande shifted. Patents were issued for private lots. Holders of other royal grants were not as fortunate. Many proved to be bogus. Denied were claims for the José Lerma Grant (1823); The Rancho de Ysleta Grant (1828); La Prieta Grant (1828); Rafael Rúelas Grant (1847); and the José Ygnacio Ronquillo Grant (1832). The massive Ronquillo claim covered most of the Big Bend of Texas. After silver was discovered in 1880 at the Presidio Mine in Shafter, interest in the desert lands exploded. Forged records and lost Mexican archives doomed the Ronquillo patent effort.[7]

Spanish land claims continued well into the twentieth century as evidenced by a letter from Commissioner J. T. Robison of the GLO April 18, 1928, to the Pioneer Abstract & Guarantee Title Co. as filed by the El Paso County Clerk January 25, 1938. Commissioner Robison had personally investigated Trans-Pecos Mexican and Spanish grant claims for two decades. Mexican officials in five states were unable to verify the validity of the La Prieta Grant. The Governor of Chihuahua stated in conclusion that there was no evidence of such a grant between 1828 and 1834 in either his or any other northern Mexico records. An earlier claim that the grant was made in 1750 was proved to be a modern forgery after being subjected to forensic examination. The Trustee of the Texas & Pacific Land Association, Colonel W. H. Abrams, was forced to defend his railroad's patented land against the La

Prieta claimants. He won a criminal conviction against the forgers in Dallas County. The Commissioner promised to put in the penitentiary all land swindlers, and if caught using the mail to sell bogus deeds, he would seek federal charges.

More than a thousand families in the Trans-Nueces and Trans-Pecos would eventually receive patents for land claims. Successful claimants were usually those conversant in English and privileged by legal representation and political connections. Tejano small ranchers, valley farmers and pueblo dwellers were discouraged by the process. One heir wrote that Mexican settlers "were cruelly raped of their land grants by greedy and unscrupulous land grabbers." Such sentiment was earlier expressed by President Ulysses S. Grant, describing the war with Mexico more in the European tradition of grabbing land through conflict. He considered this war "one of the most unjust, ever waged by a stronger against a weaker nation."[8]

Indian land claims were the next oldest unresolved grant claims. Stephen F. Austin, as "Commandant of the Colony on the Brazos and Colorado Rivers," negotiated an agreement with Captain Huan Movat, principal chief of the Lipan Apaches January 15, 1825. After years of negotiation the Creek Indians, through their agent, Ben Hawkins, failed to purchase a homeland from a New York company. The Texas Vigilance Committee on September 15, 1835, appointed General Sam Houston to stop the sale, which he did. A treaty with the Cherokees on February 23, 1836, by Indian Commissioners Sam Houston and John Forbes, secured the tribe's support during the revolution with promises of land to follow. The Texas Consultation on November 13, 1835, assured the tribe it would respect all "just claims" of the Indians living north of the San Antonio Road and the west of the Sabine and Angelina Rivers. The treaty was declared null and void by Congress on December 16, 1837, over Houston's objections. Treaties with the Tonkawas (1837), Lipans (1838), Comanches (1838), Kichais, Towakones, Wacos and Towash (1839) were unfulfilled. The Republic and State did nothing to address the issue.[9]

Mexico had long encouraged better relations with the civilized tribes including the designation of lands for "situating" the Eastern civilized tribes as a barrier to the "savage" tribes. The Texas Provisional Government assured the Cherokees their reservation would be free of settlement by whites and stated that they were considered an "unfortunate race of people entitled to protection" and "the just owners of the soil."[10]

When the Texas General Land Office opened in 1838 no protection of Indian reservations was made. The Congress, in November 1838, announced to "All the People of Texas" the strained relations between President Houston over Indian tribal lands. Surveys were ordered by President Mirabeau Lamar on July 23, 1842, of the reservation lands. The project was cancelled on January 27, 1844, and the territory was later made part of the Peters Colony grant. On September 5, 1850, the legislature, by Joint Resolution, requested the United States to remove all Indians in Texas and relocate them to federal reservations.[11]

Annexation temporarily excused Texas from their broken promises concerning Indian homelands. The United States had no federal lands in Texas to resettle because public land belonged to the State. The Texas legislature in 1854 made available twelve leagues in the Brazos River Basin of North Texas to serve as a federal reservation. Many tribes, including the Apaches, refused to comply with a federal relocation order. Later, most tribes were relocated to the Indian Territory. The reservation later reverted back to Texas. In 1875, the twelve leagues were declared vacant and made available for homesteads and schools. Some were patented to Republic period empresarios as premium lands.[12]

Smaller Indian tribes were normally overlooked. Members of the Coshatta, Tonkawa and Muscogees were resettled periodically. Members were given headrights ranging in size from a half to a full league. The Tiguas of Ysleta del Sur Pueblo in El Paso County received 64 square miles under the 1854 Relinquishment Act. Most participating tribal members lost the granted land after failing to pay taxes. The Pueblo Indians of Texas, the Tiguas, now designated the "Tiwa Indians of Ysleta del Sur Pueblo," in Texas since 1682, were placed under the jurisdiction of the State of Texas on April 12, 1968. Despite many attempts, the small tribe has failed to have its thirty-six mile grant validated. Eagle Pass, Texas, has become the home of the Texas Kickapoos after years of living in Nacimiento, Coahuila, Mexico. In 1989 land was acquired by the Kickapoo Tribe of Oklahoma for a village near Eagle Pass.[13]

# Chapter IX

# Homestead and Education Grants, 1845–1897

Texas homesteads were protected from creditors even before independence. From the Spanish tradition of enhanced marital property rights, Texas community property was always distinct from the English experience. Texas rights date to January 13, 1829, when the legislature of Coahuila and Texas through Decree No. 70 denied seizures by creditors of property necessary to a family, farm or business. This appealed to thousands of bankrupt Americans after The Panic of 1819. Texas homestead protection predated the United States by a quarter century. Homesteaders became a special class of citizen.[1]

Although Texas preceded the United States homestead laws, the two programs had much in common as explained by the U.S. Commissioner of the General Land Office on March 10, 1869, in a "Circular" instructing applicants in the process of obtaining a title through pre-emption, college scrip, railroad grants or purchase programs. Preemptive federal rights were first authorized September 4, 1841, and expanded for soldier bounty warrants in 1852. (Fig. 2) During the Civil War, delayed payment was extended to veterans (Act of May 20, 1862). On June 21, 1866, abandoned lands within the former rebel states of Alabama, Mississippi, Louisiana, Arkansas and Florida became patentable by loyal homesteaders. Parcels ranged in size from 40 acres to a quarter section. The Bureau of Refugees, Freedmen and Abandoned Lands administered abandoned properties from March 1865 to 1872. Parcels cost between $1.25 and $2.50 per acre plus fees between $9.00 and $18.00 depending on size and location. Western lands were priced about 20 percent higher. Preconditions such as residence, notification and cultivation similar to the Texas rules applied. Texas homesteads were always cheaper and larger than their federal counterparts.

Texas families and homes were always encouraged. On December 21, 1838, the Republic Congress authorized a "military road" to Arkansas. In return for volunteering for frontier service, recruits were promised homesteads of 160 acres within the military reservation. Individual sites were to be determined by lot. Surplus lands would be made available to others after completing a two year residency and cultivation requirement. The donated land could not be sold for five years to foster permanent settlement. Lack of funding caused the highway to be abandoned. Congress, in order to fulfill the open enlistment promise, raised the grant to 240 acres and allowed veterans to locate land anywhere in Texas on December 10, 1841.[2]

Republic families were also allowed to apply for "pre-emption grants" from the General Land Office. Such homesteads were distinguishable from the earlier family and military headrights. These grants were subject to conditions of residency as well as the normal improvements and fees for the land. The residency qualifier of three years was less than the federal five year term. If certified, the applicant, after residency, could exercise the pre-emption purchase option. Once completed and land costs paid, the settler could apply for a patent.[3]

The price of pre-emption land under the law of January 22, 1845, was fifty cents if in currency or two dollars if paid in "Late Republic" debts or promissory notes. The parcel, a half section (320 acres) was available to both married and single applicants. Selection of location had to be sworn, vouched and certified in the county. The cut-off date was January 1, 1854. On February 13, 1854, homesteads were reduced to 160 acres. The "pre-emption grant" statute was repealed August 26, 1856. On February 11, 1858, a law especially favorable to slave owners was passed. Planters could request 160 acres for every three slaves owned. The legislature hoped to extend the plantation system to a greater portion of the state. Few patent applications were filed during the Civil War. (Fig. 67) Immediately afterwards, Mexico for a short term promoted immigration to former Confederates. On September 5, 1865, Emperor Maximilian I, with the assistance of the French, encouraged the creation of a "New Virginia" by former Confederates. Four colonial sites at Cordoba, Mazatlan, Monterrey and Veracruz were established. American agents John Perkins, Alonso Ridley, John J. Luz and T. P. Oropesa recruited former Confederates. The four land agents were supervised by the "Pathfinder of the Seas" Matthew Fontaine Maury, a Virginian. Sections of land were priced at a dollar an acre, twice the Texas patented price at the time. Although over a thousand Confederates immigrated, the colonies failed after France withdrew support and the emperor was executed.[4]

After the Civil War, many moved to Texas. Immigrants needed a home. The legislature, on November 12, 1866, renewed its pre-emption homestead program, with modification. Single men had to be at least twenty-one years old. Applicants had only a year to file certificates of location. Residency remained unchanged but the county surveyor had to confirm the site was not claimed by another and it was truly a homestead. Tax and new patents cost three dollars from the GLO.[5] (Fig. 68)

All could not qualify for homesteads. Specifically excluded after the Civil War were blacks and Indians. The Texas Homestead Act was repealed before the Civil War, but when reinstated, only "white settlers" could apply. Not until 1870 was "white only" dropped. Between 1845 and 1898 almost 1,500 females claimed homesteads in their names under Texas law.[6]

After the Civil War, Texas farmers often resisted hiring former slaves. State associations promoted the introduction of foreign agricultural workers to fill the shortage of field hands. In 1868 a "Committee on Immigration" recommended the creation of an agency to seek out and transport white farm laborers. At the time, African Americans accounted for 30 percent of the population. Texas had suffered less property destruction than any other Southern state. Only Galveston and Brownsville were occupied. The inviting opportunities to European farmers were appealing.[7]

In 1866 nine San Antonio businessmen chartered a million-dollar company to exploit "state resources through immigration, investment and enterprise." The "Western Texas Colonial Land Immigration Company" was led by banker John T. Brackenridge and land owners D. G. Beaumont, C. C. Gillespie and D. M. Stapp. The same year Galveston investor John Hunter Herndon of the Buffalo Bayou, Brazos and Colorado Railway Company, and William R. Baker of the Houston and Central Railroad, formed the farm labor immigration company, the "Texas Land, Labor and Immigration Company." Four years later, Texas Speaker of the House, Ira H. Evans, with others from Corpus Christi incorporated the "Texas Land and Immigration Company" with similar objectives. The company was managed by Evans, President of the "New York and Texas Land Company."[8]

These immigration companies were dissimilar to the empresario contractors. None were entitled to premium lands for settlement. European farm immigrants did create a market for railroad scrip land. To promote this program railroads encouraged emigrant guides such as Willard Richardson's *Texas Almanac* (*Galveston Daily News*), 1869–1873, and J. Burke's *Texas Almanac and Immigrants Handbook*, 1875–1885. Coupled with soil descriptions, planting schedules, weather charts, and travel tips, such books were often the only knowledge the newcomer had about Texas. Maps were particularly valuable.[9]

The Legislature, on August 12, 1870, offered to every Texas family a quarter section homestead. Single men were eligible for an eighty acre tract under the same conditions. After establishing residence, the homesteader could survey his property and file field notes with the Land Office along with an affidavit before witnesses. (Fig. 69) A patent would follow from the General Land Office. (Fig. 70) The land cost per acre was a dollar. The homestead pre-emption privilege extended to January 1, 1875.[10]

During the 1871 Texas Democratic Convention, delegates considered methods to improve the state economy. The majority at the time favored "the immigration of the white from all quarters of the world." The Texas Constitution of March 2, 1867, had provided in Article XI, a "Bureau of Immigration" responsible for encouraging, supporting and informing "hardworking and upstanding" emigrants to relocate. The subsequent enabling act, of May 23, 1871, appropriated $30,000 for a general superintendent, staff and an annual report in that agency. The Bureau survived six years during the terms of Governors Edmund Davis and Richard Coke. Budgetary constraints closed the agency despite general approval.[11]

Bureau Superintendents Gustof Loeffler (1871) and Jerome B. Robertson (1874) reduced transport rates for qualified traveling immigrants aboard steamers and trains. Immigration offices were opened in St. Louis for the southern and western states, New York for the north and east, and in Breman, Germany and Manchester, England. The agencies interviewed applicants and issued "Certificates of Immigration Status" qualifying for travel. Farmers were sought, but lawyers and doctors were discouraged through warnings that Texas was not good for such professionals. In 1874 the Bureau published a pamphlet, "Texas: The Home for the Emigrant, From Everywhere." The guide included forty-three pages of favorable testimonials with statistics, almanacs and charts.[12]

During 1871 several more immigration companies were formed. The "Victoria Society of Washington County" was the brainchild of horticulturalist William Weston of Brenham and Waco businessman James B. Baker. It had agents in Britain to recruit farmers. The "Texas European Steamship and Land Company" was formed to "own, build and charter steamships to ply persons between Galveston and the ports of England, Ireland, Wales, Scotland and Breman, Germany." Agents were advised to exclude convicts, drunkards and the depraved. The Galveston steamship company was organized by C. W. Hurley, C. L. Beissner, E. Webster, George Lingham, S. A. Eagerly and W. Crooks. A Dallas area immigration company was formed by George A. Cutler with J. S. and G. W. Porter to do business as the "North Texas Land Company."[13]

Private immigration companies continued through 1873. The "Milam Real Estate and Emigration Association" owned by George Green, J. W. McCowen, Jr., W. M. McGregor, B. F. Ackerman and C. R. Smith, sought workers for Milam and McLennon counties. In El Paso, flour mill owner Simion Hart helped charter the "Texas Land and Colonization Company."

Fellow pardoned Confederate Joseph Magoffin, Collector for the port of El Paso, joined Hart. The region needed workers after the area grew with the Pacific railroad.[14]

Governor R. B. Hubbard delivered an oration at Philadelphia for the opening of the United States Centennial Exposition on September 11, 1876. He was moved to address the question of Texas emigration and tolerance. He boldly proclaimed that Texas invited the emigrant from whatever land, genial and honest young and old alike. The opinion that Texas disliked their Northern brothers as emigrants was denounced as base slander of a brave and generous people. He reminded the audience that the blood of Northern, Western and Southern have all been left in the struggles endured by Texas. He invited all to come to Texas and settle where the "sky is a bright as Italy and the soil always yields a fruitful harvest to those that sweat." He boasted that Texas could easily accommodate a population of forty million. Texas preferred Americans as emigrants but was open to the "Earth's oppressed and hungry."

The State Bureau of Immigration had representatives situated across the state. Most were real estate agents. These agent officials continued to assist newcomers after the Bureau closed in 1877:

| *City/County** | *President* | *Treasurer* | *Secretary* |
|---|---|---|---|
| Brownwood, Brown Co. | W.D.R. McConnell | —— | Will H. Meyers |
| "Panhandle," Carson Co. | O.H. Nelson | F. Lester | J.H. Carter |
| Henrietta, Clay Co. | J. B. Hopkins | S.M. Sears | W.B. Stickney |
| Baird, Callahan Co. | W.H. Cliett | —— | D. Richardson |
| Paint Rock, Concho Co. | G.H. Garland | T.C. Hill | J.D. Campbell |
| Clarendon, Donley Co. | B.H. White | O.P. Wood | S.T. Martindale |
| El Paso, El Paso Co. | S.W. Russell | —— | A.F. Comstock |
| Cisco, Eastland Co. | C.N. Connellee | —— | C.F. Alexander |
| Roby, Fisher Co. | W.L. Harrell | —— | R.C. Crane |
| Sherman, Grayson Co. | J.F. Evans | —— | J.J. Fairbanks |
| Mangum, Greer Co. | A.M. Dawson | R.C. Hannah | F.B. Duke |
| Big Springs, Howard Co. | G.W. Walthall | T.H. Clark | S.H. Cowan |
| Haskell, Haskell Co. | F.P. Morgan | —— | P.D. Sonders |
| Fort Davis, Jeff Davis Co. | O.M. Keesey | G.E. Geege | J. Stewart |
| Edna, Jackson Co. | J.S. McNutt | J.W. Allen | G.A. Staples |
| Anson, Jones Co. | L.M. Buie | F.M. Smith | A.H. Kirby |
| Midland, Midland Co. | G.E. Briggs | J.C. Rothbum | R.H. Zane |
| Colorado, Mitchell Co. | W. Martin | —— | P.D. Cordell |
| Marionfeld, Martin Co. | A Rawlins | H.N. Garrett | Ethan Allen |
| Brady, McCulloch Co. | T.T. Williams | —— | W. McShan |
| Sweetwater, Nolan Co. | B.F. Archer | —— | R.A. Musgrove |
| Weatherford, Parker Co. | J.R. Mackinzie | R.H. Float | J. Hoeny |
| Pecos City, Reeves Co. | S.S. Inge | R.D. Gage | C.F. Miller |
| Ballinger, Runnels Co. | J.N. Winters | S.A. Davis | C.S. Miller |
| Albany, Shackelford Co. | L.N. Bartholomew | —— | L.J. Thompson |
| Snyder, Scurry Co. | J.P. Skinner | —— | H.J. Camp |
| Abilene, Taylor Co. | M.A. Spoonts | —— | E.S. Hughes |
| San Angelo, Tom Green Co. | S.C. Robertson | R.B. Talbert | C.F. Potter |
| Throckmorton, Throckmorton Co. | J.E. Poole | —— | O.J. Kendall |

*Source: *Statistics and Information Concerning the State of Texas.... General Passenger.* Department of the Missouri Pacific RR Co., St. Louis: Woodward & Tresman Printing Co., 1889, 22–25.

Governor Richard Coke, a Civil War veteran from Virginia, after the rebellion, delivered a message to a joint session of the Texas Legislature on January 26, 1874, stating that Texas was needful of population to render productive its millions of acres of rich land. Earlier that month he published a message to "Fellow citizens of Texas" promising the "universal advantage" to incoming immigrants. Chief among the inducements were Texas' liberal homestead laws and cheap, rich productive farms. He noted immigrants were "pouring into her borders" from every quarter, old and new.

Half of the delegates to the 1875 Texas Constitutional Convention were members of the Patrons of Husbandry, or "Grange" as it was better known. The 1876 Texas Constitution, Section 56, prohibited future funding of the Bureau of Immigration. Work of that Bureau was assumed by companies. Emigrant homes for recent arrivals were established by railroad companies. The largest accommodations were in Galveston, Houston and Palestine. William W. Lang, President of the Texas State Grange, was head of the South Western Immigration Company. Grange membership rose to 40,000 and many were new homesteaders. The South Western Immigration Company assumed many functions of the Bureau of Immigration. One state agency survived the budget cuts. The Department of Insurance, Statistics and History Director A. W. Spaight published, in 1882, an "official map" of Texas for the emigrant complete with homestead laws, rainfalls and real estate values. *Resources, Soil and Climate of Texas* was distributed both in Europe and the United States.[15]

The 1876 Texas Constitution offered every homeless family a 160-acre farm if qualified. Single men were still entitled to an 80 acre plot, but the unmarried age limit was lowered to eighteen years. Preemption was restricted to bona fide settlers but speculators devised ways to take advantage of the cheap land offer. That Constitution also released the sovereign mineral interests of the State to land owners. All Texas minerals reserved since Spanish times were converted to private property. The minerals, still part of the public domain, were retained for future Texans.[16]

Groesbeck and Henderson, Land Locators, Stephenville, Erath County, advertised in 1881: "SPECIAL ATTENTION: As the time in which Land Certificates can be located is fast drawing to a close, and all the valuable public land is being rapidly taken up, we call special attention of holders of Land Certificates to these facts and urge them to have their Certificates located before they are either barred from locations or forced to locate on poor or worthless land." The Stephenville surveyors sensed time was running out for the homesteaders. The era of inexpensive homesteads was coming to a close. The scarcity of land pushed the immigrant families deeper into the high plains and Panhandle.

The price for pre-emption lands was $1.50 per acre after the new Constitution. The first application after ratification of the Constitution was in Bowie County. Between 1883 and 1887 twelve million acres were requested as pre-emption land. In 1898 the Texas Supreme Court declared the public domain exhausted. Another eight million homestead acres were patented through the twentieth century. Most were purchased as common school, university and asylum lands. The Constitution of 1876 had also reserved half the remaining public domain for the permanent school fund. When a General Land Office audit discovered insufficient unappropriated land, the homestead program was closed. The school fund was short six million acres. A million and a half acres were added from lapsed land scrip. A recalculation of the size of the state added another four million acres. Cash made up the balance of the permanent school fund deficit.[17]

The Texas public domain had come to an end. Railroad contractors had benefited the most. Their scrip was marketed to the public for decades. A substantial portion was allowed to lapse, never patented, reverting back to the State because survey costs exceeded market value. The next largest public domain disposition was for education.

The municipal government of San Felipe de Austin, five years after its founding, requested a seminary to no avail. More successful was Nacogdoches. That municipality received four sitios of land in 1833 for a public school. Despite the Mexican Constitutional directive that schools be built (and conducted in the Castilian language), none were provided. Provisional government delegates charged that Mexico had failed "to establish any public system of education, although possessed of almost boundless resources [land]." The first Texas Congress reserved three leagues of land for each county to subsidize primary education. By 1848 a tenth of the state budget was devoted to education. After more counties were organized, school acreage was increased to four leagues.[18]

By 1855 the Commissioner of the General Land Office reported that ninety-nine counties had received their promised land for public education. The reserve had grown to over 1,700,000 acres. The grant counties listed below had already completed surveys of their school lands. Acreage was in less settled regions. Newly formed counties continued to receive land until the supply ran out. The following are examples of the school lands awarded the counties[19] (Fig. 71):

| *Grant Counties* | *County of School Land* |
|---|---|
| Bexar | Bexar, Kinney |
| Brazoria | Travis, Medina, Uvalde |
| Bowie | Bowie |
| Fannin | Cooke |
| Fayette | Fayette |
| Fort Bend | Travis, Kinney |
| Galveston | McLennon |
| Gonzáles | Gonzáles |
| Harris | Harris |
| Harrison | Upshur |
| Liberty | Polk, Tyler |
| Robertson | Navarro |
| Nacogdoches | Van Zandt, Upshur |
| Washington | Bexar |
| Milam | McKennon |

Occasionally the GLO held successful land auctions. The Legislature needed a county seat for Smith County. On April 11, 1846, Commissioners purchased land for the future town of Tyler, the county seat, for $150. The twenty-eight-block town comprised a hundred acres and was named in honor of President John Tyler. Lots were auctioned off on April 20, 1852. Successful bidders had the option of paying cash or signing promissory notes payable in eight months with no interest. Single lots averaged about $400, making a nice profit for the state. (Fig. 72)

In 1839 Texas provided fifty leagues for university lands. The actual land survey was delayed until 1853. Proceeds from the sale of these lands were designated for a university fund. University lands were auctioned in the counties of Grayson, Cooke, Fannin, Hunt, Collin, McLennon and Lamar. This quarter-million acres was only the first of many grants. Special acts set aside additional acreage in Gillespie, Smith, Van Zandt and Hopkins counties for Rutersville College and universities in Marshall and Nacogdoches. Parcels normally were sold in quarter sections. As part of the railroad act of January 30, 1854, one tenth of all future railroad grants were dedicated for the university permanent fund. Auction of these lands yielded between one to three dollars an acre. Legislation in 1883 added two million more acres to the permanent school fund. These school and university lands were made available to pre-emption requests by qualified homesteaders and priced at $1.50 per acre. Unclaimed lands could be sold to ranchers. Proceeds from ranch and homestead sales were endowed in the permanent school fund and invested in 6-percent state bonds.[20]

An act of August 30, 1856, directed the governor to make up any deficiency in the fifty leagues due the university permanent fund as originally provided on January 26, 1839. Surveyors located a number of 160-acre tracts. The minimum price was raised to three dollars per acre. Terms were twenty annual payments at 8 percent interest. All purchases were required to post bonds to secure deferred payments. The proceeds were also dedicated to the permanent university fund.[21] (Fig. 73)

Texas education benefited substantially after the annexation. Two million dollars of the United States annexation bonds were appropriated January 31, 1854, to the education fund. The endowment was encroached during the Civil War. The Texas Military Board used some of the bonds to purchase war goods. For three decades, agents tried to recover the bonds. Some were returned. The endowment fund in 1869 received land from lapsed railroad scrip to restore some of the shortfall.[22]

Texas asylums for "lunatic," "orphans," and "deaf, dumb and the blind" also received land grants. Under an August 30, 1856, act, ten thousand dollars was appropriated to locate and survey 300,000 acres for the asylums. Under the Constitution of 1876, asylum lands could be sold as pre-emption land but the proceeds were to be held for the support, maintenance and improvement of the institutions and patients. Between 1881 and 1897 asylum lands were priced between one and two dollars and fifty cents an acre. Pre-emption homesteaders were the most common purchasers, but ranchers also benefitted. Asylum buildings were constructed between 1857 and 1890 in Austin, Terrell and San Antonio.[23] (Fig. 74)

Governor Lawrence Sullivan Ross, in his inaugural address to "Fellow Citizens, Senators and Representatives" on January 18, 1887, recapped the long-held policy in Texas to favor the increase of population and productivity of the soil over the immediate sale and lease of the public domain as a source of revenue. The mission was to allow every industrious man, however poor, the opportunity to become a freeholder. Grants to such yeomen farmers initially were a league and a labor but by Governor Ross' term the homestead had been reduced to only eighty acres for a single man. He noted that many of the older and well settled counties now were in possession of sterile and unproductive public land. Isolated tracts were only desirable to contiguous land owners. Many had been on the market for years. He suggested such parcels of the public domain in older counties should be set aside for pre-emption by bona fide settlers.

In 1889 unlocated county school lands totaled over twenty million acres. Parcels ranged from a low of 70 acres in Limestone County to 2,260,960 and 1,424,486 acres in Pecos and El Paso counties. Also, unsold were University Lands totaling two million acres in far West Texas. Andrews, Crockett, El Paso, Pecos and Tom Green counties had in excess of two hundred thousand acres each. Another million acres of "Common School Lands" were located in the western counties of Reeves, Winkler, Loving, Andrews, Crane and El Paso. On April 1, 1887, an Act provided for the sale of these lands for the benefit of Public Free Schools, the University and Asylums. Ranchers often acquired these tracts for about two dollars an acre, financed for forty years with 5 percent interest.

The General Land Office held over four million acres in trust for Texas students. To this endowment were added the proceeds of forty-five million acres previously sold. The Regents of the University of Texas gained control of their mineral interests. The Texas Agriculture and Military (A&M) University System received a third of the revenue. When the permanent school fund was discovered to be short by six million acres, the General Land Office made up the deficiency in cash and additional land. The greatest loss to the State was the 1876 Constitutional gratis transfer of the sovereign mineral interests to private property owners.[24]

When Governor O. M. Roberts made an address to the Special Session of the Legislature April 6, 1882, he reminded the lawmakers most of the vacant school, university, asylum and reservations to secure public debt were located in western Texas, and short of wood and water. Since the enactment of the pre-emption homestead acts, forty years earlier, only about eighteen thousand applications had been made for tracts within the western frontier, and many of those were abandoned and never patented. Only about 10,000 acres of common school lands were sold over five years. The law of 1879 allowed the purchase limit of three sections raised to seven for common school land. This gave impetus to disposition of a million acres of the public domain for ranches in less than three years.

After the closure of applications by homesteaders, Americans turned to the federal government. The Indian Territory welcomed incoming settlers. Like Texas, the United States continued to provide preference to honorably discharged soldiers and sailors. Civil War veterans who could prove loyalty to the Union and who served at least ninety days were allowed two years credit in fulfilling their three-year homestead residency requirement. The service credit was extended to veterans of the war with Spain, the Mexican border operations and World War I servicemen. The U.S. Commissioner of the General Land Office, on July 1, 1922, reported almost two hundred million acres open to homesteaders (Circular No. 837). The Commissioner reminded potential claimants that most vacant land was west of the Mississippi River, an eighth in South Dakota and quarter in Nevada. None was ever available within the original thirteen colonies or the Republic of Texas. If any prospect was interested in Texas land, the U.S. Commissioner recommended state authorities be contacted.

# Chapter X

# Internal Improvement Grants, 1836–1882

Texas ceded over thirty-six million acres to contractors for improvements to its transportation, roads and canals. Ninety percent was for railroads. One of the first public works contractors was Byrd Lockhart of Virginia, who received four leagues for a San Felipe de Austin road connecting Gonzáles and Matagorda Bay. Land commissioner José Navarro certified the land to the road builder in 1835. On December 21, 1836, the Congress appropriated land, valued at forty cents an acre, to postal contractors for past due claims for mail services rendered on behalf of the Republic. In 1838 Joseph Wilder dug a public canal for the town of New Washington located at Morgan's Point. The two foot drainage ditch cost $1.50 a rod. He was probably paid with land.[1] (Fig. 75)

Defense consumed most of the Republic's budget. Finances improved after statehood. The federal government assumed some of the work projects. The United States built a line of forts from the Red River to the Rio Grande. Army posts became stopovers for western travelers, traders and mail carriers. The way stations were essential to California pilgrims bound for the gold fields. Rio Grande crossings into Mexico became federal custom stations to control smugglers and collect duties from incoming commercial traffic.[2]

Up the Rio Grande to the head of navigation, the federal government built posts. In 1848 the Army leased from Henry Davis "Davis Landing." The thirty-acre outpost became Fort Ringgold. The community of Rio Grande City was the county seat. Thirty years later, the Davis heirs sold the property to the federal government for $20,000. All federal posts, custom houses and courts were either leased or purchased from individuals or the State because United States held no public domain in Texas. Fort Inge on the east bank of the Leona River was leased from David Murphee of San Antonio for fifty dollars a month, payable quarterly. (Fig. 76) Although the camp was abandoned in 1869, the community of Encine became the county seat of Uvalde.

Fort Davis, in the Apache Mountains on Limpia Creek, was the stopover between San Antonio and El Paso. The site, leased from John James, would serve as the county seat for both Presidio and Jeff Davis counties. Fort Concho, next to the town of Ben Ficklin, on the San Antonio–El Paso Mail Line, grew into San Angelo. The largest Texas fort during the "Indian Wars" was Fort Richardson, founded in 1868 in North Texas. The protection offered by such outposts helped settle the frontier.

In the Panhandle, after the Red River War of 1874–1875 that concluded with the Battle of Adobe Walls, the United States Army realized a need for permanent posts between Fort Supply in Indian Territory and the San Antonio headquarters. Governor Richard Coke in a message of August 10, 1876, to the Speaker of the House T. R. Bonner, responded to a request from General P. H. Sheridan for a transfer of sections of land in the northwestern portion of Texas for posts necessary for the protection of the frontier. Article 16, Section 34 of the new Constitution required a law authorizing such transfers before the Governor could sell or lease public domain for use as a U.S. fort or barracks. Fort Elliott at what became Mobeetie in Wheeler County was established in 1875 and operated for fifteen years. The site was leased rather than purchased.

The Republic could afford few projects other than defense. Works such as roads and ferries were left to private developers or county governments. County courts regulated ferries and toll bridges under a December 20, 1836, law. Roads often required public funding. The Republic on May 26, 1838, appointed a commissioner to survey a road from Bastrop to the Red River. The following year another was planned from Washington to Jasper. Both projects were never completed. A turnpike company chartered January 19, 1844, was designated to be a toll road between Houston and Austin. Although the company was given the right of eminent domain, it too, failed to develop.[3]

Internal improvement surveyors earned two certificates (320 acres) and their assistants a single (160 acres) for laying out the highway. Contractors were awarded 160 acres per mile of road completed. Appointed commissioners received a section of land for their service. Patent applications were suspended until the project was certified completed. The planned "National Road," thirty feet wide with fifteen-foot bridges, was scheduled to open by April 1, 1845. It was never completed. Congress authorized thirty-seven thousand acres for actual work performed. The empresarios Mercer and Peters, who colonized the Trinity River Valley, settled along the path of the partially completed "Military Road."[4]

Throughout the nineteenth century, road proposals were presented to the legislature. One state road, to be funded with land scrip, was authorized March 13, 1875. It was designed to be a macadamized highway through Hays County. The turnpike connected San Marcos and Austin. This project followed complaints that railroad companies were too favored with scrip by the lawmakers. Texas needed roads as much as rails.[5]

The Texas Rail Road, Navigation and Banking Company hoped to develop an inter-coastal waterway, but it never materialized. Others were more successful, such as the Colorado Navigation Company (1837) constructing a canal from Matagorda to the Colorado River; Lavaca Navigation Company (1852) for a canal between Matagorda and Lavaca Bay; and, Corpus Christi Navigation Company (1852) connecting Lavaca to the Sabine. Not until 1853 did the Legislature appropriate money for navigation companies. Unrealistic deadlines of four years required regular extensions. In 1853 the Legislature appropriated $300,000 for eighteen coastal and river projects. Half the subsidy was for navigation improvements to the Sabine, Trinity, Brazos and Colorado Rivers.[6]

On August 23, 1856, lawmakers clearly restricted the bulk of the navigation appropriation to the Colorado, Brazos, Trinity and Sabine Rivers. No other river could receive more than $20,000 and bay projects need apply for only $10,000. Counties could float bonds if they wished to improve lakes, bayous or the other navigable waterways. The Galveston and Brazos Navigation Company first earned ninety-four sections of land scrip for improvements between Galveston Bay and the Brazos River. Under the standard contract, companies had to dispose of their land within twenty-four years. Sixteen sections were initially awarded for the Aransas Pass to Corpus Christi Channel. In 1860 the Lavaca Navigation Company received forty-eight sections for a canal between Matagorda and Lavaca Bay.[7] (Fig. 77)

By 1879, the State had granted 4,261,760 acres to private companies, cities and individuals for improving navigable rivers, bayous, channels and creeks. After the projects were certified, scrip could be located, surveyed and patented by the contractors. The City of Corpus Christi received the most in scrip. Navigation scrip was issued for work on the following waterways.[8]

| *Bodies of Water* | *Land Scrip Issued* |
|---|---|
| Sabine River | 1,916 sections |
| Angelina River | 888 sections |
| Neches River | 1,733 sections |
| Galveston Bay to Brazos River | 1,226 sections |
| Matagorda Bay to Lavaca Bay | 48 sections |
| Aransas River to Corpus Christi Bay | 104 sections |
| Trinity River | 684 sections |
| Pine Island Bayou | 60 sections |
| *Certificates* | *6,659 sections* |
| *Total Acreage* | *4,261,760 acres* |

Texas also subsidized ship builders. Beginning in 1854 a quarter section of land scrip was offered to ship and steamboat builders successfully constructing craft of fifty tons or more. Bonus scrip was available for vessels of greater capacity, in twenty ton increments but only if the ship was registered as a United States vessel. The State Commissioner of Claims reported sixty-four half section (320 acres) certificates, representing 20,480 acres, claimed for Texas vessels. The fleet included steamboats, sloops, schooners and sailing ships[9]:

| *Ship* | *Weight* |
|---|---|
| *Betty Powell* | 166 tons |
| *Dr. Massie* | 120 tons |
| *Mary Ella* | 128 tons |
| *Skinner* | 64 tons |
| *Mary Falvey* | 112 tons |
| *Sam* | 100 tons |
| *Union* | 100 tons |
| *Texas* | 175 tons |
| *Falcon* | 75 tons |
| *A. Hawley* | 200 tons |
| *A.B.* | 75 tons |
| *Welshman* | 100 tons |
| *Sarah Johnson* | 50 tons |
| *Mary Heill* | 225 tons |
| *Uncle Mose* | 50 tons |

In 1827 the State of Coahuila and Texas granted driller Leon R. Aleny a six year monopoly for building artesian wells. The State offered scrip to drillers for artesian wells capable of flowing fifty gallons of potable water per minute. The standard award was eight sections. For wells deeper than four hundred feet, bonus sections at the rate of one per hundred feet were available. Wells on the roads between San Antonio to El Paso; Corpus Christi to Rio Grande City; Corpus Christi to Brownsville; and San Antonio to Laredo made inland travel less hazardous. Bids for wells were announced in newspapers for Austin, San Antonio, Corpus Christi, Brownsville and Galveston prior to the awards. The 1858 program ended with the Civil War.[10]

During the Civil War the State "Military Board" renewed the Texas shipbuilding effort. The Houston Navigation Company refitted the *Bayou City*, a postal transport armed with guns converted from the captured United States Revenue Cutter *Henry Dodge*. The *Bayou City* participated in the Battle of Galveston on New Year's Day, 1863. The vessel was reflagged as a Confederate vessel and the State was reimbursed. The State Military Board, under a December 16, 1863, Act, issued 7 percent bonds with land scrip exercisable "twelve years after the close of the present war." No evidence of land ever being patented with such scrip is known. It is unlikely since the Fourteenth Amendment to the U.S. Constitution repudiated all rebel debt.[11]

An Act of December 15, 1863, allowed land scrip to encourage the construction of iron, cotton and wool factories as well as the manufacture of arms, niter, sulphur and powder. A certificate was earned for each thousand dollars of goods produced. The following companies, none of which survived past 1879, earned Civil War land scrip[12]:

| *Companies* | *Scrip Certificates (Half Sections)* |
|---|---|
| Texas Powder | 12 |
| Waco Manufacturing | 58 |
| Theodore Koester | 19 |
| Concordia Cotton Mill | 83 |
| Comal Manufacturing Company | 47 |
| Sulphur Fork Iron Works | 97 |
| Cherokee Furnace Company | 33 |
| *Total Certificates* | *349* |
| *Total Acreage* | *111,680* |

The Brazos Manufacturing Company, incorporated May 28, 1864, in Robertson County, had nineteen stock subscribers who each contributed fifty or a hundred bales of cotton in exchange for their shares. Land scrip was one of the incentives for the investment. The wool and flour factory was built by Captain Charles P. Slater, C.S.A., with slave laborers, on Pine Oak Creek, five miles east of Hearne. European equipment and millstones were imported through the Union blockade. All arrived too late. Delayed delivery denied the company any scrip. The Brazos Manufacturing Company did receive preliminary certification for its plant. Survey and field notes for the six hundred acre plat were filed May 12, 1864.[13] (Fig. 78)

By 1875, the Legislature realized the capital city needed more water to grow. A February 27, 1875, act authorized twenty sections for each mile of canal constructed between Austin and the reservoir at Marble Falls on the Colorado River. The ten-foot-wide ditch was five feet deep. After the ditch was excavated two and half miles, the water company received twenty sections of land for every mile completed thereafter. After the canal was approved by the state engineer, the company received an additional twenty-five sections. The company easements were similar to those granted to railroads. The water rates were state regulated. The utility authority furnished water services free of charge to the City of Austin and the State Government. Maintenance and service of the system was the responsibility of the State.[14]

Water affected early land values more than any other factor. The Spanish always limited the width of river frontage included in grants to homesteaders. Parcels were fan shaped to equalize riverside access. Irrigated lands were the most desirable. The legislature, on December 2, 1871, granted irrigation companies eminent domain similar to railroads. The San Antonio River Valley Irrigation Company built a ditch north of Goliad. The company raised $50,000 for that project. The Pecos Irrigation, Manufacturing and Live Stock Company invested $30,000 in water projects for West Texas. General contractors drilled water wells for the system.[15]

On April 25, 1874, El Paso County was allowed to develop a network of irrigation ditches nine feet wide and five feet deep. Irrigation scrip denominated in eight-section certificates was used to pay construction companies. To qualify, a contractor had to complete five miles of ditch certified suitable for agricultural irrigation. The regional program was expanded statewide on March 10, 1875. That act had several classes of canals distinguished by width and depth of the ditch. Irrigation companies could condemn a 150 foot easement. Landowners were entitled to fair compensation. Irrigation rates were set by state officials. Once certified, the irrigation company was given an exclusive franchise. All construction was subject to oversight of State engineers.[16]

Irrigation companies submitted scrip applications according to the size ditch proposed. Although the act had several classes of ditches, only small canals were actually dug. A total of 584,000 acres in certificates were patented. Canal depths were increased and scrip awards lowered on April 21, 1876. The following scrip awards were authorized under the two acts[17]:

| ***Canals*** | ***Scrip Award (Per Mile)*** | | | |
|---|---|---|---|---|
| *Class* | *Width* | *Depth* | *1875 Act* | *1876 Act* |
| 1 (Not Built) | 30' | 4' | 16 sections | |
| 1 (Not Built) | 30' | 5' | | 8 sections |
| 2 (Not Built) | 15' | 4' | 12 sections | |
| 2 (Not Built) | 15' | 5' | | 6 sections |
| 3 | 9' | 3' | 8 sections | |
| 3 | 9' | 3' | | 4 sections |
| 4 | 6' | 2½' | 6 sections | |
| 4 | 6' | 2½' | | 2 sections |

The half million acres for water ditches were dispersed over twenty-six regions and benefited two dozen companies; the projects were completed by 1882[18]:

| *Company* | *Class 3 Ditch* | *Class 4 Ditch* |
|---|---|---|
| Ben Ficklin | 31 certificates | |
| Comanche Creek | 63 certificates | |
| Canutillo | 52 certificates | |
| Elizario | 50 certificates | |
| El Paso | 196 certificates | |
| Garza | 11 certificates | |
| Key West | 33 certificates | |
| Leona | 97 certificates | |
| Mud Creek | 9 certificates | |
| Pinto | 24 certificates | |
| Presidio | 19½ certificates | |
| Puerta Tierra | 15 certificates | |
| Quadrilla | 50 certificates | 14 certificates |

*continued on p. 47*

| *Company* | *Class 3 Ditch* | *Class 4 Ditch* |
|---|---|---|
| Ruidosa | 21 certificates | |
| San Antonio | 9 certificates | |
| San Antonio Valley | 27 certificates | |
| San Felipe | 9 certificates | |
| San Geronimo | 9 certificates | |
| Saragosa | 9 certificates | |
| Socorro | 60 certificates | 12 certificates |
| Torres | 25 certificates | |
| Toyah | 12 certificates | |
| Vaughan | 11 certificates | |
| Ysleta | 34 certificates | |
| Total certificates (sections) | 513 | 399.5 |
| Total acres | | 584,000 |

The first Texas railroad chartered, the Texas Railroad, Navigation and Banking Company, was never built. The second, the Harrisburg and Brazos Railroad, fared no better. The third, the Buffalo Bayou, Brazos and Colorado, of 1840, managed to complete only a few miles. (Fig. 79) Despite little progress, the legislature had chartered fourteen companies by 1852. Railroads were lured by the generous eight-section grants for every mile completed, after completing the initial twenty-five miles. Companies had to alienate patented lands within twelve years. Railroads were required to survey alternating sections for the benefit of the State free of charge. When the Civil War began, only five hundred miles were operational, and seven of the charters had lapsed.[19]

Texas needed to open its western lands to settlement. In 1853 lawmakers offered rail companies twenty sections of land for every mile completed for a transcontinental line from Arkansas to El Paso. The "Mississippi and Pacific Railroad Reserve" of land was appropriated to fund that project. The Vicksburg and El Paso Railroad Company, first chartered February 16, 1852, as the Texas Western Railroad, was formed to build the line across Texas. It was reorganized in 1856 as the Southern Pacific Railroad, not related to the California company of the same name. (Fig. 80) The New York rail company was required to post a $300,000 performance bond. In 1858 twenty miles were complete but construction halted during the Civil War. The "Southern Trans-Continental Railway Company," chartered July 27, 1870, was assigned its rights after the war. With only 5 percent down, subscribers could acquire "Scrip Stock."[20] (Fig. 81)

State and municipal governments loaned money to many Texas railroad companies. The State also invested endowment funds in railroad bonds. Rail companies could borrow $600 for every mile of line completed. This was often more valuable than the land scrip. Six railroad companies received money from the education trust fund[21] (see table).

| *Railroads* | *Loans* |
|---|---|
| Houston and Texas Railroad | $450,000 |
| Texas and New Orleans Railroad | $430,000 |
| Buffalo Bayou, Brazos and Colorado Railroad | $420,000 |
| Houston and Brazoria Railroad | $300,000 |
| Southern Pacific Railroad | $150,000 |
| Washington County Railroad | $66,000 |
| Total Bonds | $1,816,000 |

After the Civil War, only a thousand miles of track remained. Most rail equipment was inoperable. Between 1869 and 1873 legislative subsidies to railroads was suspended. Although railroad land grants were reinstated at the rate of twenty sections per mile completed, the 1873 Panic slowed construction. Railroad grants were again suspended on April 22, 1882. The final portion of the transcontinental railroad was completed in 1883. The five thousand miles of line cost Texas thirty-two million acres. The railroad holding companies consolidated all lines into three companies. These companies held patents for twenty million acres from the scrip. Southern Pacific (fourteen lines), Missouri Pacific (four lines) and Texas and Pacific (seven lines) netted about $1.34 an acre from the sales of some of the land. Most of their acreage was transferred to land holding companies.[22]

Some have questioned if Texas received full value for land awarded to build its railroads. Governor James Stephen Hogg long condemned the railroads for taking advantage of the State. He termed their real estate holding companies "parasites." The Texas and Pacific conveyed its real estate to the Texas and Pacific Land Company. The Illinois and Great Northern placed property in the New York and Texas Land Company. (Fig. 82) The New York land syndicate of 1846 sprang up after West Texas was secure following the Mexican War. Texas federal judge John C. Watrous assisted three New Yorkers, James G. Minor, J.N. Reynolds and Joseph L. Williams, in forming the holding company. Watrous provided legal advice in the company's purchase of four hundred league headright certificates, representing claims to over one million six hundred thousand acres along the upper Rio Grande and Puerco (Pecos) Rivers. The land, 3,049,430 acres, was sold in 1879 for almost five million dollars. Railroad historian A. G. Reed concluded that the railroad scrip program in general was sound and fair to the public. The value of the land awarded was less than the actual cost of construction. Many West Texas communities owe their existence to the railroads. Governor Hogg's complaints did result in the denial to alien corporations.[23]

The Legislature of Texas lobbied the federal government to build a "first class" deep water port capable of berthing ocean carriers and naval vessels. The United States Corps of Engineers was assigned the task of building an inland waterway along the Texas coastline. In 1894 the Texas Legislature assisted the United States in its purchase of land for canals and harbors in furtherance of the waterway.[24]

# Chapter XI

# Panhandle and Western Grants, 1879–1900

During Reconstruction vast amounts of real estate were forfeited for delinquent property taxes. At tax auctions, foreclosed real estate often passed back to the state for lack of buyers. Interest in land was slight unless near railroad terminals or ports. The official price for land was lowered from a wartime high of two dollars an acre to only fifty cents. In spite of these constraints, Texas was relatively well off as compared to the South in general. Immigration continued and the population grew. Former Texas Supreme Court Justice George W. Smith published a broadside enticing emigrants from the Midwest to Texas. Numerous benefits awaited newcomers, including fertile soil, high crop yields, abundant water and timber, moderate climate, good transportation and cheap land. The Houston lawyer turned realtor listed as business references Governor E. J. Davis, federal judges and lawmakers. (Fig. 83)

Between 1871 and 1876 the Texas Bureau of Immigration published brochures for those interested in relocating to Texas. Highlighted were cheap homesteads, creditor protection and fertile land. After the Bureau closed for lack of funding, railroad marketing departments continued the promotionals. The Great Northern Railroad published "Lone Star Guide." The International and Great Northern Railroad printed in 1880 "Homes in Texas" with guidance on picking a residence and farm. *Burke's Texas Almanac and Immigration Handbook* informed thousands annually of the benefits of farming in Texas. The Santa Fe Railroads ran excursion trains called "Specials for Land Prospectors," complete with cheap lodging for prospective settlers.[1]

Simultaneous with the influx of new emigrants were foreign speculators fully aware of the good cattle range at depressed prices. Out of state investors used local agents and nameless holding companies to conceal their activities. Governor James S. Hogg championed the causes of the "Patrons of Husbandry" including homestead exemptions, railroad regulations, low interest and limits on speculation. Hogg supported the passage of two "Alien Landowner Prohibition" laws, dated April 13, 1891, and April 12, 1892. Each prohibited "foreign" corporations from owning land. These laws were not repealed until the mid-twentieth century.[2]

A fire caused one of the largest transfers of public land in Texas. Speculators were ready. In 1875 delegates of the Constitutional Convention expressed interest in another state house. On February 20, 1879, the "Capitol Board" recommended selling three million acres in the Panhandle to fund the project. At most, the land was worth no more than $1,650,000. The old capitol building was destroyed by fire November 9, 1881, placing the project on a fast track. The "Capital Reserve," as the Panhandle land was known, was selected from the "best lands" in ten counties in the high plains. Leagues were marked off in Deaf Smith, Parmer, Lamb, Castor, Bailey, Hockley, Dallam, Hortley, Cochran and Oldham counties. The tracts were offered in exchange for the construction of the new capitol building. Few bid. The contract was awarded to Matheas Schnell of Rock Island, Illinois, in 1882. Fifty thousand acres were also surveyed for architect fees. This second tract was in Oldham County, and sold February 20, 1879, for $27, 750 or fifty-five cents an acre.[3]

The contractor, Matheas Schnell, assigned its "Capitol Reserve" land to Taylor, Babcock and Company to raise capital for the construction project. John V. Farwell, of the Chicago investment house Taylor, Babcock, organized in 1884 the English-based "Capitol Freehold and Investment Company, Ltd." Their real estate venture, named the "Capitol Syndicate," intended to ranch the property while land values appreciated. The Syndicate adopted modern ranching methods on its "XIT" Ranch. Barbed wire and windmills well demonstrated the fertility of the high plains soil for livestock and farming. The "XIT" had a million dollar livestock herd. The Syndicate floated a million pound sterling bond secured by deeds of trust against the real estate to finance the ranching operations. The bonds yielded 7 percent.[4]

The "Capitol Syndicate" business model proved valid. By 1909 the real estate holding company was free of debt and held its land free and clear. Truck farms prospered with good water, seed selection and modern cultivation methods and won many prizes at the State Fair of Texas in 1887. The Oldham County Immigration Association promoted the Panhandle towns of Amarillo and Texline, located along the Denver and Fort Worth Railroad line. Older towns moved toward the line in order to take advantage of the new rail terminals. In 1890 the Syndicate subdivided 80,000 acres for public sale.

Multiple sections had been sold to large-scale ranchers such as George W. Littlefield's "Yellow House," W. E. Halsell's "Spring Lake" and the Matador Ranch near Amarillo. Unimproved grazing land brought a dollar an acre. Fenced farms went from $3 to $5 an acre. After the "XIT" cattle herd was liquidated, the balance was sold off in the 1950s.[5]

Sale of Texas's "upper stovepipe" to the United States after annexation changed the shape of the state. Disposal of the "Capitol Reserve" shaped the state's future. The new capitol was completed at double its estimated construction costs. The $3,200,000 price tag, which converts to $1.07 per acre, confirmed the good bargain struck by the lawmakers. Railroads, water and increased population opened the Texas Panhandle. Only after the public domain was no longer available did the market value of raw land begin to rise. After the public domain was depleted, economic opportunity in the form of oil and gas reserves doubled with land as the coin of the realm. Latecomers to Texas redirected their wagons to the Indian Territory. The federally managed Oklahoma land boom was welcomed by disappointed Texas home seekers.

According to Texas historian Walter Prescott Webb in his book *The Great Plains*, barbed wire was instrumental in settling the High Plains. J. F. Glidden's barbed wire, patented in 1879, was distributed throughout Texas by Sanborn and Walter. It often cost more to enclose farmland than it did to buy it. By 1882 over forty-six million acres were deeded to homestead famers who purchased corresponding rolls of fencing. Surveys and fencing divided the frontier.[6]

As deadlines approached for the railroads to dispose of their land scrip to third parties, land offices scrambled to protect holdings. The most obvious buyers were ranch operators. In North Texas, Scandinavian Svante Magnus Swenson bought scrip from the Buffalo, Brazos and Colorado Railroad. His Throckmorton Ranch grew after the purchase of school lands. The "SMS" ranching empire costs averaged less than a dollar an acre, and land prices were going up.[7]

The merger of International Houston with the Great Northern Railroad resulted in the transfer of three million acres of land to its real estate trust. The assignee was an affiliated real estate holding company, the Texas Land Company. The $4.6 million dollar entity reorganized into the New York and Texas Land Company, with offices in Austin and New York. In 1882 its board sold 637,440 acres of its land for $887,654 to the Francklyn Land and Cattle Company. The property was scattered over Carson, Greg, Hutchison and Roberts counties. Ranch operations were conducted as the "White Deer Lands." School land purchases at fifty cents an acre were added to their holdings. Two decades after its formation, the White Deer sold tracts to other ranchers. Between 1903 and 1924, White Deer Lands sold quarter section parcels to small farmers for $3.00 an acre. Terms were 20 percent down with the balance over five years at 6 percent. In 1919 oil was discovered on some of the property. In 1957 White Deer was completely liquidated.[8]

One railroad scrip saga was particularly complex. The Memphis, El Paso and Pacific Railroad extended its charter after the Civil War. Explorer, politician and speculator, John Charles Frémont gained control of its successor company and began to raise capital in Europe, through the sale of railroad bonds. (Fig. 84) Little of the five million dollars raised benefited the rail company. The company went into receivership. In 1873 the federally chartered Texas and Pacific Railroad acquired the transcontinental right of way of the successor company to the Memphis, El Paso and Pacific Railroad. It assumed the bonded debt incurred by Frémont. The railroad's bonds and scrip were transferred to a real estate holding company August 7, 1876, the Franco-Texan Land Company. (Fig. 85) The company's inflated land scrip was manipulated so that the French creditors seemed protected. The French bondholders received $100 stock for each thirteen acres of scrip but the land was valued at $8.00 an acre. The land was valued at $5,340,000, eight times its actual worth. The 640,000 acres in Parker, Palo Pinto, Stephens, Callahan, Shackelford, Mitchell, Taylor, Nolan, Jones and Fisher counties were offered at a dollar an acre, despite its eight dollar alleged valuation to the court. The purpose of the Land Company was to acquire, locate, lease and sell lands, ostensibly for the bondholders. Promoting immigration was essential in creating a market for their real estate. Profits were to be split 95 percent to shareholders and 5 percent to directors; however directors diverted most of the profits through fees to themselves as agents, advisors and officers. The bulk of the proceeds went to the insiders rather than French shareholders. A few Frenchmen travelled to Texas. Upon their arrival at the corporate offices in Weatherford, they demanded thirteen acres of land. Most were refused and lawsuits followed. A fire destroyed most of the Company's records. Allegations of embezzlement followed. In settlement, shareholders were promised $13.35 a share payable in three installments. Land was sold at $3.00 an acre to wind down the bankrupt company.[9] (Fig. 86)

The Fort Worth and Denver Railroad's agents directed home buyers to their holdings in Archer City, Henrietta, Clarendon, Clairemont and Dumas. Many future oilmen started from land purchased from this line. The Texas and Pacific was instrumental in the growth of Odessa, Big Spring and Pecos. The Missouri, Kansas and Texas, from its emigration offices in St. Louis, Cincinnati, Louisville and New York sold passage to many would-be Texas settlers. The "KATY" excursion, tagged the "Pioneer Line," brought thousands of buyers from the Midwest. The Houston and Texas Central passed through the Indian Territory. Thousands of guides were distributed to home-seekers traveling the "Central Route" from Oklahoma to Texas. De Córdova, Wither and

Company, Land Agents with offices in Austin, Houston, Dallas and Galveston advertised a quarter million acres suitable for farming and ranching priced between a dollar and two an acre. Their promotion read "Tickle the soil with a hoe, and she will laugh out crops with so much ease that the hard working immigrant from the old world ... will scarcely credit his senses."[10]

The line between Hempstead and Dallas opened in 1872. Dallas became the transportation and warehouse hub for North Texas. During the Republic era, the "Military Highway" had been surveyed along this same route. Dallas, founded in 1844, was strategically placed at the Trinity River crossing. The 1846 town of merchants, mills and warehouses was thriving by the Civil War.

Another North Texas town owing its existence to the railroad was Denison. The "KATY" arrived in 1873. A half dozen railroads converged at this gateway to the Indian Territory. To the city's west was the old trading post of Preston, terminus of the old "Military Road." Midwestern land promoters hawked Denison as the natural jumping-off spot for all bound for Texas. Families from Ohio, Missouri and Kentucky arrived aboard the excursion trains. Land "sharpies" met them at the station. Promoters of the "Ohio, Kentucky and Texas Land Company" offered for only one dollar a 25' × 100' lot in Grayson County. Their town site "Mineral City" was pictured on promotional maps. Buyers could have, for another dollar, a warranty deed. The 1876 purchaser got little more than an empty promise of land and his train trip. (Fig. 87)

Land frauds had long plagued the General Land Office. Governor Richard Coke in his January 12, 1875, message to a joint session reminded the lawmakers the "bad men" had constantly perpetuated through forgery and fraud, evils against the State of Texas. Such acts consumed hours of investigation and research to clear beclouded titles. Sadly the miscreants escaped punishment because the crimes were difficult to prove. He suggested to the lawmakers that a Land Office detective agency be considered. Budgetary constraints defeated the proposal.

The Iron Mountain and Southern ran its "Grand Texas Excursion" in conjunction with the Ohio and Mississippi, Texas, Pacific and Houston, and Texas Central. Real estate broker Henry H. Hanson, Swan Creek, Ohio, in 1878 encouraged all to get aboard for Texas "to make a first class investment ... at the least possible expense, as well as those seeking recreation, the pleasure of hunting." Round-trip tickets were good for forty days. Beginning in Cincinnati, connections were available from river steamers along the Ohio and Mississippi. Travelers could bring up to two hundred pounds of baggage, checked to their final destination, for the price of their ticket. (Fig. 88)

Many cities were created by the railroads. Arlington, in Tarrant County, located on the Texas and Pacific near Bird's Fort, was founded in 1878. Lots were bought in bulk by real estate brokers such as William Jesse Boaz, a Fort Worth developer. From his office in Arlington Heights at the "Flatiron Building" he advertised, in 1892, three dozen lots. He paid less than $2,000 for the parcel. Jay Gould's heir, George J. Gould of Lakewood, New Jersey, president of the railroad, deeded lots to the Boaz Company in 1893. (Fig. 89)

# Chapter XII

# Speculation

Colonizers and speculators filled the void of the frontier. Abundant land constrained market value, except in populated areas. Real estate speculators, especially foreign, were contrary to the Republic's ideal. Section 10 of the Constitution made null many late-date purchases from the State of Coahuila and Texas. Forever named in infamy was New Yorker John T. Mason and similarly situated speculators. Others denied grants were the heirs of James Bowie and Benjamin R. Milam, as well as Thomas J. Chambers and Samuel M. Williams. All were denied the benefits of their nefarious land grabs.[1]

The Republic's program to grant land to veterans and first families chilled the Texas real estate market for decades. The oversupply of land certificates depressed values to pennies on the dollars. Railroad scrip aggravated the market depression. Discounts ran as high as 90 percent. Seldom did bids reach the government price of fifty cents an acre. Eastern financiers such as Nicholas Biddle, Jay Cooke, and the Collector of the Port of New York, Samuel Swartwout, sought land empires in Texas. Michel Menard's Galveston City Company was one of the few financial successes. Galveston became a sister port to New Orleans and the largest city in Texas. Menard's investors were handsomely rewarded while others took notice.[2]

Dr. William P. King, through the Southern Land Company of Holly Springs, Mississippi, purchased thousands of acres in North Texas. The company opened an office in 1839 in San Augustine. New Yorker Warren Ferris was hired to survey 400,000 acres of the promised Cherokee tribal lands in the Three Forks region of the Trinity River. Ferris explored what became Dallas, Kaufman, Van Zandt, Hunt, Rockwall, Collin and Denton counties. King died before the project was completed. His successor, John Neely Bryan, persuaded settlers of Bird's Fort to relocate to a bluff above the Trinity River, and the site became Dallas, at the head of navigation of the Trinity River.[3]

Samuel Swartwout and associates formed his namesake town along the Trinity River in present day Polk County. The organizers, James Morgan, Arthur Garner and Thomas Bradley, placed fifty acres each in the venture. The site was located at "Garner's Ferry." (Fig. 90) Sam Houston invested in their venture. Bradley, from San Augustine, was the local agent for James Morgan, from New York. Morgan had served as Lorenzo de Zavala's land agent in 1834, and founded "Morgan's Point" on the peninsula between Galveston and San Jacinto Bays. That land had been purchased from Nicholas Clopper in 1832 and would become part of the Houston Ship Channel. "Swartwout" was the typical model city plan divided into 86 blocks of 60' × 120' lots. Main streets were 80 feet wide with secondary roads of 50 feet.[4] (Fig. 91)

Nicholas Clopper, an Austin colonist, operated his Texas trading store from 1827 at Clopper's Point, before selling to James Morgan. He and his son moved to Matagorda Bay where they founded the "City of Portland" in 1841 on the Colorado River near Tres Palacios Bay. The two thousand acres included both town and commercial blocks. (Fig. 92) The Galveston engraved stock certificates was denominated in dollars and could be exchanged for lots. The town failed to grow. On Mission Bay, Stuart Perry planned "Port Preston," which he advertised in 1840 as a "little colony of Carolinians," on the road to San Antonio. A promotional piece advertised that it was located on the way to the silver mines of Chihuahua. Although chartered on January 21, 1839, it did not survive. Up Matagorda Bay, between La Grange and Bastrop, the town of Rutersville, founded in 1839, grew as a college town.[5]

The brother of Galveston developer Pierre J. Menard partnered with merchants Samuel May Williams and Thomas F. McKinney in 1838 to launch the town of Menard on the west bank of the Neches River. The $50,000 company surveyed 1,408 lots for their development. Shares could be redeemed for lots. Agent Stephen H. Everitt of Bevil sold the securities to speculators. (Fig. 93) Also located on the Neches River was Georgia, organized by Thomas McKinney. Neither Georgia or Menard proved successful. More fortunate was Sabine City (Sabine Pass) organized in 1839. Incorporators of the 2,060-lot venture included Sam Houston, Philip A. Sublett, George W. Hockley, John S. Roberts, Albert G. Kellogg, Niles F. Smith and Sidney Albert Johnston. (Fig. 94) The town, chartered June 15, 1861, was annexed by Port Arthur in 1878. That same group formed the "Town of Hamilton" in 1839, on the Sabine River. It too was successful.[6]

The "Town of Louisville" was promoted by Samuel S. Davis, Summer Bacon and Almanzon Huston. Huston had served as the Texas Quartermaster General in 1837. Huston owned the Nacogdoches to Huntsville Stage Company. Shareholders could take lots, valued in $250 and $500 certificates. (Fig. 95) Davis was a Representative from San Augustine while Summer Bacon served as the Texas agent of the American Bible Society. The town failed to develop. Also in East Texas, "Magnolia Town Company," organized in 1840, capitalized on the military post at Fort Houston, also on the Trinity River. Company agent S. Payne of San Augustine saw the depot grow, until it was bypassed by the railroad.[7]

The Edwards Brothers, surviving the 1826 Fredonian Rebellion, returned to Texas in 1838 and laid out two towns, opposite each other, on the Sabine River. "Fredonia" and "Cotton Plant" were planned to be agricultural depots. The four-hundred-share joint ventures entitled holders to receive five of the two thousand lots in exchange for stock. The company advertised in the Nacogdoches and San Augustine newspapers. The towns were never built.[8]

Cities were surveyed above almost every bluff on the Trinity River. Most were little more than a town name and field notes. An Arkansan floating the river in 1842 wrote that "on nearly all of the Bluffs speculators have marked out town sites with high sounding names." One, Coshutte, was set ten miles north of Liberty in 1839. Originally known as "Tanner's Bluff," the town was sold by four promoters, Samuel Whiting, William M. Logan, William P. Harris and Robert Wilson. Coshutte advertised churches, seminaries, schools, a court house, market and town hall, but none were built. Presidents of the Republic loaned their prestige to promote towns such as Mirabeau B. Lamar's Copano Bay and Anson Jones's Manhattan. Both failed.[9]

English speculators long participated in the Texas land boom. Pumphrey Burnett backed the port of Tres Palacios in Matagorda County. First known as Tidehaven, the 1845 company, officed at 141 Leadenhall Street, London, England. The £50 lots were divided into thirty lot blocks varying in size from 25' × 100' to 25' × 125'. Owners had five years to build or lose ownership. The covenant period started after the owner took possession. (Fig. 96) The promotion failed, partially due to a title dispute.

The continuous line of town promotions sustained the demand for Texas maps and guides. Francis Moore updated Stephen F. Austin's seminal map. Moore's Houston *Telegraph and Texas Register* reported that although there were "many vicious and corrupt men" in the state, the newer class of emigrant "is of a respectable character" and Texas society was becoming more civil. A guide by George Bonnell, in 1840, was pleased to announce that the "wearing of concealed weapons is so unusual." He warned newcomers not to be "Loaded down with pistols and Knives" because locals will only laugh. Land compared favorably to other parts of the nation. Acreage costs were a tenth of the price of property in the Midwest. He advised emigrants to locate below the frontier. Most importantly, the buyers were cautioned to avoid persons of doubtful character selling property.[10]

Illinois minister Orceneth Fisher published a traveler's guide in 1893. The Methodist preacher assured his readers that "Not all in Texas are desperados and outlaws." He was amazed at the "lovely surface" of the land and noted that the farther west one journeyed, "the beauty of the scenery greatly increases." He also admonished everyone to stay clear of speculators. The minister's price point was no more than fifty cents an acre. Hunt and Randel's guide detailed the changing character of Texas and its population. Descriptions of 35 counties along with 150 city previews came with the full endorsement of General Sam Houston and GLO Commissioner Thomas L. Ward. The 1845 Hunt and Randel map became the accepted standard during early statehood.[11]

Naturally the new railroad towns had emigrant hotels, and were the first to capture the interest of newcomers. Such stations connected the population centers. Dr. Richard Rodgers Peebles of the mercantile firm J. S. Shackelford, Galveston, donated right-of-way to the Houston and Central Railroad. Peebles' Hempstead Town Company sold lots beginning in 1857. (Fig. 97) Buyers could pay 10 percent down with the balance due over three years. Speculators could pay nothing down with the balance due at 10 percent interest in a year. This second form was a no risk option. After full payment all received warranty deeds. (Fig. 98) After the Houston and Central made it to Dallas in 1872, Hempstead became the central station for traffic between Houston and Dallas.[12]

Plans to render the Trinity River navigable date to the Republic. Nevertheless, Dallas prospered as a transportation and distribution center. Crucial to that success was Sarah Horton Cockrell's iron bridge, built with private funds. The bridge spanned the flood plain of the Trinity River and was strategically positioned at the center of Dallas. Completed in 1872, the bridge was sold to the city in 1878, after six years of private ownership. Mrs. Cockrell reinvested her profits in lots, hotels and mills, to become a significant commercial force in North Texas. (Fig. 99)

From the time of "Champ d'Asile," founded by Napoleonic veterans in 1817, Texas has drawn social visionaries. The "wild" of the wilderness crushed most utopian dreamers. Both Robert Owen's attempt at a Texas "New Harmony' and abolitionist Benjamin Lundy's freedmen colony on the Nueces progressed no farther than the planning stage. French socialist Étienne Cabet was only slightly more successful. He purchased ten thousand acres in the Peters Colony in 1847 as a "Promised land, and a new Paradise on Earth." Named "Icaria," the Utopian settlement never exceeded several hundred. Seventy colonists arrived in Texas in 1848. The hundred thousand acres, near present-day Junction, was quickly abandoned, and colonists returned to New Orleans. The French socialist

Victor Prosper Considerant attempted a "Charles Fourier" commune in 1855 along the north bank of the Trinity River. The experiment collapsed due to lack of organization and funding after two years. The site, "La Réunion," populated by members of the "Société de Colonisation Européo-Américaine au Texas," was on the chalk bluff in Oak Cliff overlooking Dallas. Morman Lyman Wight's "Zodiac" on the Colorado River north of Austin, was slightly more successful, but was destroyed by floods in 1858.[13]

The Clarendon Land Investment and Agency Company of London sold land in Donley County to Methodist evangelist Lewis Henry Carhart and W.A. Allen in 1878. The English real estate company had acquired 343 sections of railroad scrip, and subdivided some into lots and farms. The town of "no drinking" Methodists was a Western oddity. Nicknamed "Saint's Roost" by the cowboys, Donley became the county seat in 1887. The Fort Worth and Denver City Railway helped sales of the acreage by the Clarendon Land Investment and Agency Company. The $13.50 acre land was offered in 1889. Deeds were signed by the U.S. General Consul in London. That same year Roman Catholic priests founded Mariensfield (Stanton) with scrip purchased from the Texas and Pacific Railroad. The community survived. Quakers settled in Crosby and Lubbock counties with moderate success. Breakfast cereal king Charles William Post, created a Panhandle model community in 1906 for the benefit of temperate farmers and factory workers. The 200,000-acre development still exists in Garza County.[14]

A constraining factor from the beginning for the Texas real estate market was the lack of third party funding. Not until the end of the century was home financing available. State banks were outlawed in Texas. Commercial banking only came to Texas after the Civil War. Savings associations first appeared in 1876. Cooperative lending institutions distributed profits from real estate loans, net of expenses and losses, to depositors. The first was in Taylor, Texas, and was supported by the real estate department of the International Great Northern Railroad, "The Texas Land Company" which financed railroad lot sales. The 1890 chartered "East-Side Building and Loan Company" served home buyers in Denison, a Houston and Central Railroad town. That thrift had capital of $65,000 when incorporated. (Fig. 100)

Third party financing made Arthur E. Stillwell's Kansas City, Pittsburg and Gulf Railway town project, "Port Arthur Land Company" viable. The 66,000-acre coastal development was marketed in Holland. The $8.00 land was overvalued to the immigrant farmer and dairymen. The hundred dollar stock entitled shareholders to select lots. In 1897 the overpriced land proved a windfall to the immigrants after oil was discovered at Spindletop. Soon Sun Oil built a refinery. The farming community evolved into the petrochemical industry along the Houston Ship Channel.

City government changed in 1912 by a Constitutional Amendment that permitted Texas home rule for populations in excess of five thousand. The automobile and highway system that followed opened up regions previously unpopulated. Abandoned towns revived. Colonial "Anáhuac" sprang back with the "Anáhuac Townsite" Company, to become the county seat of Chambers County in 1907. The town's incorporators William Duncan Willcox, George R. Fahring and Francis M. Hamilton invested $40,000. All went well until the Great Depression crushed the economy. (Fig. 101)

Anáhuac is a natural conclusion of the Texas land odyssey. French explorer Jean-Baptiste Bénard de La Harpe landed along that coast in the eighteenth century. A hundred years later Mexican General Mier y Terán built a fort prior to his recommendation to close immigration to Americans. Fort Anáhuac's disturbances were a harbinger to the Texas Revolution. For years the town's growth was curtailed by competing developers. Speculator Thomas Jefferson Chambers was assassinated by a rival after the Civil War. Charles Willcox, a relative of the alleged assassin, was involved in the "Anáhuac Townsite." The town succeeded after the discovery of oil and the opening of the Houston Ship Channel. The unexpected growth and prosperity of Anáhuac parallels Texas in general.

# Conclusion

The "animating pursuit of speculation" continues today in Texas. Profits are less common than public outcry against development. The 1830 Tomás de la Vega Brazos River Grant at Waco Village is the classic example of Texas land speculation. The venture traces its roots to Stephen F. Austin's partner, Samuel May Williams. By power of attorney he bought and sold the Mexican Grant of Tomás de la Vega in 1832. (Fig. 24) After several transfers, patents were finally issued to William Dillard, C. Gafford and John Harman, each for a league. Texas Federal Judge John C. Watrous helped organize the Alabama land syndicate. Thomas J. Chambers also owned of one of de la Vega's leagues at Waco. The sales agent for these transactions was Jacob de Córdova of Galveston. The managing partner of the syndicate was Thomas M. League of Galveston, Samuel May Williams' brother-in-law. Both governors Sam Houston and Sul Ross were later involved in the Waco land. The Alabama syndicate brought eviction proceedings against squatters. One trespasser refused to leave, retained noted attorney Judah P. Benjamin of New Orleans, and the case was eventually heard by the U.S. Supreme Court. The land syndicate's titles were upheld, but Judge Watrous faced impeachment for official misconduct related to his speculation. Although he prevailed, Watrous' reputation was forever tainted for his questionable land dealings.[1]

The Tomás de la Vega leagues illustrate the continuing struggle between Texans and speculators. Public favor has swayed, depending on the peace and prosperity of the time. By the end of the century the struggle resulted in a unique blend of Texas capitalism and western populism, as recounted in the movie *Giant*. That film showcased the mutation of some Texas cattlemen into oilmen and philanthropists. More legal protection exists today than ever before for Texas homeowners, debtors and conservationists.

From the time of Royal grants issued under the "Laws of the Indies," homesteaders in the land of the Tejas knew their duty as landowners. Except during war or depression, land grants have been subject to preconditions. Even recipients of large blocks such as railroads and empresarios understood that they could retain only a portion. Most had to be dispersed to third parties within a specific time. Land barons, foreigners and corporations were usually denied direct ownership by both the Republic and State. Lawmakers, when forming the Republic, set aside large tracts for the benefit of veterans, students, the disabled and even a few native tribes. From Spanish times, land abandoned or held by disloyals was subject to forfeiture. Citizens were expected to contribute annually to public projects, civil defense and construction of community buildings. All had to defend their own and their neighbor's property against invaders, hostile tribes or enemies of the state. In the beginning, Texas land was the coin of the realm. Land remains Texas's primary resource as well as a repository of its heritage. Like Shangri-La and Valhalla, the ideal of Texas would exist even if the kingdom were only a vision. Now, the myth and reality have merged into a culture of freeholders fiercely protective of their land against all enemies, domestic and foreign.

# Illustrations

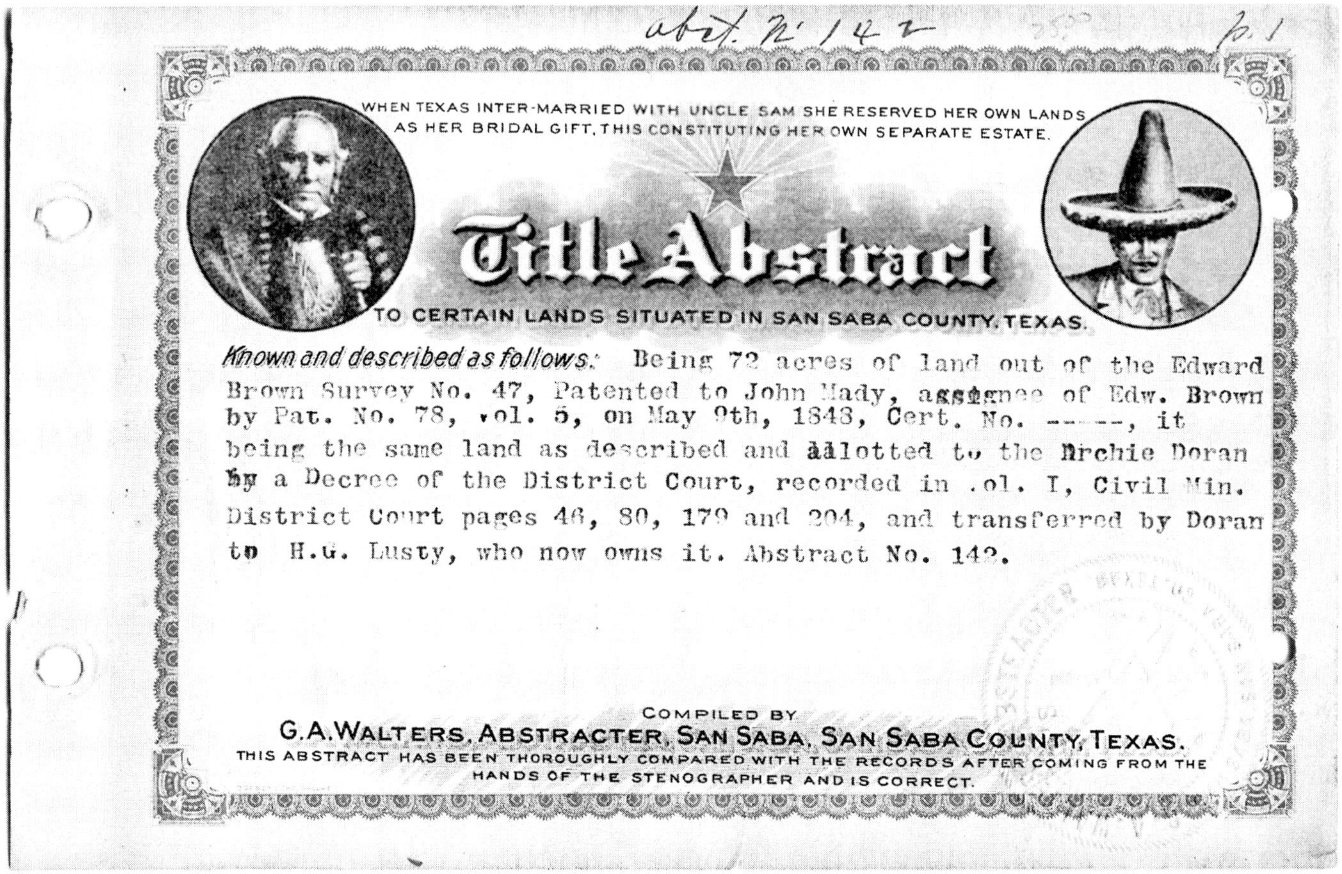

abst. N 142 p. 1

WHEN TEXAS INTER-MARRIED WITH UNCLE SAM SHE RESERVED HER OWN LANDS AS HER BRIDAL GIFT, THIS CONSTITUTING HER OWN SEPARATE ESTATE.

Title Abstract

TO CERTAIN LANDS SITUATED IN SAN SABA COUNTY, TEXAS.

*Known and described as follows:* Being 72 acres of land out of the Edward Brown Survey No. 47, Patented to John Mady, assignee of Edw. Brown by Pat. No. 78, vol. 5, on May 9th, 1848, Cert. No. ------, it being the same land as described and allotted to the Archie Doran by a Decree of the District Court, recorded in vol. I, Civil Min. District Court pages 46, 80, 179 and 204, and transferred by Doran to H.G. Lusty, who now owns it. Abstract No. 142.

COMPILED BY
G.A. WALTERS, ABSTRACTER, SAN SABA, SAN SABA COUNTY, TEXAS.
THIS ABSTRACT HAS BEEN THOROUGHLY COMPARED WITH THE RECORDS AFTER COMING FROM THE HANDS OF THE STENOGRAPHER AND IS CORRECT.

**Figure 1. Letterhead of G. A. Walters, Abstracter, San Saba, Texas, "Lands, the Texas-Bridal Gift of a Separate Estate in the Republic's Marriage to the United States" [ca. 1930]. The San Saba Title Company letterhead well illustrates the merger of Anglo and Spanish real estate law. This forward page describes the result of a multipage record of a parcel in the Texas Hill Country tracing back to an original land patent by the General Land Office to Edward Brown for army service beginning in June 1836. As was common, the veteran sold and assigned his land grant of one section to a third party, John Mody, who received title from Governor George T. Wood in 1848. Mody, to save the filing fee, did not record his deed in San Saba County until 1871. The property was situated between Waller Creek, the San Saba River and the Colorado River. The abstract contains the surveyor's sketch, his field notes and certification to the Bexar Land District Office in San Antonio. All predated the issuance of the patent.**

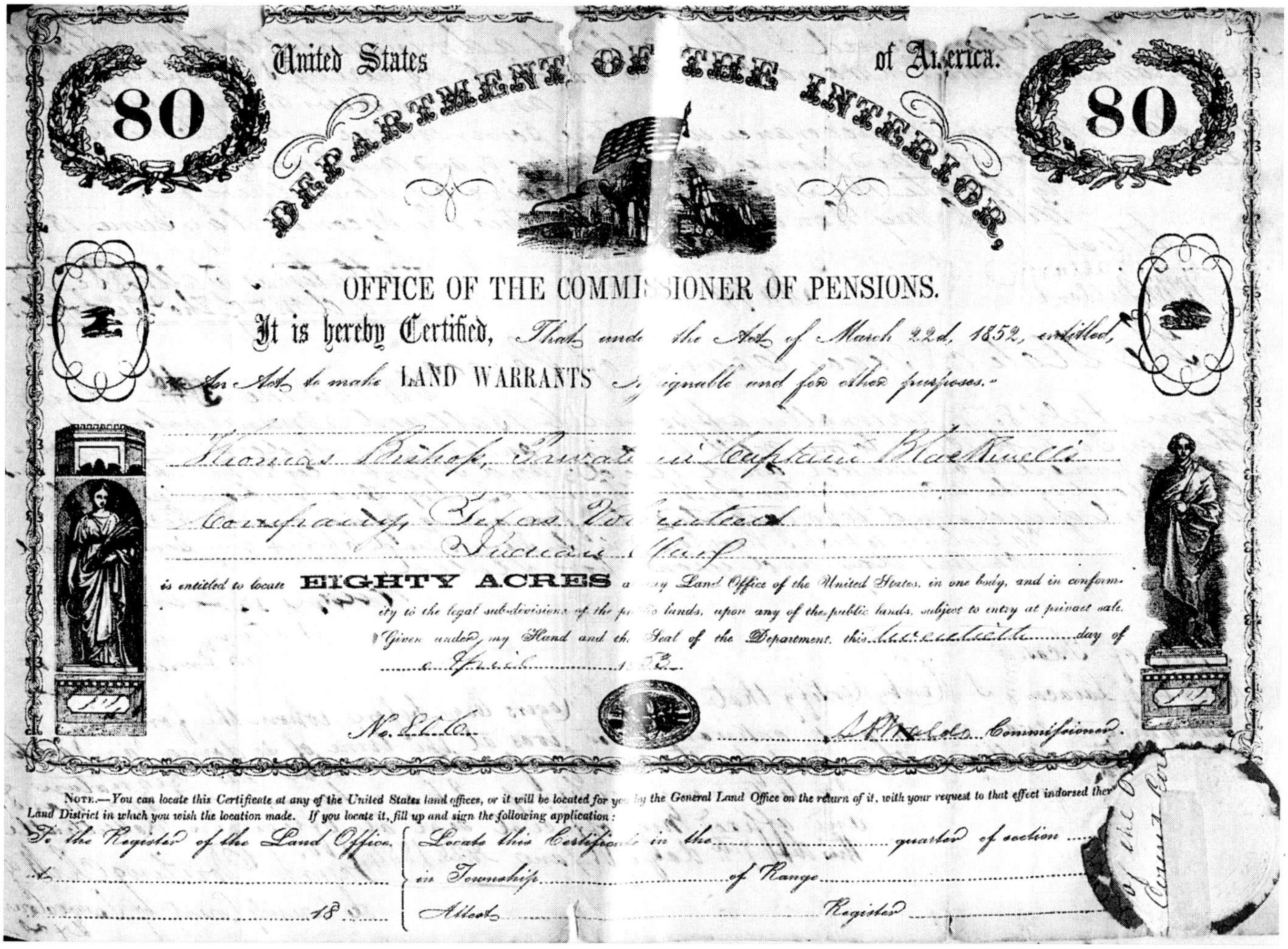

80 United States of America. 80

DEPARTMENT OF THE INTERIOR,

OFFICE OF THE COMMISSIONER OF PENSIONS.

It is hereby Certified, That under the Act of March 22d, 1852, entitled, "An Act to make LAND WARRANTS assignable and for other purposes."

Thomas Bishop, Private in Captain Blackwell's Company, Texas Volunteers, Indian War,

is entitled to locate EIGHTY ACRES at any Land Office of the United States, in one body, and in conformity to the legal subdivisions of the public lands, upon any of the public lands, subject to entry at private sale.

Given under my Hand and the Seal of the Department, this ........ day of ........ 18..

No. ........ ........ Commissioner.

NOTE.—You can locate this Certificate at any of the United States land offices, or it will be located for you by the General Land Office on the return of it, with your request to that effect indorsed thereon. Land District in which you wish the location made. If you locate it, fill up and sign the following application:

To the Register of the Land Office. Locate this Certificate in the ........ quarter of section ........ in Township ........ of Range ........

At ........ 18.. Attest ........ Register ........

Figure 2. United States Land Warrant for 80 acres to Texas U.S. Volunteer, 1853. Military land bounties have a long tradition in the United States as well as Mexico. During the time between the Revolution and before the Civil War (1789–1858), the acreage size of the bounty depended on the veterans rank—a hundred acres for a private, and up to 1,100 acres for a major general. This was an English tradition, discontinued after the Civil War. The illustrated 80-acre bounty from the U.S. Commission of Pensions, Department of the Interior, was awarded in 1853 for the honorable completion of service in Captain Blanchard's Company of Texas Volunteers during the Indian Campaigns. The recipient, Private Thomas Bishop, could locate his bounty land within any U.S. Land District. The State of Texas had no such office because the federal government never held any public domain within the sovereign territory.

*Núm.* 1.

# ESTADO QUE MANIFIESTA LA FUERZA

## que deben tener las cinco compañias que se consideran necesarias para la guarnicion del estado de Chihuahua, con espresion de los haberes y gratificaciones que deberán disfrutar.

| *COMPAÑIAS.* | *FUERZA.* | | *HABER EN el año.* Pesos. R. G. |
|---|---|---|---|
| Chihuahua | 1. | . . Capitan | 1.500. 0. 0. |
| | 1. | . . Teniente 1.° | 800. 0. 0. |
| | 1. | . . Idem. 2.° | 700. 0. 0. |
| | 1. | . . Alferez 1.° | 600. 0. 0. |
| | 1. | . . Idem 2.° | 500. 0. 0. |
| | 1. | . . Capellan | 500. 0. 0. |
| | 1. | . . Armero | 270. 0. 0. |
| | 4. | Sargentos con 360 ps. cada uno al año | 1.440. 0. 0. |
| | 2. | Tambores ó clarines con 144 ps. al año | 288. 0. 0. |
| | 8. | Cabos con 300 ps. cada uno al año. | 2.400. 0. 0. |
| | 120. | Soldados con 240 ps. cada uno al año, | 28.800. 0. 0. |
| | | Gratificacion anual | 500. 0. 0. |
| | 7.134. | Plazas. Haber en el año, | 38.298. 0. 0. |
| Janos | 1. | . . Capitan, | 1.500. 0. 0. |
| | 1. | . . Teniente | 800 0. 0. |
| | 1. | . . Alferez 1.° | 600. 0. 0. |
| | 1. | . . Idem 2.° | 500. 0. 0. |
| | 1. | . . Capellan | 500. 0. 0. |
| | 1. | . . Armero | 270. 0. 0. |
| | 3. | Sargentos con 360 ps. cada uno al año | 1.080. 0. 0. |
| | 1. | Tambor ó clarin | 144. 0. 0. |
| | 6. | Cabos con 300 ps. cada uno al año | 1.800. 0. 0. |
| | 80. | Soldados con 240 ps. cada uno al año, | 19.200. 0. 0. |
| | | Gratificacion anual | 500. 0. 0. |
| | 6. 90. | Plazas. Haber en el año, | 26.894. 0. 0. |
| S. Elzeario. | 6. 90. | Esta compañia tiene la misma fuerza y haber que la anterior | 26.894. 0. 0. |
| Norte | 6. 90. | Es igual en todo á la anterior | 26.894. 0. 0. |
| S. Buenaventura | 1. | . . Capitan | 1.500. 0. 0. |
| | 1. | . . Teniente | 800 0. 0. |
| | 1. | . . Alferez 1.° | 600. 0. 0. |
| | 1. | . . Idem 2.° | 500. 0. 0. |
| | 1. | . . Capellan | 500. 0. 0. |
| | 1. | . . Armero | 270. 0. 0. |
| | 2. | Sargentos con 360 ps. cada uno al año, | 720. 0. 0. |
| | 1. | Tambor ó clarin | 144. 0. 0. |
| | 6. | Cabos con 300 ps. cada uno al año, | 1.800. 0. 0. |
| | 56. | Soldados con 240 ps. cada uno al año, | 13.440. 0. 0. |
| | | Gratificacion anual | 500. 0. 0. |
| | 6. 65. | Plazas. Haber en el año, | 20.774. 0. 0. |

## *RESUMEN GENERAL.*

| | | | |
|---|---|---|---|
| Chihuahua | 7.134. | Plazas vencen en el año | 38 298. 0. 0. |
| Janos | 6. 90. | Plazas idem | 26.894. 0. 0. |
| S. Elzeario. | 6. 90. | Plazas idem | 26.894. 0. 0. |
| Norte | 6. 90. | Plazas idem | 26.894. 0. 0. |
| S. Buenaventura | 6. 65. | Plazas idem | 20.774. 0. 0. |
| Total fuerza | 31.469. | Plazas. Total haber en el año, | 139.754. 0. 0. |

***México Febrero* 3 *de* 1826.**

**Figure 3. Mexican Presidial Companies in Chihuahua, 1826. For over a century, the governments of Spain and Mexico provided companies of soldiers garrisoned at presidios to protect the roads, pueblos and missions. Funding and staffing was never sufficient for the task. In 1826 the State government of Chihuahua City had only 120 soldiers, 4 sergeants and a few officers to garrison five presidios. The Texas post, San Elizario, below El Paso del Norte, had only a handful of troops. Many garrison soldiers married locals and acquired rancheros. As the region became settled, more Europeans came and commercial centers developed along the Royal Roads.**

Figure 4. Lipan Warrior, Emory's Boundary Survey, 1857. The Lipan Apaches dominated much of Western Texas when the Anglo-Americans first appeared. Their economic impact dwindled with the appearance of credit and commercial trade in lieu of the barter system. As the horseman reflects, the Lipan adopted much from the European soldiers, such as weapons, dress and tack. By the end of the nineteenth century, Spanish officers were recommending the removal of tribes such as the Lipans. Afterwards, a series of treaties were negotiated, including some by Empresario Stephen F. Austin. Promises of permanent homelands were often included but not honored. The native traditions emphasized temporary possession of land held in common with use of resources such as water, vegetation and game. European land traditions were centered on titled ownership and exclusive possession.

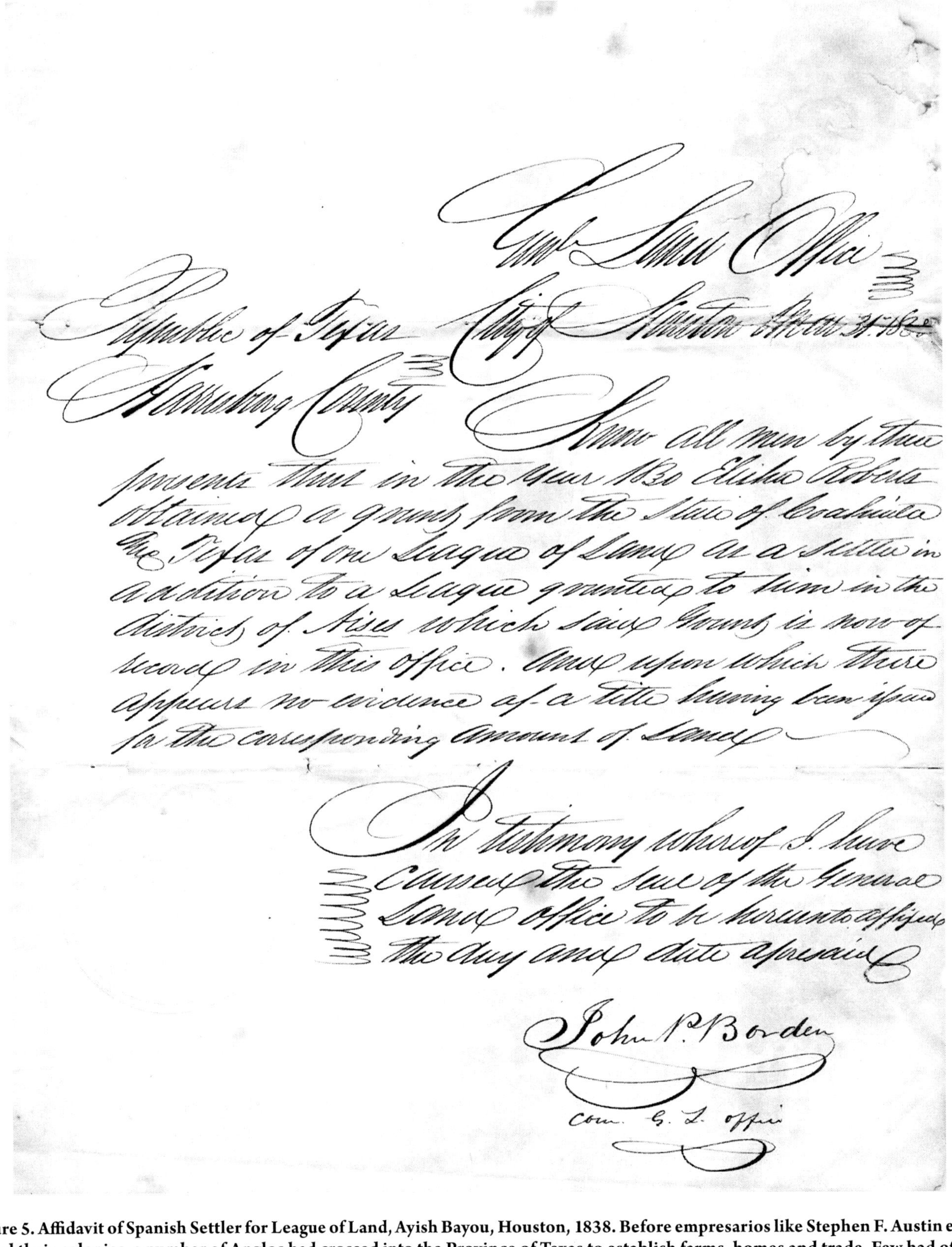

Genl Land Office

Republic of Texas City of Houston Novr 31st 18[illegible]

Harrisburg County

Know all men by these presents that in the year 1830 Elisha Roberts obtained a grant from the State of Coahuila & Texas of one League of Land as a Settler in addition to a League granted to him in the district of Ayish which said Grant is now of record in this Office. And upon which there appears no evidence of a title having been issued for the corresponding Amount of Land

In testimony whereof I have caused the seal of the General Land Office to be hereunto affixed the day and date aforesaid

John P. Borden

Com. G. L. office

**Figure 5. Affidavit of Spanish Settler for League of Land, Ayish Bayou, Houston, 1838. Before empresarios like Stephen F. Austin established their colonies, a number of Anglos had crossed into the Province of Texas to establish farms, homes and trade. Few had official approval or title. Such a settler was Elisha Roberts of Tennessee, who arrived in 1824 and set up a farm and had a cotton gin east of Ayish Bayou, near present day San Augustine. By 1831 he was the municipality's *alcalde*. After the Texas Revolution, the Republic, in its constitution, promised to recognize Spanish and Mexican homesteads within Texas, if the citizen was loyal to the Texas cause and did not aid the enemy, Mexico. After proving his loyalty and good character, Roberts received a patent for a league of land, effective September 7, 1836. Commissioner John P. Borden, of New York, issued the patent for the General Land Office.**

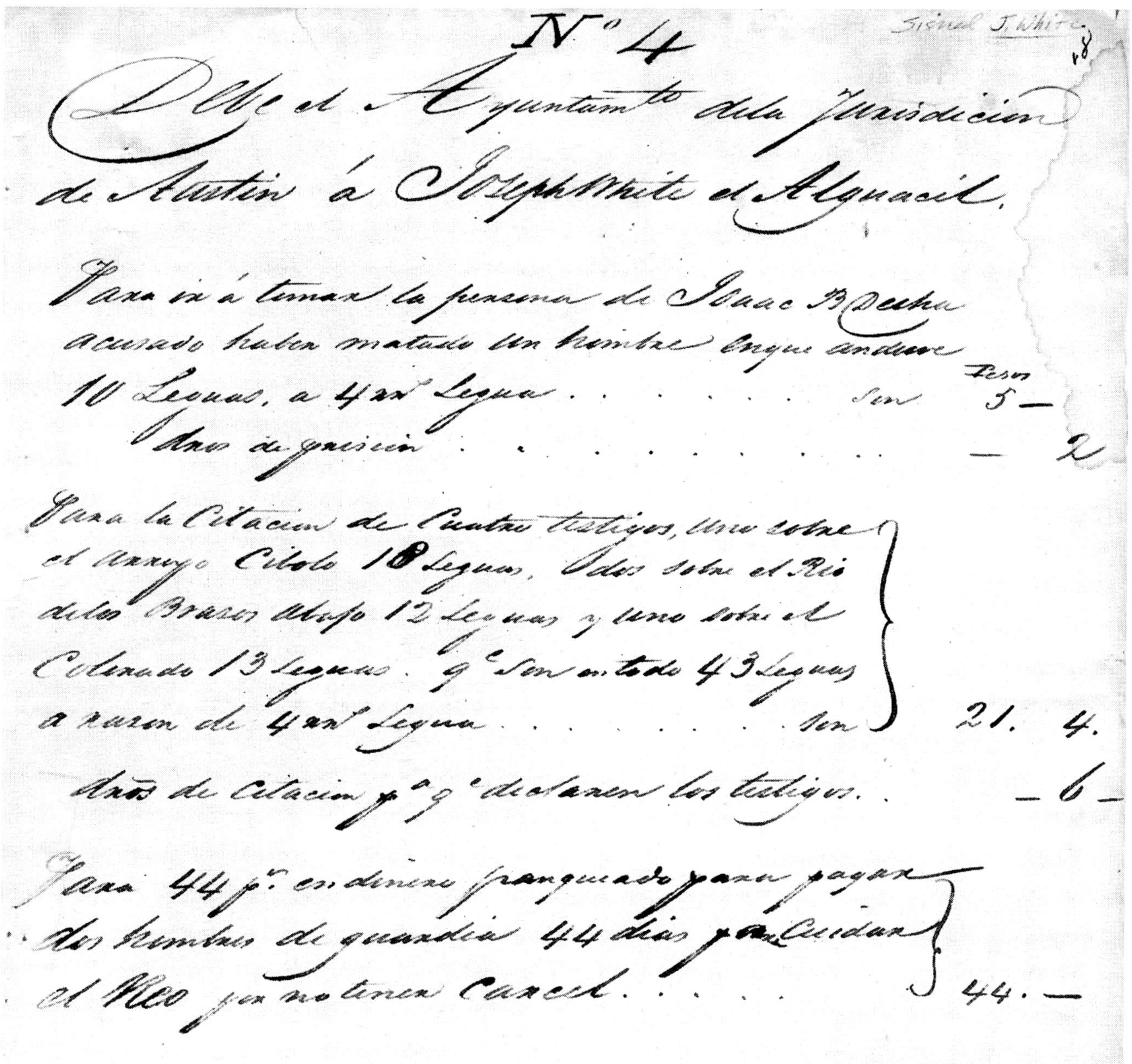
No 4
Signed J. White
Debe el Ayuntamto dela Jurisdicion de Austin á Joseph White el Alguacil.

Para ir á tomar la persona de Isaac B Decha acusado haber matado un hombre en que anduve 10 Leguas, a 4 rrs Legua . . . . . . . Son Pesos 5 —
Dros de prision . . . . . . . . — 2

Para la Citacion de Cuatro testigos, uno sobre el Arroyo Cibolo 18 Leguas, Dos sobre el Rio delos Brazos Abajo 12 Leguas y uno sobre el Colorado 13 Leguas. qe son en todo 43 Leguas a razon de 4 rrs Legua . . . . . . Son 21. 4.
Dros de Citacion pa qe declaren los testigos. . . — 6 —

Para 44 ps en dinero franqueado para pagar dos hombres de guardia 44 dias pa Cuidar el Reo por no tener Carcel. . . . . . 44. —

14 de Agosto de 1828 Son Pesos 71 . 4

**Figure 6. San Felipe de Austin Scrip to Sheriff for Guarding Accused Murderer, 1828. Settlers in Austin's first colony were known as the "Old Three Hundred." Georgian Joseph White, one such colonist, received his league of land in Brazoria in 1824. Soon thereafter he served as the municipality's sheriff. As sheriff he was in charge of prisoners, which was no small task, since there was no jail. He was paid 71.4 pesos by the town for capturing and guarding accused murderer Issac B. Decha. He and his men had to "look after" Decha for 44 days. White was elected *alcalde* at San Felipe in 1828.**

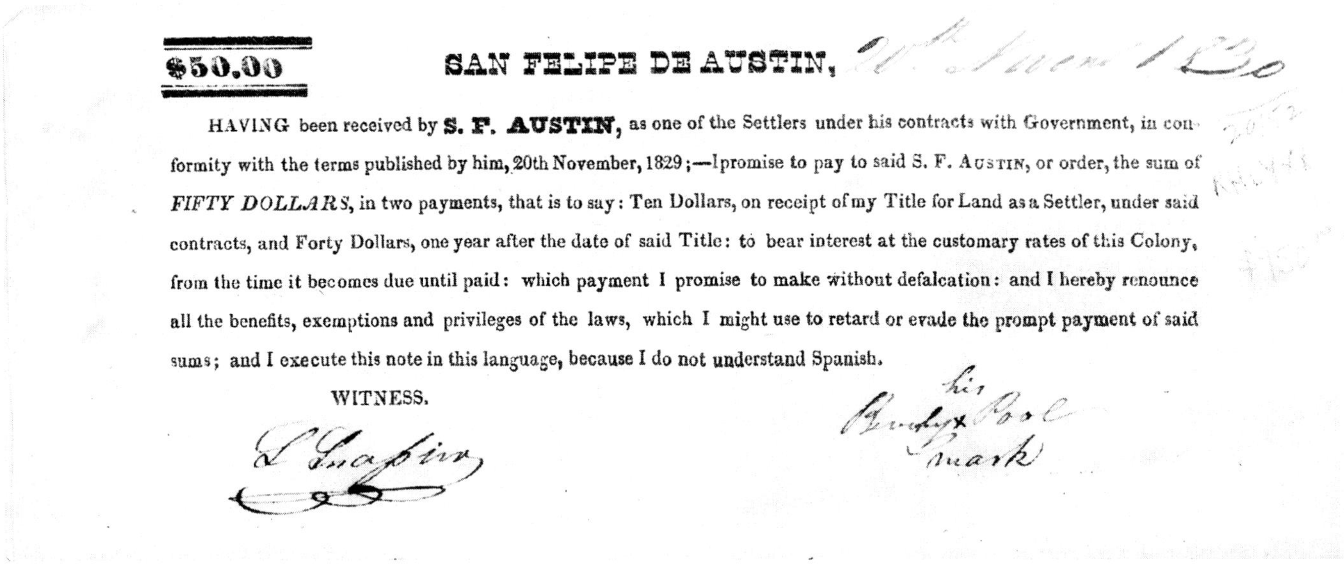

**$50,00** **SAN FELIPE DE AUSTIN,**

HAVING been received by **S. F. AUSTIN,** as one of the Settlers under his contracts with Government, in conformity with the terms published by him, 20th November, 1829;—I promise to pay to said S. F. AUSTIN, or order, the sum of *FIFTY DOLLARS*, in two payments, that is to say: Ten Dollars, on receipt of my Title for Land as a Settler, under said contracts, and Forty Dollars, one year after the date of said Title: to bear interest at the customary rates of this Colony, from the time it becomes due until paid: which payment I promise to make without defalcation: and I hereby renounce all the benefits, exemptions and privileges of the laws, which I might use to retard or evade the prompt payment of said sums; and I execute this note in this language, because I do not understand Spanish.

WITNESS.

**Figure 7. Promissory Note for Land in Austin's Colony, 1830. There were four documents required before a colonist could request a title to land in one of Empresario Stephen F. Austin's colonies. Family man Beverly Pool made his "mark" on one of those documents in 1830. The $50 promissory note was to Stephen F. Austin. Terms were $10 on receipt of his land title and $40 a year thereafter. Within the body of the note colonist Pool promised that he would not use any exemption or privilege under the law "to retard or evade the prompt payment." Contrary to Mexican law, the note was printed in English because colonists like Pool did not understand Spanish. He received his character certificate in 1835, signed by the *alcalde* of Nacogdoches. He located his grant on the road to Bexar along the Navasota River. His patent was effective July 19, 1835.**

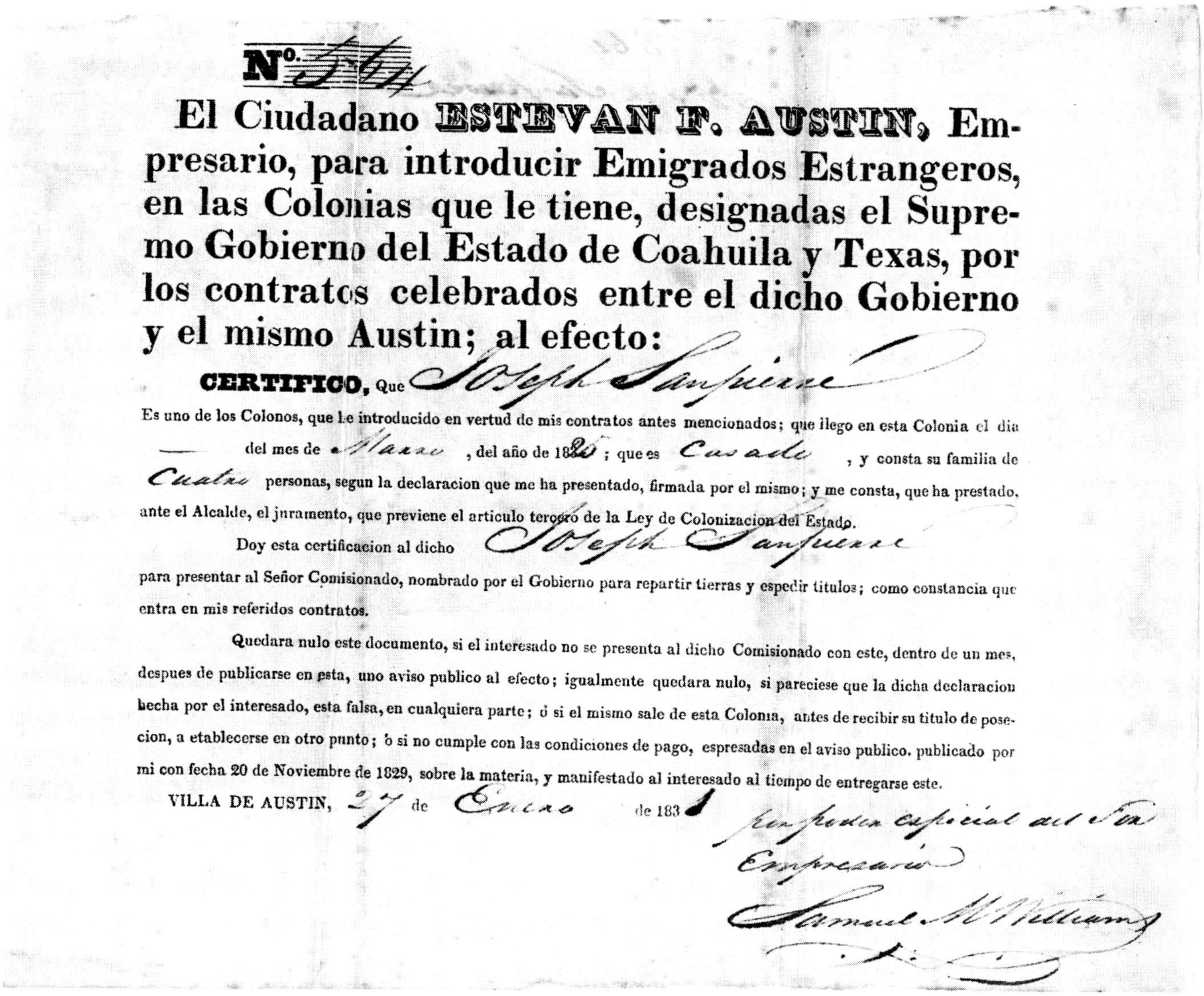

No. 564

El Ciudadano ESTEVAN F. AUSTIN, Empresario, para introducir Emigrados Estrangeros, en las Colonias que le tiene, designadas el Supremo Gobierno del Estado de Coahuila y Texas, por los contratos celebrados entre el dicho Gobierno y el mismo Austin; al efecto:

CERTIFICO, Que Joseph Sanpierre

Es uno de los Colonos, que he introducido en vertud de mis contratos antes mencionados; que ilego en esta Colonia el dia — del mes de Marzo, del año de 1825; que es Casado, y consta su familia de Cuatro personas, segun la declaracion que me ha presentado, firmada por el mismo; y me consta, que ha prestado, ante el Alcalde, el juramento, que previene el articulo tercero de la Ley de Colonizacion del Estado.

Doy esta certificacion al dicho Joseph Sanpierre para presentar al Señor Comisionado, nombrado por el Gobierno para repartir tierras y espedir titulos; como constancia que entra en mis referidos contratos.

Quedara nulo este documento, si el interesado no se presenta al dicho Comisionado con este, dentro de un mes, despues de publicarse en esta, uno aviso publico al efecto; igualmente quedara nulo, si pareciese que la dicha declaracion hecha por el interesado, esta falsa, en cualquiera parte; ó si el mismo sale de esta Colonia, antes de recibir su titulo de posecion, a etablecerse en otro punto; ó si no cumple con las condiciones de pago, espresadas en el aviso publico, publicado por mi con fecha 20 de Noviembre de 1829, sobre la materia, y manifestado al interesado al tiempo de entregarse este.

VILLA DE AUSTIN, 27 de Enero de 1831

por poder especial del Sor Empresario

Samuel M. Williams

Figure 8. Austin Colony Emigrant Certificate, 1831. The second colonial document was the Certificate of Entry to Texas. This followed the settler filing a character certificate. Joseph San Pierre applied for a certificate in San Felipe de Austin in 1825. An imprint by G.B. Cotten, in Spanish, certified San Pierre's status in 1831. Austin's administrator in his absence was Samuel May Williams, who signed and verified the character of the emigrant. The next colonial documents were a location certificate describing the land the settler located. The final was a certified deed executed by the Land Commissioner, known as a "Testimonio." San Pierre received title to a labor in present-day Fort Bend County dating back to August 24, 1824, and a league in Jackson County, June 15, 1831.

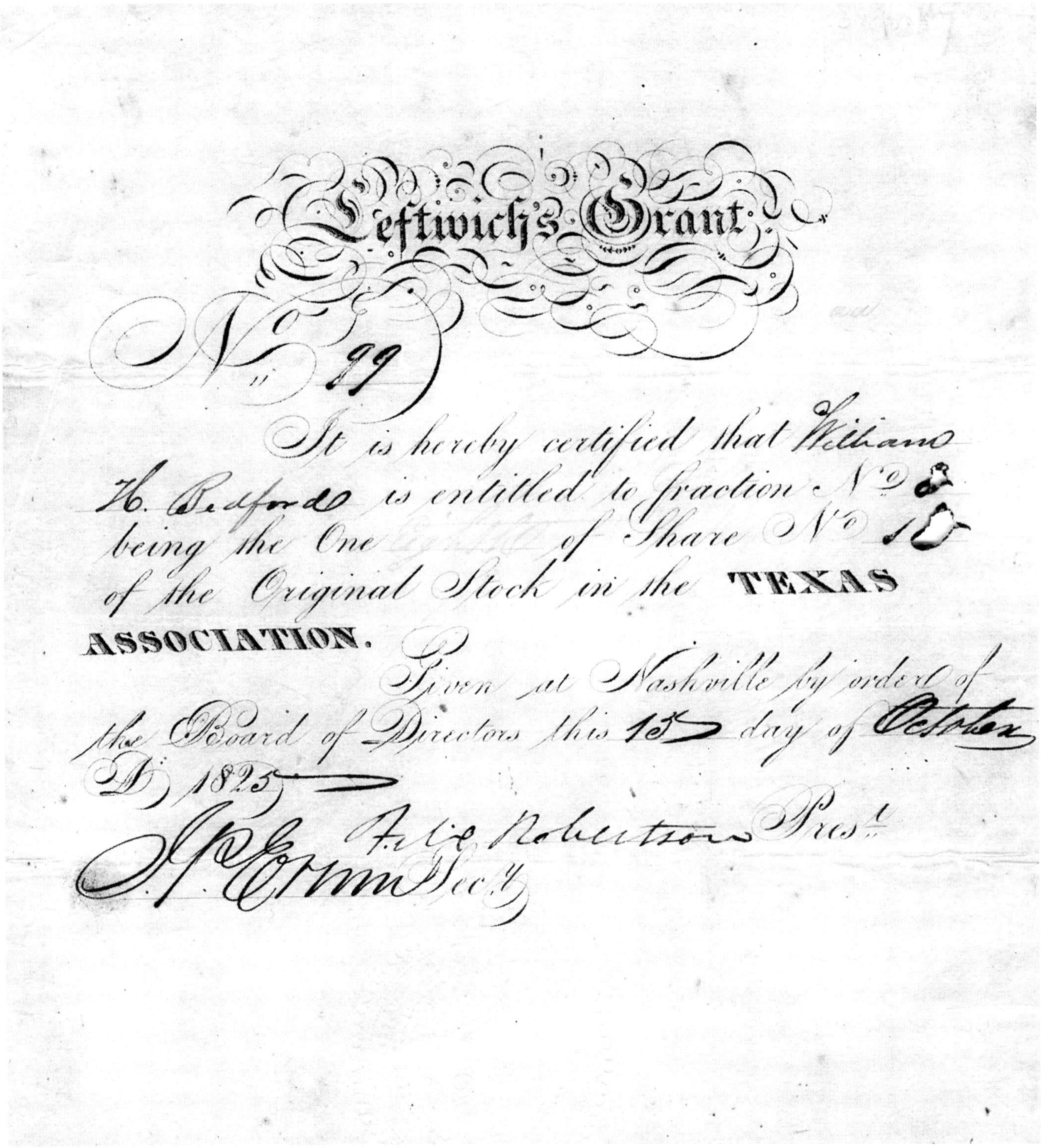

Leftwich's Grant

No. 29

It is hereby certified that William H. Bedford is entitled to fraction No. 8 being the One Eighth of Share No. 1[illegible] of the Original Stock in the TEXAS ASSOCIATION.

Given at Nashville by order of the Board of Directors this 15th day of October A.D. 1825.

Felix Robertson Presdt.

J.P. Erwin Secy.

**Figure 9. Fractional Share Certificate in Leftwich's Grant, "Texas Association," 1825. In 1822, over fifty residents of Davidson County, Tennessee, formed the "Texas Association" and decided to secure an empresario contract in Texas. Robert Leftwich, their agent, after arriving in Mexico City, suffered the same delays as Stephen F. Austin. After the National Colonization Act passed in the Mexican Congress, the State of Coahuila and Texas granted a concession to Leftwich, while he was in Saltillo. His colony could settle 800 families north of Austin on the Brazos River. William Bedford, after qualifying as a man of good character, acquired a ⅛ share of the Texas Association from the Association's president, Felix Robertson and secretary J.P. Erwin on October 15, 1825. The failed Anglo-backed Fredonia rebellion delayed managed settlement within the Leftwich grant. Bedford's heirs received a league of land from the Nacogdoches Land Commissioner Radford Berry, September 5, 1835.**

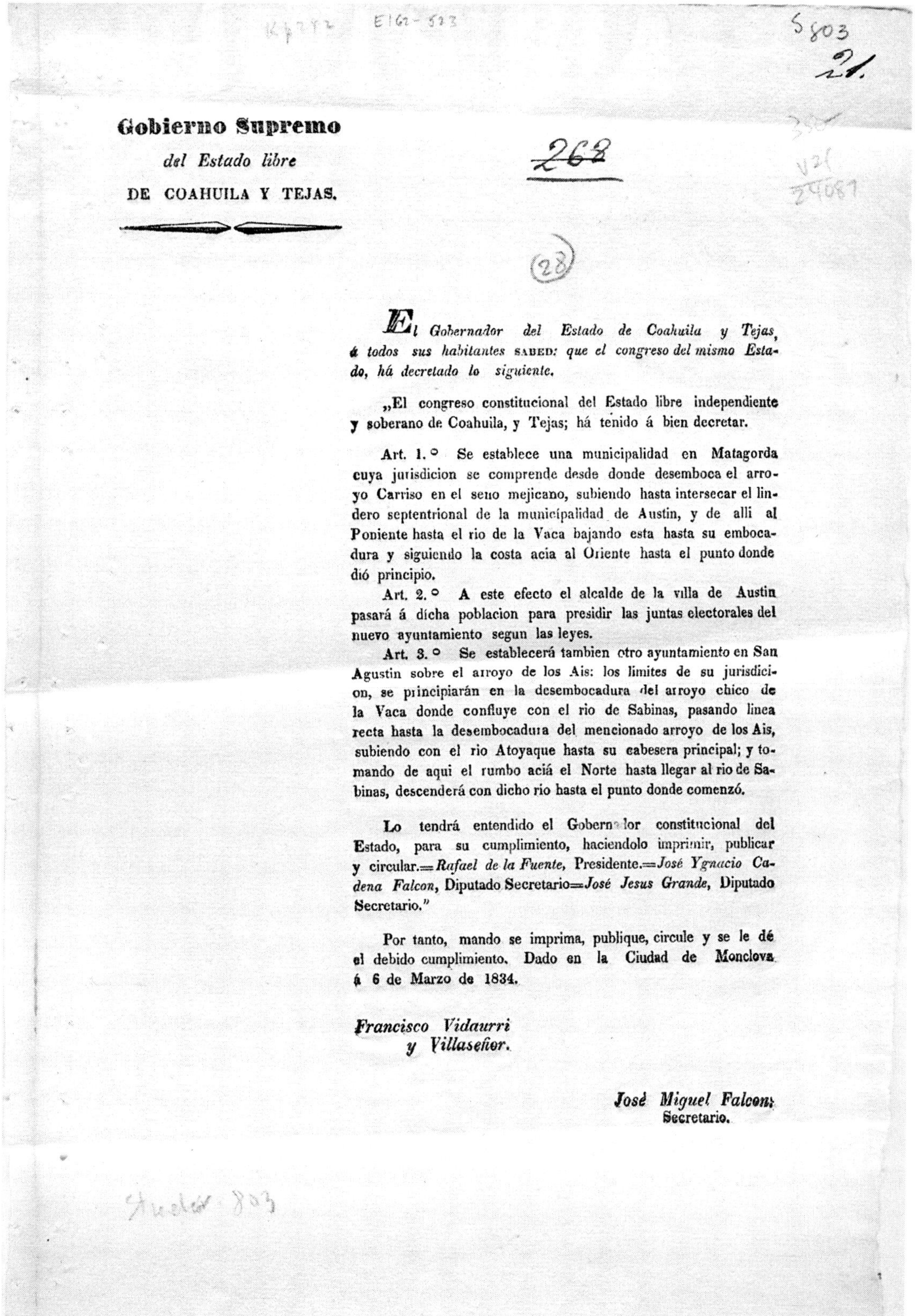

**Gobierno Supremo**
*del Estado libre*
DE COAHUILA Y TEJAS.

268

*El Gobernador del Estado de Coahuila y Tejas, á todos sus habitantes* SABED: *que el congreso del mismo Estado, há decretado lo siguiente.*

„El congreso constitucional del Estado libre independiente y soberano de Coahuila, y Tejas; há tenido á bien decretar.

Art. 1.° Se establece una municipalidad en Matagorda cuya jurisdicion se comprende desde donde desemboca el arroyo Carriso en el seno mejicano, subiendo hasta intersecar el lindero septentrional de la municipalidad de Austin, y de alli al Poniente hasta el rio de la Vaca bajando esta hasta su embocadura y siguiendo la costa acia al Oriente hasta el punto donde dió principio.

Art. 2.° A este efecto el alcalde de la villa de Austin pasará á dicha poblacion para presidir las juntas electorales del nuevo ayuntamiento segun las leyes.

Art. 3.° Se establecerá tambien otro ayuntamiento en San Agustin sobre el arroyo de los Ais: los limites de su jurisdicion, se principiarán en la desembocadura del arroyo chico de la Vaca donde confluye con el rio de Sabinas, pasando linea recta hasta la desembocadura del mencionado arroyo de los Ais, subiendo con el rio Atoyaque hasta su cabesera principal; y tomando de aqui el rumbo aciá el Norte hasta llegar al rio de Sabinas, descenderá con dicho rio hasta el punto donde comenzó.

Lo tendrá entendido el Gobernador constitucional del Estado, para su cumplimiento, haciendolo imprimir, publicar y circular.=*Rafael de la Fuente,* Presidente.=*José Ygnacio Cadena Falcon,* Diputado Secretario=*José Jesus Grande,* Diputado Secretario."

Por tanto, mando se imprima, publique, circule y se le dé el debido cumplimiento. Dado en la Ciudad de Monclova á 6 de Marzo de 1834.

*Francisco Vidaurri y Villaseñor.*

*José Miguel Falcon.*
Secretario.

**Figure 10. Coahuila and Texas Decree Establishing Municipalities of Matagorda and San Augustine, 1834. After a Texas townsite became a permanent community, Mexican officials could grant the city municipality status. This entitled the town to an *alcalde* and sheriff. The port of Matagorda on the bay was founded in 1827 and became a significant port of entry. The "Gobierno Supremo" del Estado libre de Coahuila y Tejas, Francisco Vidaurri, from Monclova, granted municipality status on March 6, 1834. St. Augustine on the Arroyo de los Ais was also raised to that status in the same decree. Soon thereafter, land speculators proposed a canal for Matagorda to connect it to the bay by Caney Creek. Windmills, salt workers and homes followed.**

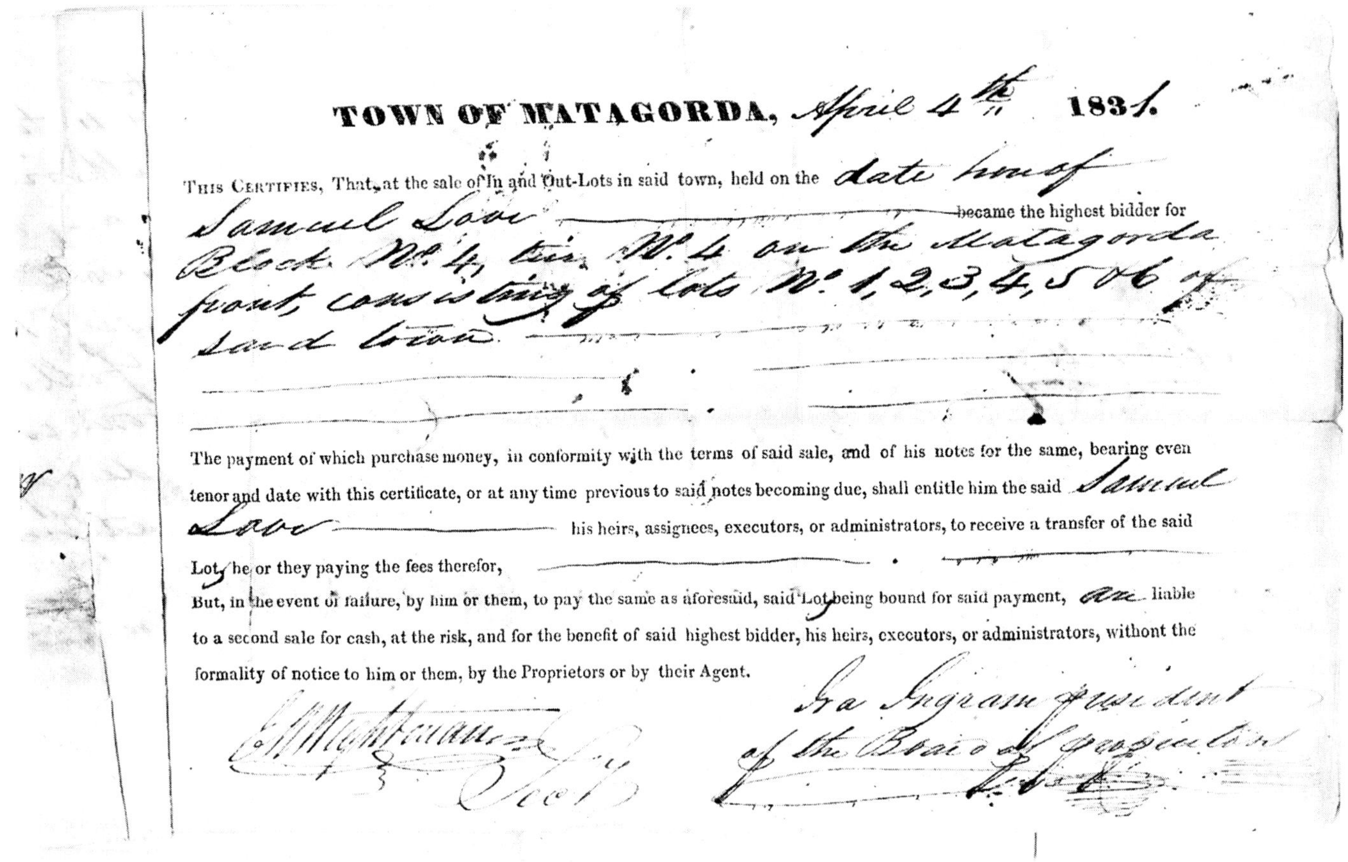

TOWN OF MATAGORDA, April 4th 1837.

This Certifies, That, at the sale of In and Out-Lots in said town, held on the date hereof Samuel Love became the highest bidder for Block No. 4, tier No. 4 on the Matagorda front, consisting of lots No. 1, 2, 3, 4, 5 & 6 of said town

The payment of which purchase money, in conformity with the terms of said sale, and of his notes for the same, bearing even tenor and date with this certificate, or at any time previous to said notes becoming due, shall entitle him the said Samuel Love his heirs, assignees, executors, or administrators, to receive a transfer of the said Lots he or they paying the fees therefor,

But, in the event of failure, by him or them, to pay the same as aforesaid, said Lots being bound for said payment, are liable to a second sale for cash, at the risk, and for the benefit of said highest bidder, his heirs, executors, or administrators, without the formality of notice to him or them, by the Proprietors or by their Agent.

E. R. Wightman Secy

Ira Ingram President of the Board of Proprietors

**Figure 11. Land Certificate for 6 Lots in Town of Matagorda, 1834. The town of Matagorda was the product of several land speculators: Elias R. Wightman, Hosea H. League, James E. Austin, Thomas M. Duke and William Selkirk. Town lots were publicly auctioned off to the highest bidder on April 4, 1837. Samuel Love won six lots. The buyers paid in installments. If the purchaser failed to make timely payments, the lots could be auctioned again. Title was issued only after all the debt was cleared. Samuel Love had already received a league of land in Austin's Third Colony (Matagorda) on July 23, 1831, after arriving from Kentucky in 1821. He received a grant for one-third of Matagorda Island before purchasing his six town lots.**

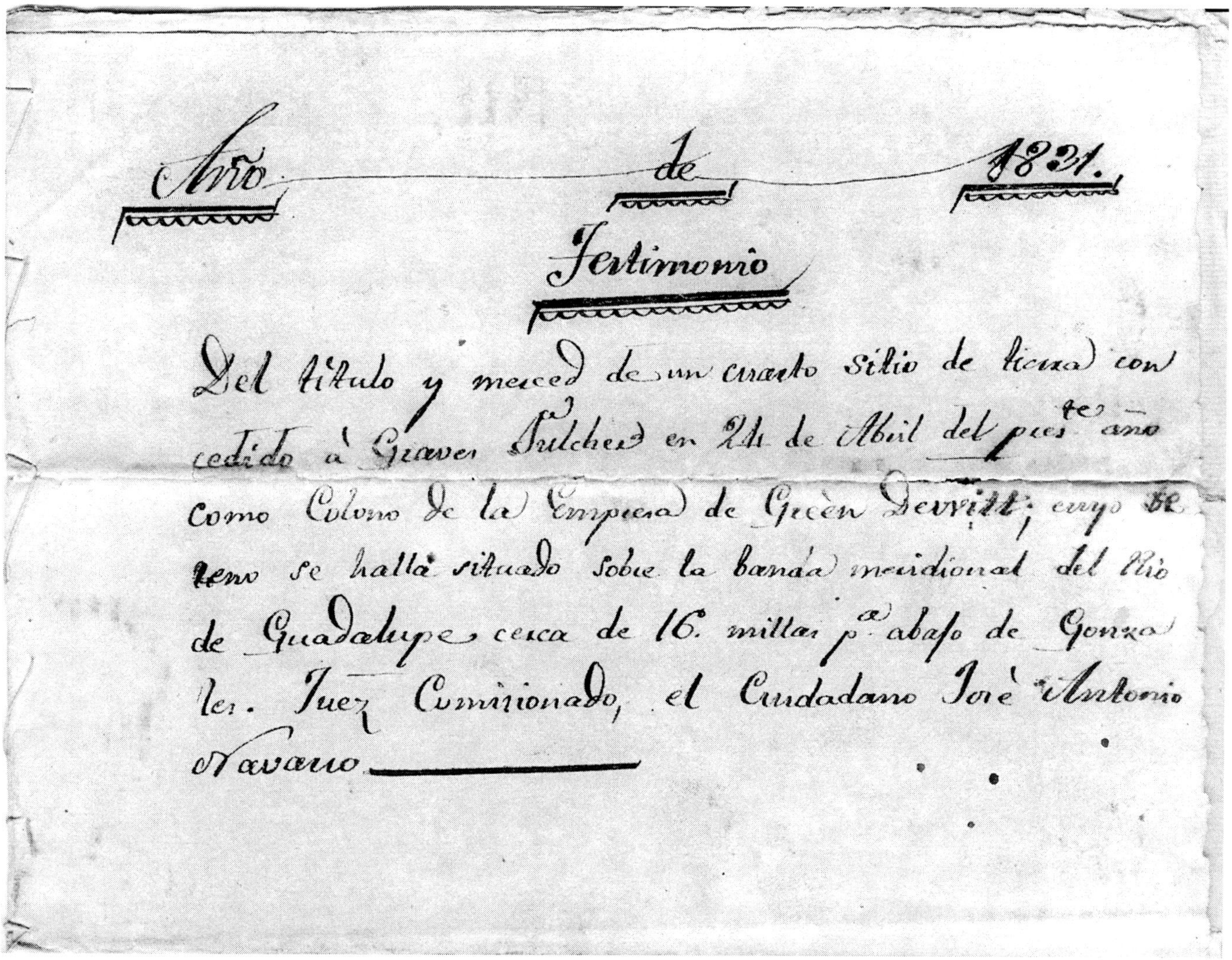

Año de 1831.

Testimonio

Del titulo y merced de un cuarto sitio de tierra con
cedido á Graves Fulcher en 24 de Abril del pres.te año
como Colono de la Empresa de Green Dewitt; cuyo te
reno se halla situado sobre la banda meridional del Rio
de Guadalupe cerca de 16. millas p.a abajo de Gonza
les. Juez Comisionado, el Ciudadano José Antonio
Navarro

Figure 12 (this page and the four following). Land Testimonio for Sitio in DeWitt's Colony, 1831. The colonist received title to his land evidenced by a deed after fulfilling all the requirements. Three copies were prepared. The "Testimonio" was the land owner's copy. This would become crucial evidence when settlers submitted requests to have patents issued by the Republic's General Land Office. Colonist Graves Fulcher from Tennessee, a single man, located on the Guadalupe River above the town of Gonzáles in DeWitt's Colony, April 24, 1831. Land Commissioner José Antonio Navarro executed the document. Benjamin and Graves Fulcher, brothers, joined together in the request for land, and were allowed to qualify as a "family," entitling them to a full league, twice their individual allotment if considered single. The league grant was jointly held as of June 31, 1831. The "Testimonio" and four-page deed was in Spanish and executed on tax-stamped paper. Stephen F. Austin had originated the tactic of single men "coupling" to form a family qualifying for the land grants as a "family." Their father, Churchill Fulshear, one of Austin's "Old 300," received a league in present-day Fort Bend County on the Brazos River and served as Austin's regidor in 1830.

**SELLO SEGUNDO: DOCE REALES.**

HABILITADO POR EL ESTADO DE COAHUILA Y TEXAS PARA EL BIENIO DE 1828 Y 29. 3 y 31

William

No. 10.
2a Clase

Sor. Comisionado = Graves Fulcher natural de los Estados Unidos del Norte ante V. premisas las solemnidades del derecho comparesco y digo: Que siendo uno de los admitidos por el Empresario Green DeWitt p. poblar los terrenos de su Colonia segun previene la Ley de Colonizacion del Estado, como consta del certificado que debidamte. incluyo, siendo como soy soltero y hayarme hasta la fha. sin el titulo de posesion del terreno q. me corresponde como poblador; à V. pido que en uso de sus facultades se sirva meterme en posesion de un Cuarto de sitio que se haya enteramte. valdio sobre la banda meridional del Rio de Guadalupe cerca de diez y seis millas p.a abajo de Gonzales en lo q.e recibirè justicia = Gonzales 22. de Abril de 1831. = Graves Fulcher. = Villa de Gonzales 22 de Abril de 1831. = Al Empresario Green DeWitt p.a que à continuacion me informe por escrito si el presentante es el verdadero dueño del certificado que incluye, legitimo èste, y verdad cuanto expone en su instancia particularmente si el terreno que pretende està enteramente valdio è incluso en los limites de su Colonia, con lo demas que se le ofrezca informar p.a proveer lo que corresponda. = Navarro. = Gonz.s y Abril 24. de 1831. = Sor. Comisionado. = En atencion al decreto anterior de V. digo: Que el suplicante es uno de los Colonos introducidos en virtud de mi contrato y con arreglo à la Ley, por cuyo motivo lo concidero acreedor à la gracia que solicita por ser legal todo cuanto expone y legitimo el certificado que incluye en su instancia como asi mismo valdio el terre

no é incluso en los limites de esta Colonia.— Green
Dewitt.— Librésele titulo de propiedad p.a que p.r me-
dio de él lo posea y disfrute con arreglo á las leyes. Por
este auto así lo proveó mandó y firmó en esta dha Villa de
Gonzales á los veinte y cuatro dias del mes de Abril de
1831; lo que certifico.— José Antonio Navarro.— En la
referida Villa de Gonz.s en el mismo dia mes y año, yo
el C. José Antonio Navarro Comisionado particular por
el Supremo Gobierno del Estado de Coahuila y Tejas para
el repartimiento y posesion de tierras valdias en esta
Colonia contratada por el Empresario Ciudad.o Green
Dewitt con dho. Supremo Gobierno, consecuente al De-
creto que antecede y por cuanto haberse recivido á
Graves Fulcher como Colono en la Empresa de Coloni-
zacion arriba mencionada segun consta por el informe
anterior del Empresario, habiendo dicho Graves Fulcher
Justificado que es soltero como por Encontrarse en su
persona los requisitos que previene la Ley de Colonizaci-
on del Estado de 24. de Marzo de 1825. de conformi-
dad con la citada Ley, la contrata, instrucciones q.e me
rigen de fha 4. de Septiembre de 1827, y comision que me
ha sido conferida p.r el Exmo. Sõr. Gob.or del Estado
en oficio de 29. de Enero del pres.te año de 1831. En nom
bre del mismo Estado concedo, confiero y meto en po
sesion real, actual, corporal y virtual al expresado Gra-
ves Fulcher de un cuarto sitio de tierra, cuyo terreno
habiendo sido medido por el Agrimensor Cientifico
Byrd Lockhart nombrado previam.te en la forma le-
gal resultó estar en la situacion y con los linderos si-
guientes.— Situado en la margen por la banda me-
ridional del Rio de Guadalupe p.a abajo de Gonza

les; comenzando à una Estaca plantada en la Barran
ca de dicho Rio de la q.e demora un Olmo del diametro
de 16. pulgadas S. 20.° O. à 5. v.s de distancia y un nogal
de Castilla de 9. pulg.s N. 20.° E. à 5. v.s de distancia de
cuyo punto corre la linea Superior 1600. varas al rumbo
N. 86.° V. donde se hizo el rincon Noueste señalandolo
un mezquite del diametro de 8. pulgadas que demora del
S. 9.° E. à 11½ v.s de distancia, y de alli S. 4.° V. 2496. v.s
se hizo la mojonera Suoueste de la que demora un ro-
ble del diametro de 12. pulg.s N. 72.° E. à la distancia
de 4. varas de la que siguiendo en demanda del Rio S.
86.° E. 2512 v.s se planto en la barranca una estaca
de la que demora un nogal de Castilla del diametro de
15. pulg.s S. 40.° E. à 4 eslabones de distancia y otro ydem
de 24. pulgadas S. 50.° E. à 7. eslabones de distancia
cuyos linderos incluras las bueltas del Rio q.e impor
tan 2250 v.s à los diferentes Rumbos completan el q
arto de sitio al punto de comenzar, quedando clasi-
ficado de en cuatro Vigesimas quintas partes de sitio,
de temporal, y lo demas de agostadero. = Lo que sir
ve de calificacion p.a el precio que por el debe pagar
al Estado segun el Articulo 22. de dicha Ley, bajo
las penas alli establecidas, quedando advertido que
dentro del termino de un año debe construir mojo-
neras permanentes en cada angulo del terreno, y
que debe poblarlo y cultivarlo de conformidad con lo pre
venido por la referida ley. = Por tanto usando de las fa
cultades que me son concedidas por la propia ley
è instrucciones consiguientes, expido el presente ins-
trumento y mando que se saque testimonio de el
y se entregue al interesado para que posea y disfrute di-
cho terreno, el, sus hijos, herederos y subcesores, ò qui

604

en de él ó de [illegible] causa ó derecho hubiere, lo q.e firmo con dos testigos de mi asist.a conforme á la ley hoy dia de la fha. — José Antonio Navarro — De asist.a Victoriano Zepeda — De asist.a José Ramon Bedford.

Concuerda en todas sus partes con el titulo original q.e queda protocolado en el libro Becerro de esta Colonia, de cuyo original se mandó sacar p.a la parte hoy dia de la fha. en la forma prevenida por la Ley, á que me remito. Es dado en esta Villa de Gonz.s á los veinte y cuatro dias del mes de Abril de mil ochocientos treinta y uno, lo que certifico y firmo con dos testigos de mi asist.a

José Antonio Navarro

De asist.a Victoriano Zepeda — De asist.a José R. Bedford

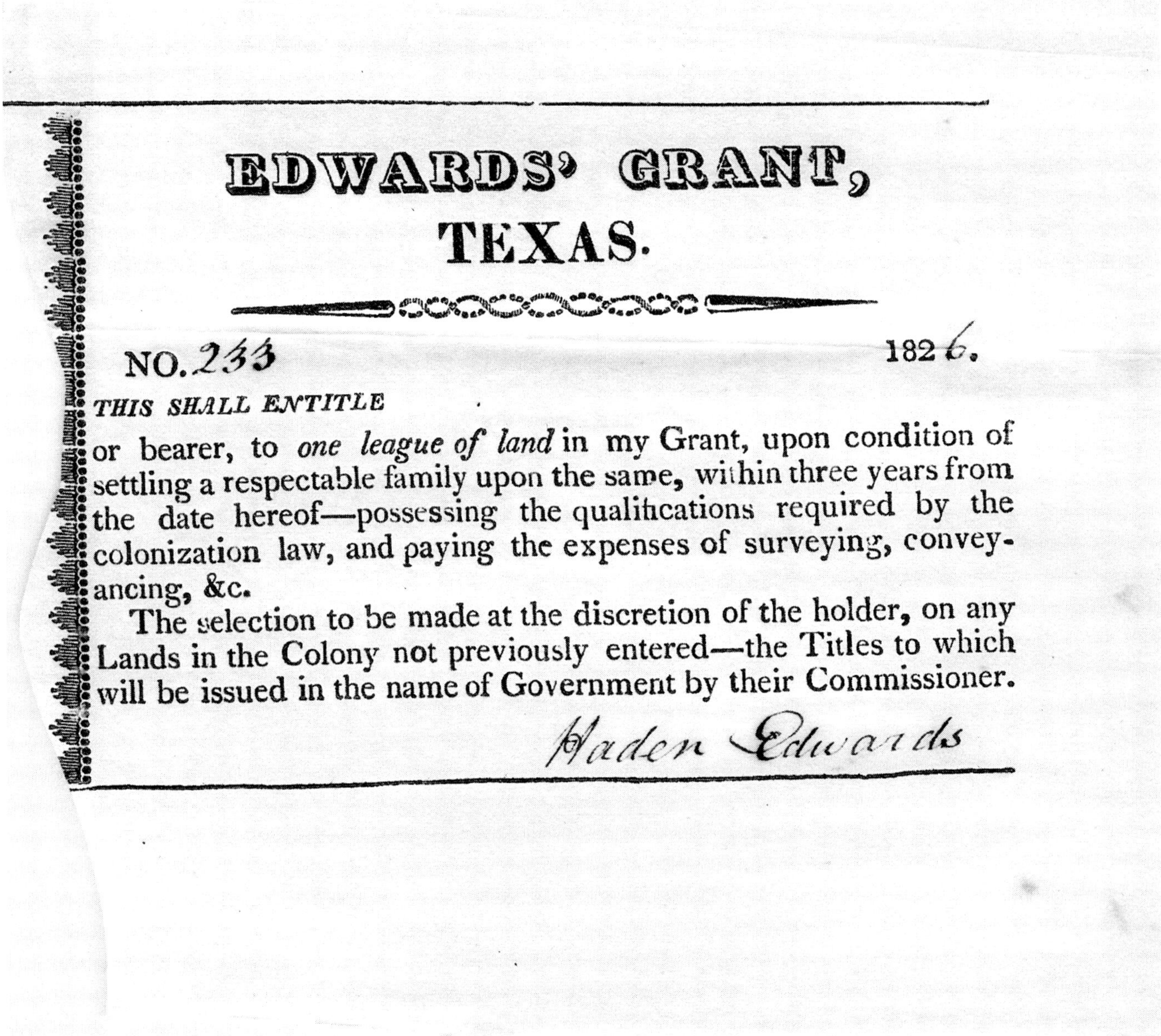

EDWARDS' GRANT,

TEXAS.

NO. 233 1826.

*THIS SHALL ENTITLE*

or bearer, to *one league of land* in my Grant, upon condition of settling a respectable family upon the same, within three years from the date hereof—possessing the qualifications required by the colonization law, and paying the expenses of surveying, conveyancing, &c.

The selection to be made at the discretion of the holder, on any Lands in the Colony not previously entered—the Titles to which will be issued in the name of Government by their Commissioner.

Haden Edwards

**Figure 13. Land Certificate [Blank] for a League in Edward's Grant, 1826. Haden Edwards was awarded an empresario grant in the territory of Nacogdoches April 15, 1825. Already residing within his prospective colony were numbers of undocumented settlers, living as squatters. The officials of the State of Coahuila and Texas required Edwards to give titles to such settlers if they were loyal to the government and of good character. Edwards gave notice that the squatters must submit to him proper papers establishing the validity of their claims. The time deadline was short and agitated the community. Edwards had a supply of "Edwards' Grants" forms intended to fulfill that requirement. He dated, numbered and pre-signed the grants in 1826. Before any could be issued, the Fredonian Rebellion occurred in December 1826. For his part in the insurrection, Edwards lost his empresario contract. Later, some early settlers with claims dating back to 1792 were accepted, validated and had patents issued by the Republic.**

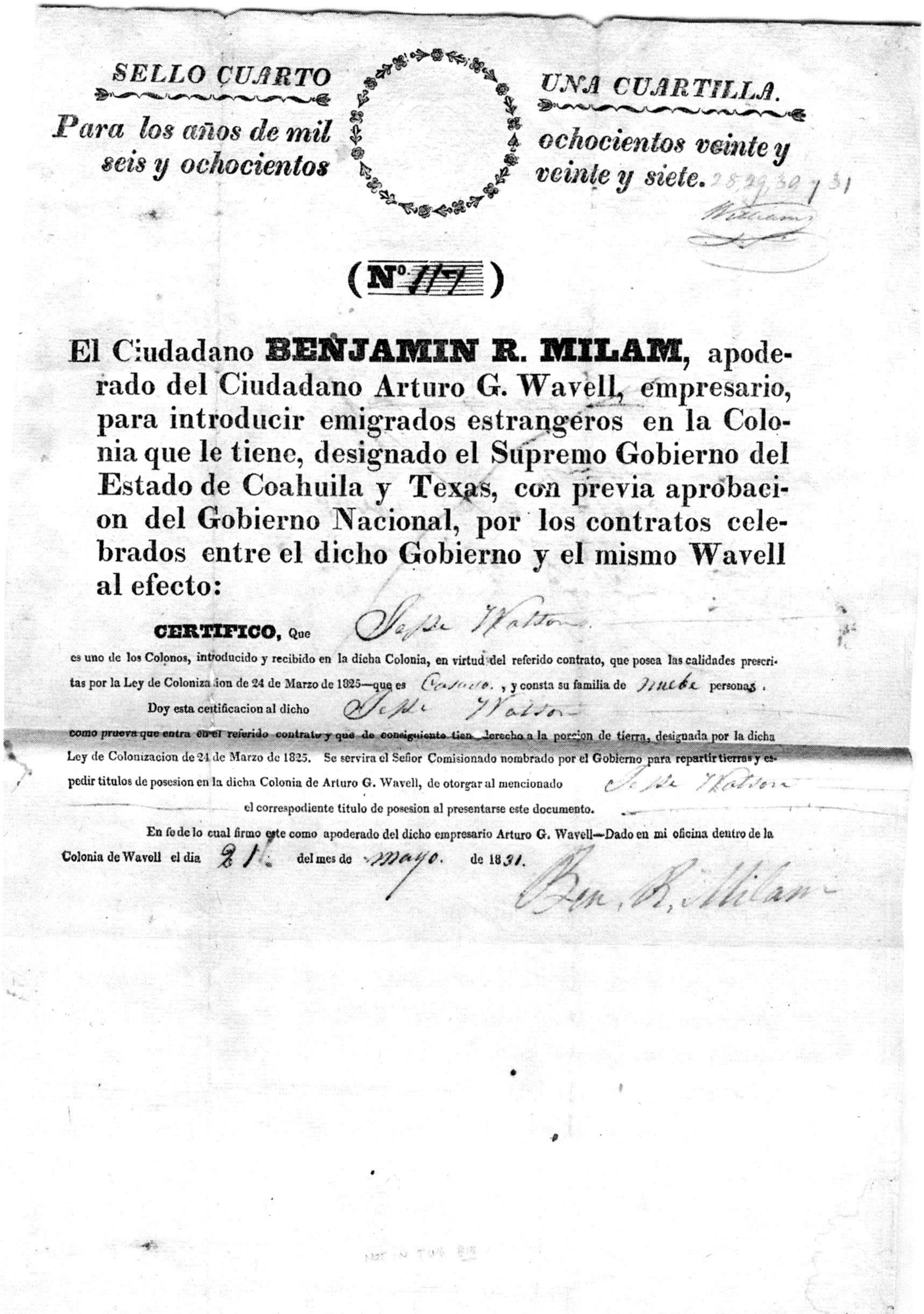

*SELLO CUARTO* — *UNA CUARTILLA.*

*Para los años de mil ochocientos veinte y seis y ochocientos veinte y siete.* 28 29 30 y 31

(Nº 117)

El Ciudadano **BENJAMIN R. MILAM**, apoderado del Ciudadano Arturo G. Wavell, empresario, para introducir emigrados estrangeros en la Colonia que le tiene, designado el Supremo Gobierno del Estado de Coahuila y Texas, con previa aprobacion del Gobierno Nacional, por los contratos celebrados entre el dicho Gobierno y el mismo Wavell al efecto:

**CERTIFICO,** Que Jesse Watson es uno de los Colonos, introducido y recibido en la dicha Colonia, en virtud del referido contrato, que posea las calidades prescritas por la Ley de Colonizacion de 24 de Marzo de 1825—que es Casado, y consta su familia de nueve personas.

Doy esta certificacion al dicho Jesse Watson como prueva que entra en el referido contrato y que de consiguiente tiene derecho a la porcion de tierra, designada por la dicha Ley de Colonizacion de 24 de Marzo de 1825. Se servira el Señor Comisionado nombrado por el Gobierno para repartir tierras y espedir titulos de posesion en la dicha Colonia de Arturo G. Wavell, de otorgar al mencionado Jesse Watson el correspodiente titulo de posesion al presentarse este documento.

En fe de lo cual firmo este como apoderado del dicho empresario Arturo G. Wavell—Dado en mi oficina dentro de la Colonia de Wavell el dia 21 del mes de mayo. de 1831.

Ben. R. Milam

**Figure 14. Land Certificate from Commissioner Benjamin R. Milam in Wavell's Colony, 1831. The Secretary of the State of Coahuila and Texas gave notice March 31, 1832, from the seat of government at Leona Vicario, that the following empresario contracts had lapsed because of their failure to introduce the required number of families within the time provided in their grants: Green DeWitt; Frost Thorn; Robert Leftwich; Benjamin R. Milam and Arthur G. Wavell. The document to Jesse Watson in Wavell's colony, dated May 31, 1831, and signed by Ben Milam on governmental tax stamped paper, in Spanish, designated him as a qualified emigrant. The effort failed to produce a land grant for Watson because of the lapse.**

# IN THE TOWN OF SAN AUGUSTINE.

ON THE twentieth DAY OF December in the year 1835

BEFORE ME, A. Hotchkiss Judge of the first instance for the jurisdiction of San Augustine and Ex-officio Notary Public, and the instrumental witnesses with whom I act according to law, appeared Daniel Hopkins citizen of the Department of Nacogdoches (whom I know, and to whose act I give faith and credit) and declared and said that he had this day bargained and sold, and by this act sells and gives, in real and public sale to David Brown citizen of the department of Nacogdoches a tract of parcel of land containing One League situated in Zavala's grant and below Grants Bluff, on the East side of the Neches River, the form and Shape of which may be seen by reference to the Plat annexed to this Sale

the title and possession of which was given to Daniel Hopkins which will be seen by reference to the original and copy of the same, which I certify to have seen, and to which I give faith as having been executed by proper authority, and according to law. And he the said Daniel Hopkins further declares that he has not heretofore sold, contracted or in any manner whatever disposed of the said land, that it is free from all incumbrance, except such dues as may be owing to the State thereon, (the purchaser hereby binding himself to discharge the obligation of the vendor to the State,) and as such he sells it to the said David Brown for the sum of One hundred dollars, which he acknowledges to have received of the said David Brown to his entire satisfaction. and declares that he made this sale in good faith, and he believe the aforesaid League of land is not worth more money than the sum he hereby acknowledge to have received, but if it should prove to be worth more, be the same much or little, he makes by this act, a perfect and irrevocable donation of the excess or overplus. therefore renounces the laws, "NON NUMERATA PECUNIA NO ENTREGA Y PRUEBH," and all other laws which might favor him in the event of an attempt on his part not to comply with the intention of this sale; and from this day henceforth and forever, he dispossess himself of, and relinquishes for himself and his heirs end successors, the dominion, possession, title, and every right to the said League of land to which he may have a claim, in favor of the purchaser the said David Brown and yields renounces and delivers it to him that he may possess, enjoy, exchange, aleniate, use and dispose of it at his pleasure, as his own, acquired by a just and legitimate title, to himself and heirs, and

**Figure 15 (this page and following page). Land Grant for a League in Zavala's Grant, San Augustine, 1835. Zavala merged his grants into the Galveston Bay and Texas Company. A league located in Zavala's grant was given to Daniel Hopkins in the Nacogdoches District. Hopkins had emigrated in 1826 and received a deed to a league in Jefferson and Jasper counties from Land Commissioner Carlos S. Taylor in November 1835. The following month he sold that land to David Browne for $100. The property was situated below Grant's Bluff on the east side of the Neches River. The sales contract was an imprint of David E. Lawhorn's Nacogdoches press. A. Hotchkiss, agent of the Galveston Bay Company, witnessed the transaction.**

successors, or whoever shall have cause or right from him or them. And to the observance of all the above binds and obliges his person and property, present and future, and submit them with them to the jurisdiction of the tribunals, which may be competent to take cognizance of this matter, in order that they may compel him to a strict compliance of the same by all the rigors of the law; all this he declares and admits , and signs with me; the instrumental witnesses being Larkin Gross and P John M Hadley, and George Bitter. all of which I certify, and sign with my assisting witnesses, according to law.

Daniel Hopkins
By his Attorney
John Forsyth

A Hotz

Witness
William Lange

Witness
John Freeman

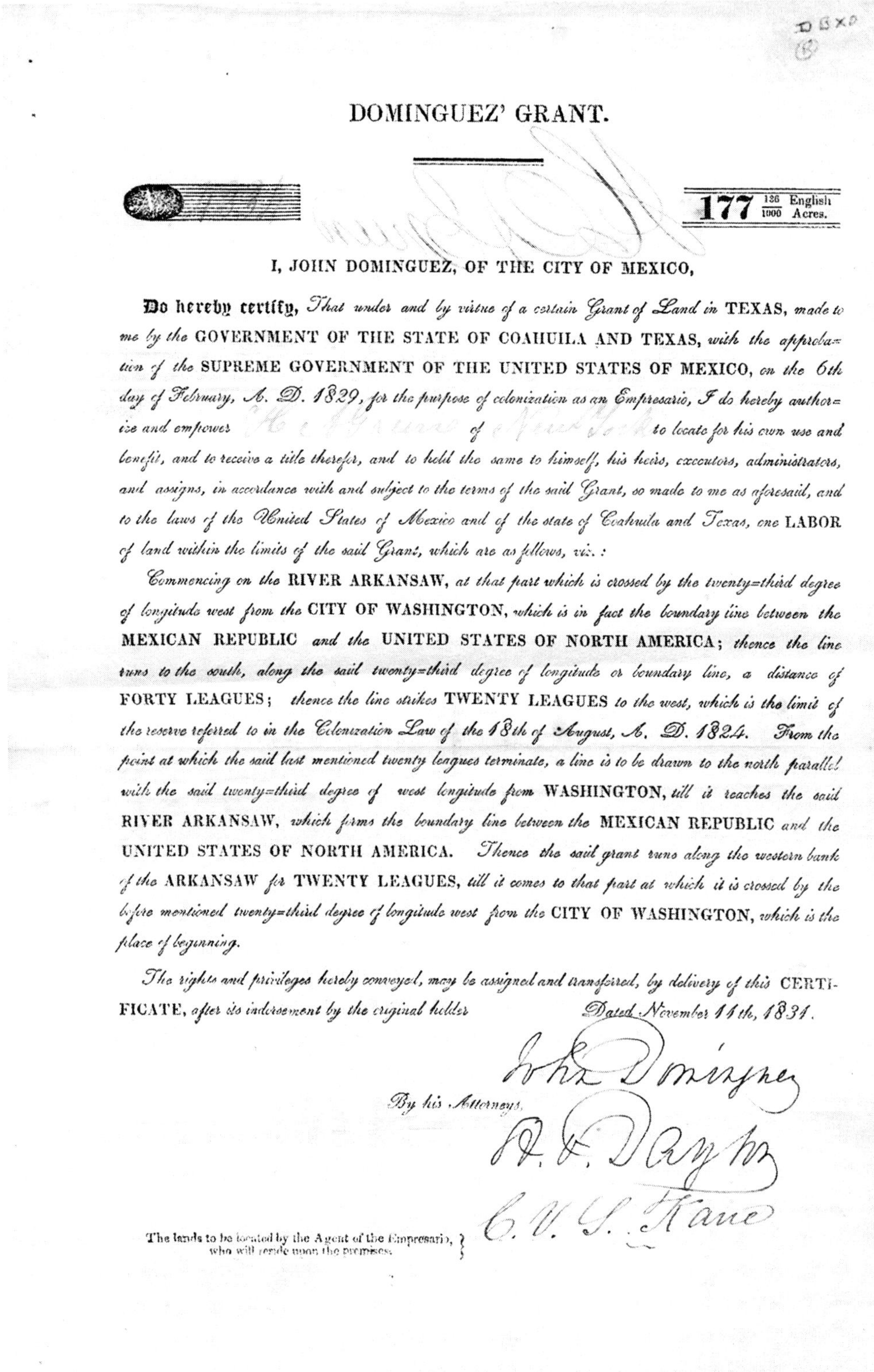

DOMINGUEZ' GRANT.

177 $\frac{136}{1000}$ English Acres.

I, JOHN DOMINGUEZ, OF THE CITY OF MEXICO,

**Do hereby certify,** *That under and by virtue of a certain Grant of Land in* TEXAS, *made to me by the* GOVERNMENT OF THE STATE OF COAHUILA AND TEXAS, *with the approbation of the* SUPREME GOVERNMENT OF THE UNITED STATES OF MEXICO, *on the 6th day of February, A. D. 1829, for the purpose of colonization as an Empresario, I do hereby authorize and empower* H. A. Green *of* New York *to locate for his own use and benefit, and to receive a title therefor, and to hold the same to himself, his heirs, executors, administrators, and assigns, in accordance with and subject to the terms of the said Grant, so made to me as aforesaid, and to the laws of the United States of Mexico and of the state of Coahuila and Texas, one* LABOR *of land within the limits of the said Grant, which are as follows, viz.:*

*Commencing on the* RIVER ARKANSAW, *at that part which is crossed by the twenty-third degree of longitude west from the* CITY OF WASHINGTON, *which is in fact the boundary line between the* MEXICAN REPUBLIC *and the* UNITED STATES OF NORTH AMERICA; *thence the line runs to the south, along the said twenty-third degree of longitude or boundary line, a distance of* FORTY LEAGUES; *thence the line strikes* TWENTY LEAGUES *to the west, which is the limit of the reserve referred to in the Colonization Law of the 18th of August, A. D. 1824. From the point at which the said last mentioned twenty leagues terminate, a line is to be drawn to the north parallel with the said twenty-third degree of west longitude from* WASHINGTON, *till it reaches the said* RIVER ARKANSAW, *which forms the boundary line between the* MEXICAN REPUBLIC *and the* UNITED STATES OF NORTH AMERICA. *Thence the said grant runs along the western bank of the* ARKANSAW *for* TWENTY LEAGUES, *till it comes to that part at which it is crossed by the before mentioned twenty-third degree of longitude west from the* CITY OF WASHINGTON, *which is the place of beginning.*

*The rights and privileges hereby conveyed, may be assigned and transferred, by delivery of this* CERTIFICATE, *after its indorsement by the original holder* *Dated November 11th, 1831.*

John Dominguez

*By his Attorneys,*

A. E. Dayton

C. V. S. Kane

The lands to be located by the Agent of the Empresario, who will reside upon the premises.

**Figure 16. Right to Locate Certificate for a Labor in Juan Domínguez's Grant, 1831. (Note that the document refers to John Dominguez. Mexicans in Anglo society used American spellings.) Juan Domínguez y Valdez received an empresario grant on February 6, 1825. Sales of the property were centered in New York. Domínguez's partners were New Yorkers who acted as agents from November 11, 1831. The grant was situated on the Arkansas River and was twenty leagues by twenty leagues. The grants were for either a league or labor of land. New Yorker H. A. Green, a sales agent for the association, received land scrip under the grant. The scrip entitled Green to locate, survey, pay dues and apply for the title. It was alleged to be a transfer of land in fee simply. To promote the land sales, Green had maps printed in New Orleans in 1836. Despite the costs incurred and marketing efforts, the empresario failed to introduce the required number of colonists by the deadline. Domínguez's contract lapsed.**

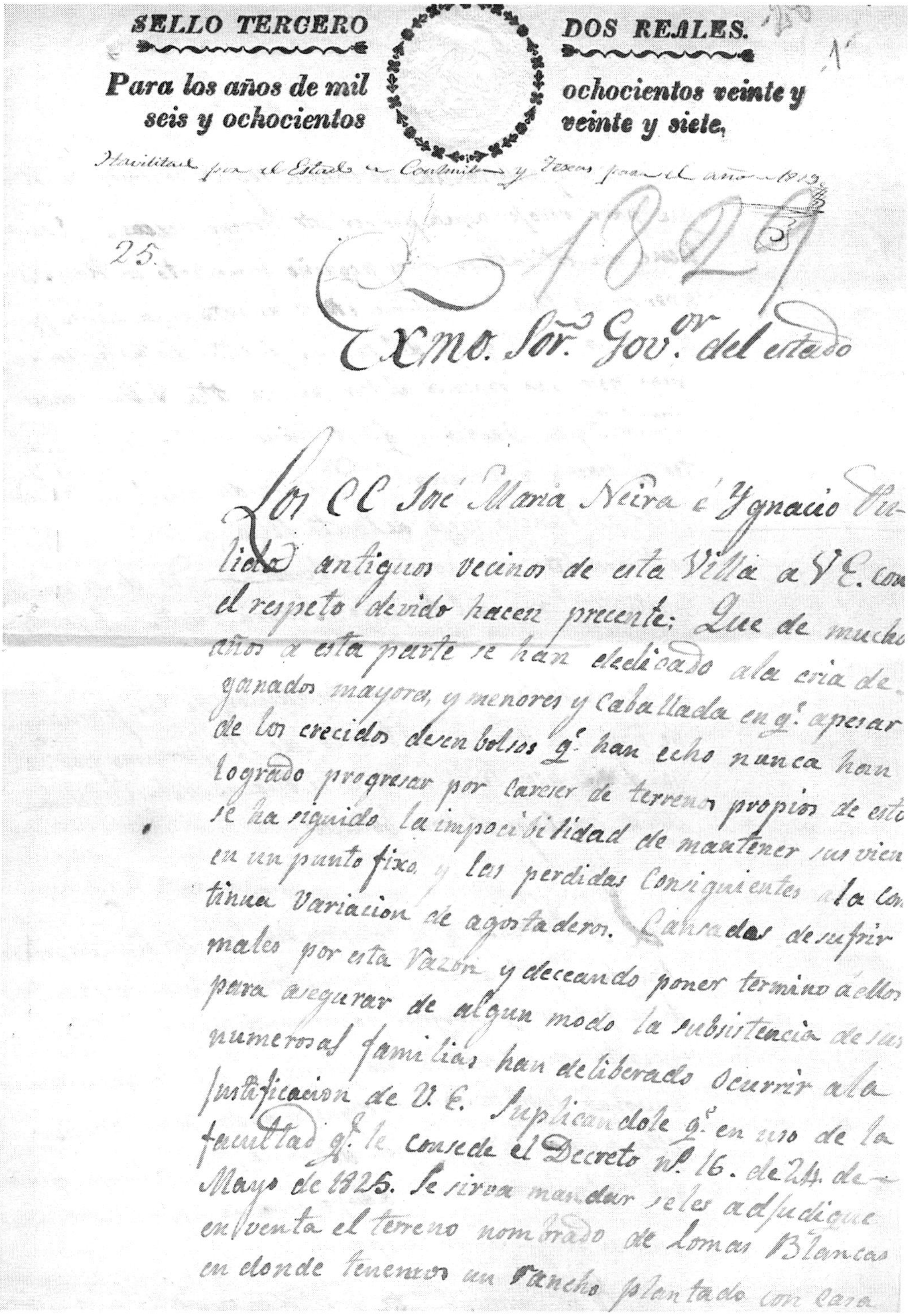

SELLO TERCERO — DOS REALES.

Para los años de mil ochocientos veinte y seis y ochocientos veinte y siete.

Habilitado para el Estado de Coahuila y Texas para el año de 1829

25

1829

Exmo. Sor. Govor. del estado

Los CC José María Neira é Ygnacio Villarreal antiguos vecinos de esta Villa a V.E. con el respeto devido hacen presente; Que de muchos años a esta parte se han dedicado ala cria de ganados mayores, y menores y caballada en q. apesar de los crecidos desenbolsos q. han echo nunca han logrado progresar por carecer de terrenos propios de esto se ha seguido la imposibilidad de mantener sus vienes en un punto fixo, y las perdidas consiguientes a la continua variacion de agostaderos. Cansados de sufrir males por esta razon y deseando poner termino a ellos para asegurar de algun modo la subsistencia de sus numerosas familias han deliberado ocurrir ala justificacion de V.E. Suplicandole q. en uso de la facultad q. le concede el Decreto no. 16. de 24. de Mayo de 1825. Se sirva mandar seles adjudique en venta el terreno nombrado de Lomas Blancas en donde tenemos un rancho plantado con casa

**Figure 17 (this page and following three). "Eleven League" Testimonio to Mexican National, 1829. Beginning in 1829, Mexico encouraged landless cattle and horse raisers near Camargo to relocate their livestock herds across the Rio Grande into the Province of Texas. The "antiquos," José María Neira and her husband Ygnacio Villareal, were granted eleven leagues in present-day Cameron County for their long-term presence and loyalty. The grant's borders were described as running from Santa Rita, to "Voila de Judas" hill (back of Judas), to the orchards of the first Geronimo near Rancho Candela. Drought had made ranching almost impossible. Ygnacio Villareal received a patent in 1873 of 5¾ leagues in Cameron County after a formal recommendation of the Bourland and Miller Commission. They took evidence from Mexican residents of ownership following the Treaty of Guadalupe Hidalgo in 1848. Other Mexican ranchers received similar grants by decree in 1833. The grants were up to five leagues priced at ten pesos per league. Ygnacio Villareal received a four-and-one-half league dated March 26, 1833, from Mexican Commissioner Don Molano, Governor of the Province of New Santander (Tamaulipas). Juan Nepomuceno Molano was council representative for Tamaulipas for the Republic of the Rio Grande insurgency in 1840.**

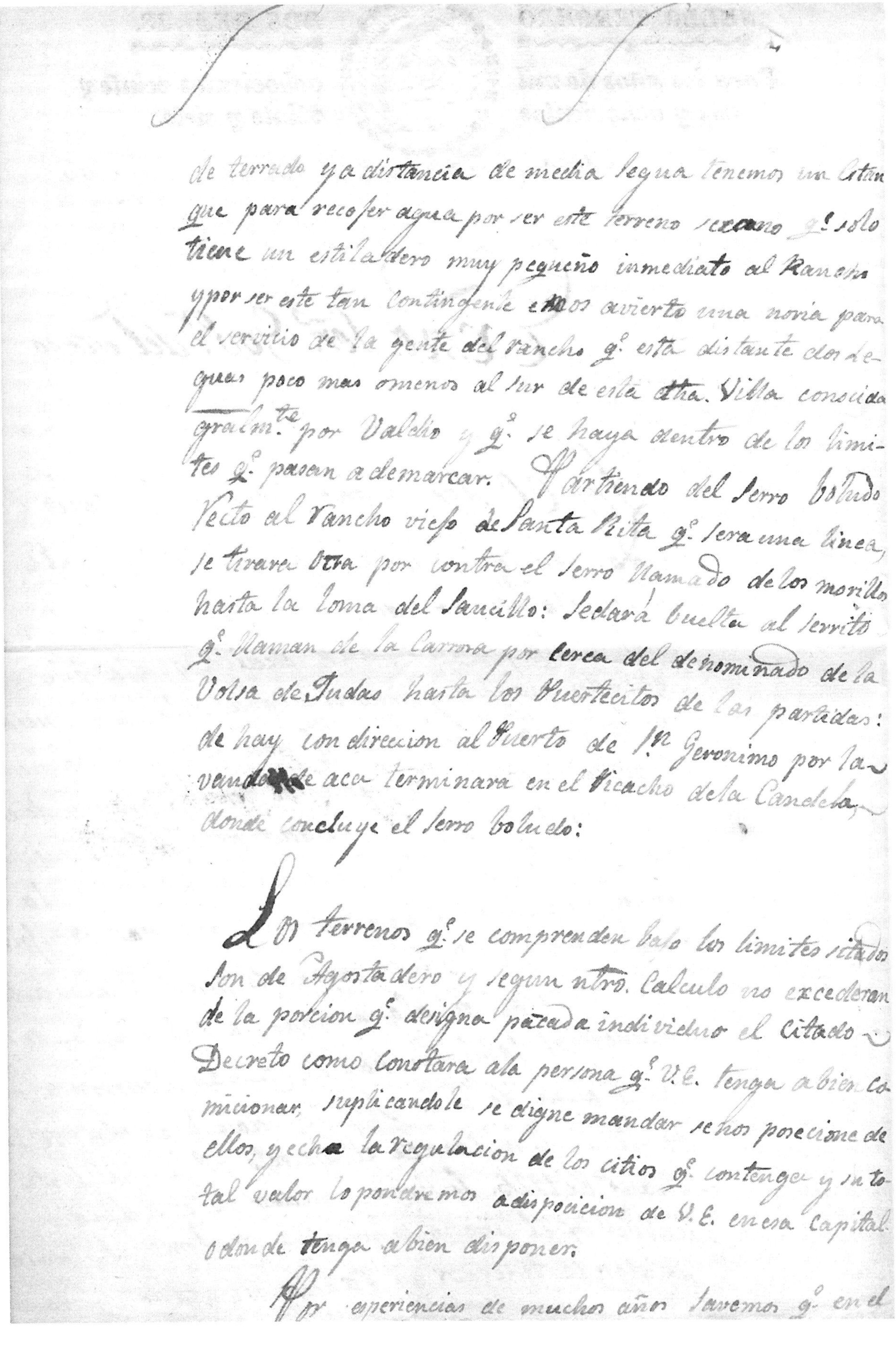

de terrado y a distancia de media legua tenemos un Estan
que para recoger agua por ser este terreno secano q.e solo
tiene un estiladero muy pequeño inmediato al Rancho
y por ser este tan contingente hemos avierto una noria para
el servicio de la gente del rancho q.e esta distante dos le-
guas poco mas o menos al sur de esta d.ha Villa conocida
gralm.te por Valdio y q.e se haya dentro de los limi-
tes q.e pasan a demarcar. Partiendo del Serro boludo
recto al rancho viejo de Santa Rita q.e sera una linea,
se tirara otra por contra el Serro llamado de los morillos
hasta la loma del Sancillo: Se dara buelta al Serrito
q.e llaman de la Carrora por cerca del denominado de la
Volsa de Judas hasta los Huertecitos de las partidas:
de hay con direccion al Puerto de S.n Geronimo por la
vanda de aca terminara en el Picacho de la Candela,
donde concluye el Serro boludo:

Los terrenos q.e se comprenden bajo los limites citados
son de Agostadero y segun ntro. Calculo no excederan
de la porcion q.e designa para cada individuo el Citado
Decreto como constara a la persona q.e V.E. tenga a bien co-
micionar, suplicandole se digne mandar se nos porcione de
ellos, y echa la regulacion de los citios q.e contenga y su to-
tal valor lo pondremos a disposicion de V.E. en esa Capital
o donde tenga a bien disponer.

Por experiencias de muchos años savemos q.e en el

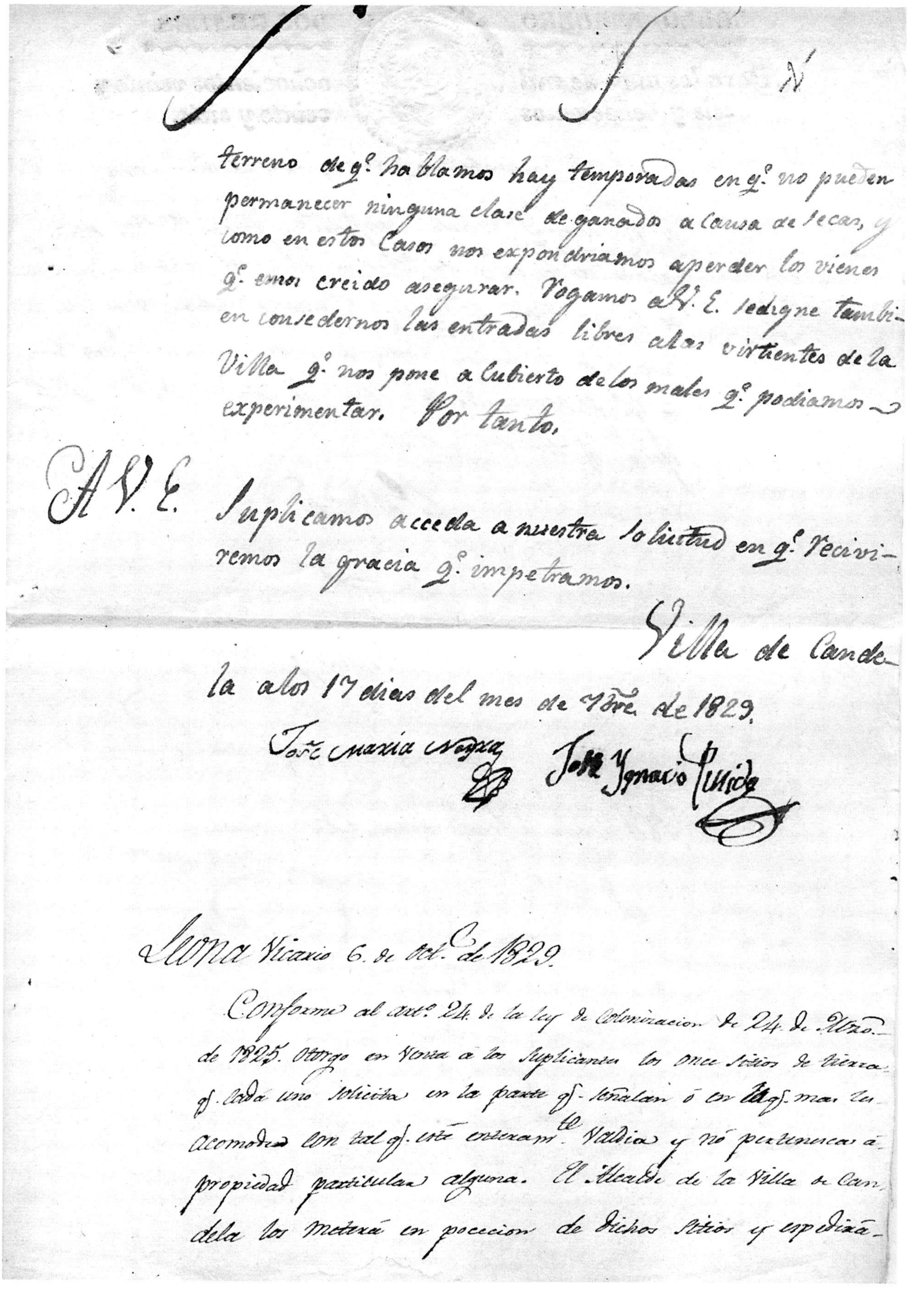

terreno de q.e hablamos hay temporadas en q.e no pueden permanecer ninguna clase de ganados a Causa de secas, y como en estos Casos nos expondriamos a perder los vienes q.e emos creido asegurar. Rogamos a V. E. se digne tambien consedernos las entradas libres a las vertientes de la Villa q.e nos pone a Cubierto de los males q.e podiamos experimentar. Por tanto.

A V. E. Suplicamos acceda a nuestra solicitud en q.e recíviremos la gracia q.e impetramos.

Villa de Candela a los 17 dias del mes de 7bre. de 1829.

José María Vergara

José Ygnacio Pineda

Leona Vicario 6. de Oct.e de 1829.

Conforme al art.o 24. de la ley de Colonizacion de 24. de Marzo de 1825. Otorgo en venta a los Suplicantes los once sitios de tierra q.e cada uno solicita en la parte q.e señalan ó en la q.e mas les acomode con tal q.e esté enteram.te valdia y nó pertenezca á propiedad particular alguna. El Alcalde de la Villa de Candela los meterá en poccecion de dichos sitios y espedirá-

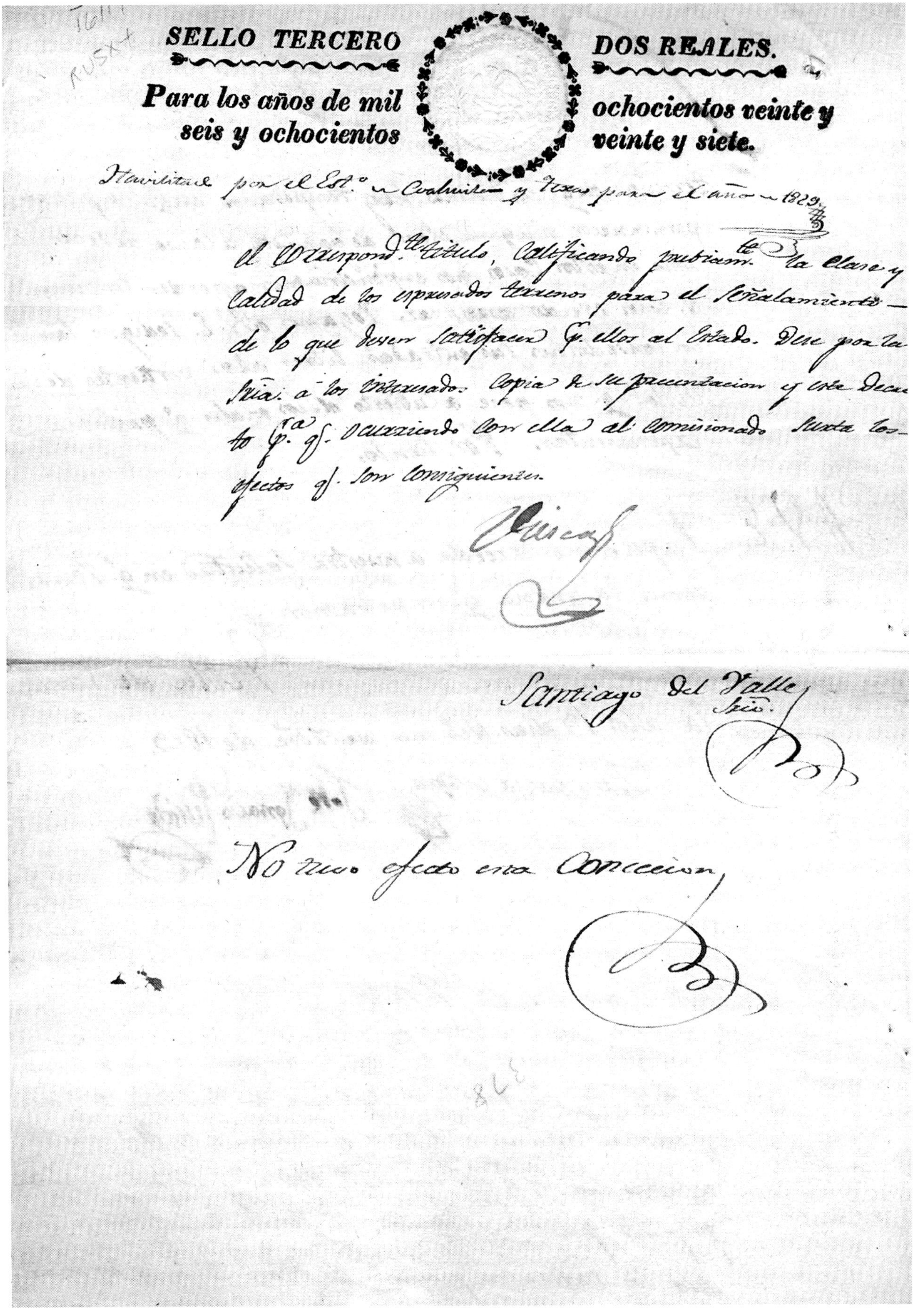

SELLO TERCERO DOS REALES.

Para los años de mil ochocientos veinte y seis y ochocientos veinte y siete.

Havilitado por el Estº de Coahuila y Texas para el año de 1829.

el correspond.te titulo, calificando previam.te la clase y calidad de los expresados terrenos para el señalamiento de lo que deben satisfacer p. ellos al Estado. Dese por la Secria. a los interesados copia de su presentacion y este decreto p.a q. ocurriendo con ella al Comisionado surta los efectos q. son consiguientes.

Viesca

Santiago del Valle
Srio.

No tuvo efecto esta concesion

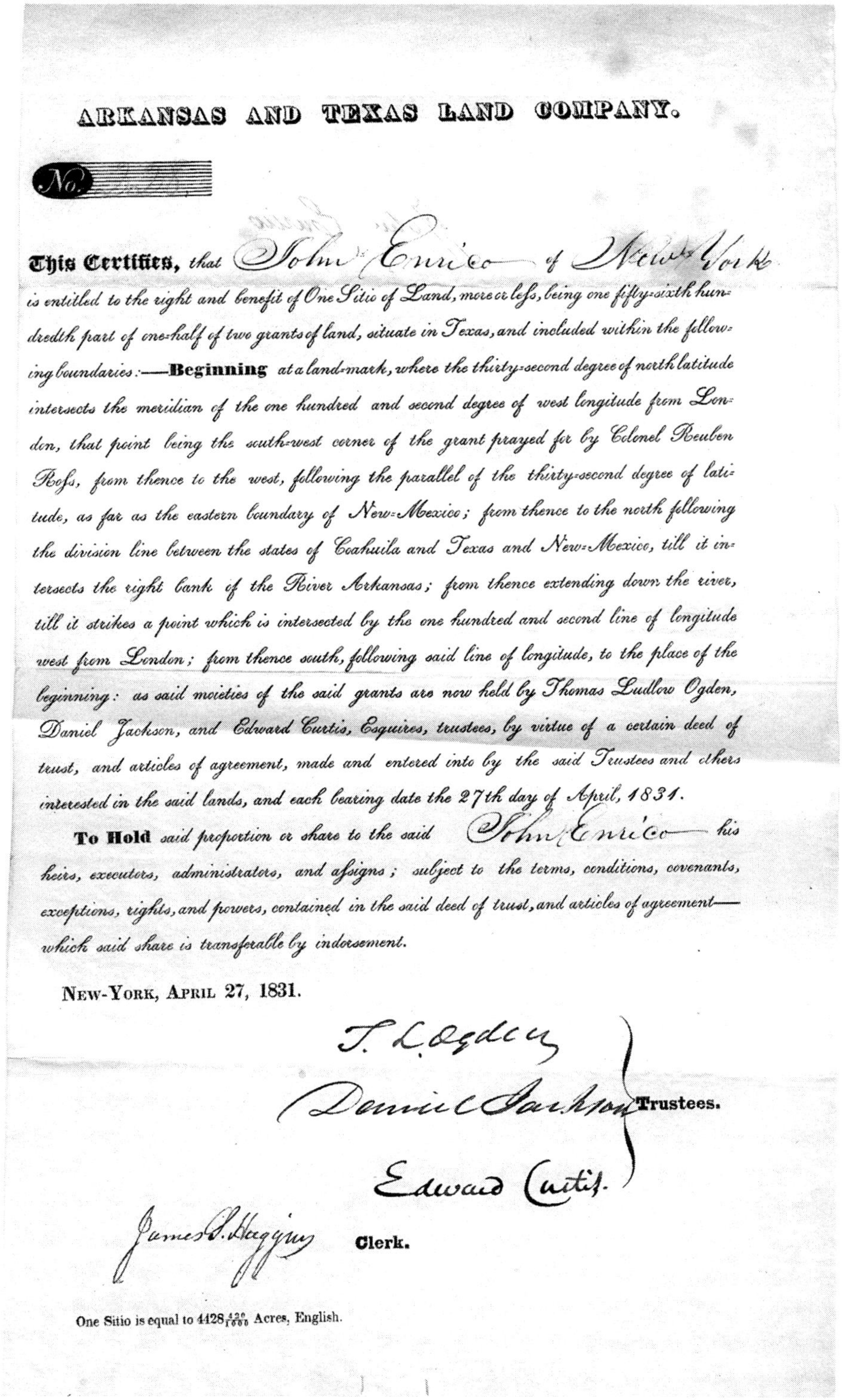

ARKANSAS AND TEXAS LAND COMPANY.

No.

**This Certifies,** *that* John Enrico *of* New York *is entitled to the right and benefit of One Sitio of Land, more or less, being one fifty-sixth hundredth part of one-half of two grants of land, situate in Texas, and included within the following boundaries:*—**Beginning** *at a land-mark, where the thirty-second degree of north latitude intersects the meridian of the one hundred and second degree of west longitude from London, that point being the south-west corner of the grant prayed for by Colonel Reuben Ross, from thence to the west, following the parallel of the thirty-second degree of latitude, as far as the eastern boundary of New-Mexico; from thence to the north following the division line between the states of Coahuila and Texas and New-Mexico, till it intersects the right bank of the River Arkansas; from thence extending down the river, till it strikes a point which is intersected by the one hundred and second line of longitude west from London; from thence south, following said line of longitude, to the place of the beginning: as said moieties of the said grants are now held by Thomas Ludlow Ogden, Daniel Jackson, and Edward Curtis, Esquires, trustees, by virtue of a certain deed of trust, and articles of agreement, made and entered into by the said Trustees and others interested in the said lands, and each bearing date the 27th day of April, 1831.*

**To Hold** *said proportion or share to the said* John Enrico *his heirs, executors, administrators, and assigns; subject to the terms, conditions, covenants, exceptions, rights, and powers, contained in the said deed of trust, and articles of agreement—which said share is transferable by indorsement.*

New-York, April 27, 1831.

T. L. Ogden
Daniel Jackson — **Trustees.**
Edward Curtis.

James B. Huggins **Clerk.**

One Sitio is equal to 4428 $\frac{426}{1000}$ Acres, English.

**Figure 18. Land Certificate for a Sitio from The Arkansas and Texas Land Company, New York, 1831. New York physician and naturalized Mexican citizen Dr. John Charles Beales married the widow of empresario Richard Exter, María Dolores Soto. Beales reactivated both the inherited Exter grant and the dormant Colonel Reuben Ross concession in the Panhandle of Texas. John Enrico of New York was Beales' North American agent, holding his power of attorney. Enrico oversaw the formation of the Arkansas and Texas Land Company in April 1831. The organizers believed Beales' Mexican status exempted his colony from the exclusion of more Anglo settlements. Most marketing was done in England. The promotional pamphlet, signed by Enrico, styled "Emigration to Texas: Proposals for Colonizing in Certain Extensive Tracts of Land in the Republic of Mexico," was printed by H. E. Carrington, Bath, England. The association's scrip certificate entitled the owner, in this case, John Enrico of New York, the rights and benefits of one sitio of land, or one fifty-sixth interest in half the described grants. The April 27, 1831, land scrip to 4,428 acres was little more than the right to locate.**

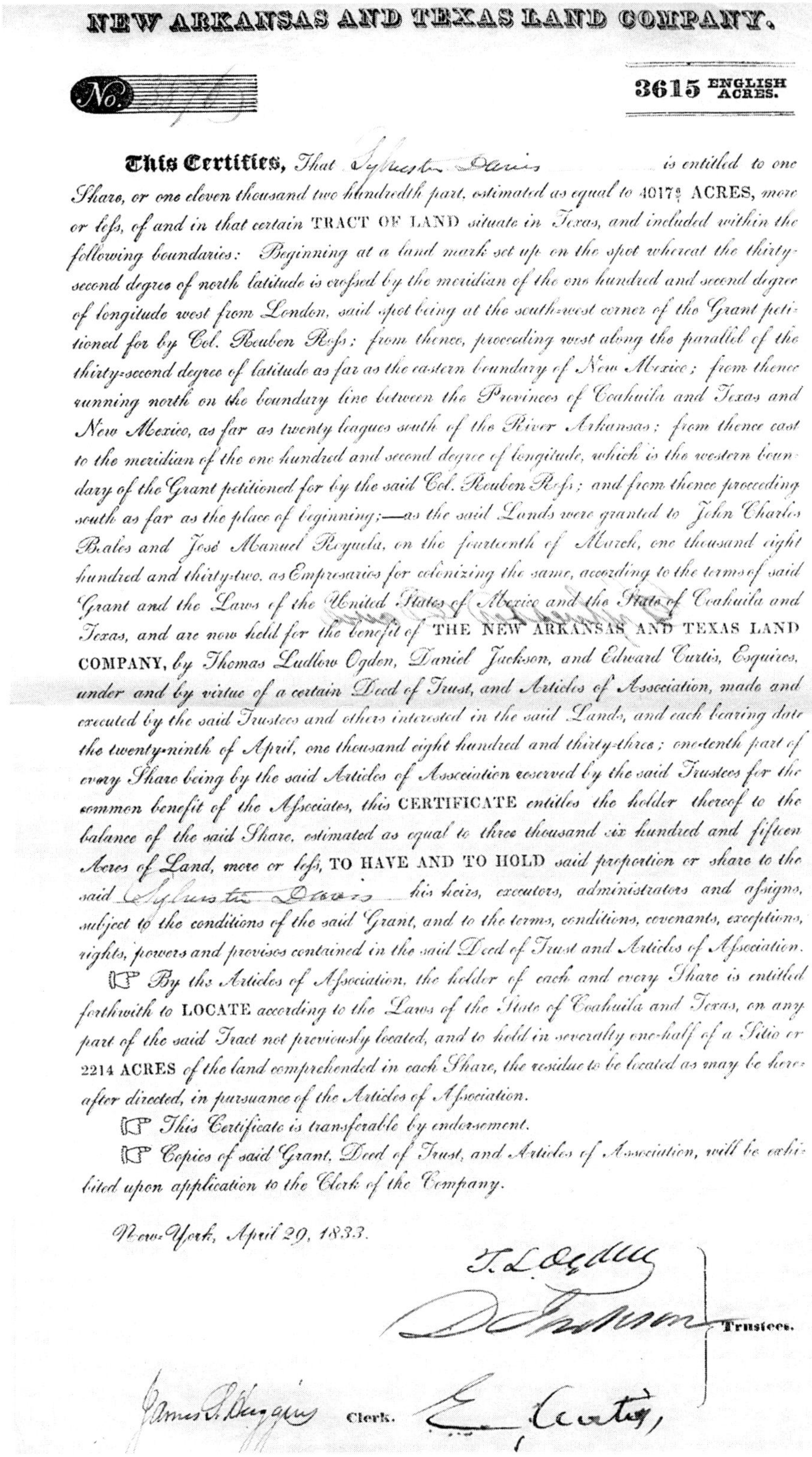

NEW ARKANSAS AND TEXAS LAND COMPANY.

No.

3615 ENGLISH ACRES.

**This Certifies,** That Sylvester Davis is entitled to one Share, or one eleven thousand two hundredth part, estimated as equal to 4017⅘ ACRES, more or less, of and in that certain TRACT OF LAND situate in Texas, and included within the following boundaries: Beginning at a land mark set up on the spot whereat the thirty-second degree of north latitude is crossed by the meridian of the one hundred and second degree of longitude west from London, said spot being at the south-west corner of the Grant petitioned for by Col. Reuben Ross; from thence, proceeding west along the parallel of the thirty-second degree of latitude as far as the eastern boundary of New Mexico; from thence running north on the boundary line between the Provinces of Coahuila and Texas and New Mexico, as far as twenty leagues south of the River Arkansas; from thence east to the meridian of the one hundred and second degree of longitude, which is the western boundary of the Grant petitioned for by the said Col. Reuben Ross; and from thence proceeding south as far as the place of beginning;—as the said Lands were granted to John Charles Beales and José Manuel Royuela, on the fourteenth of March, one thousand eight hundred and thirty-two, as Empresarios for colonizing the same, according to the terms of said Grant and the Laws of the United States of Mexico and the State of Coahuila and Texas, and are now held for the benefit of THE NEW ARKANSAS AND TEXAS LAND COMPANY, by Thomas Ludlow Ogden, Daniel Jackson, and Edward Curtis, Esquires, under and by virtue of a certain Deed of Trust, and Articles of Association, made and executed by the said Trustees and others interested in the said Lands, and each bearing date the twenty-ninth of April, one thousand eight hundred and thirty-three; one-tenth part of every Share being by the said Articles of Association reserved by the said Trustees for the common benefit of the Associates, this CERTIFICATE entitles the holder thereof to the balance of the said Share, estimated as equal to three thousand six hundred and fifteen Acres of Land, more or less, TO HAVE AND TO HOLD said proportion or share to the said Sylvester Davis his heirs, executors, administrators and assigns, subject to the conditions of the said Grant, and to the terms, conditions, covenants, exceptions, rights, powers and provisoes contained in the said Deed of Trust and Articles of Association.

☞ By the Articles of Association, the holder of each and every Share is entitled forthwith to LOCATE according to the Laws of the State of Coahuila and Texas, on any part of the said Tract not previously located, and to hold in severalty one-half of a Sitio or 2214 ACRES of the land comprehended in each Share, the residue to be located as may be hereafter directed, in pursuance of the Articles of Association.

☞ This Certificate is transferable by endorsement.

☞ Copies of said Grant, Deed of Trust, and Articles of Association, will be exhibited upon application to the Clerk of the Company.

New-York, April 29, 1833.

T. L. Ogden
D. Jackson
E. Curtis, Trustees.

James S. Huggins Clerk.

Figure 19. Land Certificate for 4,017 acres in The New Arkansas and Texas Land Company, New York, 1833. In 1833, some of the assets of the first Beales association were transferred to the New Arkansas and Texas Land Company. Added were rights to the older Beales and Royuela Grant. The new company issued certificates entitling owners interest in 4,017⅘ Mexican or 3,615 English acres and joint ownership in 2,214 acres and other assets. Trustees, attorneys and agents remained virtually the same for the old and new company. The scrip owner, Sylvester Doris, was English and probably never set foot in Texas. Again, the primary right of the certificate holder was to locate land within the granted concession. All certificates are dated April 29, 1833, in New York. None were patented by the General Land Office.

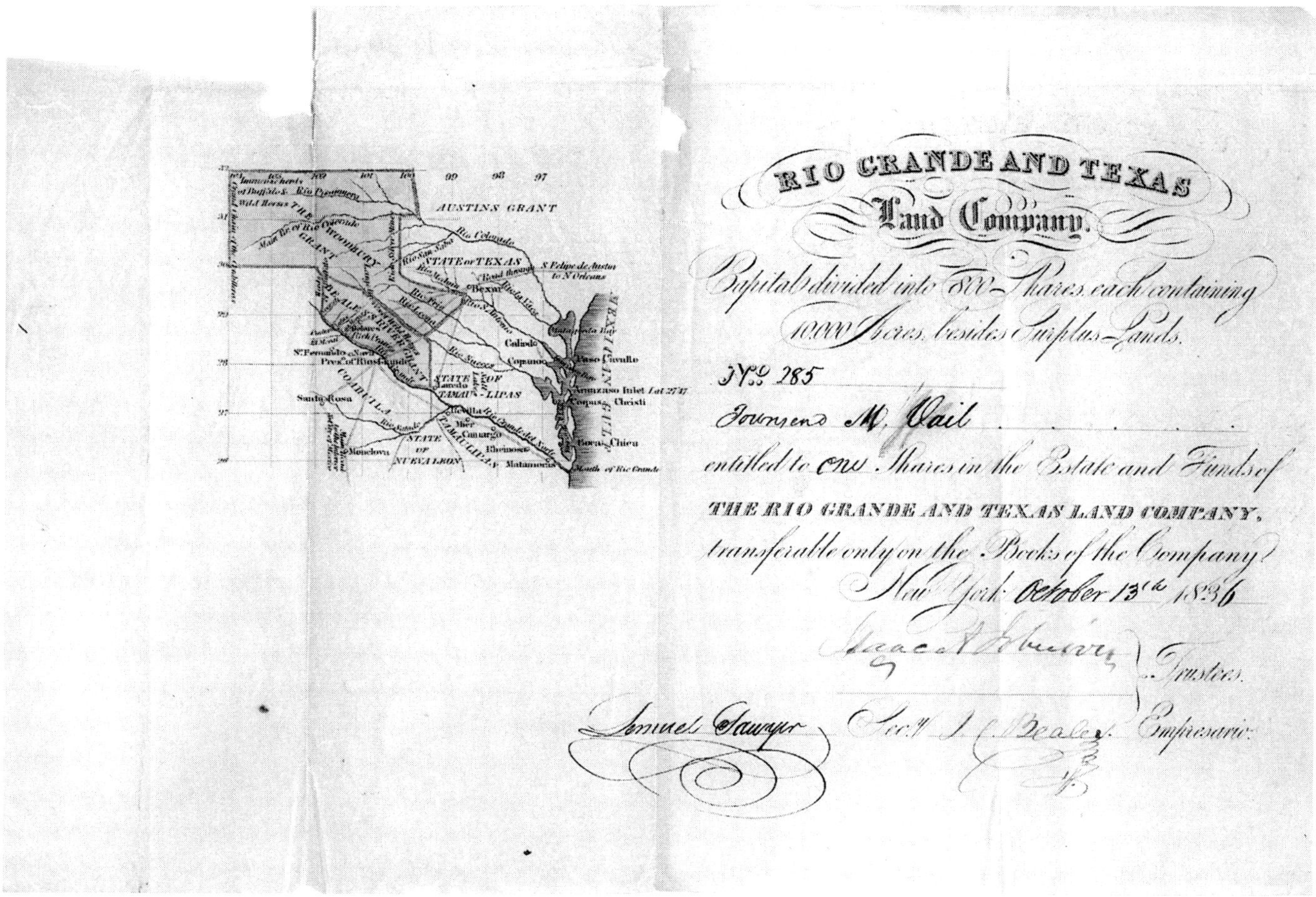


**Figure 20. Share Certificate Representing 1/800 of 10,000 acres in the Rio Grande and Texas Land Company, New York, 1836. Dr. Beales' third venture, the Rio Grande and Texas Land Company, formed April 21, 1834, in New York, received portions of the older Beales and Grant contract plus nine "Eleven League" portions purchased from the State of Coahuila and Texas belonging to his wife, Dolores. This certificate gave each owner an interest in 10,000 acres along the Rio Grande. Eight hundred shares were authorized. Scripholder M. Dail may have been one of the hundred-plus colonists who ventured to the town site, named Dolores, along Las Moras Creek. The colony included Anglos, Germans and Mexicans. They came in several waves from New York beginning in 1834. Drought, Indian raids and the Texas Revolution doomed the colony. The map on the certificate shows the grant in relationship to the other western colonies. Dail's certificate is dated October 13, 1836, after the revolution. In December 1846 the "Texas Land Company" merged with the New York and Texas Land and Emigration Association through the efforts of the "Rio Grande" officer James S. Curtis and Judge John C. Watrous.**

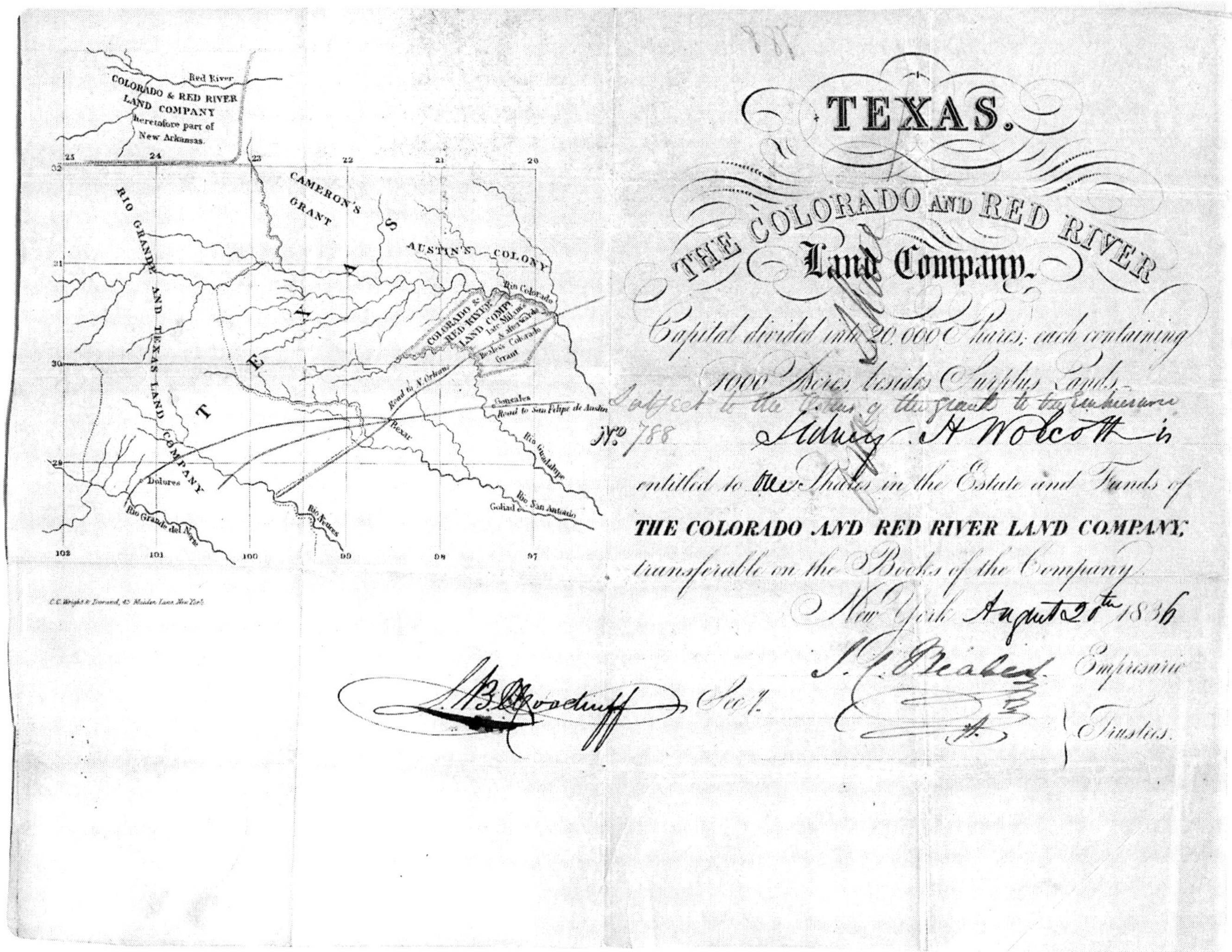


Figure 21. Share Certificate Representing 1,000 acres in the Colorado and Red River Land Company, New York, 1836. The New Arkansas and Texas Land Company transferred its holdings, known as the Beales Colorado Grant and located on that river and the Guadalupe, to the Colorado and Red River Land Company. Beales signed the share certificates as empresario. All four of his ventures produced income for the organizers, sales agents and attorneys. None received deeds and Beales failed to earn his contractual premium lands because too few colonists settled. The revolution interrupted the marketing of this grant.

GALVESTON BAY & TEXAS LAND COMPANY

No. 533

This Certifies.

4428 402/1000 Acres.

SCRIP No. 533 for ONE SITIO, containing 4428 402/1000 Eighteen[?] Acres

That the Subscribers as the Trustees and Attorneys of LORENZO DE ZAVALA, JOSEPH VEHLEIN and DAVID G. BURNET, have given and do hereby give to Rodman Moulton and his legal representatives the bearer hereof, their consent to the location of, and holding in severalty, ONE SITIO, of Land within the limits of four adjoining tracts of land in TEXAS, heretofore severally granted to the said Lorenzo De Zavala on the 12th of March 1829, Joseph Vehlein on the 21st December 1826, and 17th November 1828, and David G. Burnet on the 22 December 1826, as EMPRESARIOS for COLONIZING the same according to the terms of the said grants, and the LAWS of the UNITED STATES of MEXICO, and the STATE of COAHUILA and TEXAS, which said several Tracts are now united in one common interest, and placed under the direction and management of the Subscribers, as the ATTORNEYS and Trustees of the said EMPRESARIOS, by virtue of and according to their several DEEDS of Indenture, dated the 16th October 1830, and to the articles of Association of said COMPANY.

The four tracts of Land aforesaid, comprehend all the LAND not settled according to LAW, and the terms of said Grants, lying within the following limits, (excepting the town of Nacogdoches;) Beginning at the Westerly boundary of the UNITED STATES of AMERICA on the Gulph of MEXICO, thence running Northerly on the Westerly side of the Sabine River to the road leading from NATCHITOCHES to NACOGDOCHES thence running Westerly along said Road a distance of Twenty Spanish Leagues from the boundary line to the suburbs or vicinity of Nacogdoches, then proceeding from said Town of Nacogdoches Northwardly a distance of fifteen Spanish Leagues, where leaving free on one side, the Twenty boundary leagues in a parallel with the River Sabine and the dividing line of the UNITED STATES of the North, shall be placed a LAND MARK, and from which a right line shall be drawn to the West until it strikes the Rivulet named NAVASOTO, from thence the line shall descend upon the left margin of said Rivulet, following its course until it meets the Road leading from BEXAR to NACOGDOCHES, thence running along said road till it comes to a point thereon lying due North of the source of the Waters of the Rivulet St. JACINTO, thence running due South to the source of the Waters of the said River, thence it shall follow the left bank of the St. JACINTO to GALVESTON BAY, thence by the Westerly side of said BAY to the GULPH of MEXICO, excluding the ISLAND of St. LOUIS, and thence by the said GULPH of MEXICO to the place of beginning.

The location of said land is to be made under the SUPERVISION and direction of the Agents of the Trustees and Attorneys of the EMPRESARIOS aforesaid residing on the land, who, after making a record of the same shall make report thereof to the Commissioner appointed by the GOVERNMENT, to the intent that the holder of this Scrip upon the surrender thereof may have his land SURVEYED, and receive his title thereto in severalty from said Commissioner, according to Law: SUBJECT to the payments required by the LAWS of the STATE. This scrip being Indorsed by the original holder is Transferable by delivery. Copies of the Original GRANTS and subsequent conveyances and articles of association of the COMPANY as well as the Colonization laws before referred to, will be exhibited upon application to either of the Subscribers hereto.

New-York 16. October 1830

Trustees & Attorneys.

Sec'y.

Figure 22. Land Scrip Certificate for Sitio in the Galveston Bay and Texas Land Company, New York, 1830. In the tradition of Dr. Beales but in a grander fashion, the Galveston Bay and Texas Land Company was the most ambitious of all the early land schemes. The marketed certificates were the equivalent of 4,428 and 402/1,000 acres, undivided, in the grants originally awarded to Zavala, Vehlein and Burnet by the State of Coahuila and Texas. The land scrip came in both labor and league denominations. Large blocks were sold to other speculators. The Union Land Company acquired twenty-eight leagues in 1831. In 1834 the Trinity Land Company held 142 leagues. Neither company was successful in their sales or settlement objectives. Scrip sold for as little as a nickel on the secondary market. Titles were issued to some colonists by the Republic. Deeds referenced the empresario grants of Zavala, Vehlein and Burnet rather than the Galveston Bay Company. The company hired the most prominent attorneys in Texas to validate its questionable land claims and rights for premium lands. Retained representatives included President Sam Houston, Judge John C. Watrous and Attorney General James Pinckney Henderson.

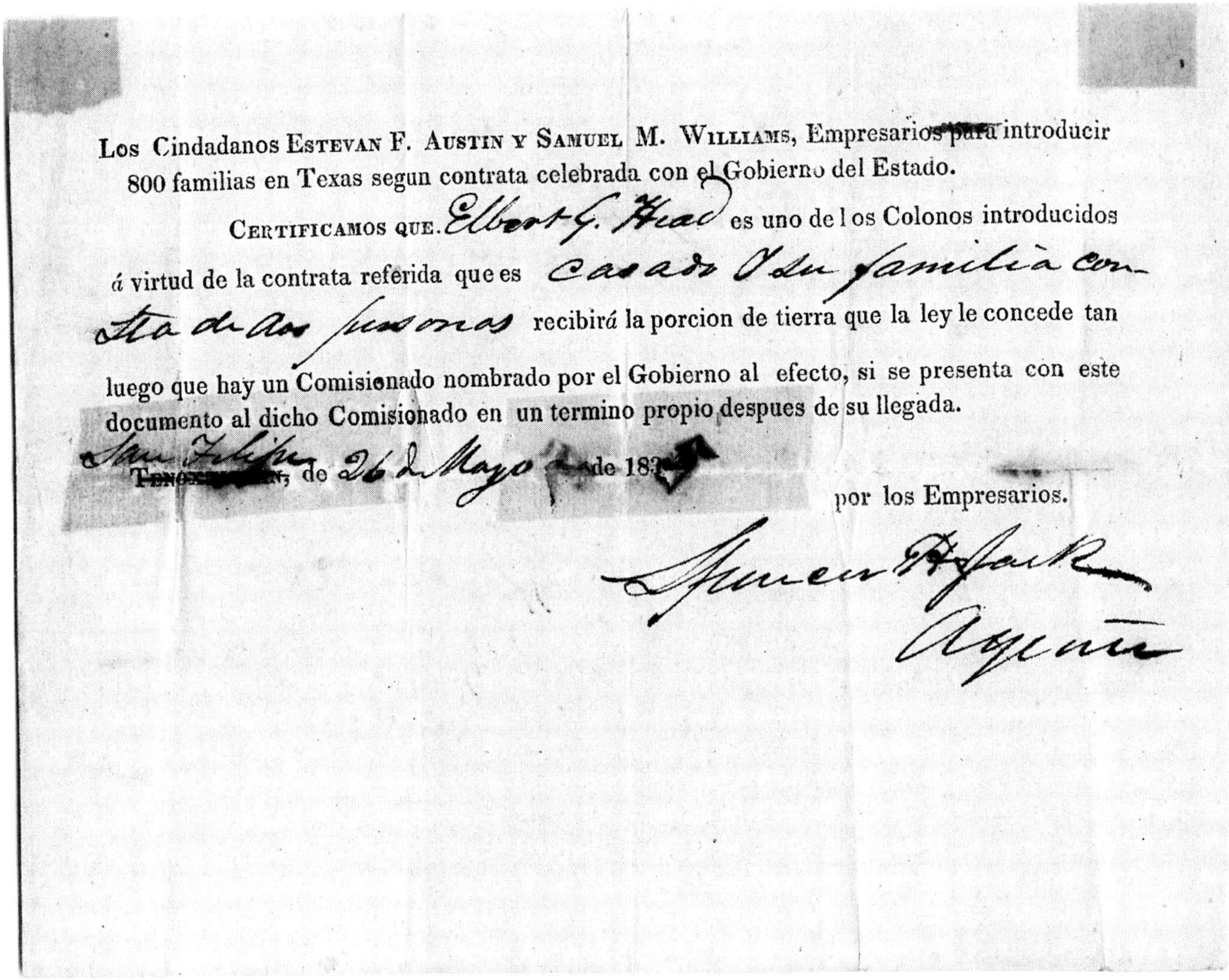

Los Cindadanos Estevan F. Austin y Samuel M. Williams, Empresarios ~~para~~ introducir 800 familias en Texas segun contrata celebrada con el Gobierno del Estado.

Certificamos que. *Elbert G. Head* es uno de los Colonos introducidos á virtud de la contrata referida que es *casado y su familia consta de dos personas* recibirá la porcion de tierra que la ley le concede tan luego que hay un Comisionado nombrado por el Gobierno al efecto, si se presenta con este documento al dicho Comisionado en un termino propio despues de su llegada.

*San Felipe* ~~Tenox[illegible]~~, de *26 de Mayo* de 183[illegible]

por los Empresarios.

*Spencer H. Jack*
*Agente*

**Figure 23. Colonist Certificate to Settle in Austin and Williams Upper Colony, 1834. Austin's final grant with his partner S. M. Williamson was known as the Upper Colony. It conflicted with the Sterling Roberson grant, causing litigation for years. Settler Elberd Head was admitted as an emigrant to the Upper Colony on May 26, 1835. Although he died in 1838, his heirs received a first-class grant for a league in what became Limestone County. The emigrant certificate was in Spanish as required by Mexican law. The certificate was issued from San Felipe de Austin. Litigation between Empresario Sterling Robertson and owners of the "Upper Colony" went on for years. Spencer Houston Jack was appointed agent for settling families in the "Upper Colony" in 1834 at Tenoxtitlan on the Brazos, presently in Burleson County. Before Austin, Travis County was selected as the permanent capital, Tenoxtitlan was expected to be the seat of government.**

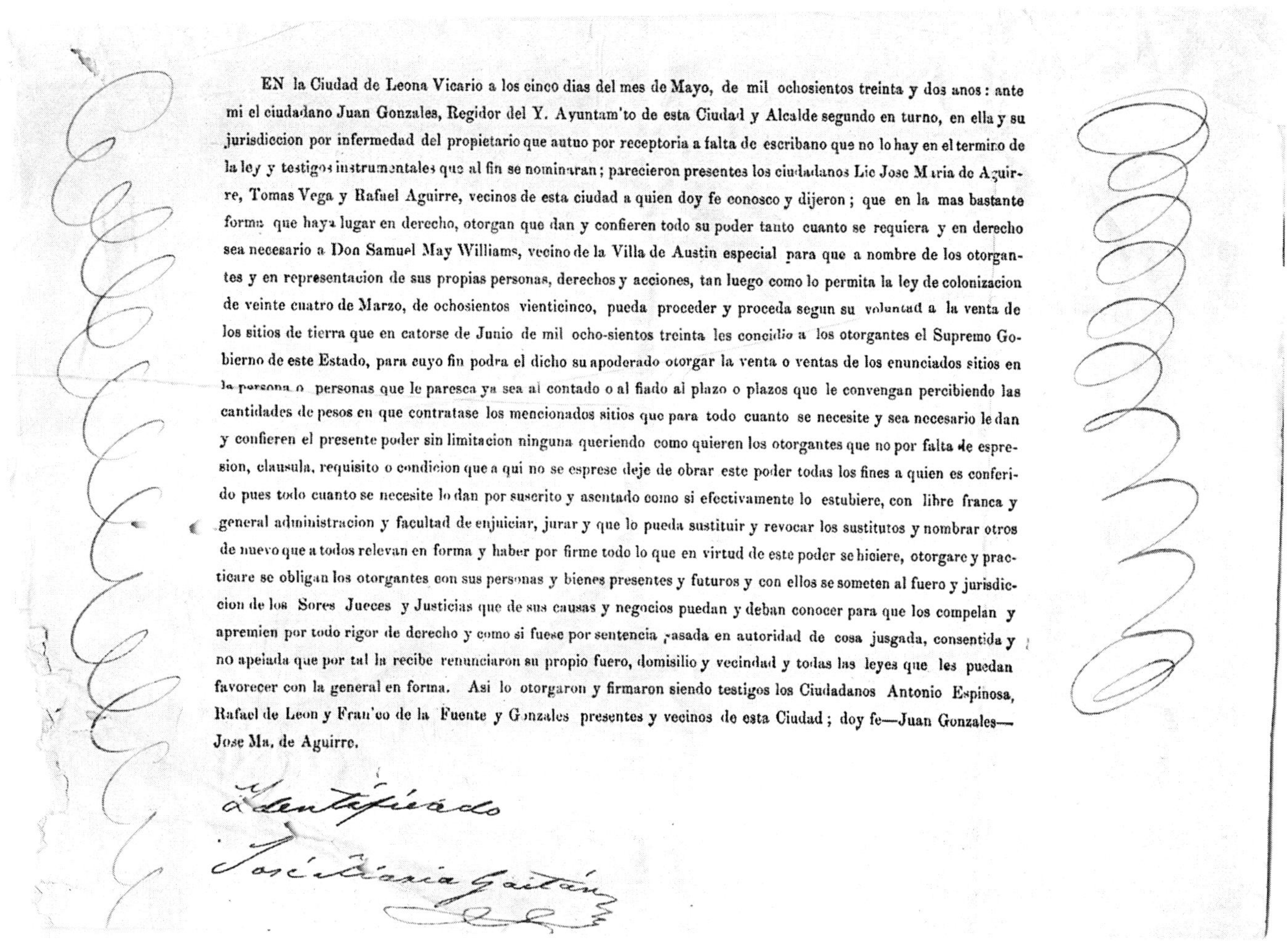

EN la Ciudad de Leona Vicario a los cinco dias del mes de Mayo, de mil ochosientos treinta y dos anos: ante mi el ciudadano Juan Gonzales, Regidor del Y. Ayuntam'to de esta Ciudad y Alcalde segundo en turno, en ella y su jurisdiccion por infermedad del propietario que autuo por receptoria a falta de escribano que no lo hay en el termino de la ley y testigos instrumentales que al fin se nominaran; parecieron presentes los ciudadanos Lic Jose Maria de Aguirre, Tomas Vega y Rafael Aguirre, vecinos de esta ciudad a quien doy fe conosco y dijeron; que en la mas bastante forma que haya lugar en derecho, otorgan que dan y confieren todo su poder tanto cuanto se requiera y en derecho sea necesario a Don Samuel May Williams, vecino de la Villa de Austin especial para que a nombre de los otorgantes y en representacion de sus propias personas, derechos y acciones, tan luego como lo permita la ley de colonizacion de veinte cuatro de Marzo, de ochosientos vienticinco, pueda proceder y proceda segun su voluntad a la venta de los sitios de tierra que en catorse de Junio de mil ocho-sientos treinta les concidio a los otorgantes el Supremo Gobierno de este Estado, para cuyo fin podra el dicho su apoderado otorgar la venta o ventas de los enunciados sitios en la persona o personas que le paresca ya sea al contado o al fiado al plazo o plazos que le convengan percibiendo las cantidades de pesos en que contratase los mencionados sitios que para todo cuanto se necesite y sea necesario le dan y confieren el presente poder sin limitacion ninguna queriendo como quieren los otorgantes que no por falta de espresion, clausula, requisito o condicion que a qui no se esprese deje de obrar este poder todas los fines a quien es conferido pues todo cuanto se necesite lo dan por suscrito y asentado como si efectivamente lo estubiere, con libre franca y general administracion y facultad de enjuiciar, jurar y que lo pueda sustituir y revocar los sustitutos y nombrar otros de nuevo que a todos relevan en forma y haber por firme todo lo que en virtud de este poder se hiciere, otorgare y practicare se obligan los otorgantes con sus personas y bienes presentes y futuros y con ellos se someten al fuero y jurisdiccion de los Sores Jueces y Justicias que de sus causas y negocios puedan y deban conocer para que los compelan y apremien por todo rigor de derecho y como si fuese por sentencia pasada en autoridad de cosa jusgada, consentida y no apeiada que por tal la recibe renunciaron su propio fuero, domisilio y vecindad y todas las leyes que les puedan favorecer con la general en forma. Asi lo otorgaron y firmaron siendo testigos los Ciudadanos Antonio Espinosa, Rafael de Leon y Fran'co de la Fuente y Gonzales presentes y vecinos de esta Ciudad; doy fe—Juan Gonzales—Jose Ma. de Aguirre.

Identificado

Jose Maria Gaitan

**Figure 24. Power of Attorney Authorizing Samuel May Williams to Sell Land Under Mexican Colonization Law of March 24, 1825. (Tomás de la Vega Grant on Brazos River at Waco Village), 1832. Perhaps the most litigated of all Texas land speculation is the José María Aguirre, Rafael Aguirre and Tomás de la Vega "Eleven League Grant" situated at the location of present-day Waco. Purchased by the three native Mexicans on May 2, 1832, at Leona Vicario, it was acquired through a power of attorney given to Austin's partner, Samuel May Williams. A series of sales followed, including to Michael B. Menard et al., for the benefit of Sophia St. John, a relative of Austin. Thomas Jefferson Chambers acquired a couple of leagues. An Alabama land syndicate purchased three leagues. The land agent was Jacob de Córdova. After the syndicate attempted to evict all squatters from their grant, litigation followed and continued for years, ending up in the U.S. Supreme Court, which confirmed the validity of the Tomás de la Vega Grant. The grant was authenticated by Juan González, *regidor* and *alcalde* of the State of Coahuila at Lenona Vicario. The tax-sealed document cost twelve reals. This power of attorney is a copy taken from the original by Juan Gonzáles, Regidor, May 5, 1832. The eleven-league grant was conveyed by Luke Lesassier, *alcalde* of San Felipe de Austin on October 4, 1833. He was also Samuel May Williams's law partner.**

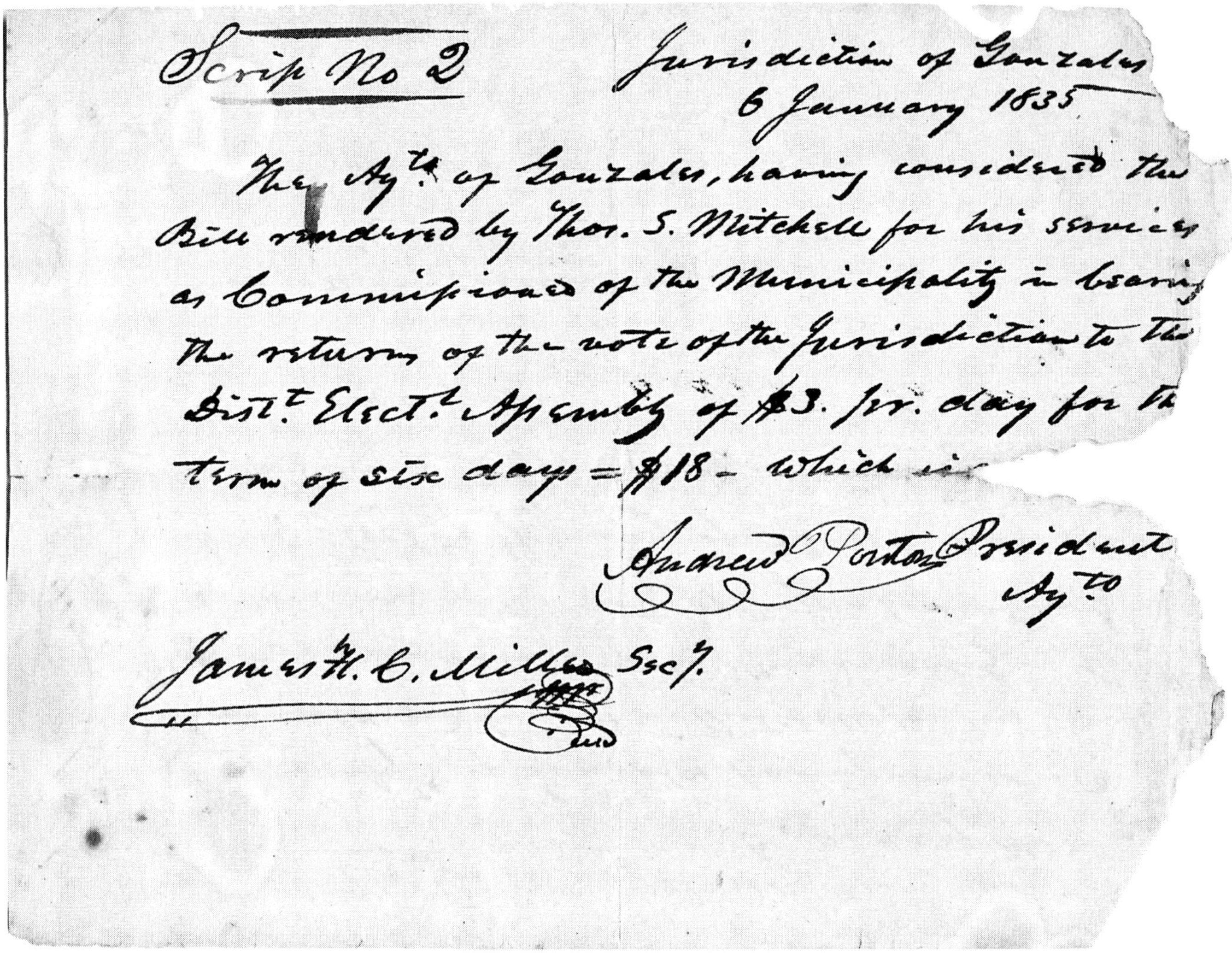
Scrip No 2

Jurisdiction of Gonzales
6 January 1835.

The Ayto. of Gonzales, having considered the Bill rendered by Thos. S. Mitchell for his services as Commissioner of the Municipality in bearing the returns of the vote of the Jurisdiction to the Distt. Electl. Assembly of $3. pr. day for the term of six days = $18 - which is

Andrew Ponton President
Ayto

James H. C. Miller Secy.

Figure 25. Scrip Certificate from Municipality of Gonzáles, 1835. Early Texans and their municipalities depended on barter, credit and scrip to conduct business. On January 6, 1835, the Jurisdiction of Gonzáles issued Scrip No. 2 for $18.00 to Thom. S. Mitchell to reimburse him for "bearing" the returns of the district election to the assembly. The signer, *alcalde* of Gonzáles, Andrew Ponton, was a member of the Texas Committee of Safety. Municipal land holdings backed up the scrip as security. Ponton patented a quarter-league, as a single man, in DeWitt's Colony in 1832, in present-day Lavaca County. Mitchell was the son of Eli Mitchell of Pennsylvania, who received a quarter-section in Austin's third colony and participated in the Battle of Gonzáles in October 1835.

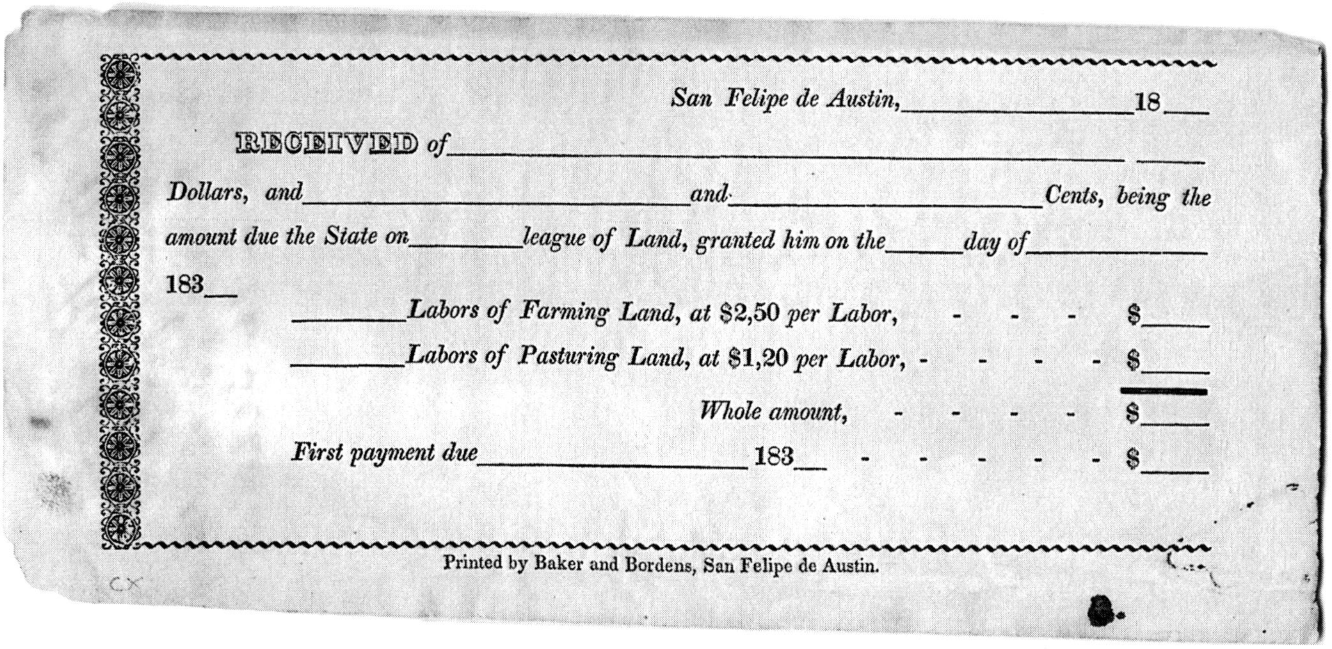

San Felipe de Austin,_______________18___

RECEIVED *of*________________________________________

*Dollars, and*____________________*and*____________________*Cents, being the amount due the State on*________*league of Land, granted him on the*_____*day of*____________ 183__

________*Labors of Farming Land, at $2,50 per Labor,* - - - $_____

________*Labors of Pasturing Land, at $1,20 per Labor,* - - - - $_____

*Whole amount,* - - - - - $_____

*First payment due*________________ 183__ - - - - - - $_____

Printed by Baker and Bordens, San Felipe de Austin.

**Figure 26. Receipt for Government Dues on Land [Blank], San Felipe de Austin, 1838. Government dues on land transactions as well as customs were the primary internally generated revenue source for the Texas government. Most dues on land were paid over several years. Unpaid amounts outstanding to Mexico were assumed by the Government of Texas after the revolution. The blank receipt prepared by Baker and Borden, San Felipe de Austin, was designed to evidence payment by land owners. A labor of farm land cost $2.50 and pasture land was $1.20. Installment terms continued. Despite being ordered to close down in 1835, the Texas Land Commission remained open in Nacogdoches, Bexar and San Felipe for a time. Funds collected were remitted to the Provisional Government.**

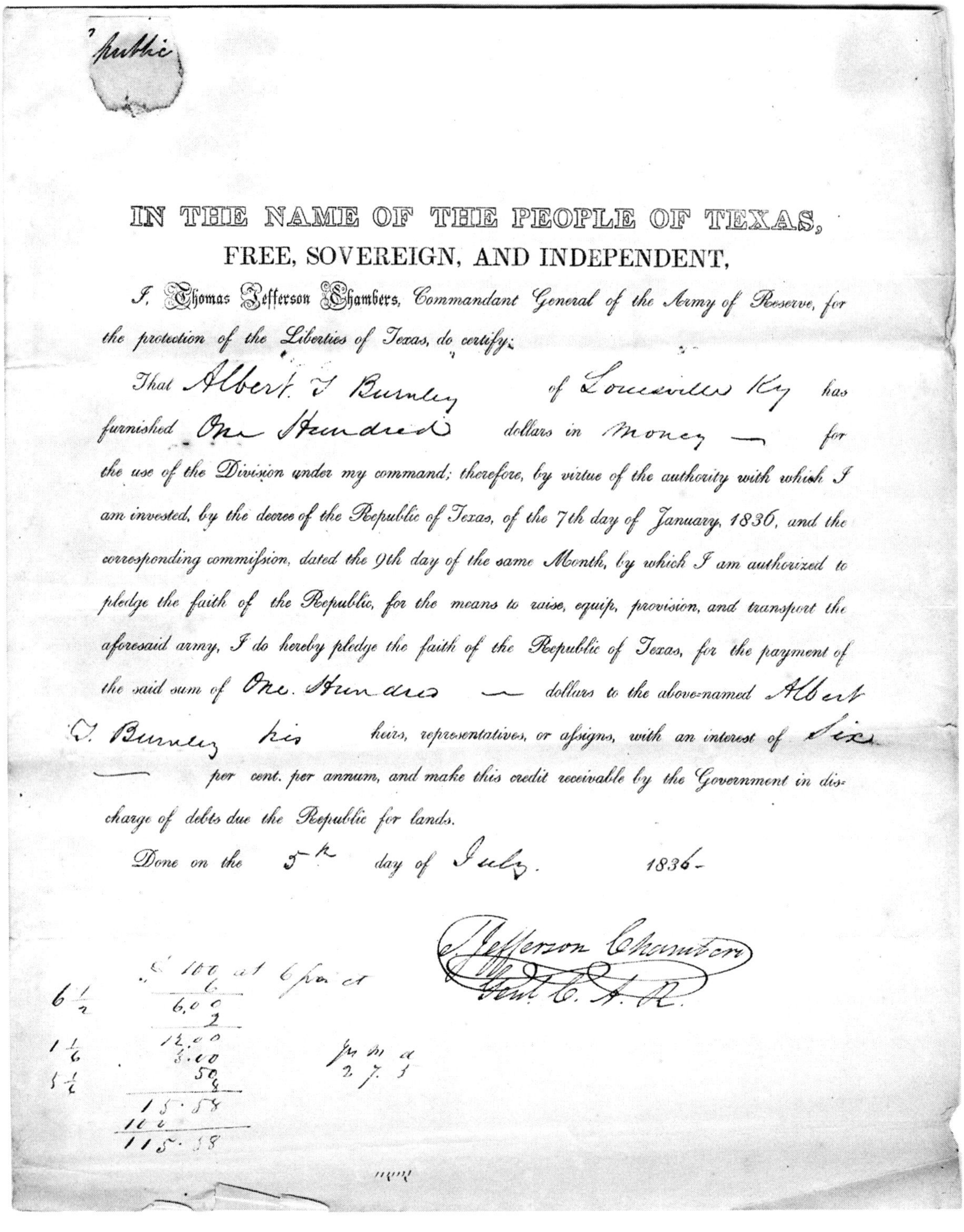

public

IN THE NAME OF THE PEOPLE OF TEXAS,

FREE, SOVEREIGN, AND INDEPENDENT,

I, Thomas Jefferson Chambers, Commandant General of the Army of Reserve, for the protection of the Liberties of Texas, do certify;

That Albert T Burnley of Louisville Ky has furnished One Hundred dollars in Money — for the use of the Division under my command; therefore, by virtue of the authority with which I am invested, by the decree of the Republic of Texas, of the 7th day of January, 1836, and the corresponding commission, dated the 9th day of the same Month, by which I am authorized to pledge the faith of the Republic, for the means to raise, equip, provision, and transport the aforesaid army, I do hereby pledge the faith of the Republic of Texas, for the payment of the said sum of One Hundred — dollars to the above-named Albert T. Burnley his heirs, representatives, or assigns, with an interest of Six — per cent. per annum, and make this credit receivable by the Government in discharge of debts due the Republic for lands.

Done on the 5th day of July. 1836.

J. Jefferson Chambers
Genl. C. A. R.

**Figure 27. Promissory Note by General Jefferson Chambers, Agent for Government of Texas, 1836. Naturalized Mexican citizen Thomas Jefferson Chambers from Virginia, land speculator and attorney, became the Surveyor General of Texas in 1829. As compensation, in 1830 he received from Mexico an "Eleven League Grant" and empresario contract shared with Juan Antonio Padilla in East Texas. As Mexican citizens, the two were exempt from General Terán's suspicion of Anglo immigration. The grant still lapsed. Mexico established a high court to review cases in the Province of Texas, and Chambers was appointed Chief Justice. His $3,000 salary was payable in land at the rate of $100 a league in 1834, of which he located thirteen. During the Texas Revolution, in return for raising over 1,000 volunteers for the Army, he was appointed Major General of the Army of Reserve. The illustration is a debt instrument issued by Chambers while performing that function in July 1836. The debt was payable in Texas currency plus interest. Chambers used his own credit to assure payment, and discounted many of the notes for pennies on the dollar. Chambers could use unpaid notes to pay government dues on his vast real estate holdings.**

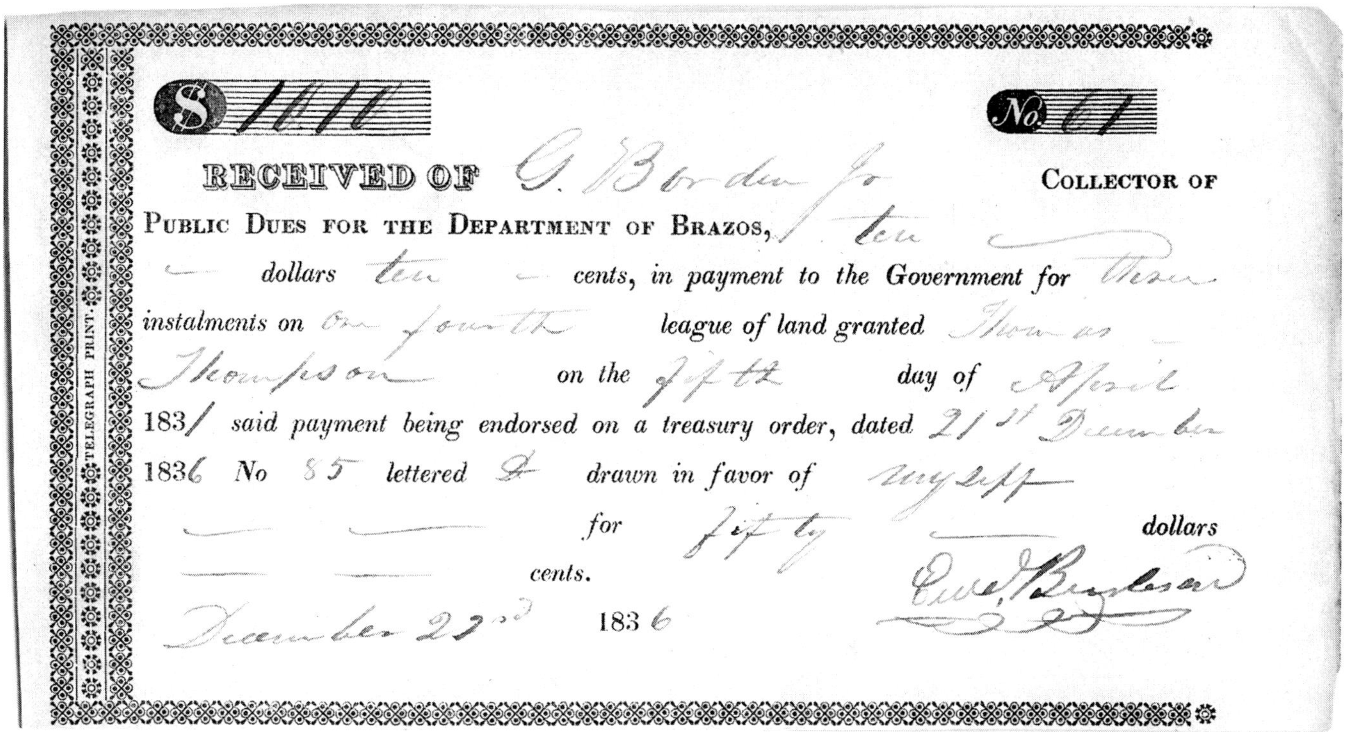
$ 10/10 No.

RECEIVED OF G. Borden Jr COLLECTOR OF PUBLIC DUES FOR THE DEPARTMENT OF BRAZOS, ten dollars ten cents, in payment to the Government for these instalments on One fourth league of land granted Thomas Thompson on the fifth day of April 1831 said payment being endorsed on a treasury order, dated 21st December 1836 No 85 lettered D drawn in favor of myself for fifty dollars cents.

December 22nd 1836

Edwd Burleson

TELEGRAPH PRINT.

**Figure 28. Receipt for Government Dues on Land, Department of Brazos, 1836. Collectors for the Republic of Texas continued to receive payments of government dues dating to the Mexican period. Full payment remained a requirement for issuance of a land patent to settlers, veterans and land scrip holders. Gail Borden, Collector for the Department of the Brazos, was naturally the most involved because of the number of settlers introduced by Austin. Thomas Thompson, as a single colonist, received a league in Austin's second colony, dating to April 5, 1831. For that acreage on the west side of the Colorado River he paid the $10.10 in government dues to Gail Borden on December 22, 1836. Collector Borden later transferred a fifty-dollar Republic treasury order to Edward Burleson. At the time Burleson was Colonel in the frontier rangers. The young nation, with only a limited cadre of officials, often turned collected funds into treasury notes and gave them to commanders to pay and supply troops, bypassing the Treasury.**

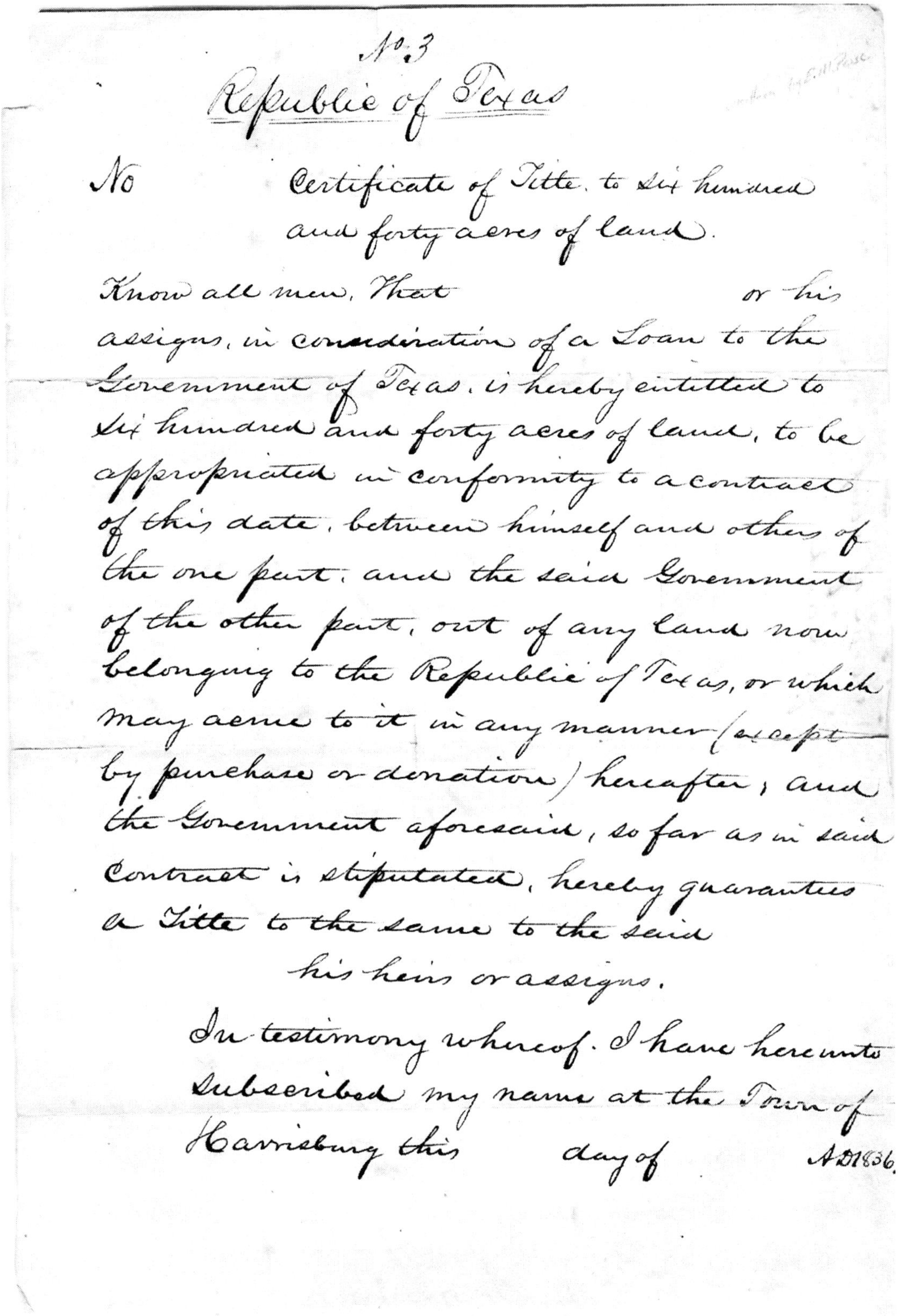

No. 3

Republic of Texas

No Certificate of Title. to Six hundred and forty acres of land.

Know all men, That or his assigns, in consideration of a Loan to the Government of Texas, is hereby entitled to Six hundred and forty acres of land, to be appropriated in conformity to a contract of this date, between himself and others of the one part, and the said Government of the other part, out of any land now belonging to the Republic of Texas, or which may accrue to it in any manner (except by purchase or donation) hereafter, and the Government aforesaid, so far as in said Contract is stipulated, hereby guarantees a Title to the same to the said his heirs or assigns.

In testimony whereof. I have hereunto Subscribed my name at the Town of Harrisburg this day of A.D. 1836.

Figure 29. Title Certificate [Blank] for 640 Acres, Houston, 1836. The majority of Texas troops, contractors and agents remained unpaid. The Texas treasury was empty. All that was in abundance was land. From the beginning the Government of Texas encouraged creditors and soldiers to take land as payment for goods and services. Before the victory at San Jacinto, scrip certificates were tendered to army contractors such as McKinney & Williams. The illustrated blank Republic of Texas "Certificate of Title to Six hundred and forty acres of land," No. 3, was prepared at Harrisburg between the first of 1836 and April 16, 1836. After that date the town was burned by General Santa Anna. Acting Secretary of Treasury Elisha Marshall Pease probably drafted the form.

# TEXIAN LOAN.

THREE HUNDRED AND TWENTY DOLLARS.

CERTIFICATE No. 579.

**Received,** *of* Geo Hancock THIRTY-TWO DOLLARS, *the First Instalment on a Loan of* Three Hundred and Twenty Dollars, *made by him this day to the Government of Texas for* FIVE YEARS, *bearing Interest at the rate of* EIGHT PER CENTUM PER ANNUM, *payable annually. Public Notice to be given, according to contract, when the other Instalments will be required, at which time they may be paid or not; at the option of the said* Geo Hancock *or his Assignee.*

*For the amount paid, Land in Texas may be taken at* FIFTY CENTS *per Acre, with the guarantees and conditions of the contract aforesaid.*

**In Testimony whereof,** *we have hereunto set our hands, and affixed our seals, in the City of* NEW-ORLEANS, *this Eleventh day of January, one thousand eight hundred and thirty-six.*

S. F. Austin L.S.

B. T. Archer L.S.

Wm. H. Wharton L.S.

COMMISSIONERS ON THE PART OF TEXAS.

GOVERNMENT OF TEXAS.

SIX HUNDRED AND FORTY ACRES OF LAND.

PRINTED BY BENJAMIN LEVY—NEW-ORLEANS.

**Figure 30. Land Scrip Certificate for Texas Loan, January 11, 1836, at 50¢ an Acre. More formal printed loan documents and land scrip forms were available early in the Republic's history. The first loan program, known as the "Texian Loan," of January 11, 1836, was documented on a form printed by Benjamin Levy of New Orleans. The $320.00 loan was in fact a subscription to purchase the $320.00 bond, in payments of $32.00. The partial payment entitled the creditor to land scrip, valued at fifty cents an acre, as an option. The half-section option hopefully converted the debt to an option. Both the high interest rate of 8 percent and generous land feature clearly reflected the level of risk assigned to any debt issued by the new Republic. The creditor, George Duncan Hancock, from Tennessee, was in Texas during the revolution. He also received two sections as bounty land for military service in 1836. His land was located in Lampasas County. The three loan commissioners were notable Texans who travelled to the United States to sell "Texian Loans."**

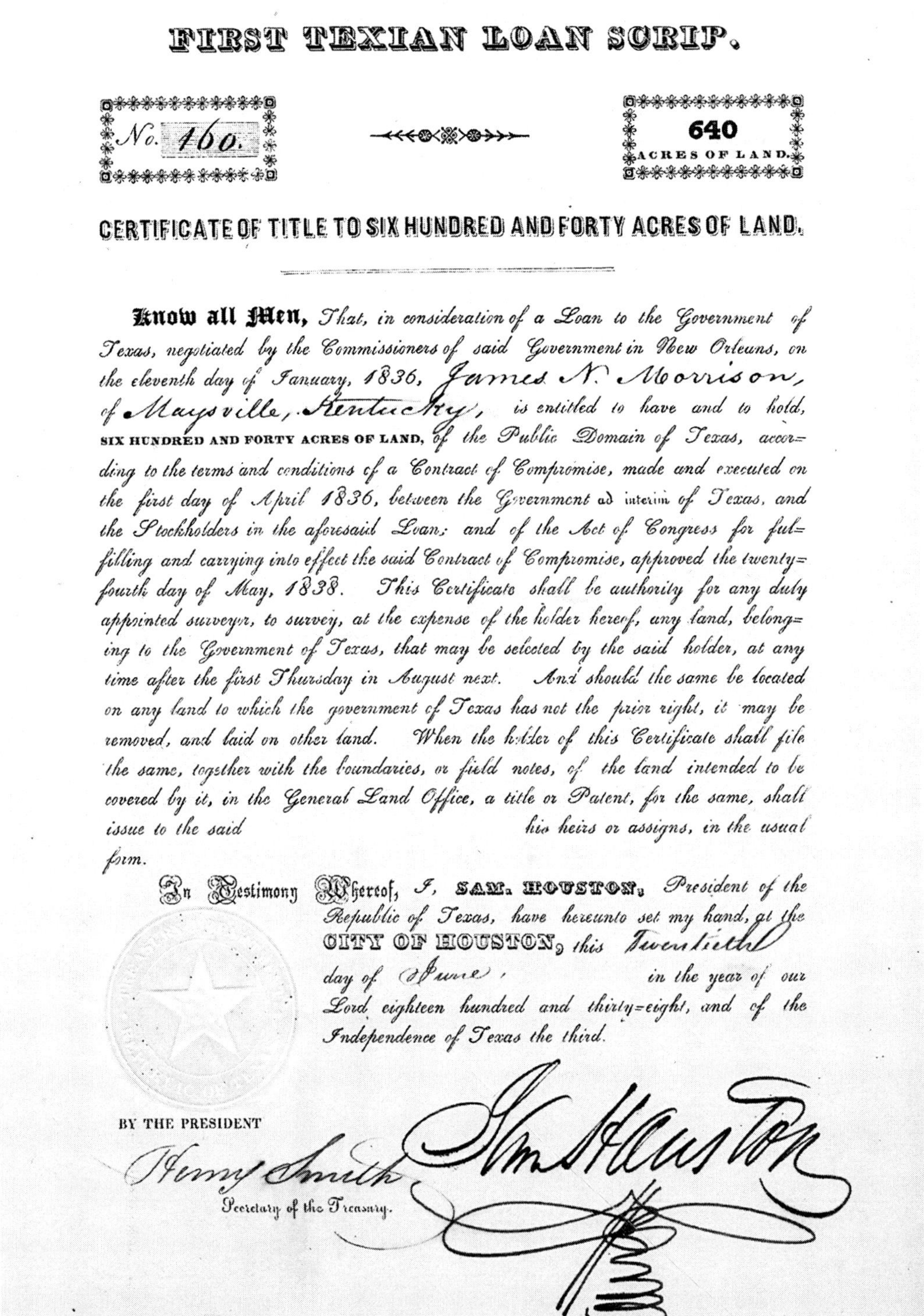

FIRST TEXIAN LOAN SCRIP.

No. 160.

640 ACRES OF LAND.

CERTIFICATE OF TITLE TO SIX HUNDRED AND FORTY ACRES OF LAND.

**Know all Men,** That, in consideration of a Loan to the Government of Texas, negotiated by the Commissioners of said Government in New Orleans, on the eleventh day of January, 1836, James N. Morrison, of Maysville, Kentucky, is entitled to have and to hold, SIX HUNDRED AND FORTY ACRES OF LAND, of the Public Domain of Texas, according to the terms and conditions of a Contract of Compromise, made and executed on the first day of April 1836, between the Government ad interim of Texas, and the Stockholders in the aforesaid Loan; and of the Act of Congress for fulfilling and carrying into effect the said Contract of Compromise, approved the twenty-fourth day of May, 1838. This Certificate shall be authority for any duly appointed surveyor, to survey, at the expense of the holder hereof, any land, belonging to the Government of Texas, that may be selected by the said holder, at any time after the first Thursday in August next. And should the same be located on any land to which the government of Texas has not the prior right, it may be removed, and laid on other land. When the holder of this Certificate shall file the same, together with the boundaries, or field notes, of the land intended to be covered by it, in the General Land Office, a title or Patent, for the same, shall issue to the said his heirs or assigns, in the usual form.

In Testimony Whereof, I, SAM. HOUSTON, President of the Republic of Texas, have hereunto set my hand, at the CITY OF HOUSTON, this Twentieth day of June, in the year of our Lord eighteen hundred and thirty-eight, and of the Independence of Texas the third.

BY THE PRESIDENT

Henry Smith
Secretary of the Treasury.

Sam Houston

Figure 31. Title Certificate for 640 Acres, First Texian Loan, January 11, 1836, Houston. If a creditor of the "Texian Loan" elected to take land scrip in lieu of repayment of the bond, certificates of title were issued. Public complaints and Congressional disapproval forced the terms of the loan to be modified, thereby removing any location and time preference to scrip holders over the veterans and colonists. The compromise, agreed to April 1, 1836, was not approved by Congress until May 1, 1838. On June 20, 1838, President Sam Houston and Secretary of the Treasury Henry Smith issued "Certificates of Title to Six Hundred and Forty Acres of Land." The General Land Office opened later that year. Creditor James N. Morrison of Kentucky received the scrip but no record of patented land was discovered. The value of the scrip decreased because of oversupply.

WARRANT No. 1. BOND No. Texian Loan Bond for $1000, payable in years. Dividend Warrant for 183 Commissioners.

WARRANT No. 2. BOND No. Texian Loan Bond for $1000, payable in years. Dividend Warrant for 183 Commissioners.

WARRANT No. 3. BOND No. Texian Loan Bond for $1000, payable in years. Dividend Warrant for 183 Commissioners.

WARRANT No. 4. BOND No. Texian Loan Bond for $1000, payable in years. Dividend Warrant for 183 Commissioners.

WARRANT No. 5. BOND No. Texian Loan Bond for $1000, payable in years. Dividend Warrant for 183 Commissioners.

WARRANT No. 6. BOND No. Texian Loan Bond for $1000, payable in years. Dividend Warrant for 183 Commissioners.

WARRANT No. 7. BOND No. Texian Loan Bond for $1000, payable in years. Dividend Warrant for 183 Commissioners.

WARRANT No. 8. BOND No. Texian Loan Bond for $1000, payable in years. Dividend Warrant for 183 Commissioners.

WARRANT No. 9. BOND No. Texian Loan Bond for $1000, payable in years. Dividend Warrant for 183 Commissioners.

WARRANT No. 10. BOND No. Texian Loan Bond for $1000, payable in years. Dividend Warrant for 183 Commissioners.

WARRANT No. 11. BOND No. Texian Loan Bond for $1000, payable in years. Dividend Warrant for 183 Commissioners.

WARRANT No. 12. BOND No. Texian Loan Bond for $1000, payable in years. Dividend Warrant for 183 Commissioners.

WARRANT No. 13. BOND No. Texian Loan Bond for $1000, payable in years. Dividend Warrant for 183 Commissioners.

WARRANT No. 14. BOND No. Texian Loan Bond for $1000, payable in years. Dividend Warrant for 183 Commissioners.

WARRANT No. 15. BOND No. Texian Loan Bond for $1000, payable in years. Dividend Warrant for 183 Commissioners.

# TEXIAN LOAN,

No. 1000 Dollars.

ONE THOUSAND DOLLARS. TEXIAN LOAN.

Under Act of Congress, Passed November 18th, 1836.

Know all Men by these Presents,

*That the* GOVERNMENT OF THE REPUBLIC OF TEXAS *acknowledges to owe to* ______ *legal representatives or assigns,* ONE THOUSAND DOLLARS, *current money of the* United States of North America, *which said sum of money the said Government promises to pay to said* ______ *legal representatives or assigns, in* ______ *years from the date hereof, with interest at the rate of* ______ *per centum per annum, payable annually at* ______ *on presentation of this* BOND *and delivery of the* CORRESPONDING DIVIDEND WARRANT, *hereto annexed; And for the faithful and punctual payment of the said principal sum, and the interest to accrue thereon, the said Government doth* HEREBY PLEDGE THE PUBLIC FAITH THEREOF, *and all the proceeds of the sales of the Public Domain, and all Taxes assessed on Lands, which may accrue to this Government, after the expiration of the year 1838.*

THIS BOND IS NEGOTIABLE BY SIMPLE ENDORSEMENT.

In Testimony Whereof, *the* President *and* Secretary *of* State *of the Republic of Texas have signed these presents, and the* Secretary *of the* Treasury *has countersigned the same, and caused the Great Seal of said Republic to be hereunto affixed, at* ______ *this* ______ *day of* ______ *Eighteen hundred and thirty-seven*

______ President.

______ Secretary of State.

______ Secretary of the Treasury.

Under Act of Congress, Passed November 18th, 1836.

PRINTED BY WM. M'KEAN,::::NEW-ORLEANS.

WARRANT No. 16. BOND No. Texian Loan Bond for $1000, payable in years. Dividend Warrant for 183 Commissioners.

WARRANT No. 17. BOND No. Texian Loan Bond for $1000, payable in years. Dividend Warrant for 183 Commissioners.

WARRANT No. 18. BOND No. Texian Loan Bond for $1000, payable in years. Dividend Warrant for 183 Commissioners.

WARRANT No. 19. BOND No. Texian Loan Bond for $1000, payable in years. Dividend Warrant for 183 Commissioners.

WARRANT No. 20. BOND No. Texian Loan Bond for $1000, payable in years. Dividend Warrant for 183 Commissioners.

WARRANT No. 21. BOND No. Texian Loan Bond for $1000, payable in years. Dividend Warrant for 183 Commissioners.

WARRANT No. 22. BOND No. Texian Loan Bond for $1000, payable in years. Dividend Warrant for 183 Commissioners.

WARRANT No. 23. BOND No. Texian Loan Bond for $1000, payable in years. Dividend Warrant for 183 Commissioners.

WARRANT No. 24. BOND No. Texian Loan Bond for $1000, payable in years. Dividend Warrant for 183 Commissioners.

WARRANT No. 25. BOND No. Texian Loan Bond for $1000, payable in years. Dividend Warrant for 183 Commissioners.

WARRANT No. 26. BOND No. Texian Loan Bond for $1000, payable in years. Dividend Warrant for 183 Commissioners.

WARRANT No. 27. BOND No. Texian Loan Bond for $1000, payable in years. Dividend Warrant for 183 Commissioners.

WARRANT No. 28. BOND No. Texian Loan Bond for $1000, payable in years. Dividend Warrant for 183 Commissioners.

WARRANT No. 29. BOND No. Texian Loan Bond for $1000, payable in years. Dividend Warrant for 183 Commissioners.

WARRANT No. 30. BOND No. Texian Loan Bond for $1000, payable in years. Dividend Warrant for 183 Commissioners.

## AN ACT

TO AUTHORIZE THE PRESIDENT TO NEGOTIATE A LOAN, ON THE BONDS OF THE GOVERNMENT, NOT EXCEEDING FIVE MILLIONS OF DOLLARS.

SECTION 1. *Be it enacted by the Senate and House of Representatives of the Republic of Texas, in Congress Assembled,* That the President of this Republic be, and he is hereby fully authorized to issue Bonds of this Republic for the sum of one thousand dollars each, not exceeding five millions of dollars, which Bonds shall be signed by the President and Secretary of State, and countersigned by the Secretary of the Treasury; shall be negotiable by simple endorsement, and shall bear an interest on the face thereof at a rate not exceeding ten per cent. per annum, to be paid to the holders thereof, at such times and places as may be stipulated in said Bonds; said Bonds to be prepared as soon as possible, under the direction of the President, and made redeemable in thirty years from the day of date.

SECTION 6. *Be it further enacted, etc.,* That said Commissioners are hereby authorized to negotiate two millions of dollars of said Bonds, redeemable in a less time than thirty, but not for a shorter period than five years.

SECTION 7. *Be it further enacted, etc.,* That if any Bank, or Banks, shall become the purchaser, or purchasers, of any portion of said Bonds, then and in that case said Commissioners are hereby authorized to stipulate that the Notes of said Bank, or Banks, shall be received at par, in payment of all public dues of this Republic, to the amount of their loan or purchase of said Bonds, so long as said Bank, or Banks, continue solvent and specie paying; and if any Bank, or Banks, become the purchaser, or purchasers, of any portion of said Bonds, the said Commissioners shall specify on the face of said Bond or Bonds, that they are redeemable and payable in the Notes of said Bank or Banks.

SECTION 8. *Be it further enacted, etc.,* That if any Bank, or Banks, which may purchase said Bond, or Bonds, or any portion of them, shall fail, stop payment, or refuse to redeem its or their Notes with specie, then and in that case the Government of Texas shall have the privilege of terminating the loan with said Bank at any time, by payment of the principal and interest of the same.

SECTION 9. *Be it further enacted, etc.,* That said Commissioners are hereby authorized to give to the purchasers of said Bonds, the privilege of at any time taking the amount of their loans or purchases in land, at the minimum government price, or if the public lands are sold at auction, the said lenders or purchasers shall be allowed to bid, and pay the amount of their bids, with any of such Bonds as they may have purchased.

SECTION 10. *And be it further enacted, etc.,* That for the punctual payment of the interest, and final redemption of said Bonds, the public faith is hereby solemnly pledged, and also all the proceeds of the sales of the public domain, and all the taxes on lands, which may accrue to this Government after the year 1838, are hereby reserved and appropriated for that special purpose.

**Figure 32. $1,000 Texian Bond [Blank] November 18, 1836, With Right to Purchase Land, Columbia, 1836. By the end of the first year, the Republic's financial needs were overwhelming. A five million dollar bond issue was authorized by Congress on November 18, 1836. The bonds were to be marketed in financial centers in the United States and Europe by two loan commissioners. In addition to interest coupons, pledges of the proceeds of the sales of the public domain after 1838 were made to the bondholder, and he could elect to tender the bond in payment for government land at auction. The bonds sparked little interest because of the uncertain conditions in Texas.**

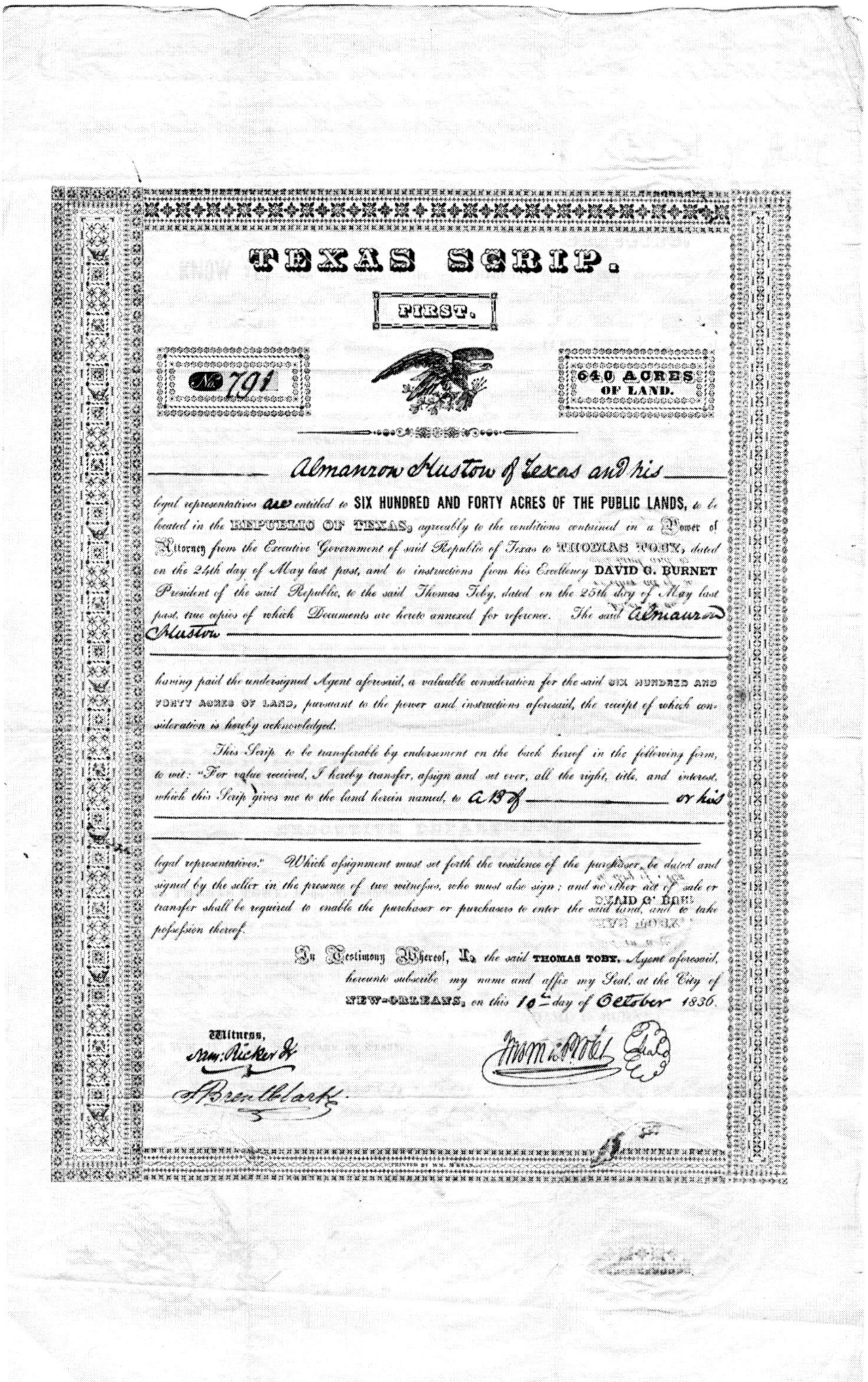
TEXAS SCRIP.

FIRST.

No. 791

640 ACRES OF LAND.

Almanzon Huston of Texas and his legal representatives are entitled to SIX HUNDRED AND FORTY ACRES OF THE PUBLIC LANDS, to be located in the REPUBLIC OF TEXAS, agreeably to the conditions contained in a Power of Attorney from the Executive Government of said Republic of Texas to THOMAS TOBY, dated on the 24th day of May last past, and to instructions from his Excellency DAVID G. BURNET President of the said Republic, to the said Thomas Toby, dated on the 25th day of May last past, true copies of which Documents are hereto annexed for reference. The said Almanzon Huston having paid the undersigned Agent aforesaid, a valuable consideration for the said SIX HUNDRED AND FORTY ACRES OF LAND, pursuant to the power and instructions aforesaid, the receipt of which consideration is hereby acknowledged.

This Scrip to be transferable by endorsement on the back hereof in the following form, to wit: "For value received, I hereby transfer, assign and set over, all the right, title, and interest, which this Scrip gives me to the land herein named, to A B C or his legal representatives." Which assignment must set forth the residence of the purchaser, be dated and signed by the seller in the presence of two witnesses, who must also sign; and no other act of sale or transfer shall be required to enable the purchaser or purchasers to enter the said land, and to take possession thereof.

In Testimony Whereof, I, the said THOMAS TOBY, Agent aforesaid, hereunto subscribe my name and affix my Seal, at the City of NEW-ORLEANS, on this 10th day of October 1836.

Witness,
Wm. Ricker Jr.
A. Brentlbart

Thom. Toby

Figure 33 (this page and page following). First Texas Scrip Certificate for 640 Acres to Thomas Toby & Bros., 50¢ an Acre, October 10, 1836, New Orleans. Toby and Brothers of New Orleans were appointed the General Agents of the Republic for financial matters including loans and the sale of land scrip. A half-million acres of the public domain was reserved to satisfy the sale of land scrip in 640-acre parcels. In addition to new sales, creditors were asked to accept "Texas Scrip" in payment of debts. Neither old nor new creditors were very receptive. After discounts in value, the General Agency was dissolved in December 1837. The Quartermaster General of the Texas Army Almanzon Huston received "Texas Scrip" to satisfy unpaid military contractors. Huston received his certificates from Thomas Toby, General Agent in New Orleans October 10, 1836. The scrip was endorsed by Huston to creditor Charles A. Lacotte, Esquire, of Natchez, Mississippi, November 1836.

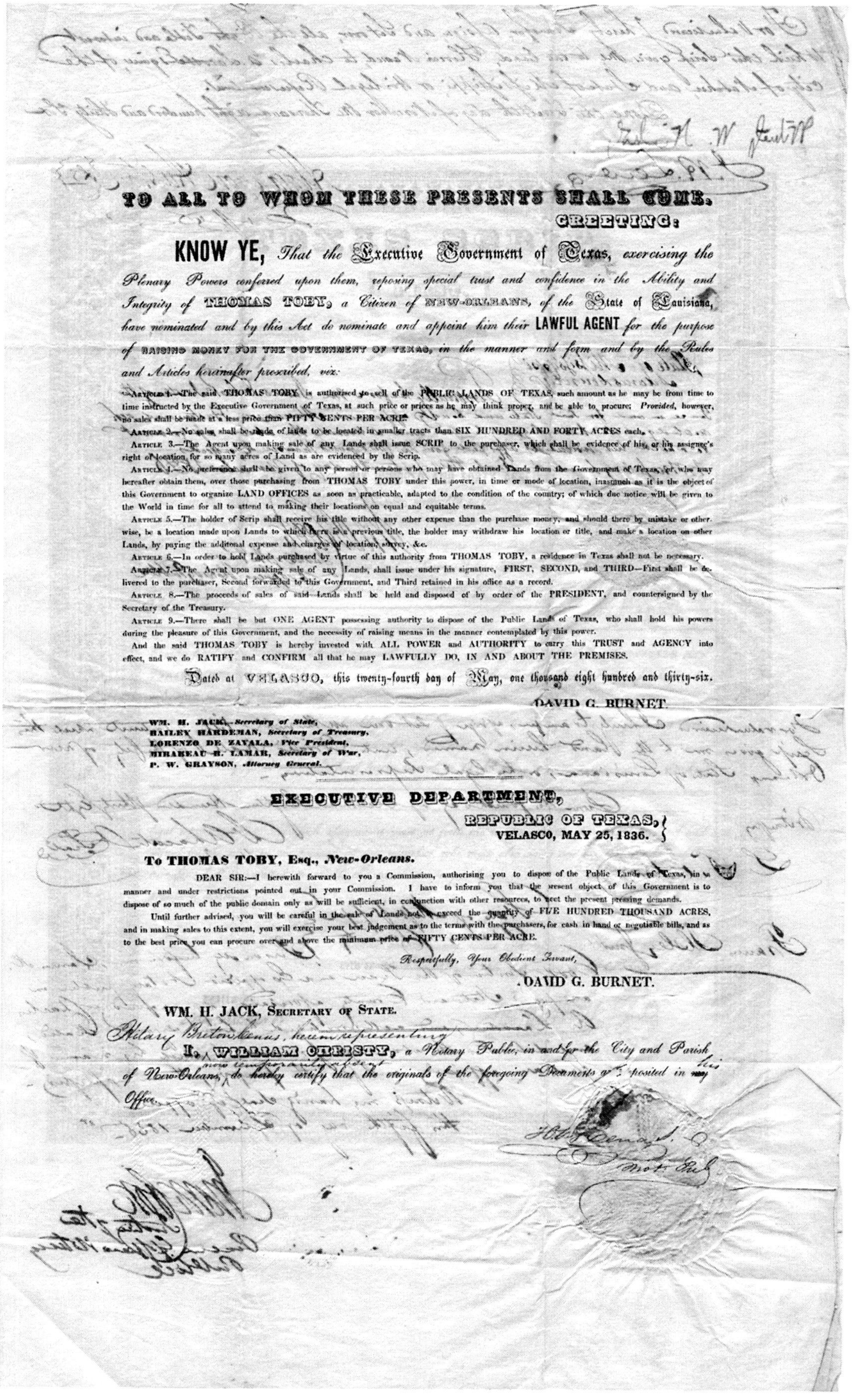

TO ALL TO WHOM THESE PRESENTS SHALL COME,

GREETING:

**KNOW YE,** *That the* Executive Government *of* Texas, *exercising the Plenary Powers conferred upon them, reposing special trust and confidence in the Ability and Integrity of* THOMAS TOBY, *a Citizen of* NEW-ORLEANS, *of the* State *of* Louisiana, *have nominated and by this Act do nominate and appoint him their* **LAWFUL AGENT** *for the purpose of* RAISING MONEY FOR THE GOVERNMENT OF TEXAS, *in the manner and form and by the Rules and Articles hereinafter prescribed, viz:*

Article 1.—The said THOMAS TOBY is authorised to sell of the PUBLIC LANDS OF TEXAS, such amount as he may be from time to time instructed by the Executive Government of Texas, at such price or prices as he may think proper, and be able to procure; *Provided*, however, no sales shall be made at a less price than FIFTY CENTS PER ACRE.

Article 2.—No sales shall be made of lands to be located in smaller tracts than SIX HUNDRED AND FORTY ACRES each.

Article 3.—The Agent upon making sale of any Lands shall issue SCRIP to the purchaser, which shall be evidence of his, or his assignee's right of location, for so many acres of Land as are evidenced by the Scrip.

Article 4.—No preference shall be given to any person or persons who may have obtained Lands from the Government of Texas, or who may hereafter obtain them, over those purchasing from THOMAS TOBY under this power, in time or mode of location, inasmuch as it is the object of this Government to organize LAND OFFICES as soon as practicable, adapted to the condition of the country; of which due notice will be given to the World in time for all to attend to making their locations on equal and equitable terms.

Article 5.—The holder of Scrip shall receive his title without any other expense than the purchase money, and should there by mistake or otherwise, be a location made upon Lands to which there is a previous title, the holder may withdraw his location or title, and make a location on other Lands, by paying the additonal expense and charges of location, survey, &c.

Article 6.—In order to hold Lands purchased by virtue of this authority from THOMAS TOBY, a residence in Texas shall not be necessary.

Article 7.—The Agent upon making sale of any Lands, shall issue under his signature, FIRST, SECOND, and THIRD—First shall be delivered to the purchaser, Second forwarded to this Government, and Third retained in his office as a record.

Article 8.—The proceeds of sales of said Lands shall be held and disposed of by order of the PRESIDENT, and countersigned by the Secretary of the Treasury.

Article 9.—There shall be but ONE AGENT possessing authority to dispose of the Public Lands of Texas, who shall hold his powers during the pleasure of this Government, and the necessity of raising means in the manner contemplated by this power.

And the said THOMAS TOBY is hereby invested with ALL POWER and AUTHORITY to carry this TRUST and AGENCY into effect, and we do RATIFY and CONFIRM all that he may LAWFULLY DO, IN AND ABOUT THE PREMISES.

Dated at VELASCO, this twenty-fourth day of May, one thousand eight hundred and thirty-six.

DAVID G. BURNET.

WM. H. JACK, *Secretary of State,*
BAILEY HARDEMAN, *Secretary of Treasury,*
LORENZO DE ZAVALA, *Vice President,*
MIRABEAU B. LAMAR, *Secretary of War,*
P. W. GRAYSON, *Attorney General.*

EXECUTIVE DEPARTMENT,

REPUBLIC OF TEXAS,
VELASCO, MAY 25, 1836.

**To THOMAS TOBY, Esq., *New-Orleans.***

DEAR SIR:—I herewith forward to you a Commission, authorising you to dispose of the Public Lands of Texas, in a manner and under restrictions pointed out in your Commission. I have to inform you that the present object of this Government is to dispose of so much of the public domain only as will be sufficient, in conjunction with other resources, to meet the present pressing demands.

Until further advised, you will be careful in the sale of Lands not to exceed the quantity of FIVE HUNDRED THOUSAND ACRES, and in making sales to this extent, you will exercise your best judgement as to the terms with the purchasers, for cash in hand or negotiable bills, and as to the best price you can procure over and above the minimum price of FIFTY CENTS PER ACRE.

*Respectfully, Your Obedient Servant,*

DAVID G. BURNET.

WM. H. JACK, Secretary of State.

I, WILLIAM CHRISTY, *a Notary Public, in and for the City and Parish of New-Orleans, do hereby certify that the originals of the foregoing Documents are deposited in this Office.*

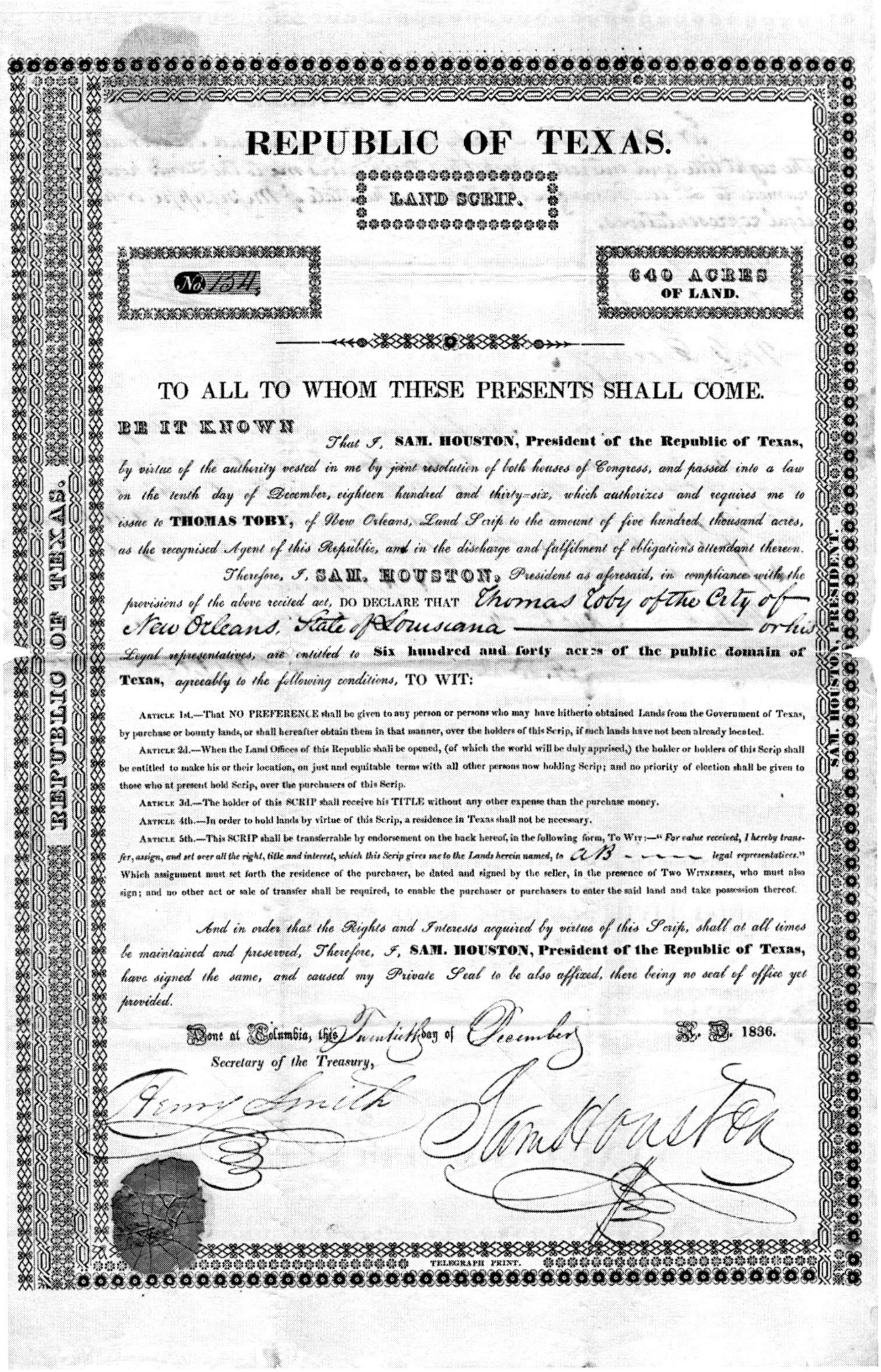

REPUBLIC OF TEXAS.

LAND SCRIP.

No. 134

640 ACRES OF LAND.

TO ALL TO WHOM THESE PRESENTS SHALL COME.

BE IT KNOWN That I, SAM. HOUSTON, President of the Republic of Texas, by virtue of the authority vested in me by joint resolution of both houses of Congress, and passed into a law on the tenth day of December, eighteen hundred and thirty-six, which authorizes and requires me to issue to THOMAS TOBY, of New Orleans, Land Scrip to the amount of five hundred thousand acres, as the recognised Agent of this Republic, and in the discharge and fulfilment of obligations attendant thereon.

Therefore, I, SAM. HOUSTON, President as aforesaid, in compliance with the provisions of the above recited act, DO DECLARE THAT Thomas Toby of the City of New Orleans, State of Louisiana or his Legal representatives, are entitled to Six hundred and forty acres of the public domain of Texas, agreeably to the following conditions, TO WIT:

Article 1st.—That NO PREFERENCE shall be given to any person or persons who may have hitherto obtained Lands from the Government of Texas, by purchase or bounty lands, or shall hereafter obtain them in that manner, over the holders of this Scrip, if such lands have not been already located.

Article 2d.—When the Land Offices of this Republic shall be opened, (of which the world will be duly apprised,) the holder or holders of this Scrip shall be entitled to make his or their location, on just and equitable terms with all other persons now holding Scrip; and no priority of election shall be given to those who at present hold Scrip, over the purchasers of this Scrip.

Article 3d.—The holder of this SCRIP shall receive his TITLE without any other expense than the purchase money.

Article 4th.—In order to hold lands by virtue of this Scrip, a residence in Texas shall not be necessary.

Article 5th.—This SCRIP shall be transferrable by endorsement on the back hereof, in the following form, To Wit:—"*For value received, I hereby transfer, assign, and set over all the right, title and interest, which this Scrip gives me to the Lands herein named, to* A B — *legal representatives.*" Which assignment must set forth the residence of the purchaser, be dated and signed by the seller, in the presence of Two Witnesses, who must also sign; and no other act or sale of transfer shall be required, to enable the purchaser or purchasers to enter the said land and take possession thereof.

*And in order that the Rights and Interests acquired by virtue of this Scrip, shall at all times be maintained and preserved, Therefore, I,* SAM. HOUSTON, President of the Republic of Texas, *have signed the same, and caused my Private Seal to be also affixed, there being no seal of office yet provided.*

Done at Columbia, this Twentieth day of December A. D. 1836.

*Secretary of the Treasury,*

Henry Smith

Sam Houston

TELEGRAPH PRINT.

REPUBLIC OF TEXAS.

SAM. HOUSTON, PRESIDENT.

**Figure 34. Republic of Texas Land Scrip Certificate for 640 Acres, 1836. To satisfy the commitment Congress had made to scrip holders, the government ordered Republic of Texas Land Scrip certificates in 640 acre parcels from Telegraph Print. Beginning in December of 1836, President Sam Houston and Secretary of the Treasury Henry Smith executed the scrip at Columbia. The certificates were issued to the General Agent Thomas Toby of New Orleans (500,000 acres) and David White of Mobile (100,000 acres). By endorsement, Toby and White transferred to creditors. An April 18, 1837, report to the President complained that White's agency in Mobile refused to render reports and dishonored government drafts drawn on it. The Toby Agency in New Orleans fared little better, as it did not provide an accounting of the transactions and had resorted to selling scrip with up to three-year credit for payment. The program was a failure, although some creditors were persuaded to take land scrip, much discounted, as payment against the debts of the Republic. The agents received a 7½ percent commission on the face of land scrip accepted as payment.**

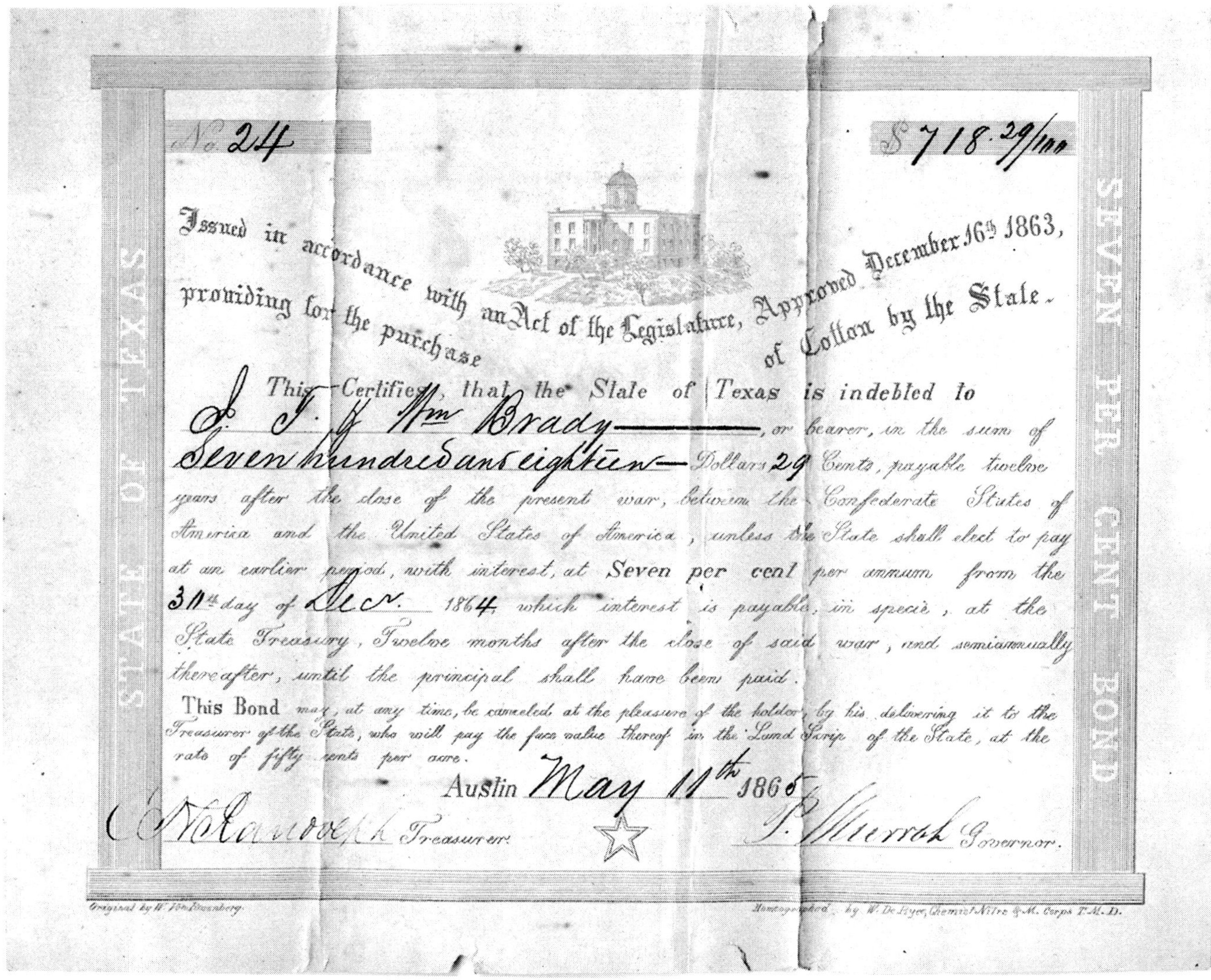

No. 24 $718 29/100

STATE OF TEXAS

SEVEN PER CENT BOND

Issued in accordance with an Act of the Legislature, Approved December 16th 1863, providing for the purchase of Cotton by the State.

This Certifies, that the State of Texas is indebted to J. T. & Wm Brady, or bearer, in the sum of Seven hundred and eighteen Dollars 29 Cents, payable twelve years after the close of the present war, between the Confederate States of America and the United States of America, unless the State shall elect to pay at an earlier period, with interest, at Seven per cent per annum from the 31st day of Decr. 1864 which interest is payable in specie, at the State Treasury, Twelve months after the close of said war, and semiannually thereafter, until the principal shall have been paid.

This Bond may, at any time, be canceled at the pleasure of the holder, by his delivering it to the Treasurer of the State, who will pay the face value thereof in the Land Scrip of the State, at the rate of fifty cents per acre.

Austin May 11th 1865

Treasurer Governor

**Figure 35. "Cotton Bond" with Land Scrip at 50¢ an Acre, 1863. Texas had no debt when the Civil War began, but was short of credit. The Texas legislature authorized a two million dollar bond issue December 16, 1863, to fund the Texas Military Board in its purchase of cotton, military supplies and provisions. The homeographic print by W. DeRyce, Chemist Nitre & Mining Corps, Trans-Mississippi Department of the Confederacy, was signed by Governor Pendleton Murray. The bond was decorated with a view of the old capitol building. The creditor was given the right to purchase land at fifty cents an acre in lieu of the repayment of principle and interest. The May 11, 1865, document was executed during the last days of the Texas Confederate State. The holders, J.T. and Wm. Brody, purchased a number of bonds at the war's end for speculative purposes. This bond for $718.25 could be converted to over 1,400 acres.**

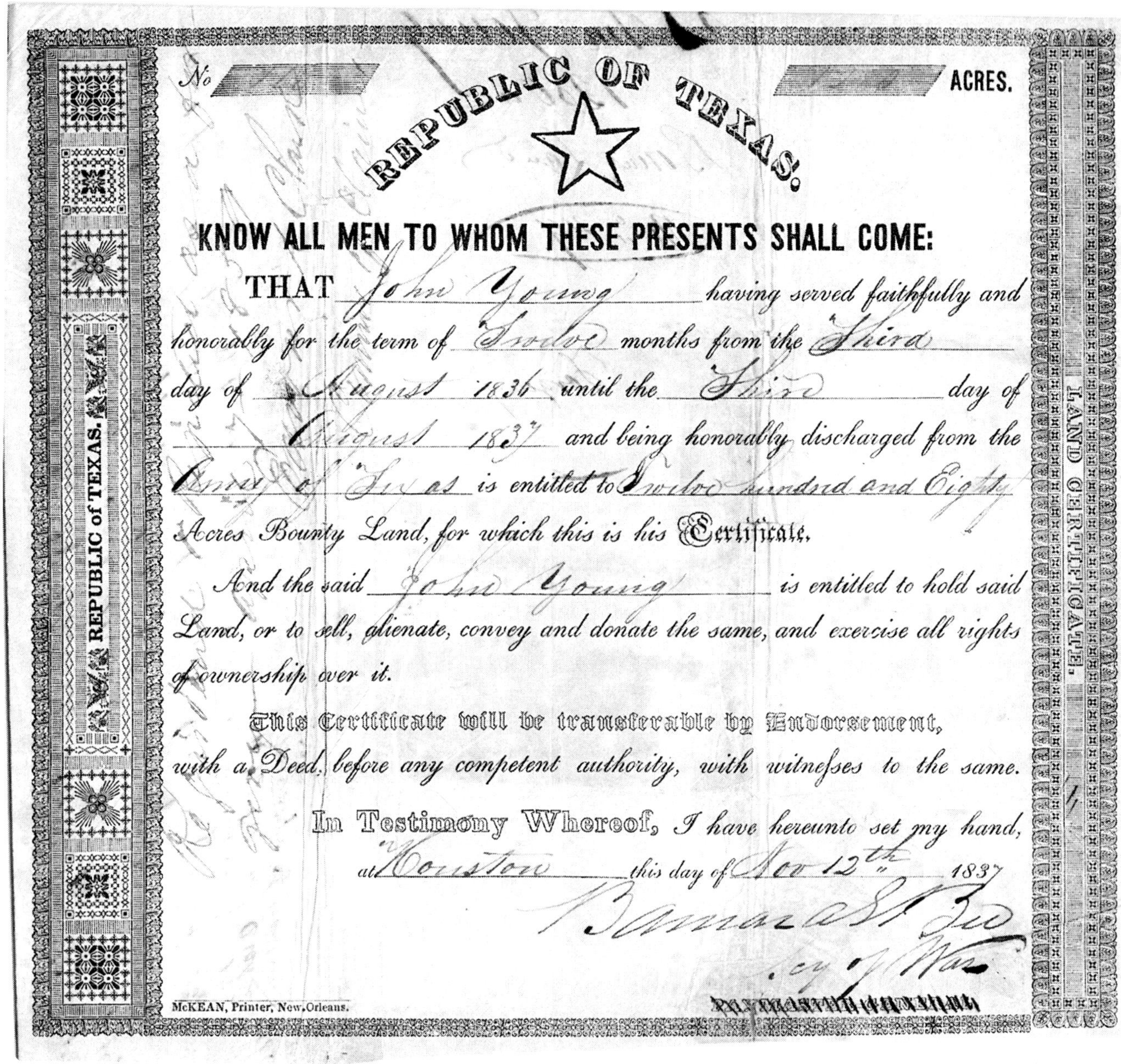

No ___ ACRES.

REPUBLIC OF TEXAS.

KNOW ALL MEN TO WHOM THESE PRESENTS SHALL COME:

THAT *John Young* having served faithfully and honorably for the term of *Twelve* months from the *Third* day of *August 1836* until the *Third* day of *August 1837* and being honorably discharged from the *Army of Texas* is entitled to *Twelve hundred and Eighty* Acres Bounty Land, for which this is his Certificate.

And the said *John Young* is entitled to hold said Land, or to sell, alienate, convey and donate the same, and exercise all rights of ownership over it.

This Certificate will be transferable by Endorsement, with a Deed, before any competent authority, with witnesses to the same.

In Testimony Whereof, I have hereunto set my hand, at *Houston* this day of *Nov 12th 1837*

*Barnard E. Bee*
*Secy of War*

REPUBLIC of TEXAS.

LAND CERTIFICATE.

McKEAN, Printer, New-Orleans.

**Figure 36. Certificate of Honorable Service in Army of Texas and 1,280 Acres of Bounty Land, Houston, 1837. John Young married the heir to the Santa Anita Spanish land grant. For service during the revolution in 1836 and 1837, he received two sections of land. As proof, he received a discharge of honorable service from the War Department, November 12, 1837. After his death, his heirs filed a warrant with the General Land Office to patent his 1,280 acres. The application was rejected for lack of an adequate survey. His widow, Doña Salomé Ballí Young, a native of Mexico, apparently never refiled. Salomé Ballí was already one of the largest ranchers in South Texas, operating the Santa Anita Ranch on El Camino Real, from Reynosa to the Nueces. This fifteen-league Spanish Grant, dating to 1798, is in Hidalgo County.**

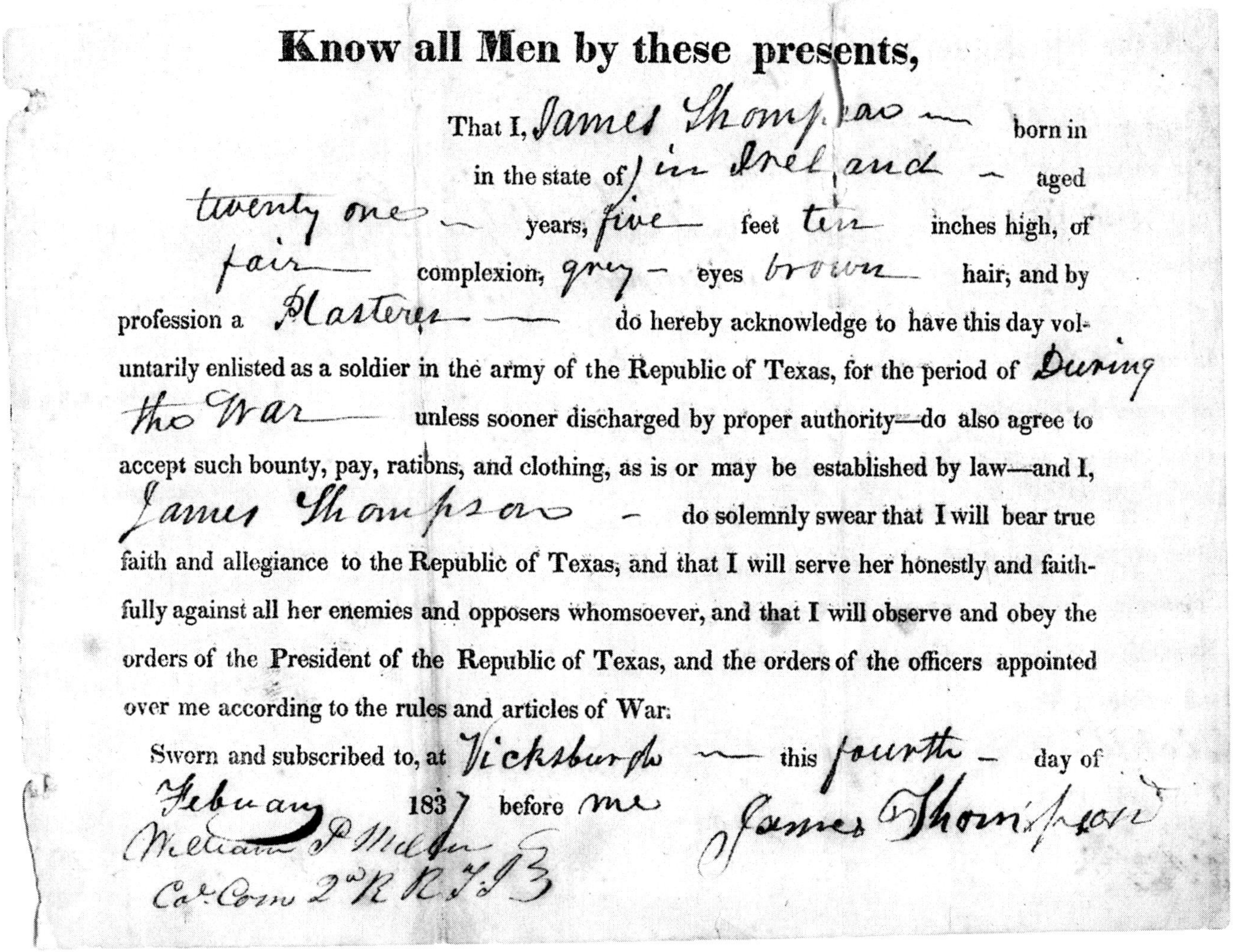

**Know all Men by these presents,**

That I, James Thompson — born in in the state of/ in Ireland — aged twenty one — years, five feet ten inches high, of fair complexion, grey — eyes brown hair, and by profession a Plasterer — do hereby acknowledge to have this day voluntarily enlisted as a soldier in the army of the Republic of Texas, for the period of During the War unless sooner discharged by proper authority—do also agree to accept such bounty, pay, rations, and clothing, as is or may be established by law—and I, James Thompson — do solemnly swear that I will bear true faith and allegiance to the Republic of Texas, and that I will serve her honestly and faithfully against all her enemies and opposers whomsoever, and that I will observe and obey the orders of the President of the Republic of Texas, and the orders of the officers appointed over me according to the rules and articles of War.

Swern and subscribed to, at Vicksburgh — this fourth — day of Febuary 1837 before me

William P. McL[illegible]
Col Com 2d R R T [illegible]

James Thompson

**Figure 37. Enlistment in Army of Texas "During the War," Vicksburg, Mississippi, 1837. After the victory at San Jacinto and establishment of the Republic, Texas had to maintain a relatively large standing army to defend its independence. A formal peace treaty was never executed. Recruiters sought men in southern states. Irish plasterer James Thompson enlisted February 4, 1837, at Vicksburg, Mississippi. He swore "faith and allegiance" during the War. No record confirms if Thompson completed his service.**

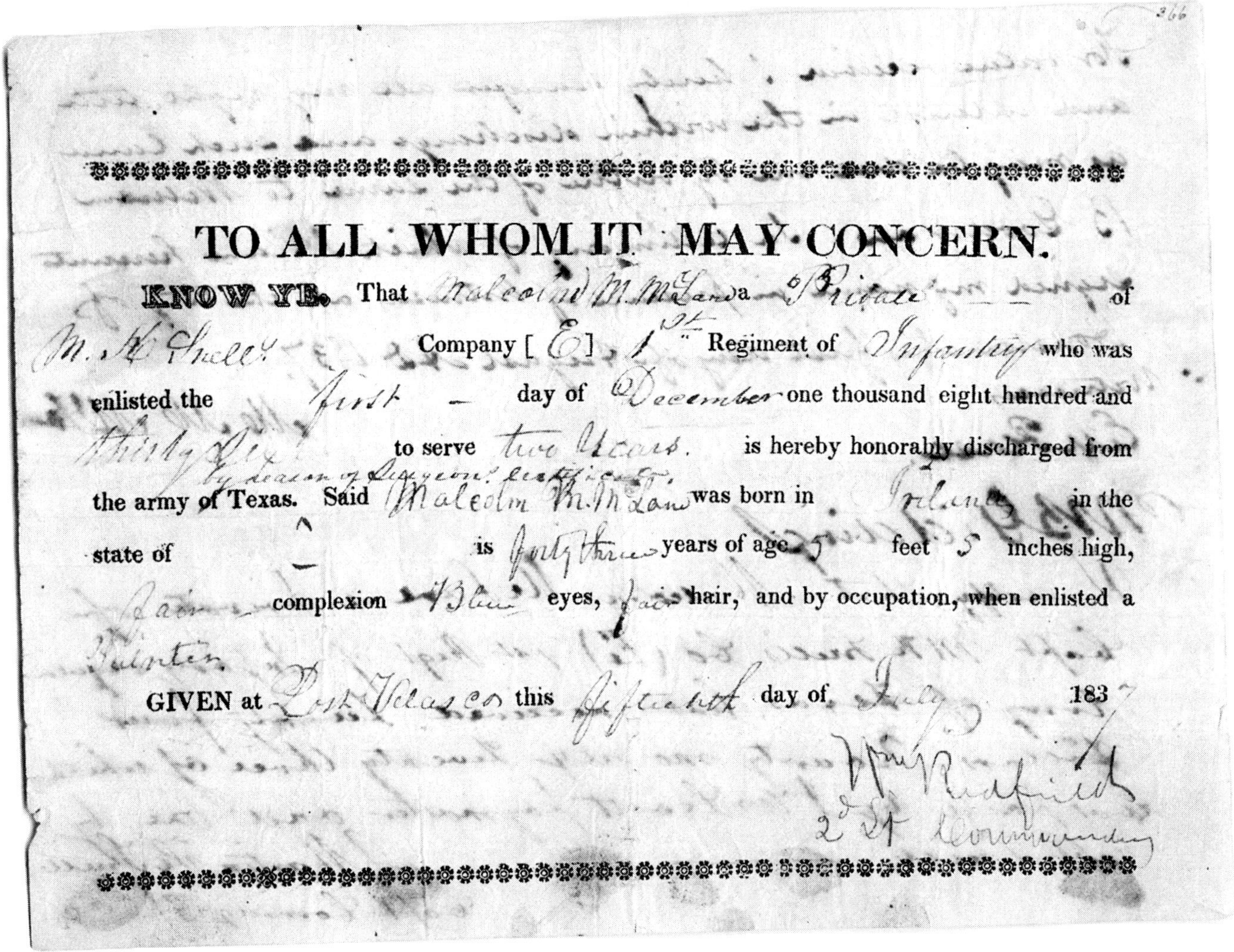
TO ALL WHOM IT MAY CONCERN.

KNOW YE. That Malcolm M. McLane a Private — of M. K. Snell's Company [ E ], 1st Regiment of Infantry who was enlisted the first — day of December one thousand eight hundred and thirty six to serve two Years. is hereby honorably discharged from the army of Texas. by reason of Surgeon's certificate. Said Malcolm M. McLane was born in Ireland in the state of — is forty three years of age 5 feet 5 inches high, fair complexion Blue eyes, fair hair, and by occupation, when enlisted a Painter.

GIVEN at Post Velasco this fifteenth day of July 1837

Wm. Redfield
2d Lt Commanding

Figure 38. Medical Discharge for Honorable Service in Army of Texas, Post Velasco, 1837. Muster rolls and discharge certificates were essential to Texas veterans in applying for their bounty lands. Malcolm M. McLane was a member of Captain Martin K. Snell's Infantry Company "F" until discharged at Velasco on July 15, 1837, for medical reasons. Medical discharges were equivalent to honorably completed service for bounty purposes. During McLane's enlistment, Snell's Company served as honor guards at the funeral of Stephen F. Austin, December 29, 1836. As was common, Private McLane assigned his "rights, title and interest" in bounty lands. The recipient, William B. Goodman, would later patent a half-section for his own service at Fort Bend on December 16, 1845. E. M. Pease and W. B. Giddings witnessed the assignment to Goodman in Houston on August 1, 1837. Private McLane was due $24.00 in bounty money, of which $23.00 was repaid to the paymaster J. W. Lea for advances, and one dollar to Captain Snell for the same.

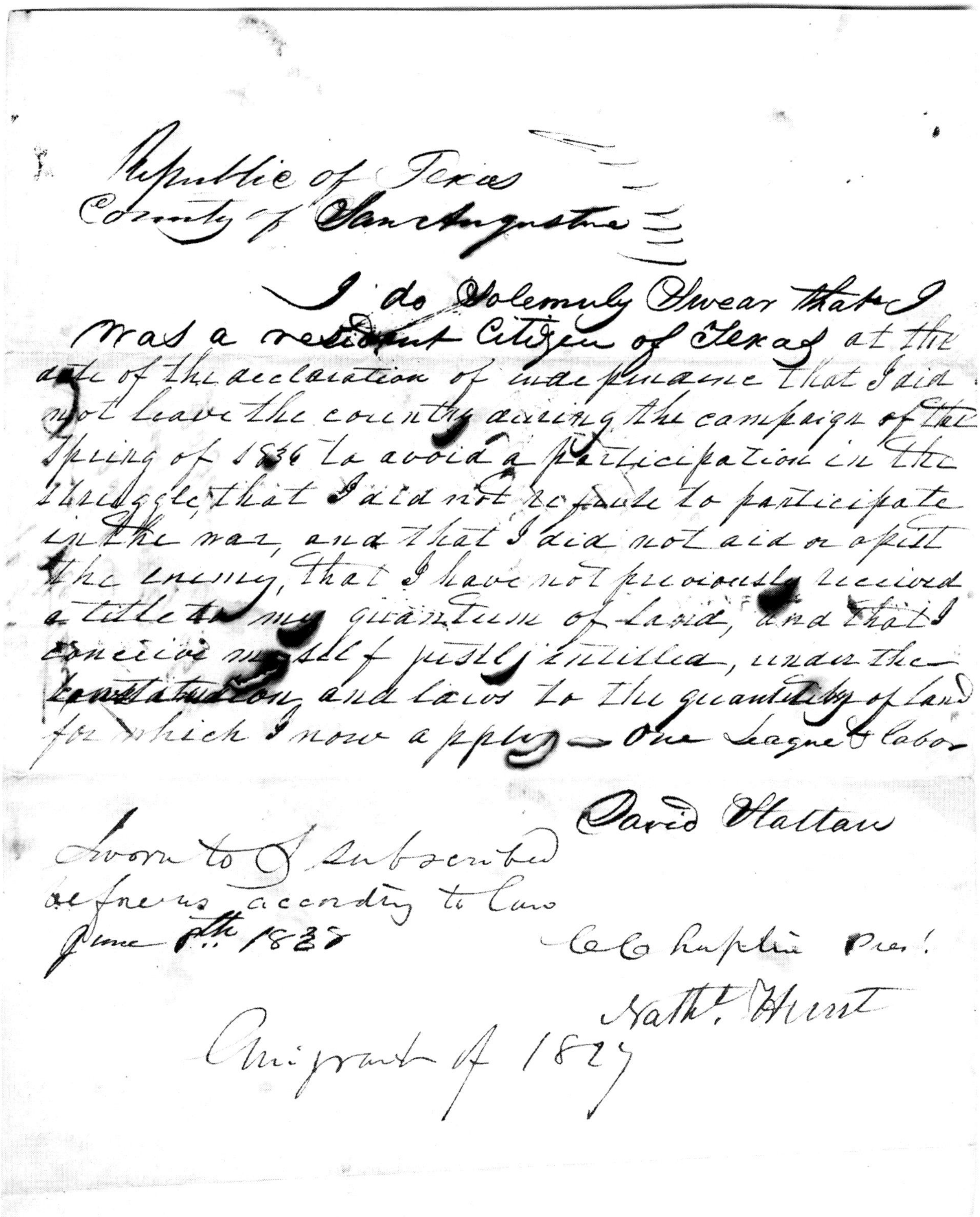
Republic of Texas
County of San Augustine

I do Solemnly Swear that I was a resident Citizen of Texas at the date of the declaration of independence that I did not leave the country during the campaign of the Spring of 1836 to avoid a participation in the struggle, that I did not refuse to participate in the war, and that I did not aid or assist the enemy, that I have not previously received a title to my quantum of land, and that I conceive myself justly entitled, under the constitution and laws to the quantity of land for which I now apply — One League & labor

David Hatton

Sworn to & subscribed before us according to Law
June 8th 1838

[illegible] Pres!

Nath! Hunt

Emigrant of 1827

**Figure 39. Constitutional First Class Grant of a League and A Labor to Original Settler, San Augustine, 1827. Colonists living in Texas on grants received from either the Spanish or Mexican governments were recognized by the Republic of Texas if loyal to Texas during the Revolution. David Hatton of San Augustine filed the appropriate oath, affidavit and application with the County Clerk on June 8, 1838. He swore he was an immigrant resident in Texas since 1827. Two witnesses confirmed his affidavit. The application was for the league and labor guaranteed for first families, referred to as "Constitutional" grants. The colonist apparently never received a patent from the General Land Office. His heir, William T. Hatton, patented a constitutional grant of a league and a labor in Live Oak and Bell counties on August 20, 1846. Tennessean Nathaniel Hunt signed Hatton's certificate as President of the San Augustine Land Commission. Hunt received a league on the west side of Ayish Bayou, in Zavala's Grant.**

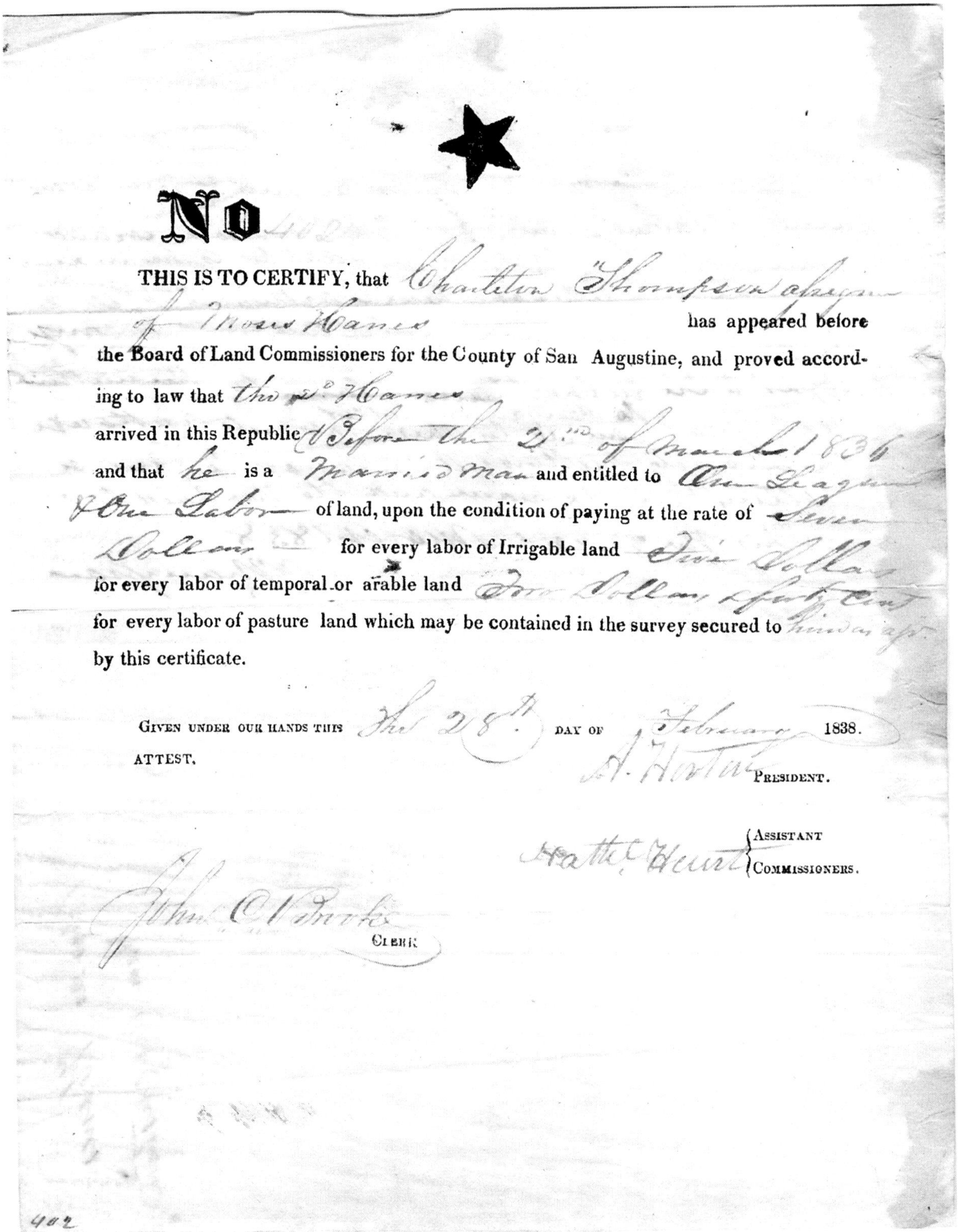

No 402

THIS IS TO CERTIFY, that Charlton Thompson assignee of Moses Hanes has appeared before the Board of Land Commissioners for the County of San Augustine, and proved according to law that the sd Hanes arrived in this Republic Before the 2nd of March 1836 and that he is a Married Man and entitled to One League & One Labor of land, upon the condition of paying at the rate of Seven Dollars for every labor of Irrigable land Five Dollars for every labor of temporal or arable land Two Dollars & forty cents for every labor of pasture land which may be contained in the survey secured to him or his asss by this certificate.

Given under our hands this the 28th day of February 1838.

Attest.

A. Horton President.

Nathl Hunt Assistant Commissioners.

John C Brooke Clerk

402

Figure 40. First-Class Headright for a League and a Labor to Head of Family Arriving Before March 2, 1836, San Augustine, 1838. Moss Hanes, as a pre-revolutionary colonist who was loyal to Texas, filed for a first-class headright with the San Augustine Board of Land Commissioners on February 28, 1838. Hanes assigned all rights to his guaranteed league and a labor to Charlton Thompson. Title was dependent upon the payment of government dues at the rate of $5.00 per labor of temporal or arable land and $2.00 for a labor of pasture land. The dues were not owed until the survey was complete and the application for title was made to the land office. Thompson transferred the claim to Benjamin F. Fuller, who received a league in San Augustine County, patented July 16, 1835, within the Zavala Grant.

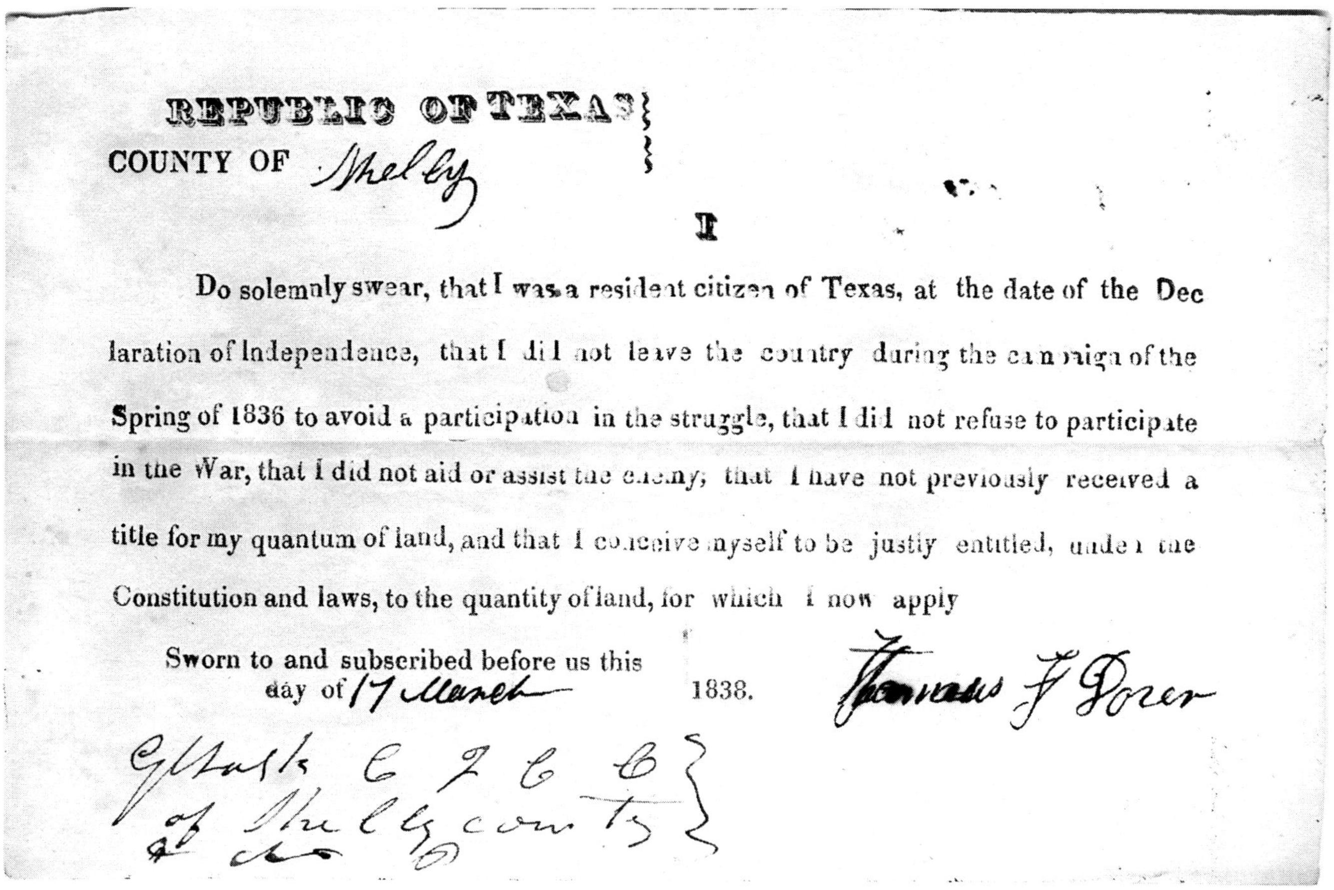

REPUBLIC OF TEXAS
COUNTY OF Shelby

I

Do solemnly swear, that I was a resident citizen of Texas, at the date of the Declaration of Independence, that I did not leave the country during the campaign of the Spring of 1836 to avoid a participation in the struggle, that I did not refuse to participate in the War, that I did not aid or assist the enemy; that I have not previously received a title for my quantum of land, and that I conceive myself to be justly entitled, under the Constitution and laws, to the quantity of land, for which I now apply

Sworn to and subscribed before us this
day of 17 March 1838.

Thomas F Doren

**Figure 41. Oath for First Class Headright, Shelby County, 1838. Loyalty oaths and pledges of future allegiance were common in early Texas as well as Mexico and the United States. First-class headrights to pre-revolutionary colonists required affirmation that the settler "did not leave the country during the campaign of the spring of 1836 to avoid participation in the struggle." Two additional conditions were required by law. The colonist had to swear he did not give aid to the enemy and he did not refuse to participate in the war. The pledge of not giving aid to the enemy was always a concern of Mexican colonists residing in the Trans-Nueces and Trans-Pecos regions. Each settler was entitled to only one portion of land and had to affirm he had not previously received a settler's grant. Thomas A. Doren gave his oath to the Shelby County Board of Commissioners on March 17, 1838. There may have been problems, as he was never patented any land.**

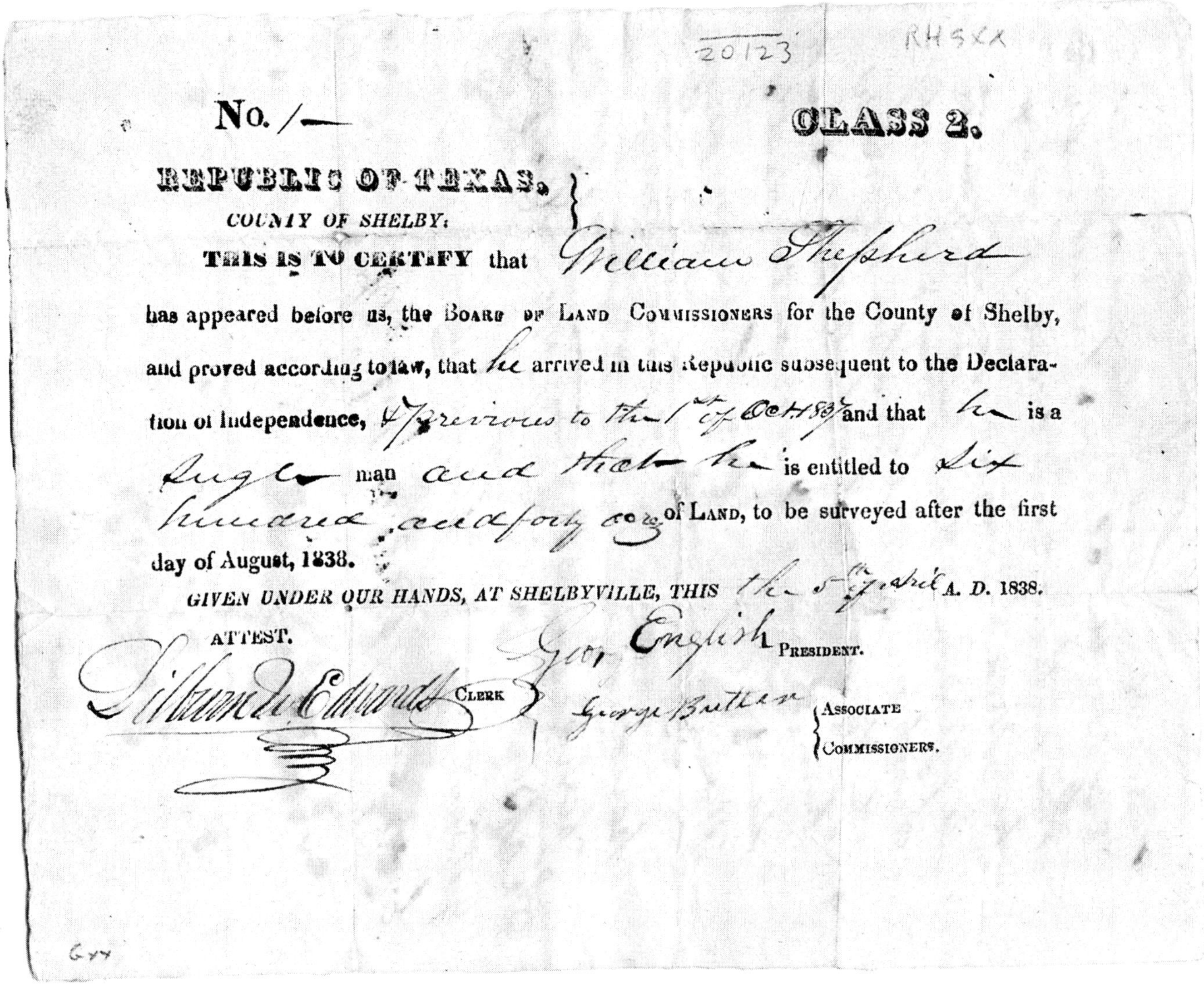

20123

RH5XX

No. 1—

CLASS 2.

REPUBLIC OF TEXAS,
COUNTY OF SHELBY:

THIS IS TO CERTIFY that William Shepherd has appeared before us, the Board of Land Commissioners for the County of Shelby, and proved according to law, that he arrived in this Republic subsequent to the Declaration of Independence, & previous to the 1st of Oct 1837 and that he is a single man and that he is entitled to six hundred and forty acres of Land, to be surveyed after the first day of August, 1838.

GIVEN UNDER OUR HANDS, AT SHELBYVILLE, THIS the 5th of April A. D. 1838.

ATTEST.

Geo English President.

Lilburn W. Edwards Clerk

George Butler Associate Commissioners.

Figure 42. Second-Class Conditional Headright for 640 Acres to a Single Man, Shelby County, 1838. The Texas Congress passed a second headright act that applied to immigrants arriving between March 2, 1836, Independence Day, and October 1, 1837. Second-class headright applicants, if married, could apply for 1,280 acres, and bachelors only one section. Shelby County settler William Shepherd claimed a single man's allotment with the Board of Land Commissioners in 1838. Later he received a patent for his second-class headright from the General Land Office, on August 7, 1838.

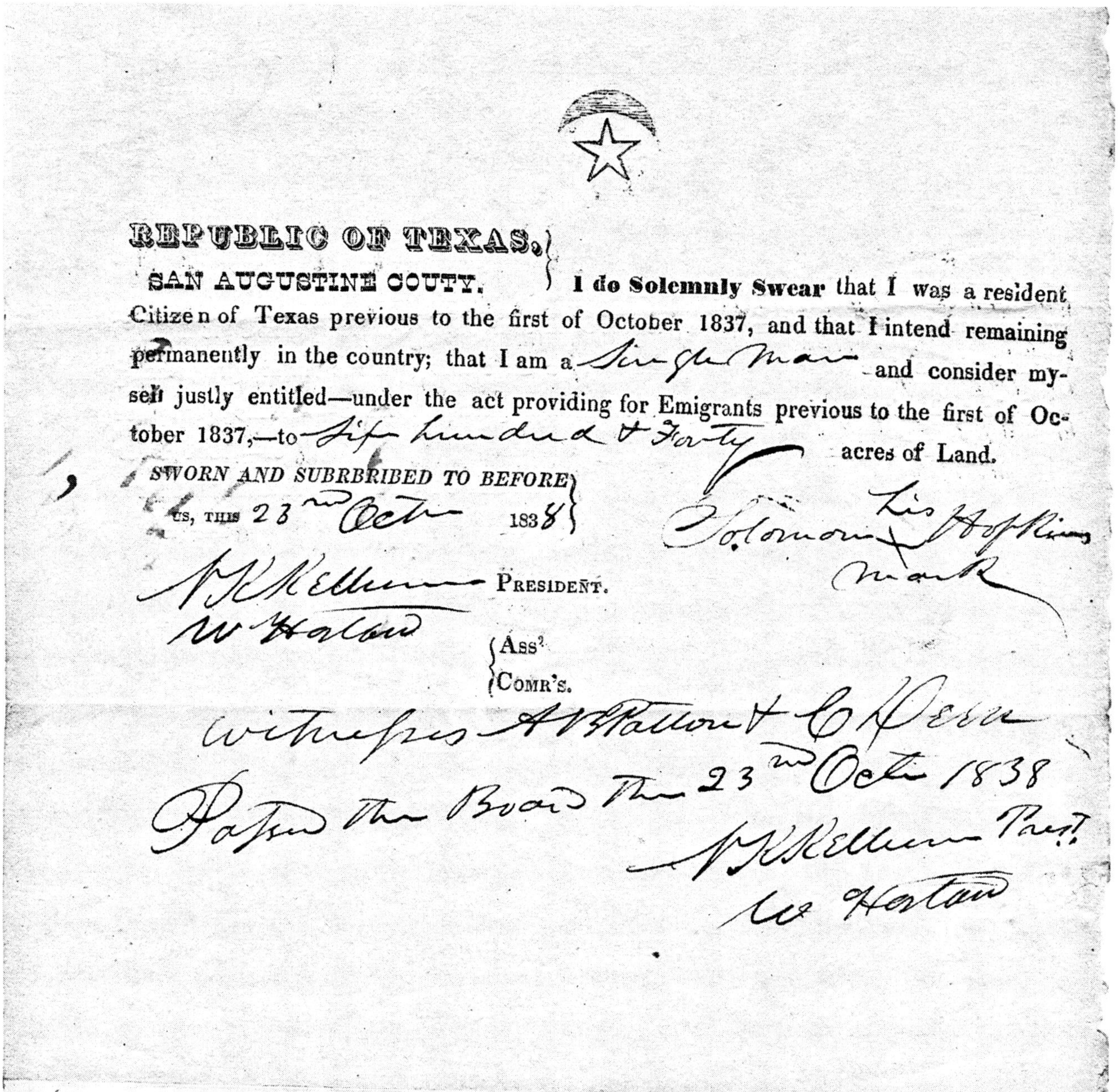
REPUBLIC OF TEXAS,
SAN AUGUSTINE COUTY. } I do Solemnly Swear that I was a resident Citizen of Texas previous to the first of October 1837, and that I intend remaining permanently in the country; that I am a Single Man and consider myself justly entitled—under the act providing for Emigrants previous to the first of October 1837,—to Six hundred & Forty acres of Land.

SWORN AND SUBRBRIBED TO BEFORE US, THIS 23rd Octr 1838

Solomon his X Hopkins mark

N K Kellum PRESIDENT.
W Horton
Ass^t Comr's.

witnesses A B Hatton & C H Dern
Passed the Board the 23rd Octr 1838
N K Kellum Prest.
W Horton

**Figure 43. Oath for Second-Class Headright, San Augustine, 1838. The required oath of second-class headright applicants arriving in Texas before October 1, 1837, included swearing he intended to remain permanently. Bachelor Solomon Hopkins went before the San Augustine Board of Land Commissioners to claim his section on October 23, 1838. After giving his oath, he made his mark, an "X," to execute the document. Hopkins also received 640 acres for his military service through discharge on March 19, 1837. He patented his section in Smith County as a second-class settler.**

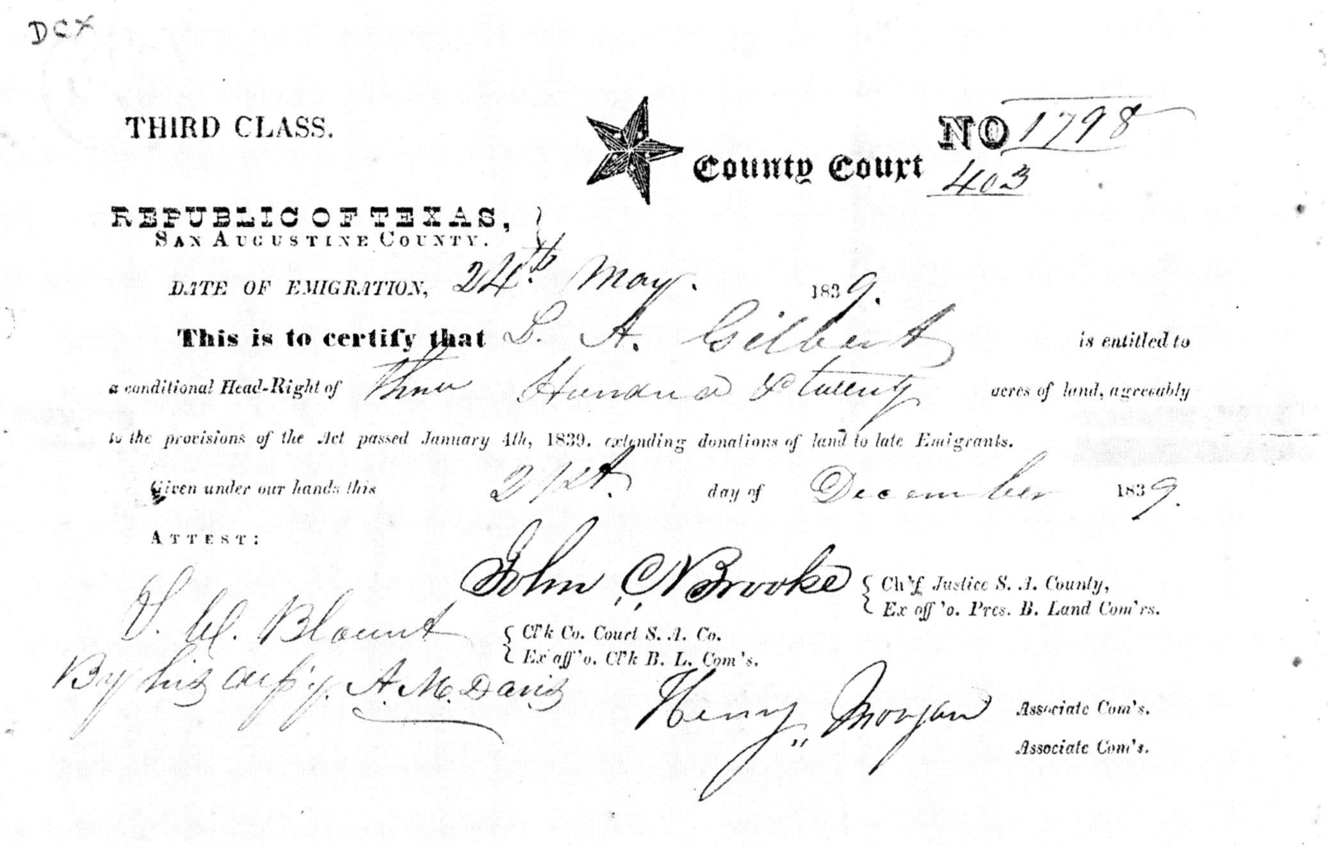

DCX

THIRD CLASS.

NO 1798

County Court 403

REPUBLIC OF TEXAS,
SAN AUGUSTINE COUNTY.

*DATE OF EMIGRATION,* 24th May. 1839.

**This is to certify that** L. A. Gilbert *is entitled to a conditional Head-Right of* Three Hundred & twenty *acres of land, agreeably to the provisions of the Act passed January 4th, 1839, extending donations of land to late Emigrants.*

*Given under our hands this* 21st *day of* December 1839.

ATTEST:

John N. Brooke { *Ch'f Justice S. A. County, Ex off'o. Pres. B. Land Com'rs.*

D. W. Blount { *Cl'k Co. Court S. A. Co. Ex off'o. Cl'k B. L. Com's.*

By his dep'y A. M. Davis

Henry Morgan *Associate Com's.*

*Associate Com's.*

**Figure 44. Third-Class Conditional Headright for 320 Acres to Late Emigrant, San Augustine, 1839. The third headright statute of January 4, 1839, reduced the family allotment to a section and only 320 acres for a single man. Operative dates for qualification were October 1, 1837, to January 1, 1840. "Late Emigrant" L. A. Gilbert, as a bachelor, applied for a half-section before the Board of Land Commissioners at San Augustine on May 24, 1839. These grants were conditional upon residency. Fraudulent claims raised the number of applications to levels exceeding the two earlier programs. Traveling examiner boards re-examined oaths and applications and invalidated a significant number of bogus claims during the aftermath of the Panic of 1837. The Red-Lander Press Office in San Augustine printed the forms. There is no evidence of Gilbert's headright ever being patented by the General Land Office.**

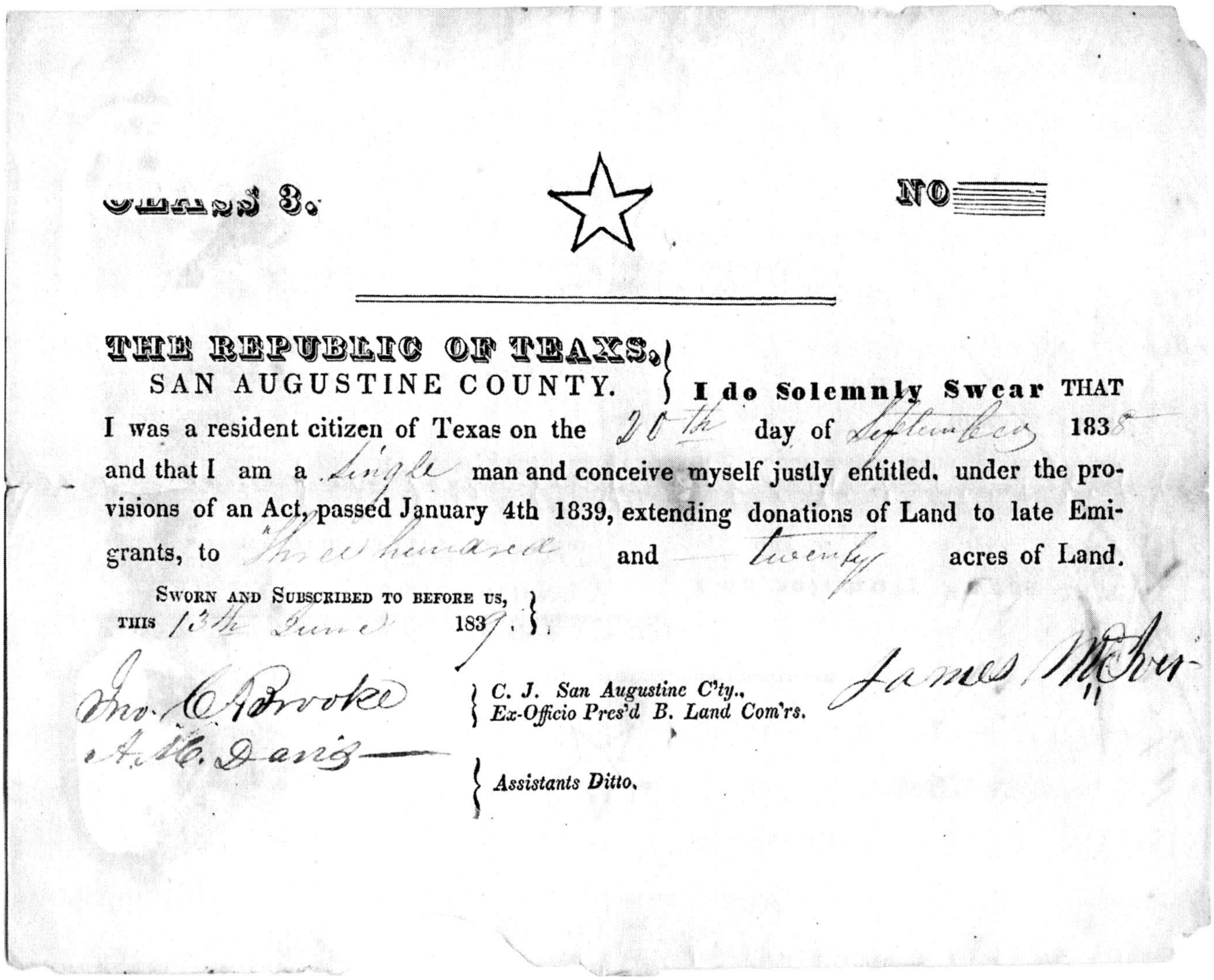

CLASS 3. ★ NO

THE REPUBLIC OF TEAXS,
SAN AUGUSTINE COUNTY.

**I do Solemnly Swear** THAT I was a resident citizen of Texas on the 20th day of September 1838 and that I am a single man and conceive myself justly entitled, under the provisions of an Act, passed January 4th 1839, extending donations of Land to late Emigrants, to three hundred and twenty acres of Land.

SWORN AND SUBSCRIBED TO BEFORE US,
THIS 13th June 1839.

James McIver

Jno. C. Brooke — *C. J. San Augustine C'ty., Ex-Officio Pres'd B. Land Com'rs.*

A. M. Davis — *Assistants Ditto.*

**Figure 45. Oath for Third-Class Headright, San Augustine, 1839. The misprinted third-class oath is known for its spelling of Texas, "TEAXS," an error of the Red-Lander Press. James McIver applied for a half-section as a single man before the San Augustine Board of Land Commissioners. He swore he was a bona fide resident of Texas September 20, 1838. The Board accepted him at his word and witnessed his signature as "justly entitled" June 13, 1839. No record exists of a third-class headright ever being patented by McIver.**

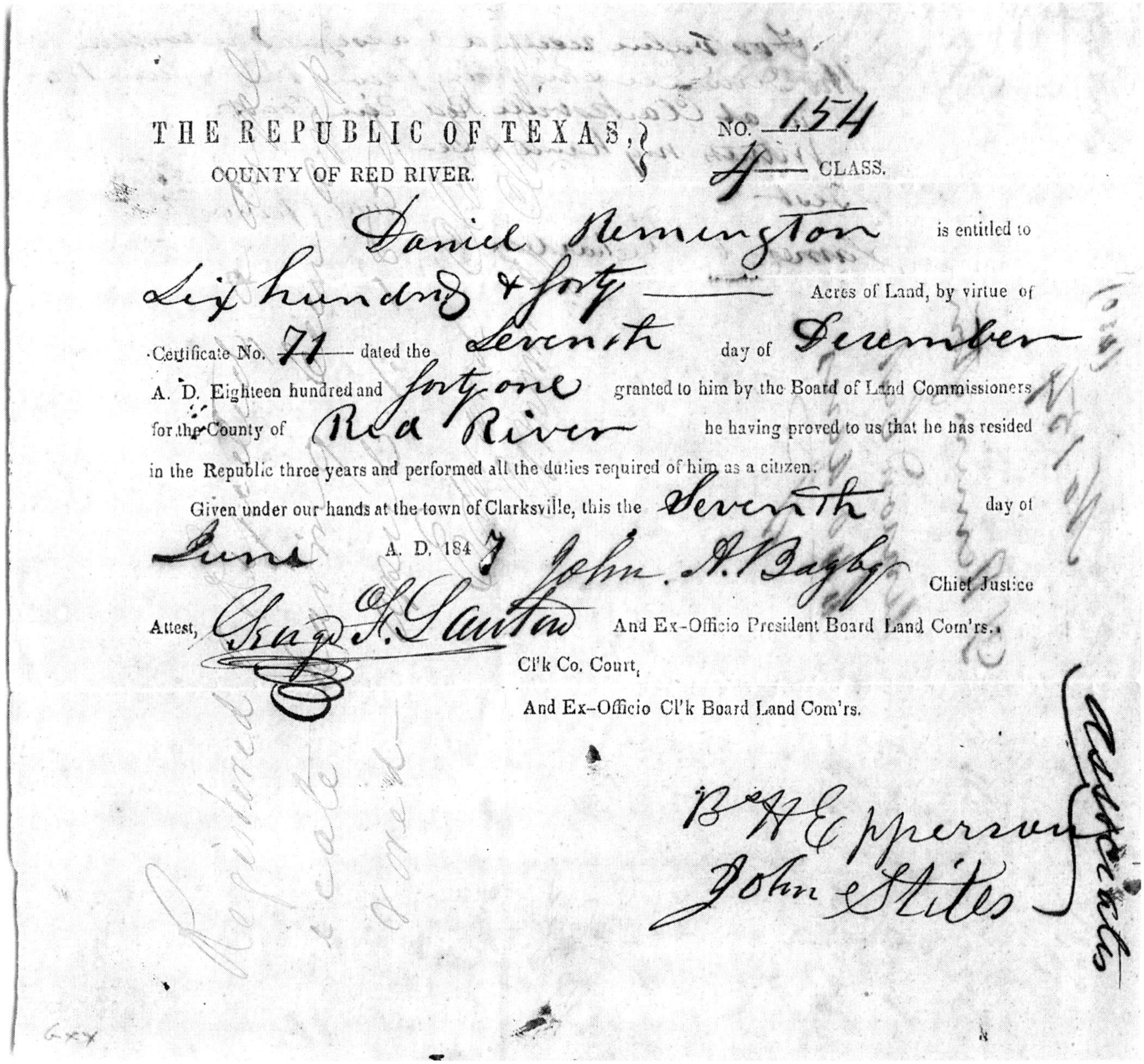
THE REPUBLIC OF TEXAS, } NO. 154
COUNTY OF RED RIVER. } 4 CLASS.

Daniel Remington is entitled to Six hundred & forty Acres of Land, by virtue of Certificate No. 71 dated the Seventh day of December A. D. Eighteen hundred and forty one granted to him by the Board of Land Commissioners for the County of Red River he having proved to us that he has resided in the Republic three years and performed all the duties required of him as a citizen.

Given under our hands at the town of Clarksville, this the Seventh day of June A. D. 1847 John A. Bagby Chief Justice

Attest, Geo. H. Lawton And Ex-Officio President Board Land Com'rs.

Cl'k Co. Court,

And Ex-Officio Cl'k Board Land Com'rs.

B. H. Epperson
John Stiles

**Figure 46. Fourth Class Conditional Headright for 640 Acres to Late Emigrant, Red River County, 1847. The final headright Act of the Republic was passed January 4, 1841, and applied to "Late Emigrants" arriving between January 1, 1840, and January 1, 1842. A fourth-class headright allotment was a section for either a family or bachelor. Added was an improvement to the land and cultivation within the three-year residency. Daniel Remington, a married man, received his warrant from the Board of Land Commissioners, Red River County, September 7, 1841. He assigned his fourth-class headright to Tomás Lee, Clarksville, Texas, June 7, 1867. The post–Civil War assignment probably contributed to the failure of the grant ever being patented.**

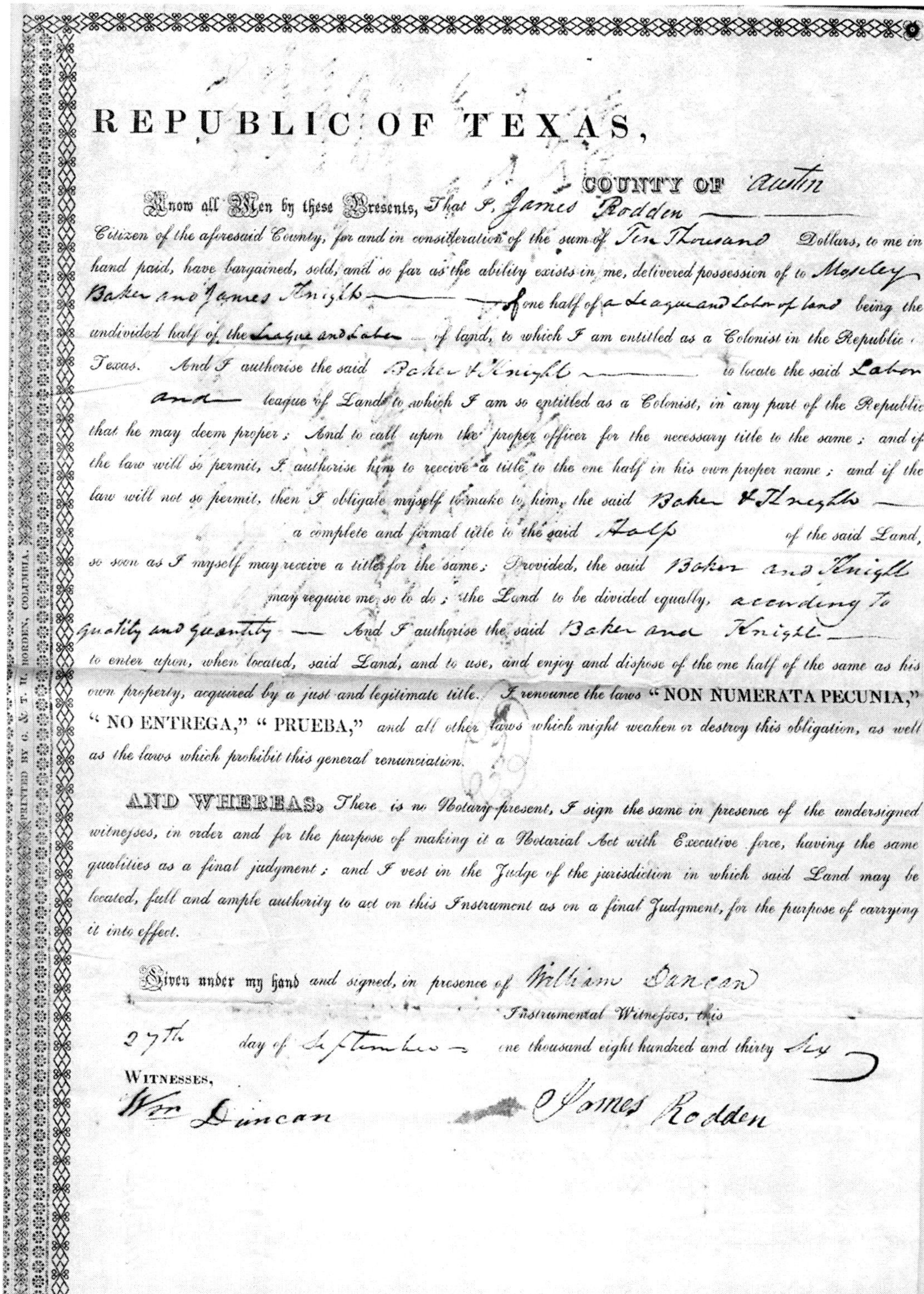

REPUBLIC OF TEXAS,

COUNTY OF Austin

Know all Men by these Presents, That I, James Rodden Citizen of the aforesaid County, for and in consideration of the sum of Ten Thousand Dollars, to me in hand paid, have bargained, sold, and so far as the ability exists in me, delivered possession of to Moseley Baker and James Knight —— one half of a League and Labor of land being the undivided half of the League and Labor — of land, to which I am entitled as a Colonist in the Republic Texas. And I authorise the said Baker & Knight —— to locate the said Labor and league of Land to which I am so entitled as a Colonist, in any part of the Republic that he may deem proper; And to call upon the proper officer for the necessary title to the same; and if the law will so permit, I authorise him to receive a title to the one half in his own proper name; and if the law will not so permit, then I obligate myself to make to him, the said Baker & Knights —— a complete and formal title to the said Half of the said Land, so soon as I myself may receive a title for the same; Provided, the said Baker and Knight may require me so to do; the Land to be divided equally, according to quality and quantity — And I authorise the said Baker and Knight —— to enter upon, when located, said Land, and to use, and enjoy and dispose of the one half of the same as his own property, acquired by a just and legitimate title. I renounce the laws "NON NUMERATA PECUNIA," "NO ENTREGA," "PRUEBA," and all other laws which might weaken or destroy this obligation, as well as the laws which prohibit this general renunciation.

AND WHEREAS, There is no Notary present, I sign the same in presence of the undersigned witnesses, in order and for the purpose of making it a Notarial Act with Executive force, having the same qualities as a final judgment; and I vest in the Judge of the jurisdiction in which said Land may be located, full and ample authority to act on this Instrument as on a final Judgment, for the purpose of carrying it into effect.

Given under my hand and signed, in presence of William Duncan Instrumental Witnesses, this 27th day of September one thousand eight hundred and thirty Six

WITNESSES,

Wm Duncan

James Rodden

PRINTED BY G. & T. H. BORDEN, COLUMBIA.

**Figure 47. Sale of ½ First-Class Headright to Land Surveyor, Austin County, 1836. The first two required documents of a colonist entering Texas before the Revolution were his character certificate and emigrant visa. Once established within an empresario's colony, the emigrant would locate and claim his league. Next, the colonist engaged a surveyor to lay out the boundaries of his land. The appointed surveyor for each land district earned $3.00 per mile run. More often than not, the surveyor would accept between a third to a half of the emigrant's grant in payment for the field notes and certificate. James Rodden located his league and labor in Austin's Colony. After the Revolution on September 27, 1836, he conveyed half his grant to James Knight and Moseley Baker in return for a survey and $10,000.00, which was an enormous sum. The property may have been the well-placed tract in Fort Bend in front of the rapids, at the site of the old fort. That tract was patented by James Knight and W. C. White.**

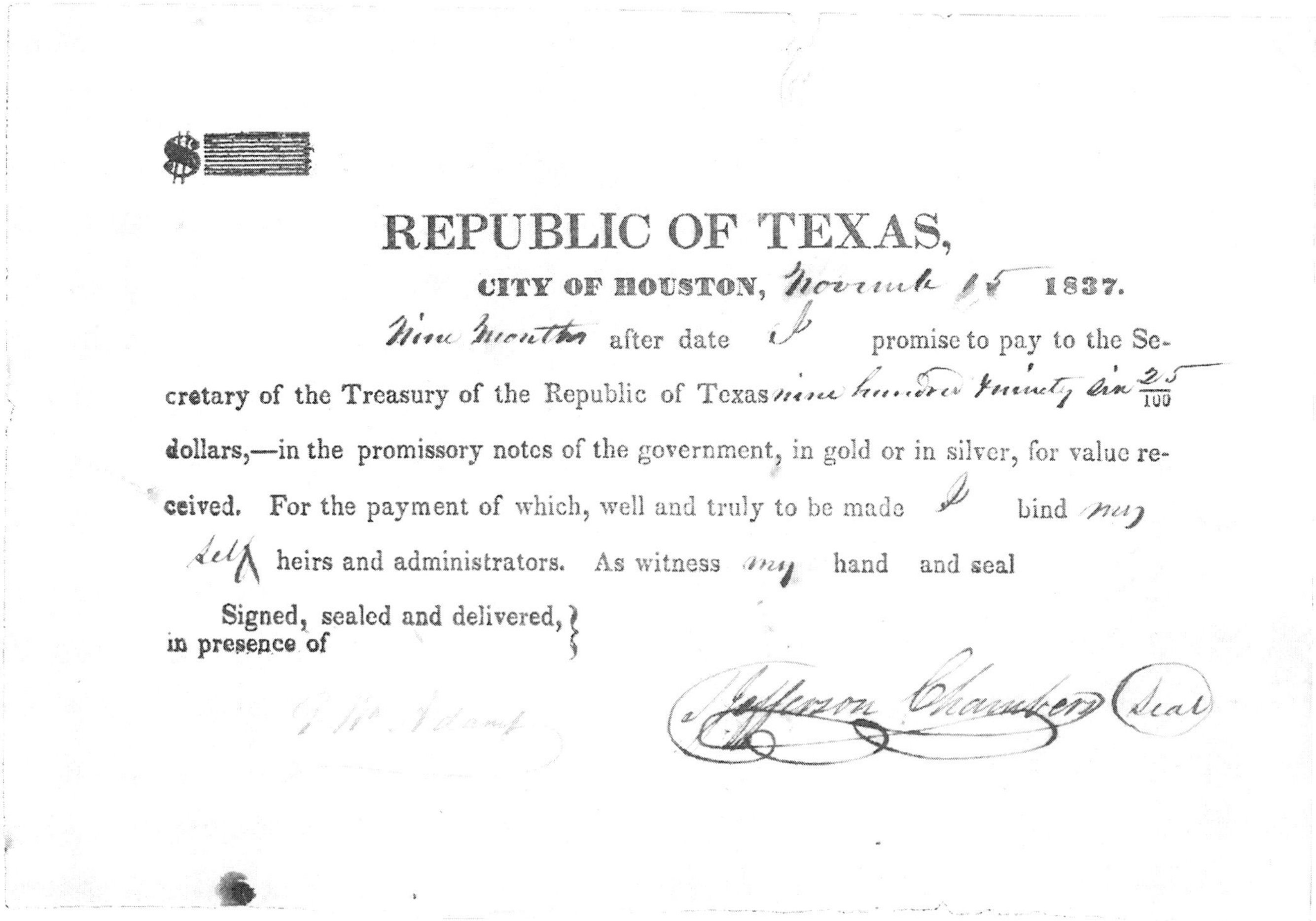

$

# REPUBLIC OF TEXAS,

CITY OF HOUSTON, November 15 1837.

Nine Months after date I promise to pay to the Secretary of the Treasury of the Republic of Texas nine hundred ninety six 25/100 dollars,—in the promissory notes of the government, in gold or in silver, for value received. For the payment of which, well and truly to be made I bind my self heirs and administrators. As witness my hand and seal

Signed, sealed and delivered, in presence of

Jefferson Chambers (Seal)

**Figure 48. Promissory Note for Lots, Galveston Island Auction, Houston, 1837. The barrier islands off the coast of Texas were part of the littoral reserve retained by both the Spanish Crown and Republic of Mexico. After independence, the Government of Texas opened the islands for settlement. It took Texas almost a century to dispose of the islands. The first sale was Galveston Island, the commercial hub of the Republic. The public auction of lots in the surveyed city of Galveston was held November 15, 1837. Land speculator Thomas Jefferson Chambers was the high bidder on 41 lots, patented February 25, 1839, after full payment was made and dues satisfied. Lot sizes ranged between ten and twenty acres. The illustrated promissory note payable to Secretary of the Treasury of the Republic could be paid with gold, silver or promissory notes of the government, at face value although substantially deflated. The $996.25 auction reflected a price of $1.50 per acre, three times the government-posted price.**

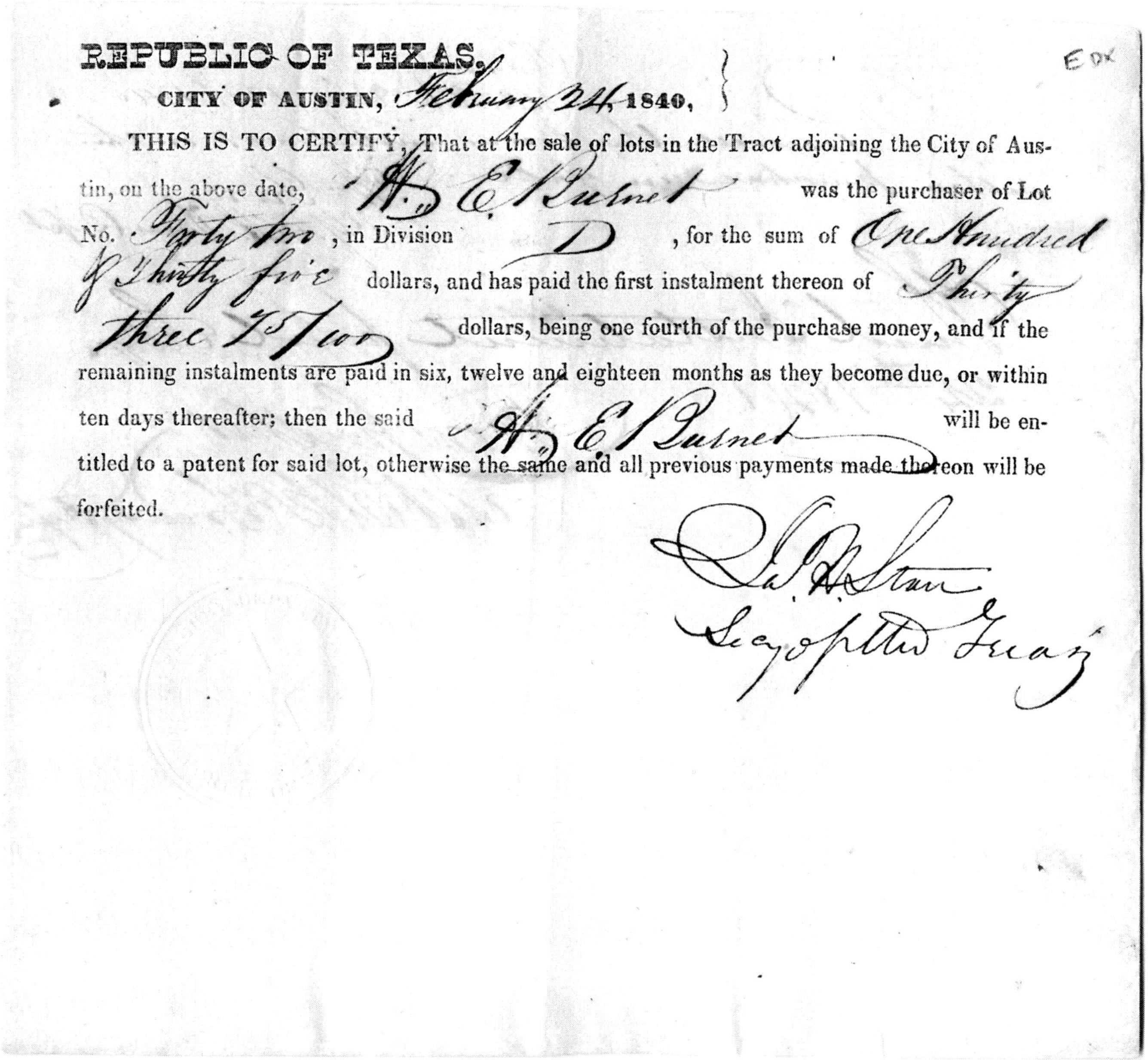

REPUBLIC OF TEXAS,

CITY OF AUSTIN, February 24, 1840,

THIS IS TO CERTIFY, That at the sale of lots in the Tract adjoining the City of Austin, on the above date, H. E. Burnet was the purchaser of Lot No. Forty two, in Division D, for the sum of One Hundred & Thirty five dollars, and has paid the first instalment thereon of Thirty three 75/100 dollars, being one fourth of the purchase money, and if the remaining instalments are paid in six, twelve and eighteen months as they become due, or within ten days thereafter; then the said H. E. Burnet will be entitled to a patent for said lot, otherwise the same and all previous payments made thereon will be forfeited.

Ja. H. Starr
Secy of the Treasy

**Figure 49. Receipt, Austin City Lots Auction, 1840. The Republic needed a centrally located seat of government to accommodate the needs of a growing nation. The future capital, named Austin, was selected. Edward Burleson surveyed 7,700 acres in the original town of Waterloo in 1839. Reserved within surveyed Austin were sufficient blocks for the government, schools, executive mansion and parks. The balance was scheduled for public auction. Two types of land were to be auctioned: town lots and outlying lots. Town lots were first auctioned in 1839, and sales continued for many years. H.E. Burnett purchased two outlying lots and signed a promissory note. He received his patent March 1, 1855, after the purchase obligation of $135.00 was paid February 24, 1841. Earlier, Edward Burnett had received military bounty lands for services in 1839. He assigned his two sections of veteran land to R.B. Jarmon, who in 1848 patented the land in Live Oak County.**

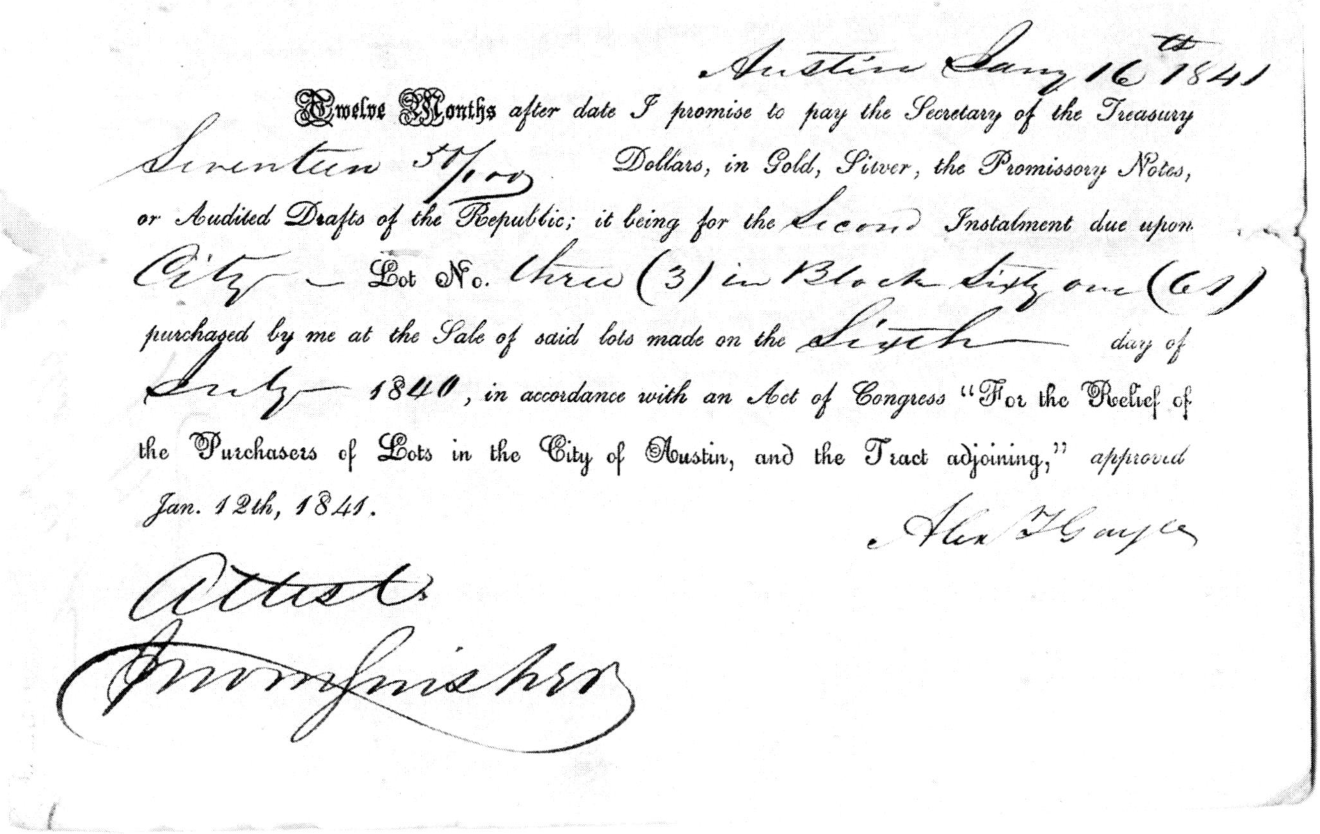
Austin Jany 16th 1841

Twelve Months after date I promise to pay the Secretary of the Treasury Seventeen 50/100 Dollars, in Gold, Silver, the Promissory Notes, or Audited Drafts of the Republic; it being for the Second Instalment due upon City — Lot No. three (3) in Block Sixty one (61) purchased by me at the Sale of said lots made on the Sixth day of July 1840, in accordance with an Act of Congress "For the Relief of the Purchasers of Lots in the City of Austin, and the Tract adjoining," approved Jan. 12th, 1841.

Alex T. Gayle

Attest.

**Figure 50. Moratorium, Austin Lots Auction, Relief Act of January 12, 1841. Economic conditions were bleak after the Austin land auction because of the continuing effect of the Panic of 1837. Austin lot buyers fell behind in their installments. The state did not want any foreclosure of city property for political reasons. Future auctions were suspended, and did not reopen until 1850. Congress, on January 12, 1841, granted a moratorium of installment payments to forestall foreclosures. Alex T. Gayle bought a number of lots. He was able to make his second installment January 16, 1841, for his July 6, 1840, purchase. The third payment was delayed. Gayle received patents between 1842 and 1849 from the General Land Office.**

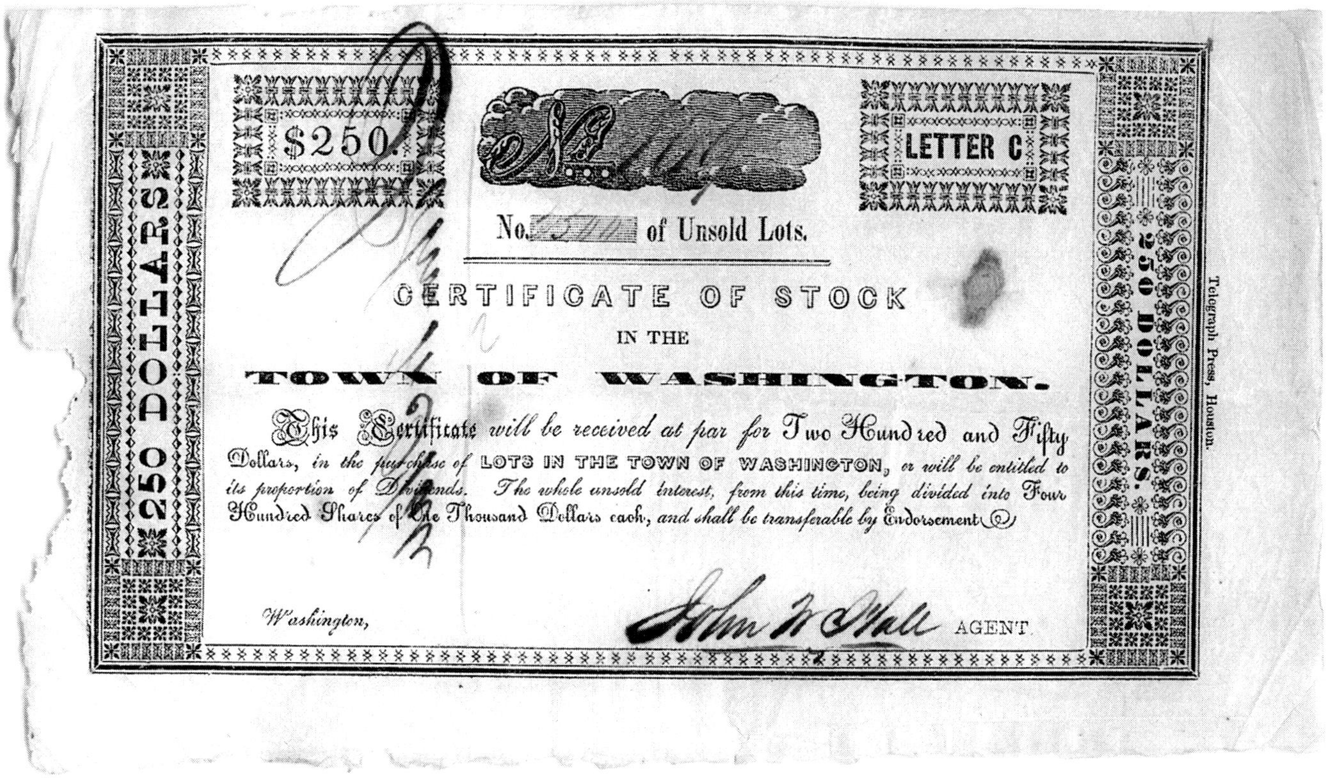


**Figure 51. $250 Stock Certificate for Town of Washington, Receivable for Lots [ca. 1835]. Andrew Robinson, one of Austin's original "Three Hundred," held a grant along the old La Bahía Road near the junction of the Navasota and Brazos rivers, where he built a ferry crossing. Robinson's son-in-law, John W. Hall, was gifted a quarter-section of the property. He surveyed the land for the Washington Town Company in 1835. In 1836 the new town was home to the General Counsel and provisional government. Hall sold stock in the company to investors and future townsfolk. The $250.00 and $1,000.00 stock entitled the owner to apply at par the certificates against the purchase of lots in the town. If held, the stockholder received a proportionate share of the company dividends. Four hundred shares were authorized.**

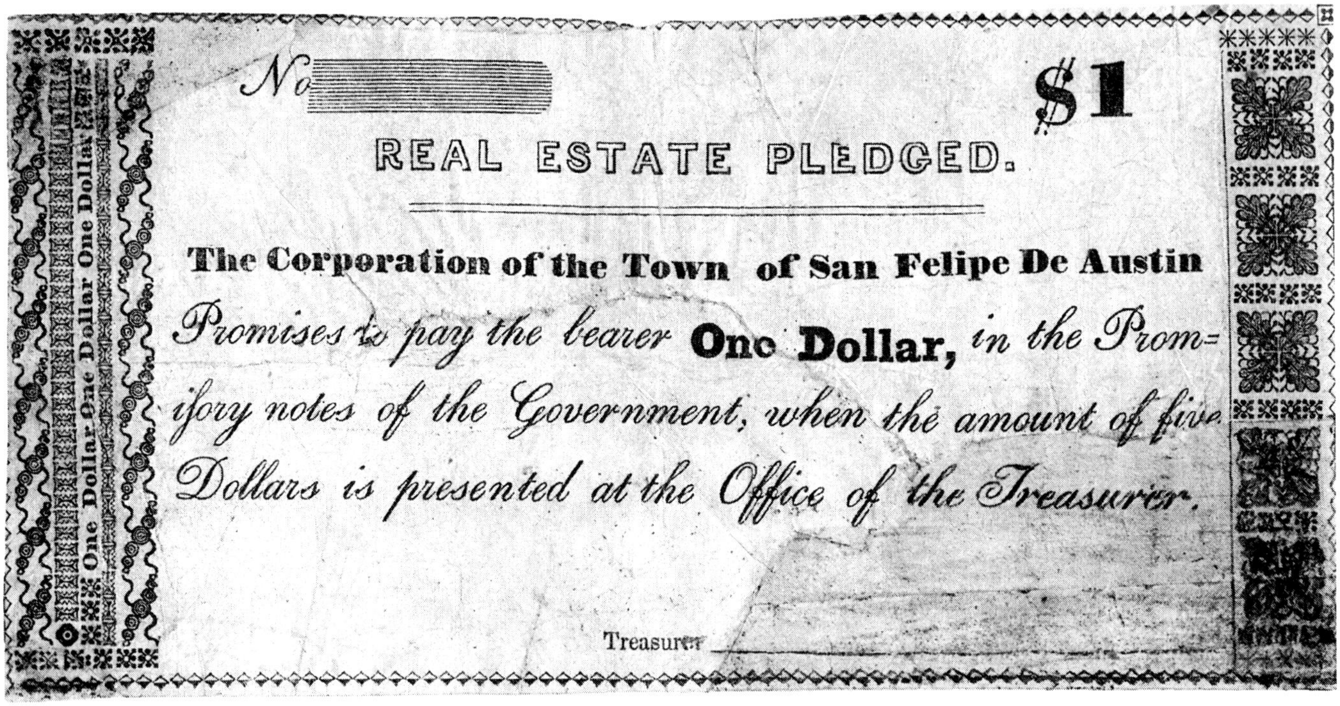


Figure 52. $1.00 Shinplaster, San Felipe de Austin, Real Estate Pledged, 1839. San Felipe de Austin, founded in 1820, was burned by General Santa Anna in 1836. The following year, townsfolk began rebuilding. The municipality was chartered by Congress. During the Panic of 1837, the town ran short of funds. In 1839 the town issued city warrants in the form of scrip to pay bills. The scrip was secured by the pledge of city real estate. The shinplaster was redeemable in Government of Texas promissory notes if presented in five dollar increments.

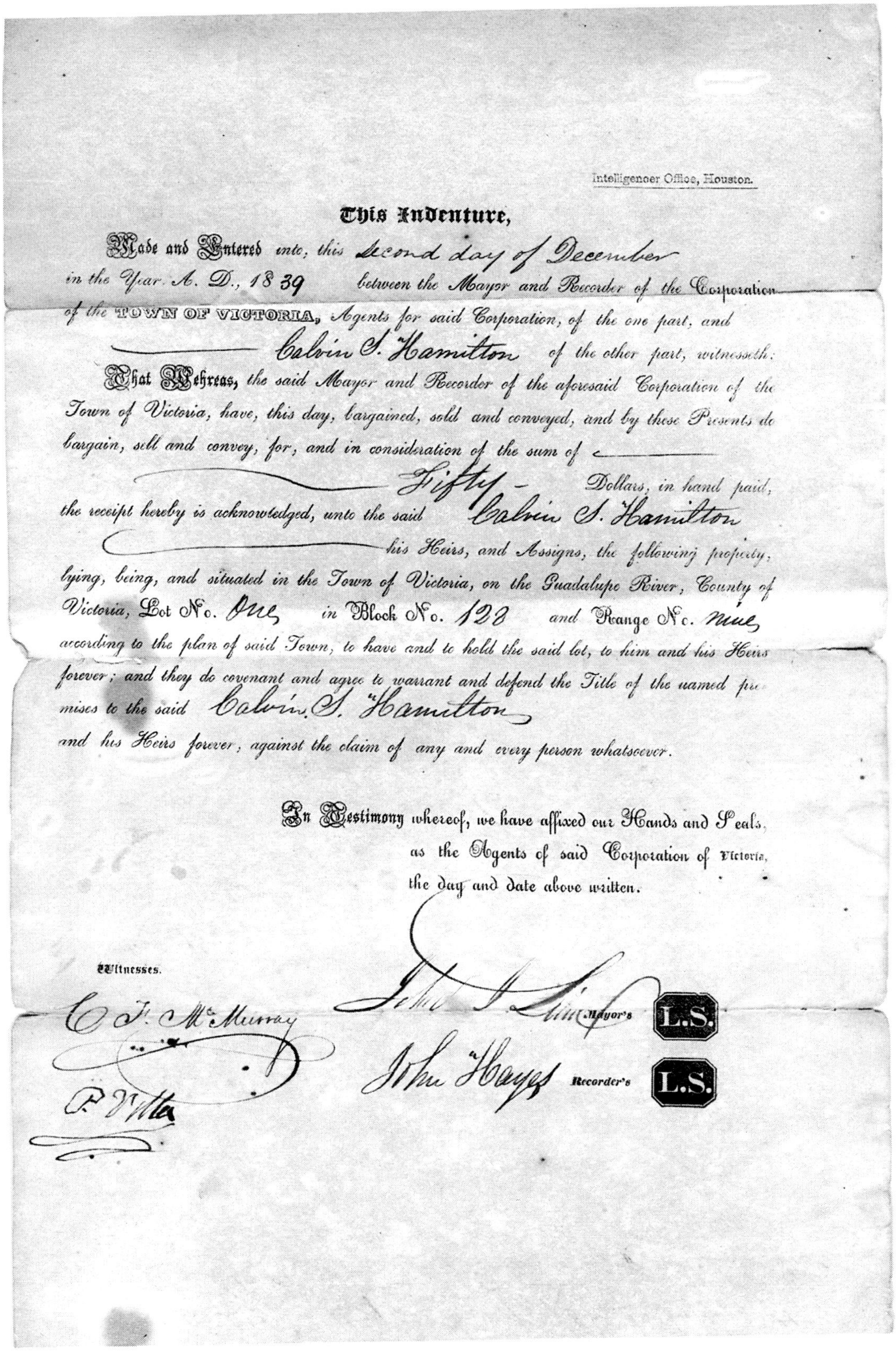

Intelligencer Office, Houston.

**This Indenture,**

Made and Entered into, this second day of December in the Year A. D., 1839 between the Mayor and Recorder of the Corporation of the TOWN OF VICTORIA, Agents for said Corporation, of the one part, and Calvin S. Hamilton of the other part, witnesseth:

That Whereas, the said Mayor and Recorder of the aforesaid Corporation of the Town of Victoria, have, this day, bargained, sold and conveyed, and by these Presents do bargain, sell and convey, for, and in consideration of the sum of Fifty – Dollars, in hand paid, the receipt hereby is acknowledged, unto the said Calvin S. Hamilton his Heirs, and Assigns, the following property, lying, being, and situated in the Town of Victoria, on the Guadalupe River, County of Victoria, Lot No. One in Block No. 128 and Range No. nine according to the plan of said Town, to have and to hold the said lot, to him and his Heirs forever; and they do covenant and agree to warrant and defend the Title of the named premises to the said Calvin S. Hamilton and his Heirs forever, against the claim of any and every person whatsoever.

In Testimony whereof, we have affixed our Hands and Seals, as the Agents of said Corporation of Victoria, the day and date above written.

Witnesses.

C. F. McMurray

P. Vitte

John L. Linn Mayor's L.S.

John Hayes Recorder's L.S.

**Figure 53. Bargain and Sale Contract for Lots, Victoria, 1839. Victoria, the city established for Martín de León's colony, was a community of Mexican and Irish immigrants. The municipality was chartered by the Republic. Calvin S. Hamilton of Massachusetts purchased lot No. 1, Block 128 in the town of Victoria, at public auction on December 2, 1839. The price was $50.00 per lot. The indenture was executed by John L. Linn, the town's first mayor.**

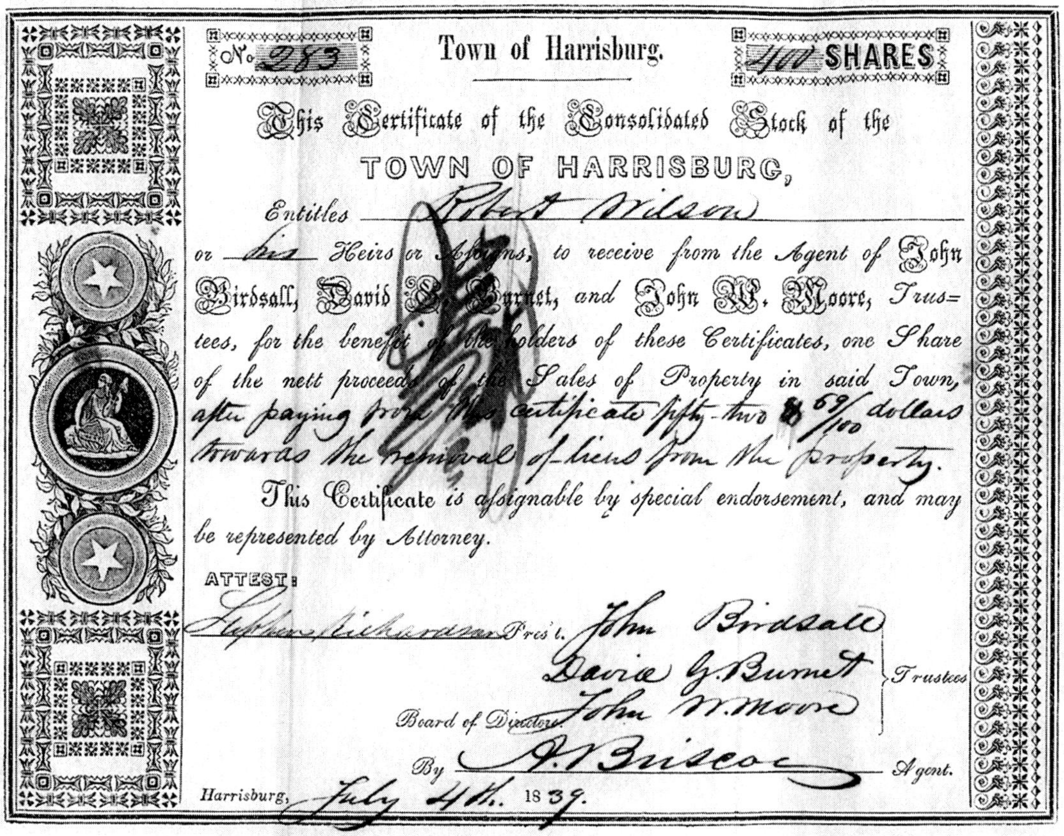
No. 283 Town of Harrisburg. 400 SHARES

This Certificate of the Consolidated Stock of the

TOWN OF HARRISBURG,

Entitles Robert Wilson or his Heirs or Assigns, to receive from the Agent of John Birdsall, David G. Burnet, and John W. Moore, Trustees, for the benefit of the holders of these Certificates, one Share of the nett proceeds of the Sales of Property in said Town, after paying from this certificate fifty-two & 59/100 dollars towards the removal of liens from the property.

This Certificate is assignable by special endorsement, and may be represented by Attorney.

ATTEST:

Stephen Richardson Pres't. Board of Directors

John Birdsall
David G. Burnet
John W. Moore
Trustees

By A. T. Briscoe Agent.

Harrisburg, July 4th. 1839.

**Figure 54. 400 Share Stock Certificate for Harrisburg [ca. 1839]. William Harris received a three-league grant from Austin on December 18, 1830. His joint owner was Robert Wilson. Their town of Harrisburg, along the Buffalo Bayou, became a municipality in 1835. Harrisburg Town Company sold shares. Robert Wilson purchased some of the lots with the condition that title liens be cleared. The purchase price of $52.59 was in addition to the removal of liens. He tendered the 400-share Certificate of the Consolidated Stock of the Town of Harrisburg. Trustees of the Town Company included signers of the Texas declaration of independence John W. Moore and David G. Burnet.**

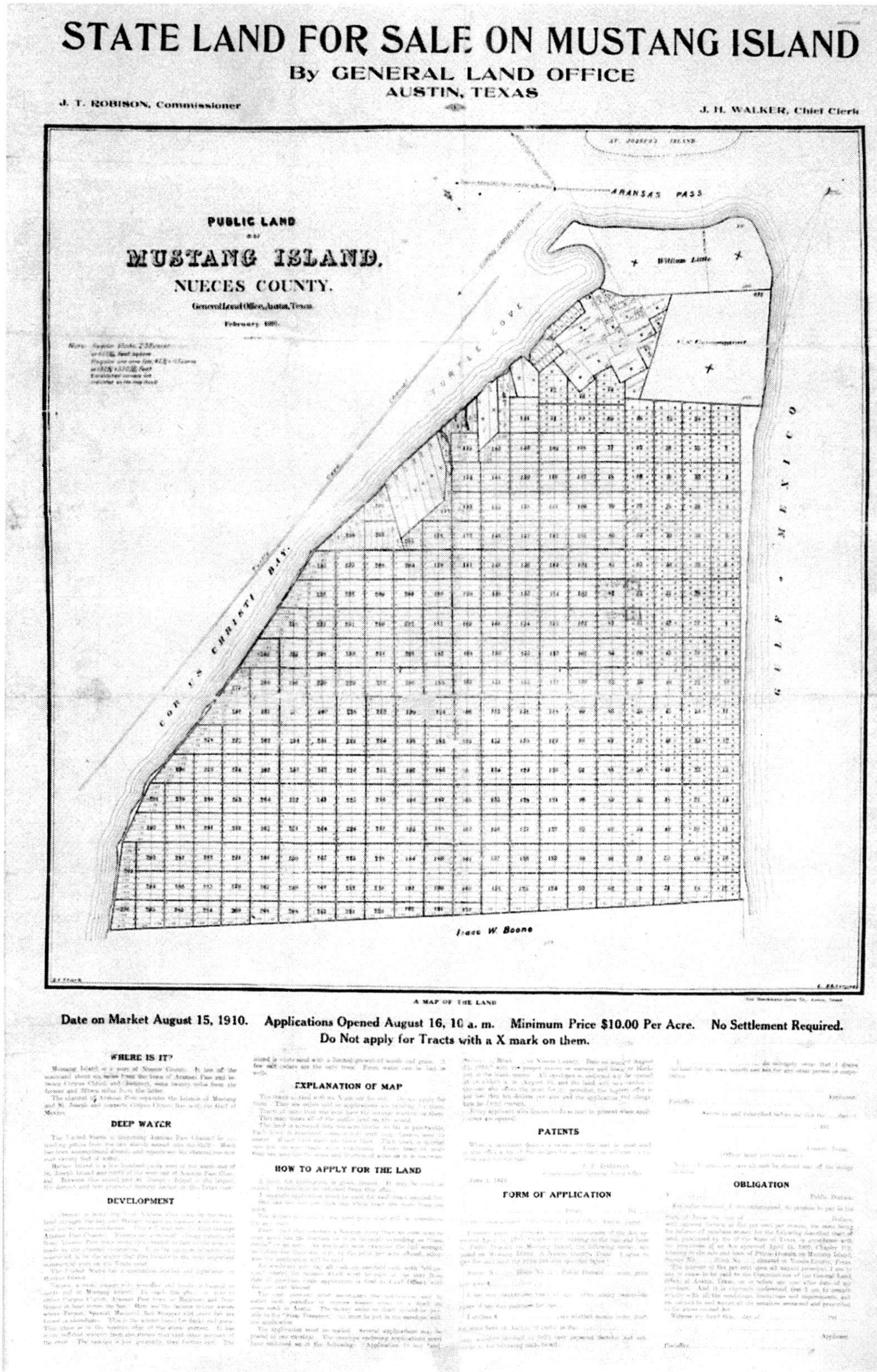


**Figure 55. Broadside Announcing Sale, Mustang Island, $10.00 Per Acre, G.L.O., 1910. Mustang Island, a barrier island on Corpus Christie Bay in Nueces County, is more than eighteen miles long. First visited by the Spanish early in the sixteenth century, it was not made available to settlers until after the Revolution, being a part of the littoral reserve. Captain Robert Mercer was the first Anglo to ranch the island. His El Mar Rancho later shared the island with a United States quarantine station and lifesaving crew. Not until 1910 did Texas offer the land for public sale. That year the General Land Office published a promotional map describing the 2,900 acres, to be sold at a minimum price of $10.00 per acre. The state printer was Von Boeckmann–Jonas Co., Austin.**

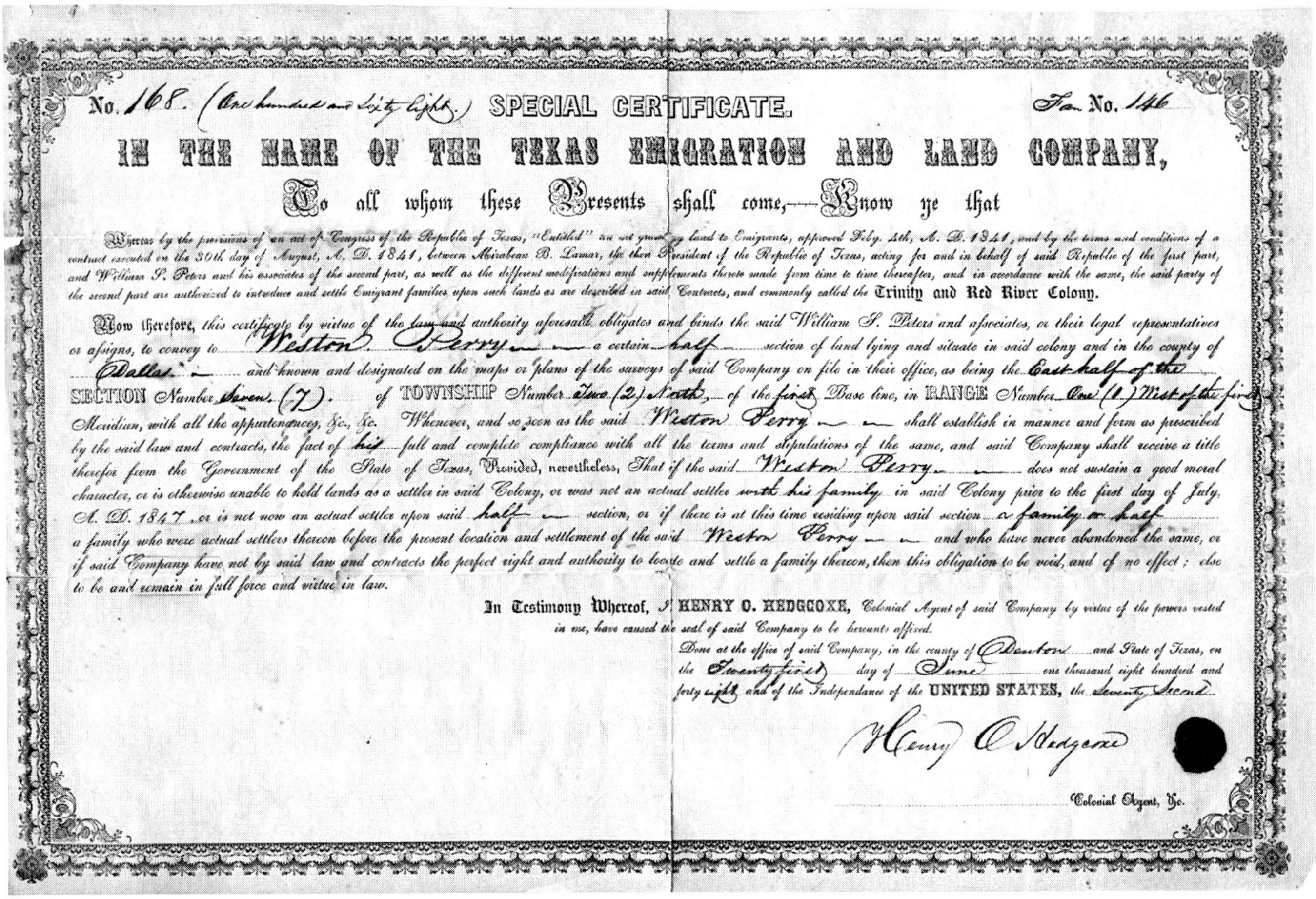

No. 168. (One hundred and Sixty eight.) SPECIAL CERTIFICATE. Fan No. 146

IN THE NAME OF THE TEXAS EMIGRATION AND LAND COMPANY,

To all whom these Presents shall come,—Know ye that

Whereas by the provisions of an act of Congress of the Republic of Texas, "Entitled" an act granting land to Emigrants, approved Feby. 4th, A. D. 1841, and by the terms and conditions of a contract executed on the 30th day of August, A. D. 1841, between Mirabeau B. Lamar, the then President of the Republic of Texas, acting for and in behalf of said Republic of the first part, and William S. Peters and his associates of the second part, as well as the different modifications and supplements thereto made from time to time thereafter, and in accordance with the same, the said party of the second part are authorized to introduce and settle Emigrant families upon such lands as are described in said Contracts, and commonly called the Trinity and Red River Colony.

Now therefore, this certificate by virtue of the law and authority aforesaid obligates and binds the said William S. Peters and associates, or their legal representatives or assigns, to convey to Weston Perry a certain half section of land lying and situate in said colony and in the county of Dallas and known and designated on the maps or plans of the surveys of said Company on file in their office, as being the East half of the SECTION Number Seven (7). of TOWNSHIP Number Two (2) North, of the first Base line, in RANGE Number One (1) West of the first Meridian, with all the appurtenances, &c., &c. Whenever, and so soon as the said Weston Perry shall establish in manner and form as prescribed by the said law and contracts, the fact of his full and complete compliance with all the terms and stipulations of the same, and said Company shall receive a title therefor from the Government of the State of Texas, Provided, nevertheless, That if the said Weston Perry does not sustain a good moral character, or is otherwise unable to hold lands as a settler in said Colony, or was not an actual settler with his family in said Colony prior to the first day of July, A. D. 1847, or is not now an actual settler upon said half section, or if there is at this time residing upon said section a family or half a family who were actual settlers thereon before the present location and settlement of the said Weston Perry and who have never abandoned the same, or if said Company have not by said law and contracts the perfect right and authority to locate and settle a family thereon, then this obligation to be void, and of no effect; else to be and remain in full force and virtue in law.

In Testimony Whereof, I HENRY O. HEDGCOXE, Colonial Agent of said Company by virtue of the powers vested in me, have caused the seal of said Company to be hereunto affixed.

Done at the office of said Company, in the county of Denton and State of Texas, on the Twenty first day of June one thousand eight hundred and forty eight and of the Independance of the UNITED STATES, the Seventy Second

Henry O Hedgcoxe

Colonial Agent, &c.

**Figure 56. Special Certificate of Title, ½ Section, Texas Emigration and Land Company (Trinity and Red River Colony), Agent Henry O. Hedgcoxe, Denton County, 1848. The North Texas Peters Colony was the result of an 1841 Republic empresario grant. For costs incurred, the contractor retained up to half the settler's grant. The association underwent several reorganizations. By 1845 probably less than 500 settlers had come to the colony, evenly divided between married and single families. Pre-existing squatters confused the land agent and surveyor. Controversy arose, feelings ran high and the legislature attempted to appease all, but failed. In 1852 the complaining colonists stormed the company's office in Collin County and forced the agent to leave. This became known as the "Hedgcoxe War." In 1848, agent Henry O. Hedgcoxe delivered "faux" land patents to qualified title applicants. The 1848 spurious patent to Weston Perry, filed in Denton, reflects that half of the land was retained by the company.**

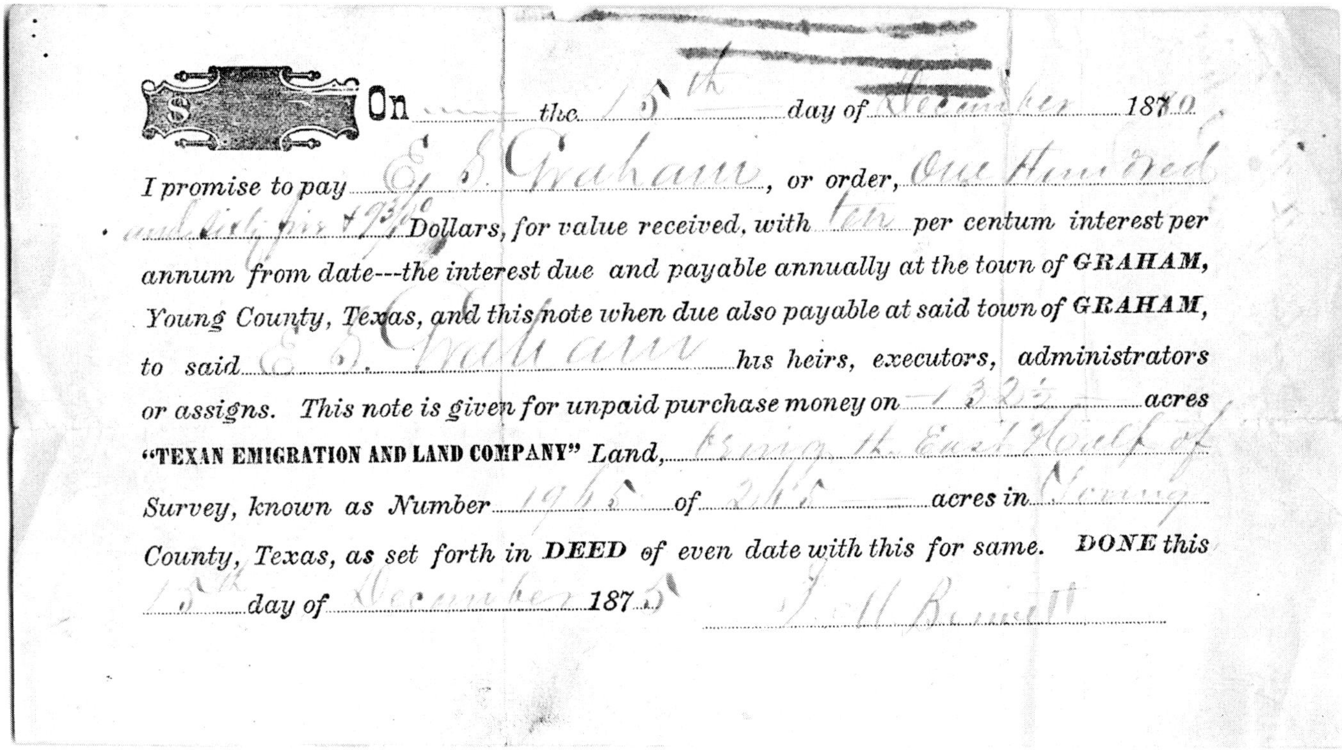

On the 15th day of December 187_

*I promise to pay* E. S. Graham, *or order,* One Hundred and sixty five & 93/100 *Dollars, for value received, with* ten *per centum interest per annum from date---the interest due and payable annually at the town of* **GRAHAM**, *Young County, Texas, and this note when due also payable at said town of* **GRAHAM**, *to said* E. S. Graham *his heirs, executors, administrators or assigns. This note is given for unpaid purchase money on* 132½ *acres* **"TEXAN EMIGRATION AND LAND COMPANY"** *Land,* being the East Half of *Survey, known as Number* 1965 *of* 265 *acres in* Young *County, Texas, as set forth in* **DEED** *of even date with this for same.* **DONE** *this* 15th *day of* December *187*5 J. M. Bennett

**Figure 57. Promissory Note for Purchase of 132½ Acres, Texas Emigration and Land Company, Young County, 1875. After negotiations with the State Legislature, the Texas Emigration and Land Company received premium lands. Most of this acreage was located in the former "Brazos River Indian Reservation," abandoned after the federal government assumed responsibility for indigenous Texans. After the Civil War, Edwin S. Graham acquired the Texas Emigration and Land Company assets, which were primarily the Brazos Reservation premium lands. Graham promoted and marketed this acreage to North Texas newcomers, priced about a dollar an acre. J. M. Bennett purchased 132½ acres for $165.93 on December 15, 1875. He paid off his promissory note in 1878. The vast acreage owned by Texas Emigration was patented by the General Land Office between 1856 and 1858.**

TEXAS ASSOCIATION No.

8000 Square miles on the Trinity River.

GRANT 1844

BY THE REPUBLIC OF TEXAS.

This Certifies that is entitled to One Share of Stock in "THE TEXAS ASSOCIATION" established for colonizing certain land in TEXAS under the Authority of the Republic. Said Share of Stock, is transferable in person or by Attorney on the Books of the Association upon the surrender of this Certificate.

This Certificate of Stock, is not liable for ANY call, except it become necessary for charges of survey of lands, acquired by the Association.

In Witness whereof is affixed the Signatures of the President & Secretary this at Louisville, Ky.

Secretary

Hart, Mapother & Co. Lithogrs. Louisville, Ky.

President.

**Figure 58. Stock Certificate for the Texas Association, Louisville, Kentucky, 1858. Former shareholder in the Peters Colony, Charles Fenton Mercer of Virginia, was a politician, railroad man and abolitionist. He received his own empresario grant from Sam Houston in 1844 and organized the Texas Association to develop the colony. To fund the venture, shares were sold in Kentucky, Tennessee, Florida and a few in Texas. The share par value was $500.00. He quickly met his 100-family settlement requirement. Mercer assigned his controlling interest in the Mercer Colony to George Hancock of Kentucky for $2,000.00 on February 27, 1852.**

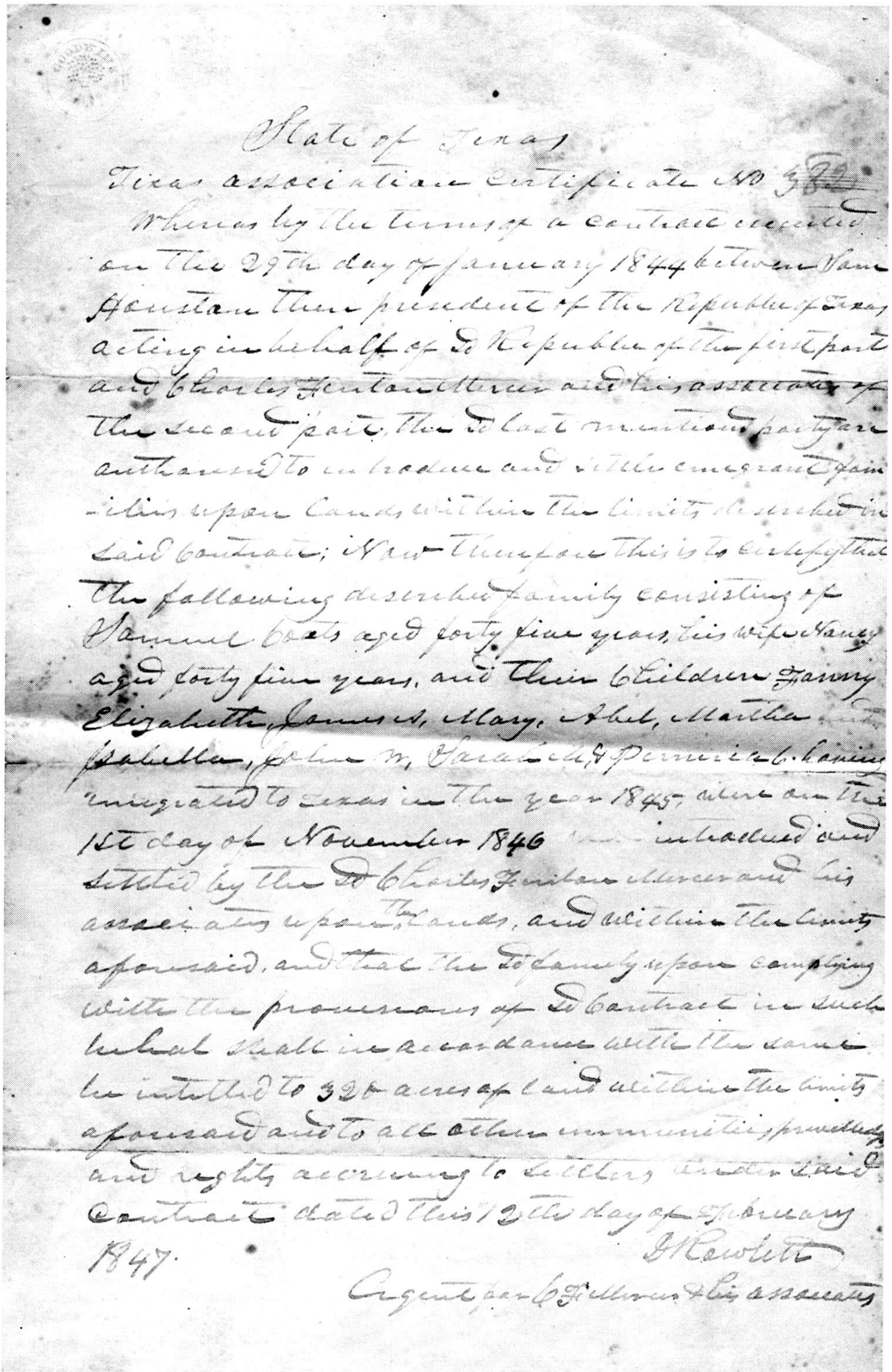
State of Texas
Texas association Certificate No 382
Whereas by the terms of a contract executed
on the 29th day of January 1844 between Sam
Houston then president of the Republic of Texas
acting in behalf of sd Republic of the first part
and Charles Fenton Mercer and his associates of
the second part, the sd last mentioned party are
authorised to introduce and settle emigrant fam-
-ilies upon Lands within the limits described in
said Contract; Now Therefore this is to certify that
the following described family consisting of
Samuel Doats aged forty five years, his wife Nancy
aged forty five years, and their Children Fanny
Elizabeth, James A, Mary, Abel, Martha,
Isabella, John W, Sarah M, & Permelia C. having
emigrated to Texas in the year 1845, were on the
1st day of November 1846 introduced and
settled by the sd Charles Fenton Mercer and his
associates upon the Lands, and within the limits
aforesaid, and that the sd family upon complying
with the provisions of sd Contract in such
behalf shall in accordance with the same
be entitled to 320 acres of land within the limits
aforesaid and to all other immunities, privileges
and rights accruing to settlers under said
Contract dated this 12th day of February
1847.
D Rowlett
Agent for C F Mercer & his associates

**Figure 59. Settlement Affidavit in the Texas Association Grant (Mercer Colony), 1846. Daniel Rowlett was a Texas investor in the Texas Association and served as Mercer's resident agent within the colony. One of his functions was to document a colonist's entry into the colony, family size and acceptability. After July 1, 1846, settlers' land allotments were reduced to only 200 acres, making proof of date of entry important. Typical residency, improvements and cultivation were prerequisites to filing for a survey and title. After patent applications were filed, the State brought suit to ascertain the validity of Mercer's contract, signed by Governor Houston a day before the law expired. After years of litigation, the settlers' right to patent were upheld. On February 12, 1847, agent Rowell confirmed the entry of Samuel Doats, a family man with children, into Mercer's colony. Doats settled November 1, 1846, and received Texas Association Certificate No. 382.**

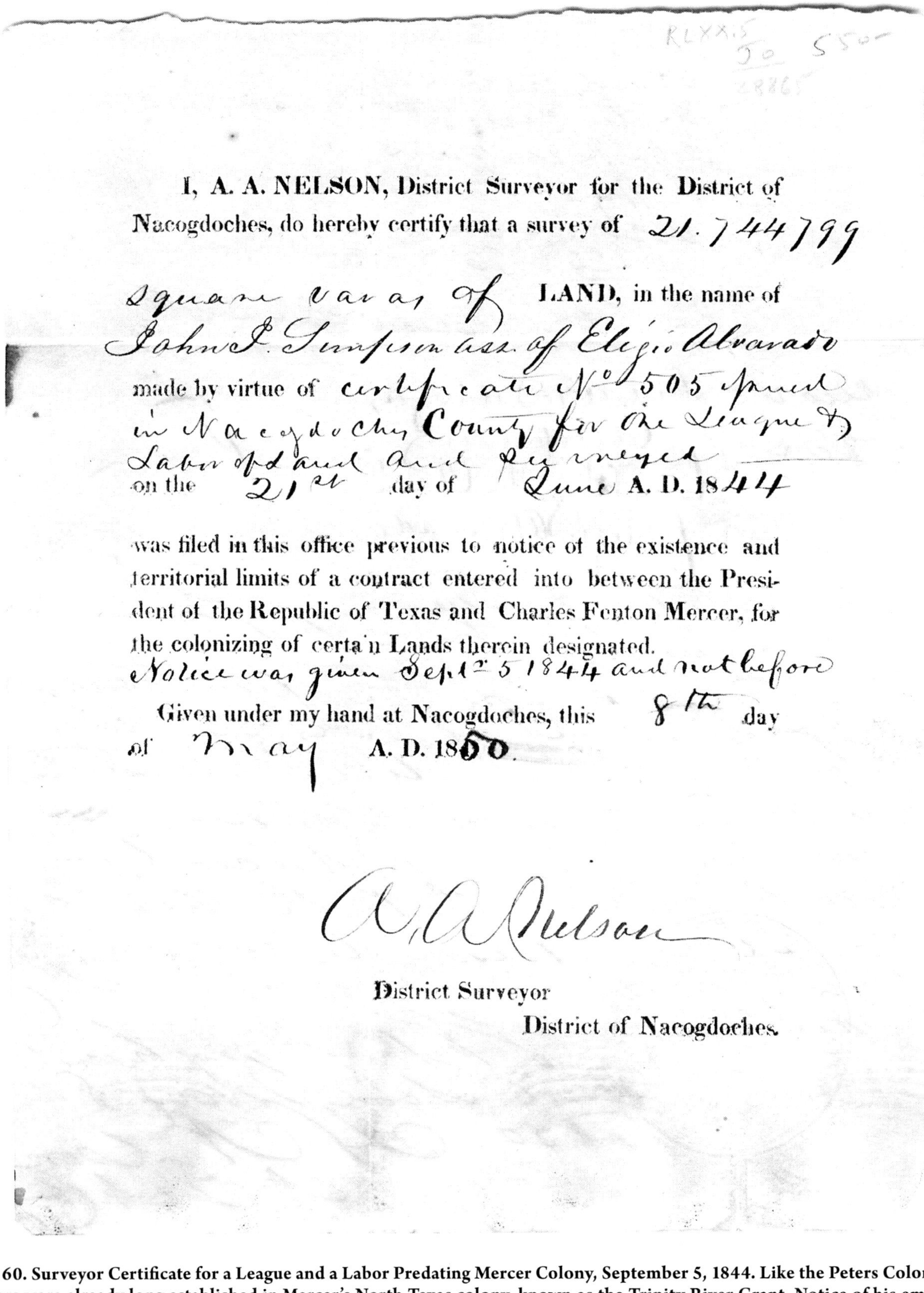

RLXX.5
50 550—
28865

I, A. A. NELSON, District Surveyor for the District of Nacogdoches, do hereby certify that a survey of 21.744799 square varas of LAND, in the name of John S. Simpson ass. of Eligio Alvarado made by virtue of certificate No 505 issued in Nacogdoches County for One League & Labor of land and surveyed on the 21st day of June A. D. 1844

was filed in this office previous to notice of the existence and territorial limits of a contract entered into between the President of the Republic of Texas and Charles Fenton Mercer, for the colonizing of certain Lands therein designated.
Notice was given Sept 5 1844 and not before

Given under my hand at Nacogdoches, this 8th day of May A. D. 1850.

A. A. Nelson

District Surveyor
District of Nacogdoches.

**Figure 60. Surveyor Certificate for a League and a Labor Predating Mercer Colony, September 5, 1844. Like the Peters Colony, many squatters were already long established in Mercer's North Texas colony, known as the Trinity River Grant. Notice of his empresario contract was made public September 5, 1844. The District Surveyor for Nacogdoches, A.A. Nelson, continued to issue field notes and certificates to undocumented settlers if their residence was established before that date. Such a resident, John S. Simpson, obtained a Nelson surveyor's certificate at Nacogdoches on May 8, 1851. Simpson received a patent for a league and a labor in the middle of Mercer's colony, along with a title dated June 11, 1859.**

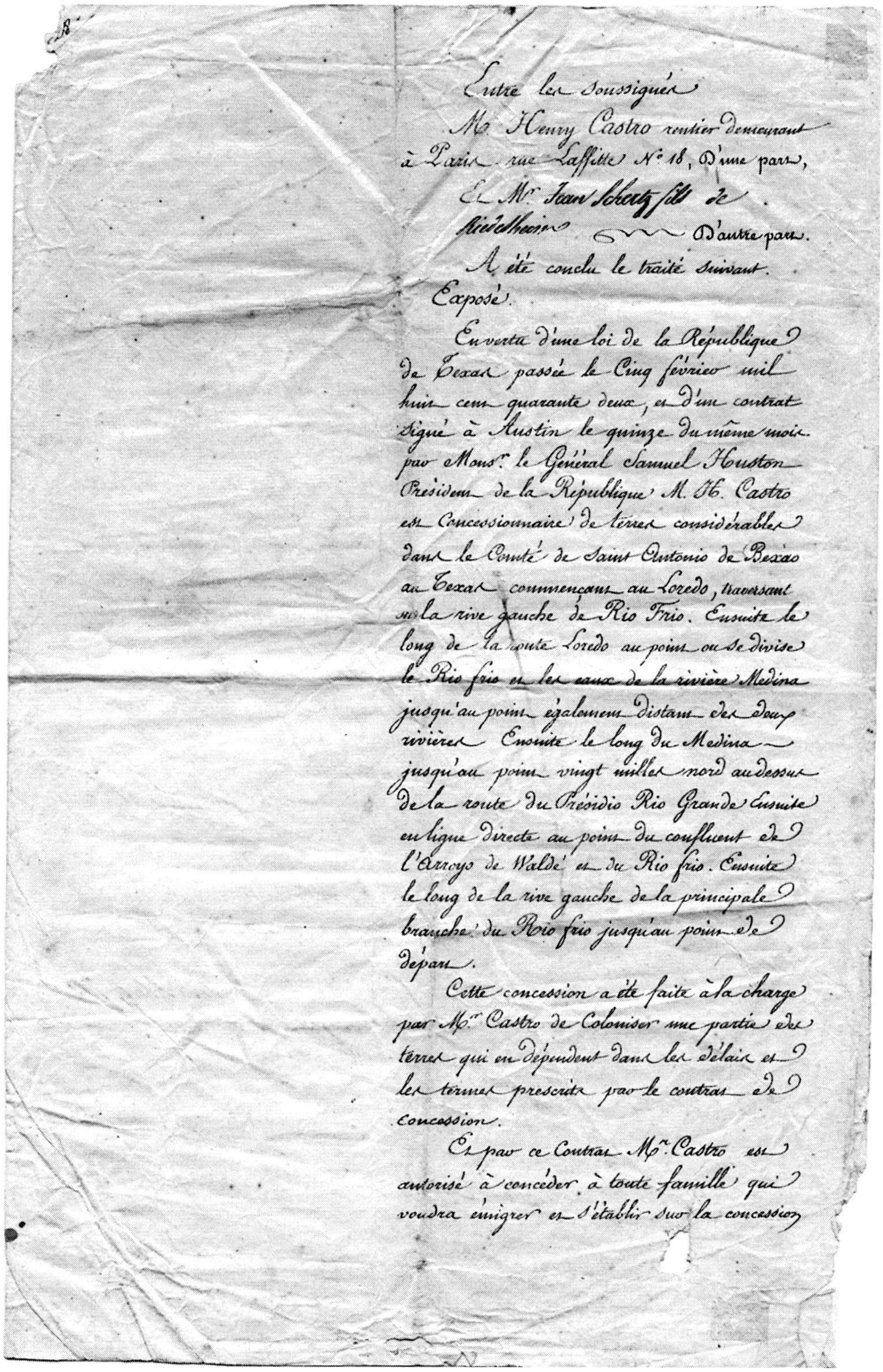

Entre les soussignés

Mr Henry Castro rentier demeurant à Paris rue Laffitte N° 18, d'une part,

Et Mr Jean Schertz fils de Riedesheim d'autre part.

A été conclu le traité suivant.

Exposé.

En vertu d'une loi de la République de Texas passée le Cinq févrieo mil huit cent quarante deux, et d'un contrat signé à Austin le quinze du même mois par Monsr. le Général Samuel Huston Président de la République M. H. Castro est Concessionnaire de terres considérables dans le Comté de Saint Antonio de Bexao au Texas commençant au Loredo, traversant sur la rive gauche de Rio Frio. Ensuite le long de la route Loredo au point ou se divise le Rio frio et les eaux de la rivière Medina jusqu'au point également distant des deux rivières. Ensuite le long du Medina jusqu'au point vingt milles nord au dessus de la route du Présidio Rio Grande Ensuite en ligne directe au point du confluent de l'Arroyo de Waldé et du Rio frio. Ensuite le long de la rive gauche de la principale branche du Rio frio jusqu'au point de départ.

Cette concession a été faite à la charge par Mr Castro de Coloniser une partie des terres qui en dépendent dans les délais et les termes prescrits par le contrat de concession.

Et par ce Contrat Mr Castro est autorisé à concéder à toute famille qui voudra émigrer et s'établir sur la concession

**Figure 61 (this page and three following). Emigrant Contract for 320 Acres, Castro Grant, Paris, France, 1841. Henri Castro of France was the appointed consul general of the Republic to France. As a result of that position, he received an empresario contract in 1842 to place colonies along the lower Rio Grande. Hostile climate as well as raids by crossing Mexican troops and bandits contributed to the failure of it to develop. His second grant along the Medina River proved more successful. Castro claimed to have invested more than $100,000 of his own wealth in the colony of French "cultivators." About twenty vessels brought French immigrants to Texas destined for Castroville. After Austin and DeWitt, Castro was the most populated colony. More than five hundred families received patents representing a quarter-million acres. Despite that, Castro was only awarded half his premium lands. The venture consumed most of Castro's personal wealth.**

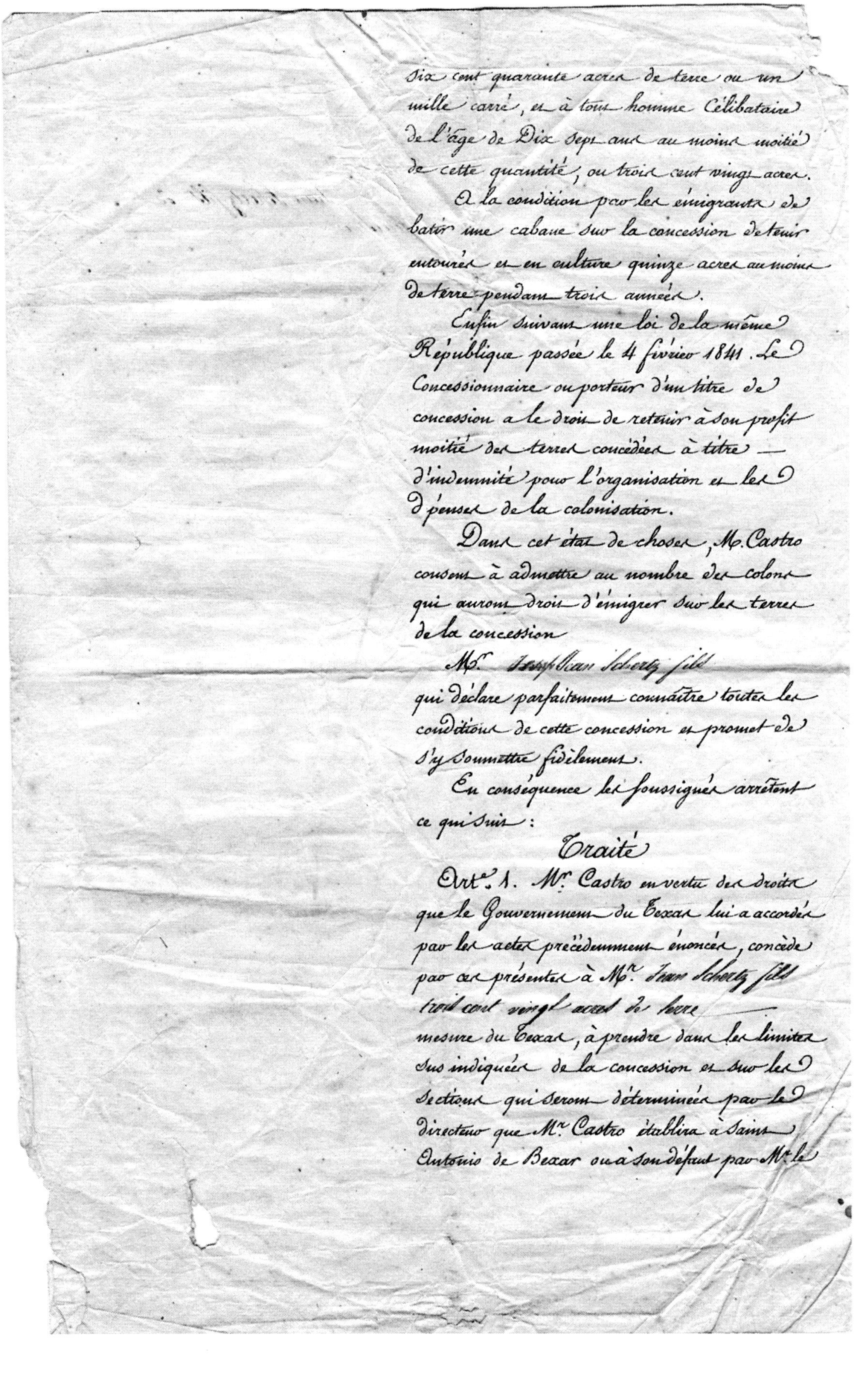

Dix cent quarante acres de terre ou un
mille carré, et à tout homme Célibataire
de l'âge de Dix sept ans au moins moitié
de cette quantité, ou trois cent vingt acres.

A la condition pour les émigrants de
bâtir une cabane sur la concession de tenir
entourées et en culture quinze acres au moins
de terre pendant trois années.

Enfin suivant une loi de la même
République passée le 4 février 1841. Le
Concessionnaire ou porteur d'un titre de
concession a le droit de retenir à son profit
moitié des terres concédées à titre —
d'indemnité pour l'organisation et les
dépenses de la colonisation.

Dans cet état de choses, M. Castro
consent à admettre au nombre des colons
qui auront droit d'émigrer sur les terres
de la concession

Mr. Joseph Jean Schertz fils
qui déclare parfaitement connaître toutes les
conditions de cette concession et promet de
s'y soumettre fidèlement.

En conséquence les soussignés arrêtent
ce qui suit :

Traité

Art. 1. Mr. Castro en vertu des droits
que le Gouvernement du Texas lui a accordés
par les actes précédemment énoncés, concède
par ces présentes à Mr. Jean Schertz fils
trois cent vingt acres de terre
mesure du Texas, à prendre dans les limites
sus indiquées de la concession et sur les
sections qui seront déterminées par le
directeur que Mr. Castro établira à Saint
Antonio de Bexar ou à son défaut par Mr. le

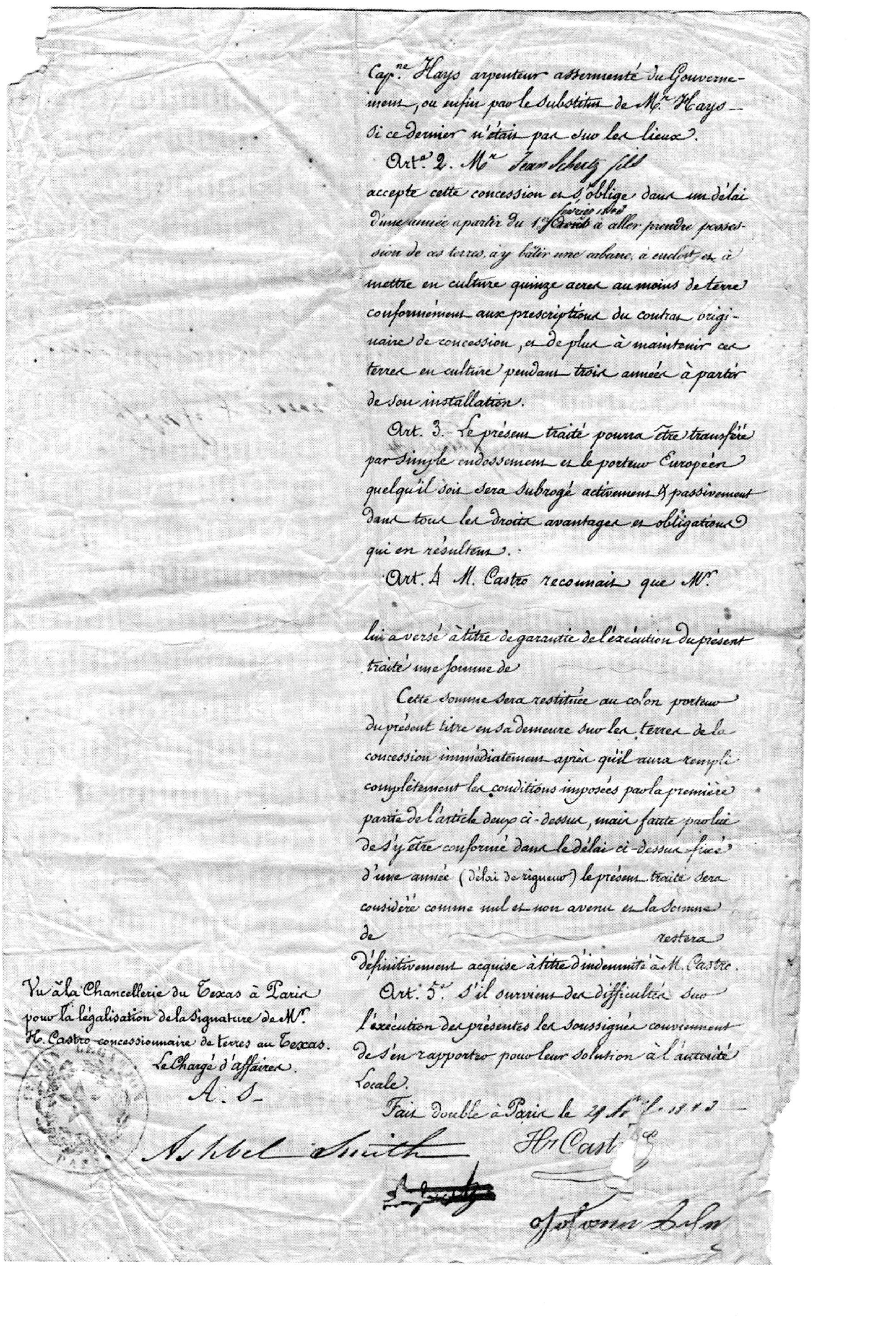

Capne. Hays arpenteur assermenté du Gouvernement, ou enfin par le substitut de Mr. Hays si ce dernier n'était pas sur les lieux.

Artle. 2. Mr. Jean Schertz fils accepte cette concession et s'oblige dans un délai d'une année à partir du 1er février 1844 à aller prendre possession de ces terres, à y bâtir une cabane, à enclore et à mettre en culture quinze acres au moins de terre conformément aux prescriptions du contrat originaire de concession, et de plus à maintenir ces terres en culture pendant trois années à partir de son installation.

Art. 3. Le présent traité pourra être transféré par simple endossement et le porteur Européen quelqu'il soit sera subrogé activement & passivement dans tous les droits avantages et obligations qui en résultent.

Art. 4 M. Castro reconnait que Mr.

lui a versé à titre de garantie de l'exécution du présent traité une somme de

Cette somme sera restituée au colon porteur du présent titre en sa demeure sur les terres de la concession immédiatement après qu'il aura rempli complètement les conditions imposées par la première partie de l'article deux ci-dessus, mais faute par lui de s'y être conformé dans le délai ci-dessus fixé d'une année (délai de rigueur) le présent traité sera considéré comme nul et non avenu et la somme de restera définitivement acquise à titre d'indemnité à M. Castro.

Art. 5e. S'il survient des difficultés sur l'exécution des présentes les soussignés conviennent de s'en rapporter pour leur solution à l'autorité Locale.

Fait double à Paris le 29 Nbre 1843

Vu à la Chancellerie du Texas à Paris pour la légalisation de la signature de Mr. H. Castro concessionnaire de terres au Texas.
Le Chargé d'affaires.
A. S.

Ashbel Smith

H. Castro

Johann Schertz

Et en vertu de la loi du Texas du 4 Février 1841, qui m'autorise à disposer de la moitié de la concession mentionnée ci-dessus, je déclare en considération de la préférence qui m'a été accordée de posséder cette concession, des dépenses de Mr H. Castro faites et à faire, des facilités qu'il m'a données pour mon passage, lui rétrocéder par ces présentes, la moitié des terres que ce Contrat mentionne, cent soixante acres

pour en jouir en toute propriété, me chargeant de remplir les obligations du Contrat en entier.

Riedsheim les jour, mois et an que dessus.

Témoins.

Johannes Schmitz

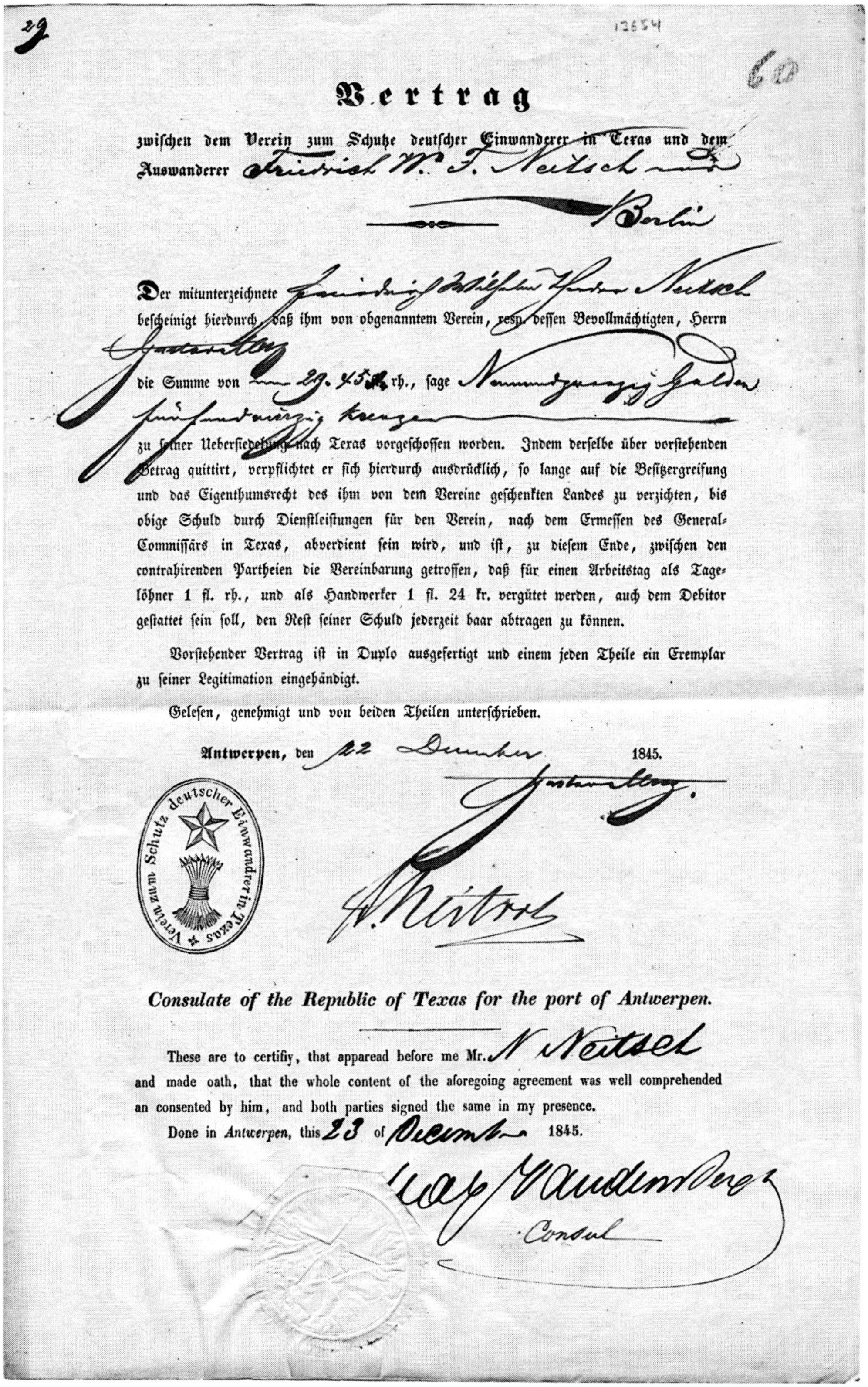

# Vertrag

zwischen dem Verein zum Schutze deutscher Einwanderer in Texas und dem Auswanderer Friedrich W. F. Neitsch aus Berlin

Der mitunterzeichnete bescheinigt hierdurch, daß ihm von obgenanntem Verein, resp. dessen Bevollmächtigten, Herrn die Summe von 29. 45 fl. rh., sage Neunundzwanzig Gulden fünfundvierzig kreuzer zu seiner Uebersiedelung nach Texas vorgeschossen worden. Indem derselbe über vorstehenden Betrag quittirt, verpflichtet er sich hierdurch ausdrücklich, so lange auf die Besitzergreifung und das Eigenthumsrecht des ihm von dem Vereine geschenkten Landes zu verzichten, bis obige Schuld durch Dienstleistungen für den Verein, nach dem Ermessen des General-Commissärs in Texas, abverdient sein wird, und ist, zu diesem Ende, zwischen den contrahirenden Partheien die Vereinbarung getroffen, daß für einen Arbeitstag als Tagelöhner 1 fl. rh., und als Handwerker 1 fl. 24 kr. vergütet werden, auch dem Debitor gestattet sein soll, den Rest seiner Schuld jederzeit baar abtragen zu können.

Vorstehender Vertrag ist in Duplo ausgefertigt und einem jeden Theile ein Exemplar zu seiner Legitimation eingehändigt.

Gelesen, genehmigt und von beiden Theilen unterschrieben.

Antwerpen, den 22 December 1845.

Verein zum Schutz deutscher Einwanderer in Texas

*Consulate of the Republic of Texas for the port of Antwerpen.*

These are to certifiy, that appeared before me Mr. N Neitsel and made oath, that the whole content of the aforegoing agreement was well comprehended an consented by him, and both parties signed the same in my presence.

Done in *Antwerpen*, this 23 of December 1845.

Consul

Figure 62. German Emigrant Contract, Antwerp, 1845. In 1844 the Adelsverein Society of Germany gained control of the Fisher-Miller empresario contract, covering much of the Texas Hill Country but still occupied by native tribes, between the Colorado and San Saba Rivers. Most emigrants elected to settle in one of the three purchased lands rather than the empresario grant within the wilderness. N. Neitsel of Berlin, Germany, signed his emigration contract with the Society at Antwerp on December 22, 1845. The certificate was witnessed by the Texas Consulate in the city. The document displays the Texas Star and Wheat as emblems of independence and industry.

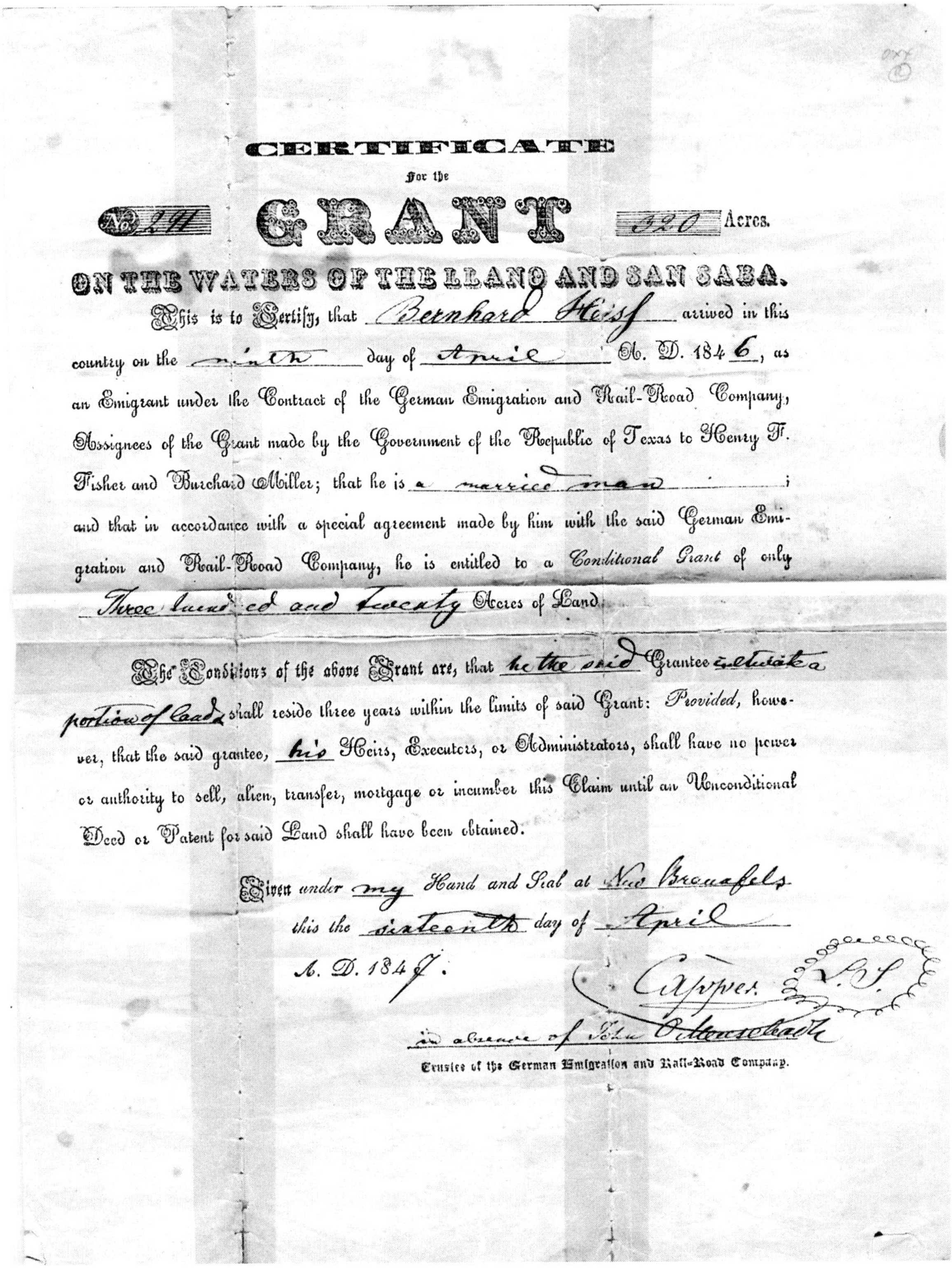

CERTIFICATE

For the

No. 241 GRANT 320 Acres.

ON THE WATERS OF THE LLANO AND SAN SABA.

This is to Certify, that Bernhard Heiss arrived in this country on the ninth day of April A. D. 1846, as an Emigrant under the Contract of the German Emigration and Rail-Road Company, Assignees of the Grant made by the Government of the Republic of Texas to Henry F. Fisher and Burchard Miller; that he is a married man; and that in accordance with a special agreement made by him with the said German Emigration and Rail-Road Company, he is entitled to a Conditional Grant of only Three hundred and twenty Acres of Land.

The Conditions of the above Grant are, that he the said Grantee [illegible] portion of Land shall reside three years within the limits of said Grant: Provided, however, that the said grantee, his Heirs, Executors, or Administrators, shall have no power or authority to sell, alien, transfer, mortgage or incumber this Claim until an Unconditional Deed or Patent for said Land shall have been obtained.

Given under my Hand and Seal at New Braunfels this the sixteenth day of April A. D. 1847.

Cappes. L.S.

in absence of John O. Meusebach

Trustee of the German Emigration and Rail-Road Company.

Figure 63. Conditional Grant of 320 Acres, German Emigration and Rail Road Company, Fisher-Miller Grant, 1847. The original Fisher-Miller contract provided for a thousand settlers from Scandinavia and Germany. The subsequent owner of the grant, the German Emigration and Railroad Company, proposed building a railroad from Indianola to the grant site, and obtained a charter to accomplish that project. Bernard Heiss arrived in Texas April 9, 1846. As a married man with a family he was entitled to a half-section under the terms of his agreement with the Society. Prior to receiving title, Heiss had to reside there for three years, under terms of the April 16, 1849, certificate from the company. More than 5,000 emigrants from Europe responded to the offer of homesteads to willing farmers. Since most preferred living around the German communities rather than in the wilderness, few patents were issued within the Fisher-Miller concession.

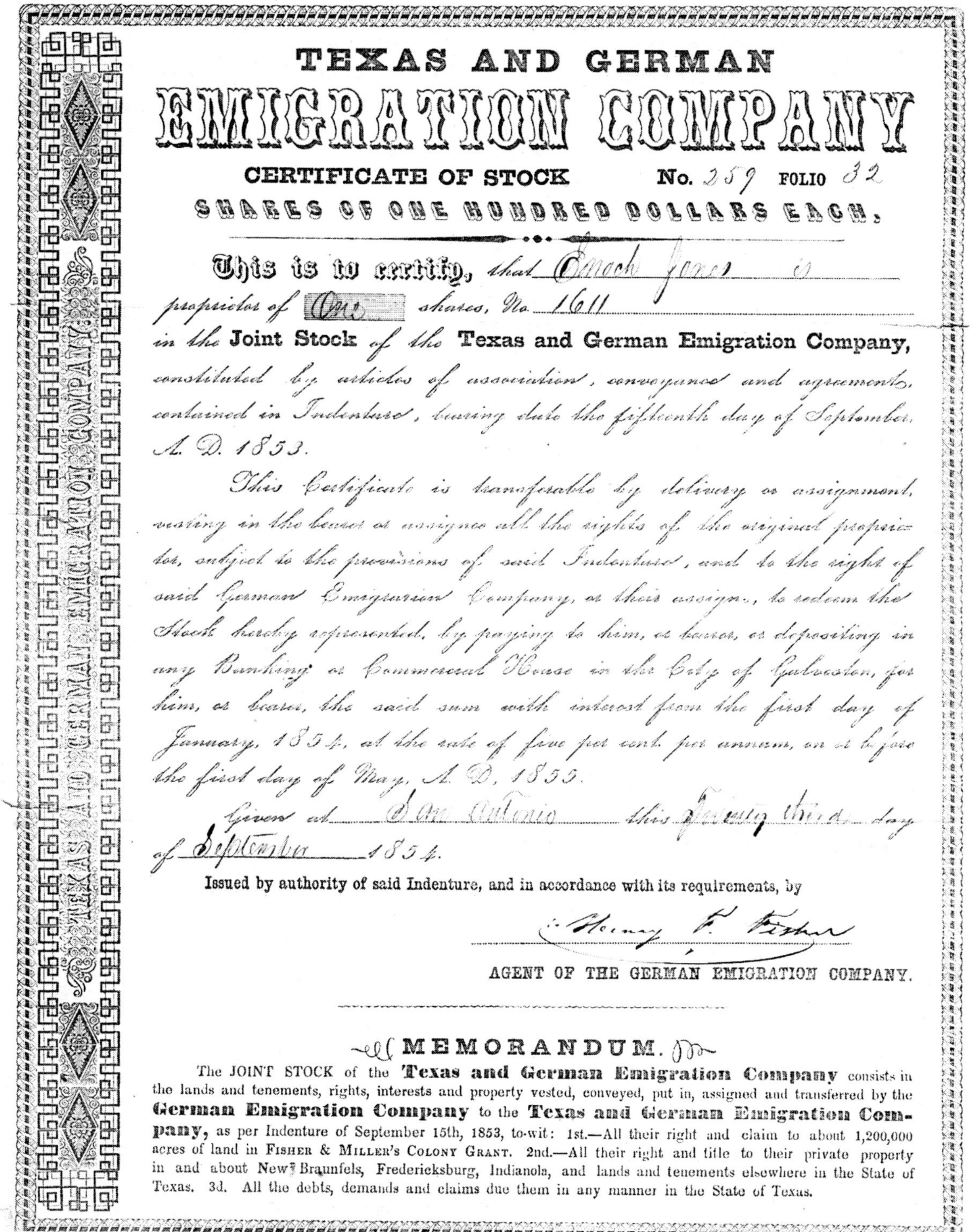

TEXAS AND GERMAN

EMIGRATION COMPANY

CERTIFICATE OF STOCK No. 259 FOLIO 32

SHARES OF ONE HUNDRED DOLLARS EACH.

This is to certify, that Enoch Jones is proprietor of One shares, No. 1611 in the Joint Stock of the Texas and German Emigration Company, constituted by articles of association, conveyance and agreement, contained in Indenture, bearing date the fifteenth day of September, A. D. 1853.

This Certificate is transferable by delivery or assignment, vesting in the bearer or assignee all the rights of the original proprietor, subject to the provisions of said Indenture, and to the right of said German Emigration Company, or their assigns, to redeem the Stock hereby represented, by paying to him, or bearer, or depositing in any Banking or Commercial House in the City of Galveston, for him, or bearer, the said sum with interest from the first day of January, 1854, at the rate of five per cent. per annum, on or before the first day of May, A. D. 1855.

Given at San Antonio this twenty third day of September 1854.

Issued by authority of said Indenture, and in accordance with its requirements, by

Henry F. Fisher

AGENT OF THE GERMAN EMIGRATION COMPANY.

MEMORANDUM.

The JOINT STOCK of the **Texas and German Emigration Company** consists in the lands and tenements, rights, interests and property vested, conveyed, put in, assigned and transferred by the **German Emigration Company** to the **Texas and German Emigration Company**, as per Indenture of September 15th, 1853, to-wit: 1st.—All their right and claim to about 1,200,000 acres of land in Fisher & Miller's Colony Grant. 2nd.—All their right and title to their private property in and about New Braunfels, Fredericksburg, Indianola, and lands and tenements elsewhere in the State of Texas. 3d. All the debts, demands and claims due them in any manner in the State of Texas.

**Figure 64. $100 Stock Certificate for The Texas and German Emigration Company, Houston, 1854. Like so many land companies before, the German Emigration Company failed and was taken over by creditor trustees. In 1853 Henry Fisher regained control of the remaining lands of his grant (1,200,000 acres), plus lots in New Braunfels, Fredericksburg and Indianola. Fisher held a promissory note and foreclosed as a result of delinquencies. Enoch Jones, as a creditor, owned a share of the new Texas and German Emigration Company, of which Henry Fisher was agent in San Antonio. The joint stock company, consisting of $100 par value shares, promised to pay creditors principal and interest from January 1, 1854, at 5 percent.**

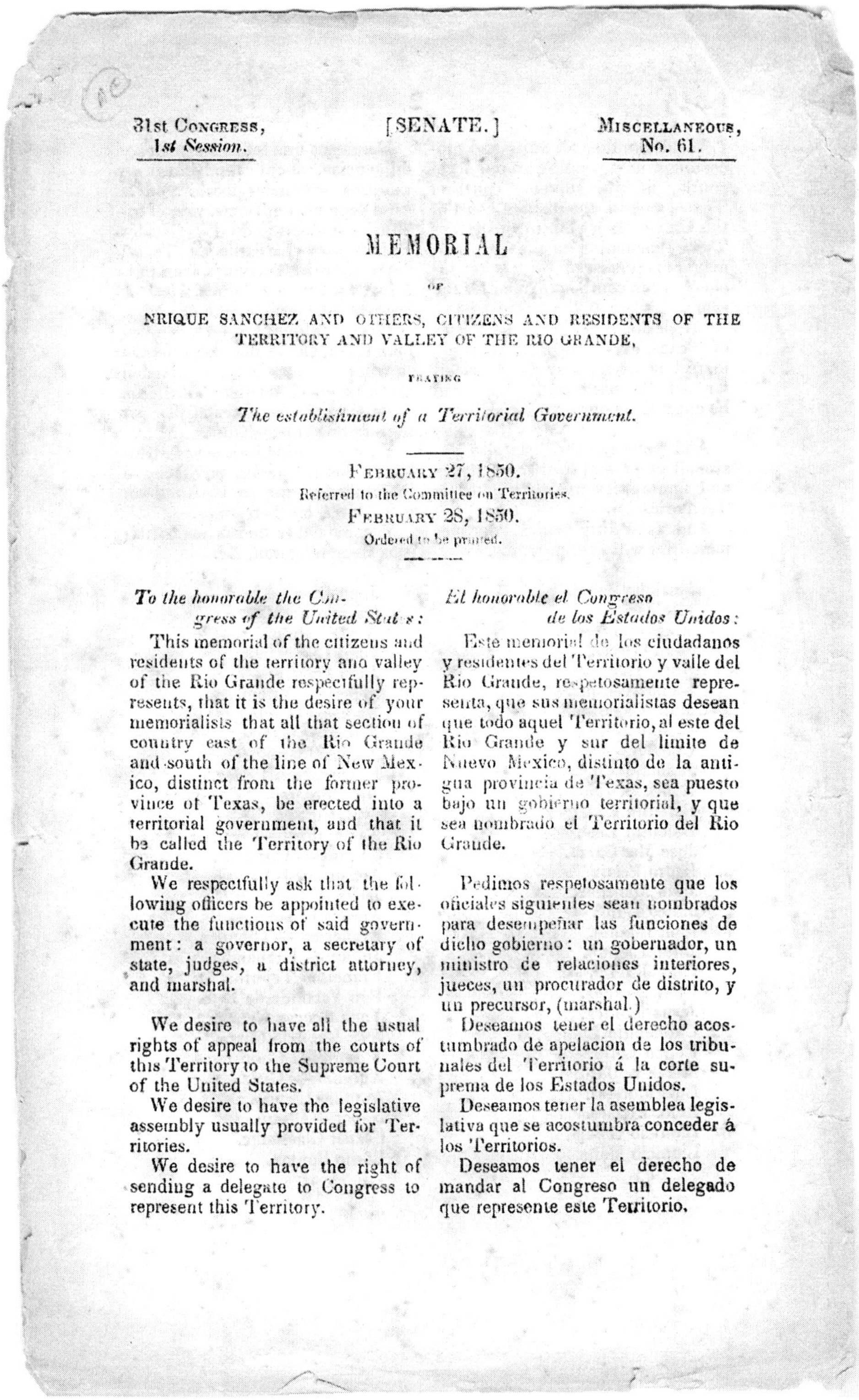

31st Congress, 1st Session. [SENATE.] Miscellaneous, No. 61.

# MEMORIAL

OF

NRIQUE SANCHEZ AND OTHERS, CITIZENS AND RESIDENTS OF THE TERRITORY AND VALLEY OF THE RIO GRANDE,

PRAYING

*The establishment of a Territorial Government.*

February 27, 1850.
Referred to the Committee on Territories.
February 28, 1850.
Ordered to be printed.

*To the honorable the Congress of the United States:*

This memorial of the citizens and residents of the territory and valley of the Rio Grande respectfully represents, that it is the desire of your memorialists that all that section of country east of the Rio Grande and south of the line of New Mexico, distinct from the former province of Texas, be erected into a territorial government, and that it be called the Territory of the Rio Grande.

We respectfully ask that the following officers be appointed to execute the functions of said government: a governor, a secretary of state, judges, a district attorney, and marshal.

We desire to have all the usual rights of appeal from the courts of this Territory to the Supreme Court of the United States.

We desire to have the legislative assembly usually provided for Territories.

We desire to have the right of sending a delegate to Congress to represent this Territory.

*El honorable el Congreso de los Estados Unidos:*

Este memorial de los ciudadanos y residentes del Territorio y valle del Rio Grande, respetosamente representa, que sus memorialistas desean que todo aquel Territorio, al este del Rio Grande y sur del limite de Nuevo Mexico, distinto de la antigua provincia de Texas, sea puesto bajo un gobierno territorial, y que sea nombrado el Territorio del Rio Grande.

Pedimos respetosamente que los oficiales siguientes sean nombrados para desempeñar las funciones de dicho gobierno: un gobernador, un ministro de relaciones interiores, jueces, un procurador de distrito, y un precursor, (marshal.)

Deseamos tener el derecho acostumbrado de apelacion de los tribunales del Territorio á la corte suprema de los Estados Unidos.

Deseamos tener la asemblea legislativa que se acostumbra conceder á los Territorios.

Deseamos tener el derecho de mandar al Congreso un delegado que represente este Territorio.

**Figure 65 (this page and following two). Memorial to Congress from Citizens and Residents of the Territory and Valley of the Rio Grande, 1850. After the Treaty of Guadalupe-Hidalgo in 1848 but before the Gadsen Purchase (Treaty of Mesilla), in 1852, residents living within the Trans-Pecos region became concerned for their land if ownership was to be determined by the laws of Texas rather than those of the United States. On February 20, 1850, a group of Hispanic residents, formerly of the State of Chihuahua, filed a Memorial with the U.S. Congress requesting severance from Texas and the creation of a new territory. Their organizational request provided for a governor, secretary of state, district attorney, marshal, legislature and representatives in Congress. They named their new government the Territory of the Valley of the Rio Grande. The one hundred citizens petitioned Congress to apply Mexican rather than Texas real estate law. All were fearful of the Texas loyalty oath covering the time of the Revolution. The petition failed.**

[ 61 ] 2

We desire that all suits and proceedings now pending in our local courts, in the supreme court of Texas, and in the district court of the United States for the district of Texas, emanating in the Territory, may be transferred by "*scire facias*" to the courts provided for the same.

We desire that the present laws of Texas, excepting such as relate to real property, may be provided for said Territory, until others can be enacted by our own legislature.

And your memorialists also desire all other and further privileges and immunities usually granted to Territories.

And, as in duty bound, your memorialists will ever pray, &c.

Deseamos que todos los juicios y diligencias, ahora pendientes en nuestros tribunales locales, en la corte suprema de Texas, y en el tribunal de distrito de los Estados Unidos para el distrito de Texas, dimanando del Territorio, sean tráspasados por "*scire facias*" á los tribunales establecidos para él.

Deseamos que las leyes que ahora rigen en Texas, esceptuando aquellas relativas á fincas, queden vigentes en el referido Territorio, hasta que otras sean decretadas por nuestra propia legislatura.

Y sus memorialistas desean tambien todos los demas privilegios é inmunidades que se acostumbran mercedar á los Territorios.

Y como deber de sus memorialistas siempre oraran, &c.

Enrique Sanchez.
Migl. Santos.
Angelino Flores.
Juan Garcia.
Anto Espanza.
Ramoz Garnaz.
Man. Cabarina.
Cosmi Forres.
Calletano Martinez.
Juan Ant. Perrez.
Bonif. O. Rodarigues.
Balentin Radaigez.
Balentin Leal.
Jose Ma. Garza.
Pedro Pelaiz.
Juan Martinez.
Mateo Luna.
Rafl. Liendo.
Anto. Liendo.
Cornelio Til.
Fran. Montes.
Jesus Montes.
Candelario Liendo.
Felipe Lollá.
Meree Lolla.
Luis Morales.
Refo. Fozacs.
Lionicio Garcia.
Lionicio Malla.

Juan Rios.
Nasario Amador.
Ygn. Mendez.
Juan Carabajal.
Juan Cabrera.
Seberiano Rubio.
Atanacio Garcia.
Leonardo Garcia.
Atanacio Rubio.
Encarnacion Perrez.
Juan Perrez.
Rafl. Cortinas.
Nessomuzeno Cortinas.
Suliant + Gonzalis.
Anastacio + Cortez.
Jesus + Gusman.
Andres Gusman.
Francisco + Ciharles.
Julian + Hernandez.
Francisco Tejerina.
Pon Vabonde da Este.
Vana Goceas Cohea.
José Ma. dela Garza.
Y Pormi la Comismo.
Antonio + Cruz.
Antonio Liendo.
Nabor + Olgun.
Caspar Glaescoke.
Berito Bontaz.

3 [ 61 ]

Jose Maria Menchan.
Santos Olibares.
Juan Belaz.
Migl. Lanaz.
Ygno. Alderetez.
Gualupe Martinez.
Anto. Fijerino.
Juan Forres.
Carlos Lasoz.
Albino Cabasosez.
Narciso Martinez.
Bicente Ballego.
Joze Ma. Ballego.
Bicente + Forres.
Juan Estrak.
Pablo Forres.
Simon Gonzales.
Grego. Briseño.
Anto. Briseño.
Ant. Losano.
Jose Riojas.
Leandro Martinez.
Luis Gonzalis.
Juan Ramirez.

Roman Sanchez.
Gregorio Rodriguez.
Lleto Sabinas.
Juan Waldez.
Juan Cantu.
Selustriano Cantu.
Jesus Morena.
Rafael Moralis.
Andres Leal.
Pantaleon Torris.
Lucias Torris.
Eustagecio Cantu.
Patricio Ramirez.
Antonio Garza.
Felipe Garza.
Selustriano Floris.
Sabas Garza.
Felipe Villerreal.
Pedro Esparza.
Carlos Esparza.
Thomas Cabrera.
Mariano Lisondo.
J. P. McDonough.
J. G. Browne.

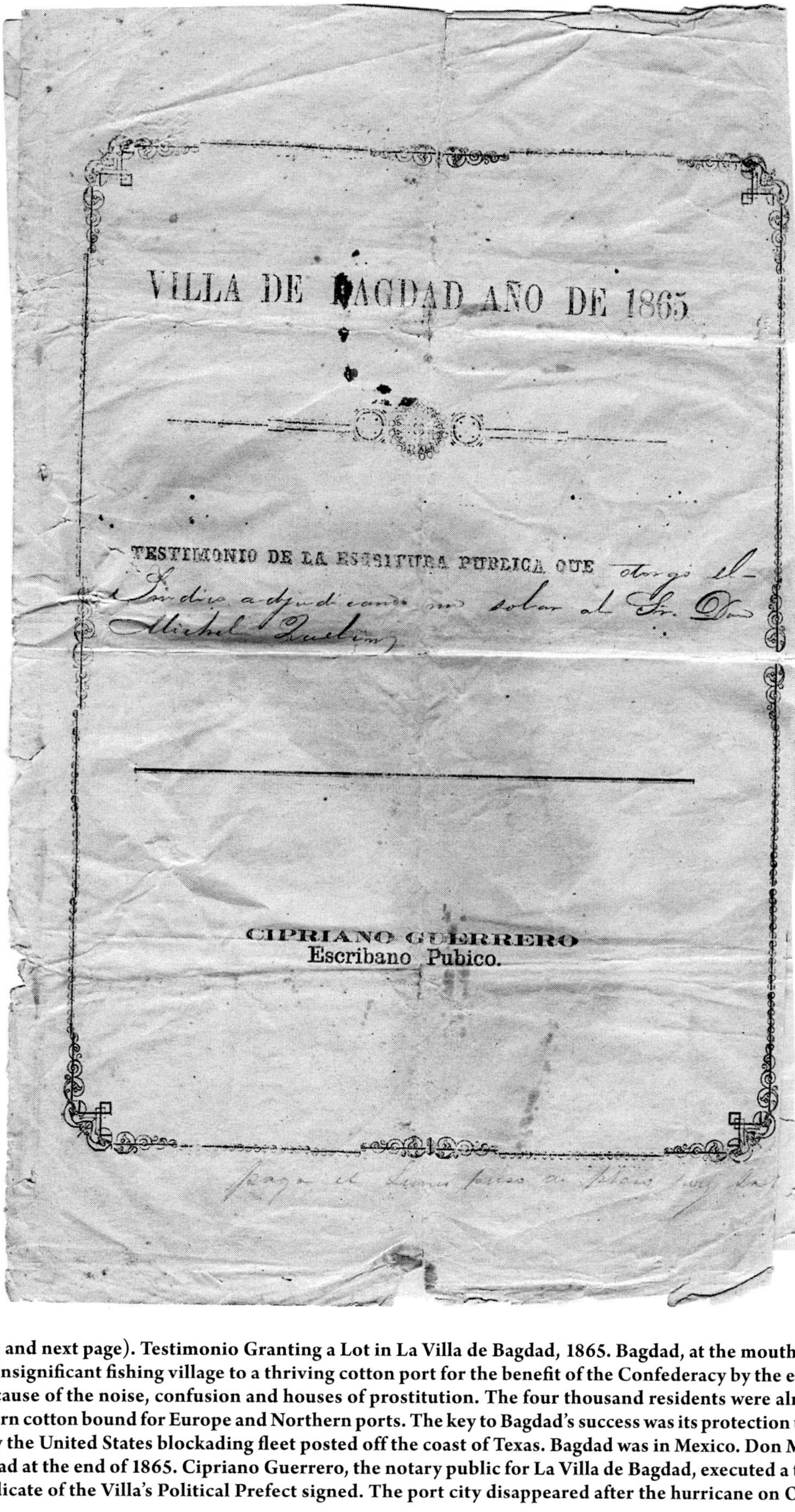
VILLA DE BAGDAD AÑO DE 1865

TESTIMONIO DE LA ESCRITURA PUBLICA QUE otorgó el Sindico adjudicando un solar al Sr. Don Michel Quelin

CIPRIANO GUERRERO
Escribano Pubico.

**Figure 66 (this page and next page). Testimonio Granting a Lot in La Villa de Bagdad, 1865. Bagdad, at the mouth of the Rio Grande, had grown from an insignificant fishing village to a thriving cotton port for the benefit of the Confederacy by the end of the Civil War. Known as Babel because of the noise, confusion and houses of prostitution. The four thousand residents were almost all involved in the export of Southern cotton bound for Europe and Northern ports. The key to Bagdad's success was its protection under international law from seizures by the United States blockading fleet posted off the coast of Texas. Bagdad was in Mexico. Don Michael Quelin purchased a lot in Bagdad at the end of 1865. Cipriano Guerrero, the notary public for La Villa de Bagdad, executed a testimonio for him. The Municipal Syndicate of the Villa's Political Prefect signed. The port city disappeared after the hurricane on October 6, 1867.**

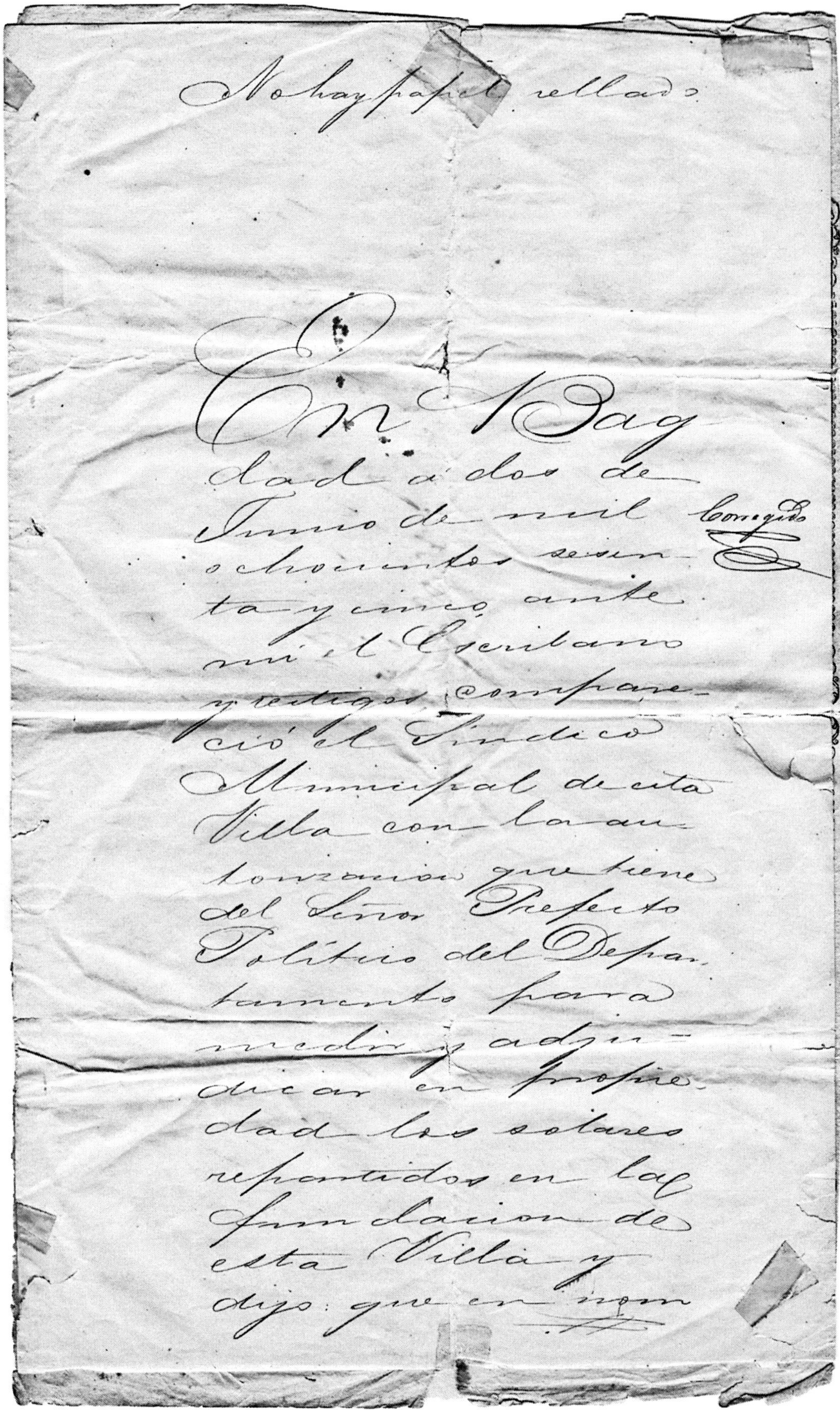
No hay papel sellado

En Bag
dad á dos de
Junio de mil
ochocientos sesen
ta y cinco ante
mí el Escribano
y testigos compare-
ció el Síndico
Municipal de esta
Villa con la au
torización que tiene
del Señor Prefecto
Político del Depar
tamento para
medir y adju-
dicar en propie-
dad los solares
repartidos en la
fundacion de
esta Villa y
dijo: que en nom

Corregido

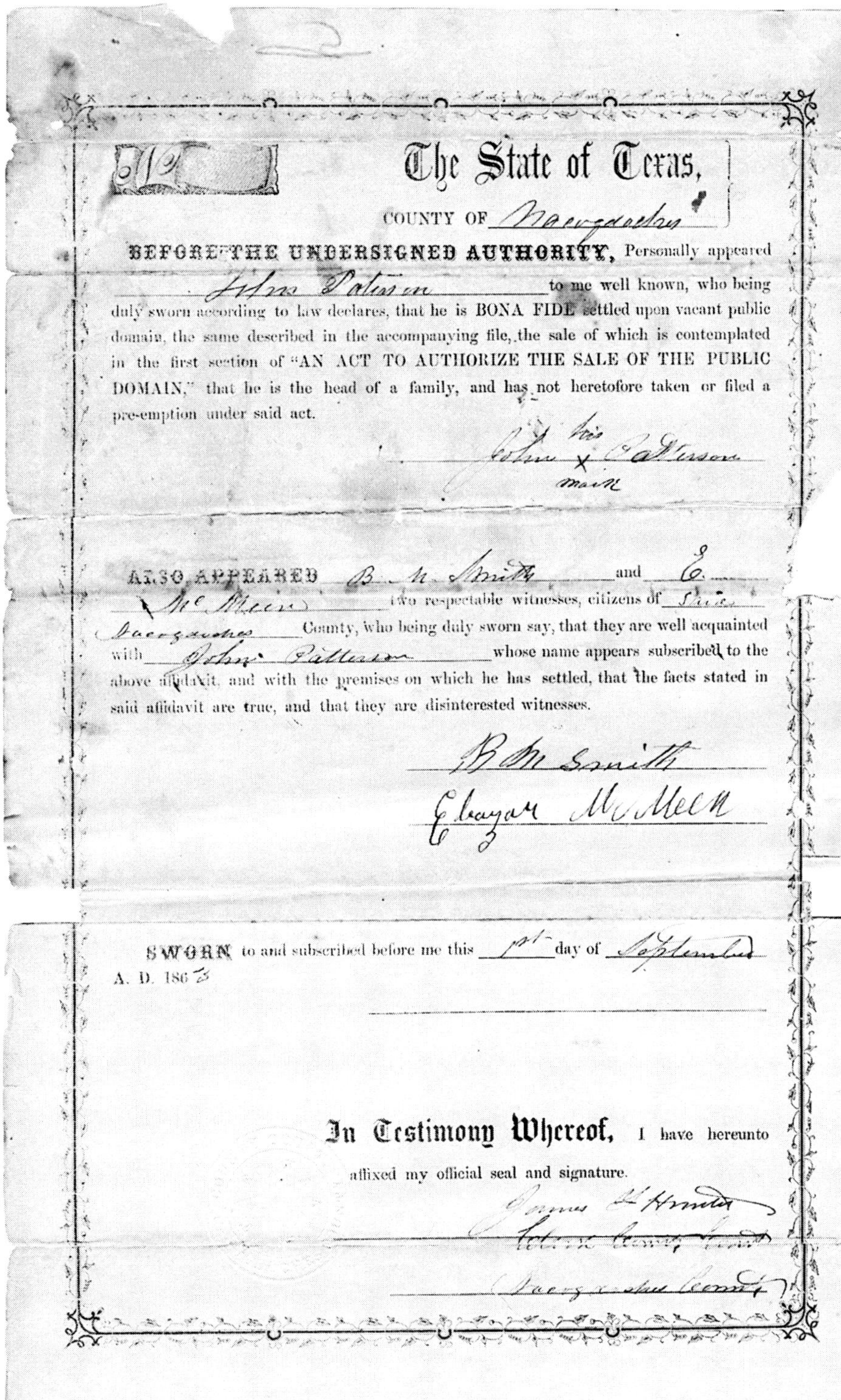

The State of Texas,

COUNTY OF Nacogdoches

BEFORE THE UNDERSIGNED AUTHORITY, Personally appeared John Paterson to me well known, who being duly sworn according to law declares, that he is BONA FIDE settled upon vacant public domain, the same described in the accompanying file, the sale of which is contemplated in the first section of "AN ACT TO AUTHORIZE THE SALE OF THE PUBLIC DOMAIN," that he is the head of a family, and has not heretofore taken or filed a pre-emption under said act.

John his x mark Patterson

ALSO APPEARED B. M. Smith and E. McMeen two respectable witnesses, citizens of State Nacogdoches County, who being duly sworn say, that they are well acquainted with John Patterson whose name appears subscribed to the above affidavit, and with the premises on which he has settled, that the facts stated in said affidavit are true, and that they are disinterested witnesses.

B M Smith

Eleazar McMeen

SWORN to and subscribed before me this 1st day of September A. D. 1863

In Testimony Whereof, I have hereunto affixed my official seal and signature.

James L. Hunter

Clk. Co. County Court

Nacogdoches County

**Figure 67. Head of Family Affidavit for Pre-Emption Land, Nacogdoches County, 1863. Private and government land sales nearly ceased during the Civil War. More common were foreclosures for delinquent Confederate and Texas taxes. Foreclosed land often was returned to the public domain. A few moved their families and slaves to Texas during the war. In 1863, John Patterson, Sr., a veteran of the Texas Revolution, applied and received bounty land for honorable service. His son applied for a homestead in Nacogdoches on September 1, 1863. He swore he was a bona fide settler on vacant public land, was head of a family and had never applied for a pre-emption, as required by "An Act to Authorize the Sale of the Public Domain." Two witnesses swore to the truth of his affidavit.**

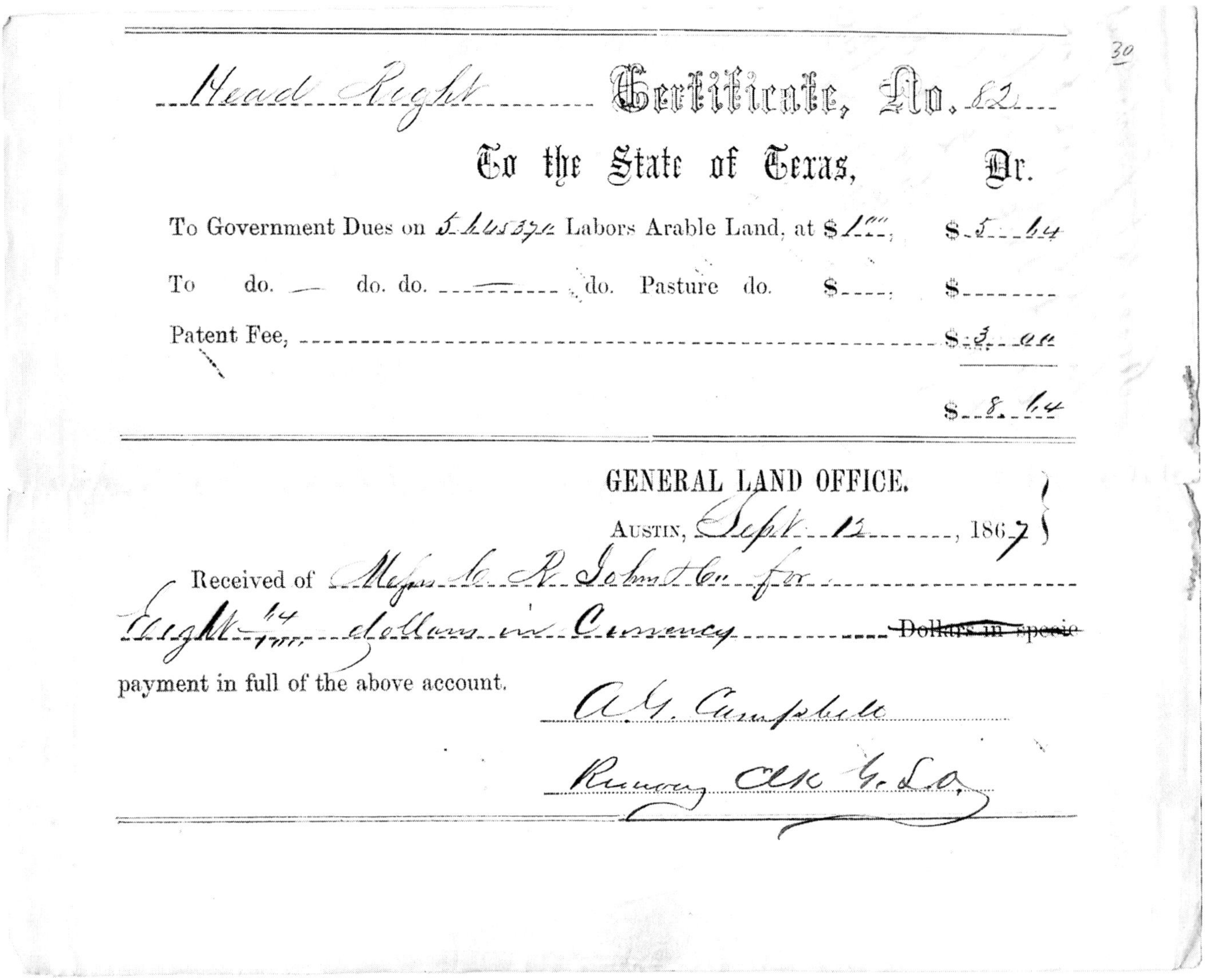

Head Right Certificate, No. 82

To the State of Texas, Dr.

To Government Dues on 5.64 37/100 Labors Arable Land, at $1.00, $5.64

To do. — do. do. ——— do. Pasture do. $ $

Patent Fee, $3.00

$8.64

GENERAL LAND OFFICE.

AUSTIN, Sept. 12, 1867

Received of Messrs C. R. John & Co. for

Eight 64/100 dollars in Currency ~~Dollars in specie~~

payment in full of the above account.

A. G. Campbell

Ransey Clk G. L. O.

**Figure 68. Receipt for Government Dues on 5.64 Labors and Patent Fee from G.L.O., Austin, 1867. After the Civil War, many Texans faced tax foreclosures for their failure to pay state taxes. Moratoriums were granted veterans and their families. C.R. John tendered $8.64 to the General Land Office to bring current the government dues outstanding on 5.64 labors of arable land acquired. Included was $3.00 for a patent to his homestead. The headright was originally issued to Samuel Highlander.**

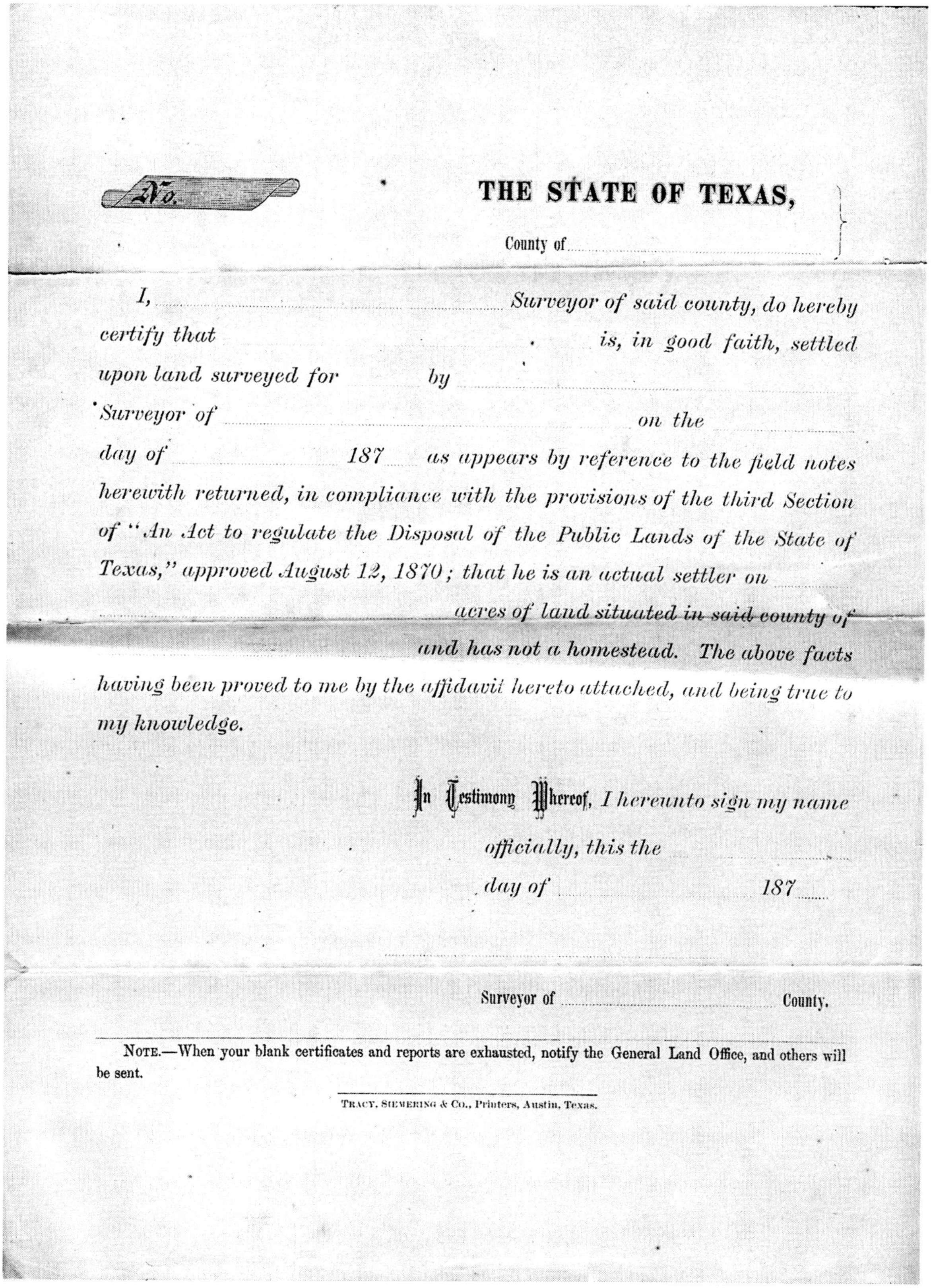

No.

THE STATE OF TEXAS,

County of ..........

*I, .......... Surveyor of said county, do hereby certify that .......... is, in good faith, settled upon land surveyed for .......... by .......... Surveyor of .......... on the .......... day of .......... 187.... as appears by reference to the field notes herewith returned, in compliance with the provisions of the third Section of "An Act to regulate the Disposal of the Public Lands of the State of Texas," approved August 12, 1870; that he is an actual settler on .......... acres of land situated in said county of .......... and has not a homestead. The above facts having been proved to me by the affidavit hereto attached, and being true to my knowledge.*

In Testimony Whereof, *I hereunto sign my name officially, this the .......... day of .......... 187....*

..........

Surveyor of .......... County.

Note.—When your blank certificates and reports are exhausted, notify the General Land Office, and others will be sent.

Tracy, Siemering & Co., Printers, Austin, Texas.

**Figure 69. Surveyor Affidavit [Blank] Under Homesteader Act of August 12, 1870. The 1879 Texas Legislature modified the pre-emption statute. Every man not possessed of state-granted homesteads or headrights was qualified to purchase pre-emption land at a dollar an acre, plus the cost of a survey, government dues and patent fee. County surveyors first had to swear that prospective homesteaders had "in good faith settled upon the land surveyed." The General Land Office supplied certificates for the county surveyor. The surveyor attached his field notes to the certificate before filing in the General Land Office.**

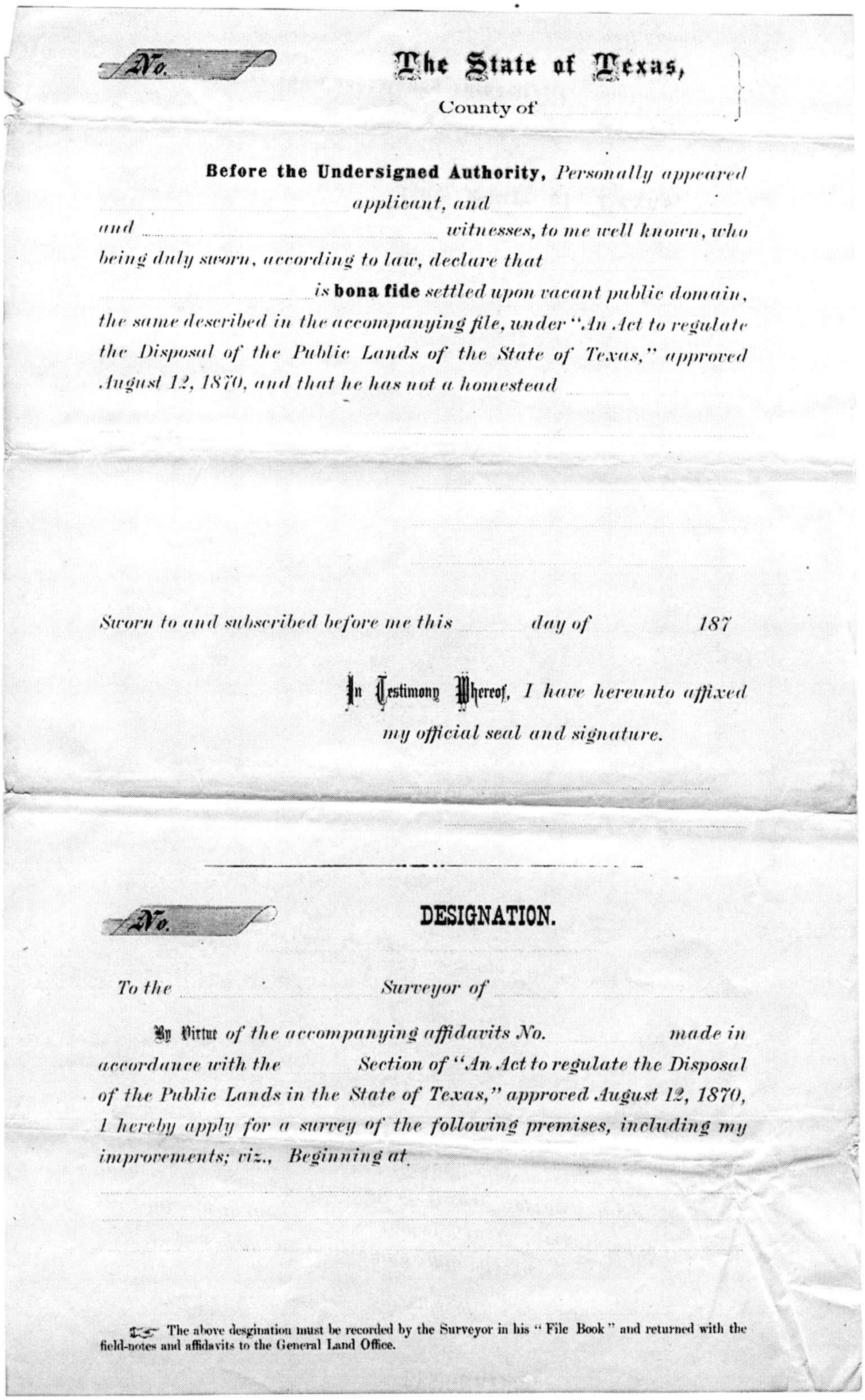

No.

**The State of Texas,**

County of

**Before the Undersigned Authority,** *Personally appeared*
*applicant, and*
*and* *witnesses, to me well known, who being duly sworn, according to law, declare that*
*is* **bona fide** *settled upon vacant public domain, the same described in the accompanying file, under "An Act to regulate the Disposal of the Public Lands of the State of Texas," approved August 12, 1870, and that he has not a homestead*

*Sworn to and subscribed before me this* *day of* *187*

In Testimony Whereof, *I have hereunto affixed my official seal and signature.*

No.

**DESIGNATION.**

*To the* *Surveyor of*

By Virtue *of the accompanying affidavits No.* *made in accordance with the* *Section of "An Act to regulate the Disposal of the Public Lands in the State of Texas," approved August 12, 1870, I hereby apply for a survey of the following premises, including my improvements; viz., Beginning at*

☞ The above designation must be recorded by the Surveyor in his "File Book" and returned with the field-notes and affidavits to the General Land Office.

**Figure 70. Settlement Affidavit [Blank] Under Homesteader Act of August 12, 1870. The first required step for claiming pre-emption land was to appear, take an oath, sign and seal before two witnesses as a bona fide settler on the vacant public land. The two subscribing witnesses had to be familiar enough with the settler to confirm all the facts as required under the Act of August 12, 1870. A county official took the oaths. Once completed, the official would inform the county surveyor of the affidavits and order a survey of the described premises and improvements. The surveyor, upon completion of his field notes, would record a copy in the "File Book." The package would be filed in the General Land Office.**

File 1919 Bexar 1st Class

No. 79 Vol. 25

IN THE NAME OF THE STATE OF TEXAS

To all to whom these Presents shall come, know ye

I L. S. Ross GOVERNOR of the STATE aforesaid, by virtue of the power vested in me by LAW and in accordance with the LAWS of SAID STATE in such case made and provided, do by these presents GRANT to Uvalde County heirs or assigns FOREVER, Three Million Fifty eight Thousand Three Hundred & Eighty five (3,058,385) Sq. vs. of LAND, situated and described as follows: In Bexar & Uvalde Counties known as sur. No. 9 on the waters of Turkey Creek a tributary of Nueces River about 15 miles S 59 W. of Uvalde, In accordance with an act Appropriating certain lands for the establishment of a general system of Education Approved Jany 26, 1839 and an act making additional appropriations of lands for the purposes of Education Approved Jany 16th 1850. Beginning at a stake on the W. line of sur. No. 3 Uvalde Co. School Land 518½ vs. from N. W. to S. W. cor. Thence N 29 W. with W. line of sd. sur. 829 vs. ... [illegible]

Thence [illegible] ... to the place of beginning. Bearings marked ...

Hereby relinquishing to the said Uvalde County and heirs or assigns FOREVER all the right and title in and to said LAND, heretofore held and possessed by the said STATE, and do hereby issue this Letter Patent for the same.

IN TESTIMONY WHEREOF I have caused the SEAL of the STATE to be affixed as well as the SEAL of the GENERAL LAND OFFICE.

DONE at the City of Austin on the Seventeenth day of April In the Year of our Lord One thousand eight hundred and Ninety

R. M. Hall Commissioner of the G. L. Office. L. S. Ross Governor.

JOS. A. NAGLE STATIONER AUSTIN, TEXAS

Figure 71. 1890 Land Patent for School Land, Uvalde County, Governor L. S. Ross, Under Acts of January 26, 1839, and January 16, 1850. Homesteaders could elect to acquire not only vacant lands in the public domain, but also patented land held for the benefit of schools, universities and asylums. Governor Sul Ross, in 1890, signed a patent for the benefit of Uvalde County schools in the amount of 3,058,385 square varas, or about 541 acres. Most were patented in half- and quarter-section parcels. Uvalde also had school lands scattered among several other West Texas counties.

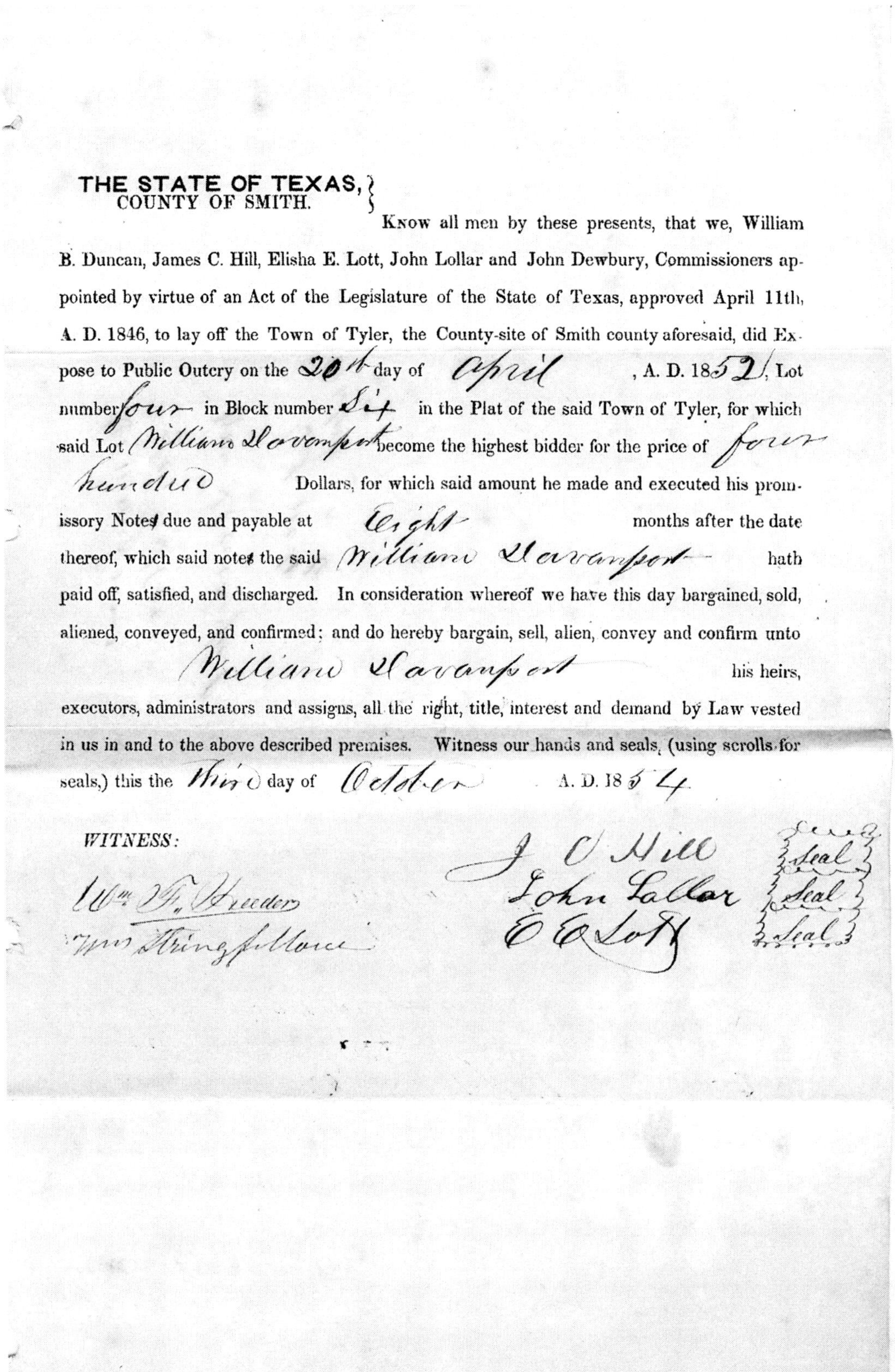

THE STATE OF TEXAS, }
COUNTY OF SMITH. }

KNOW all men by these presents, that we, William B. Duncan, James C. Hill, Elisha E. Lott, John Lollar and John Dewbury, Commissioners appointed by virtue of an Act of the Legislature of the State of Texas, approved April 11th, A. D. 1846, to lay off the Town of Tyler, the County-site of Smith county aforesaid, did Expose to Public Outcry on the 20th day of April, A. D. 1852, Lot number four in Block number Six in the Plat of the said Town of Tyler, for which said Lot William Davenport become the highest bidder for the price of four hundred Dollars, for which said amount he made and executed his promissory Note due and payable at Eight months after the date thereof, which said note the said William Davenport hath paid off, satisfied, and discharged. In consideration whereof we have this day bargained, sold, aliened, conveyed, and confirmed; and do hereby bargain, sell, alien, convey and confirm unto William Davanport his heirs, executors, administrators and assigns, all the right, title, interest and demand by Law vested in us in and to the above described premises. Witness our hands and seals, (using scrolls for seals,) this the Third day of October A. D. 1854.

*WITNESS:*

Wm. F. Freeder
Wm Stringfellow

J. C. Hill {Seal}
John Lollar {Seal}
E. E. Lott {Seal}

**Figure 72. Contract for Auctioned Town Lot in Tyler, Act of April 11, 1846, Smith County, 1852. As new counties were organized, county seats had to be chartered if none were already existing. In East Texas, after Smith County was formed by the Legislature in 1846, the State had to purchase a town site for the county seat of Tyler. The $150 price proved a bargain. The State held a public auction of lots after the survey of twenty-eight blocks. William Davenport was the high bidder on lot 4, block 6. The $400.00 purchase was evidenced by a promissory note deferring payment for eight months, signed October 3, 1854.**

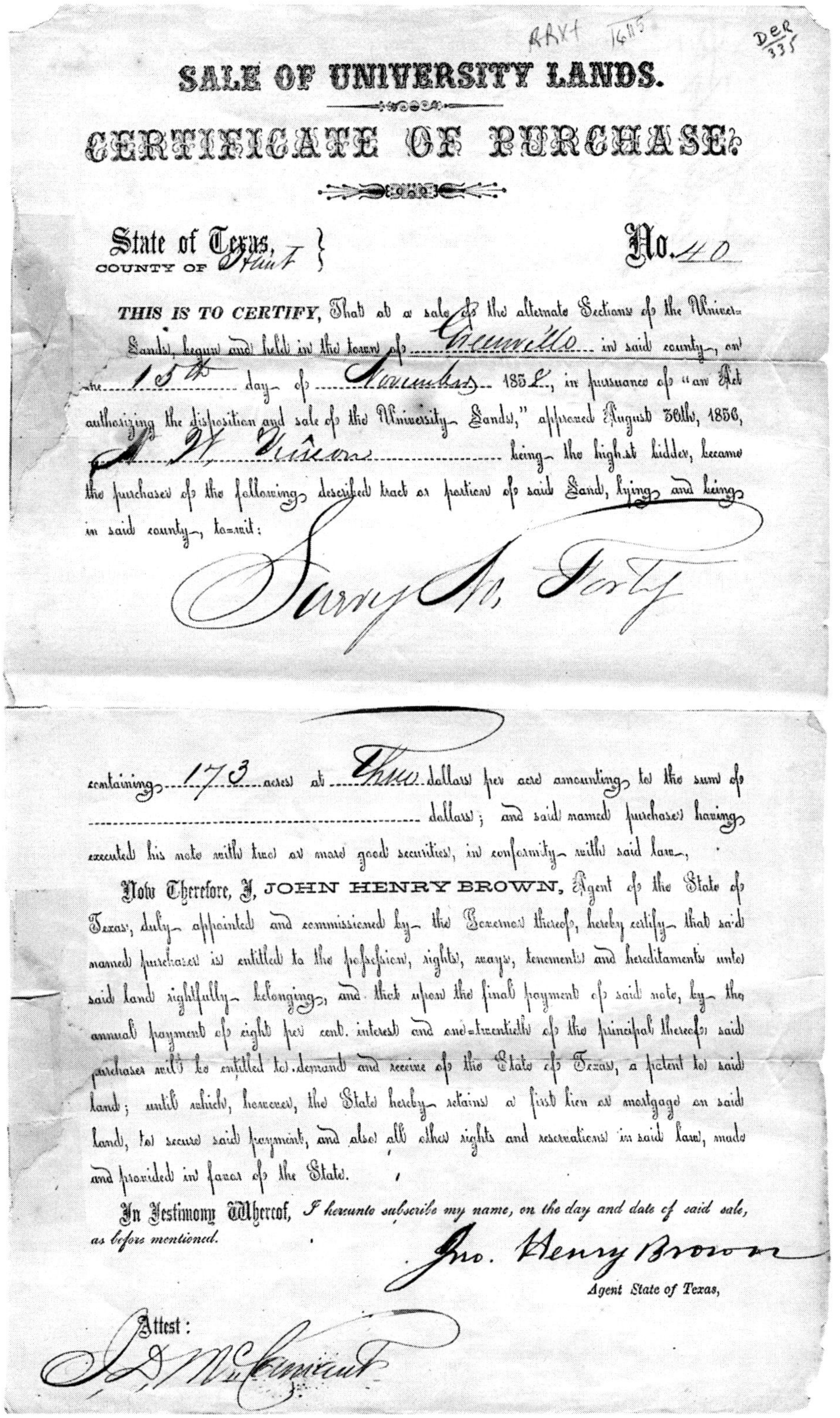

RRX4 1615 DER 335

SALE OF UNIVERSITY LANDS.

CERTIFICATE OF PURCHASE.

State of Texas, } No. 40
COUNTY OF Hunt }

*THIS IS TO CERTIFY,* That at a sale of the alternate Sections of the University Lands, begun and held in the town of Greenville in said county, on the 15th day of November 1858, in pursuance of "an Act authorizing the disposition and sale of the University Lands," approved August 30th, 1856, W. Vinson being the highest bidder, became the purchaser of the following described tract or portion of said Land, lying and being in said county, to-wit:

Survey No. Forty

containing 173 acres at Three dollars per acre amounting to the sum of ............ dollars; and said named purchaser having executed his note with two or more good securities, in conformity with said law,

Now Therefore, I, JOHN HENRY BROWN, Agent of the State of Texas, duly appointed and commissioned by the Governor thereof, hereby certify that said named purchaser is entitled to the possession, rights, ways, tenements and hereditaments unto said land rightfully belonging, and that upon the final payment of said note, by the annual payment of eight per cent. interest and one-twentieth of the principal thereof, said purchaser will be entitled to demand and receive of the State of Texas, a patent to said land; until which, however, the State hereby retains a first lien or mortgage on said land, to secure said payment, and also all other rights and reservations in said law, made and provided in favor of the State.

In Testimony Whereof, *I hereunto subscribe my name, on the day and date of said sale, as before mentioned.*

Jno. Henry Brown

*Agent State of Texas,*

Attest:

J. D. McClement

**Figure 73. Certificate of Purchase of University Lands Under Act of August 30, 1856, Hunt County, 1858. Texas had long promised land amounting to fifty leagues to help fund state universities. It took years to complete that promise. The patented land was situated all over the state, most in far West Texas and the Panhandle. University land located in Hunt County was surveyed into 160-acre parcels. A public auction was held in Greenville in 1858. Terms were favorable, allowing twenty years to pay at 8 percent interest. Almost unique as compared to other sales, successful bidders had to post a surety bond for deferred payments. Often this proviso was ignored or not enforced. Jm. Henry Brown, agent for the State, formalized the sale of 173 acres for $3.00 an acre to W. Vinson on November 15, 1858. The sale was conducted under the law of August 30, 1856, allowing the disposal of university lands to the public at auction.**

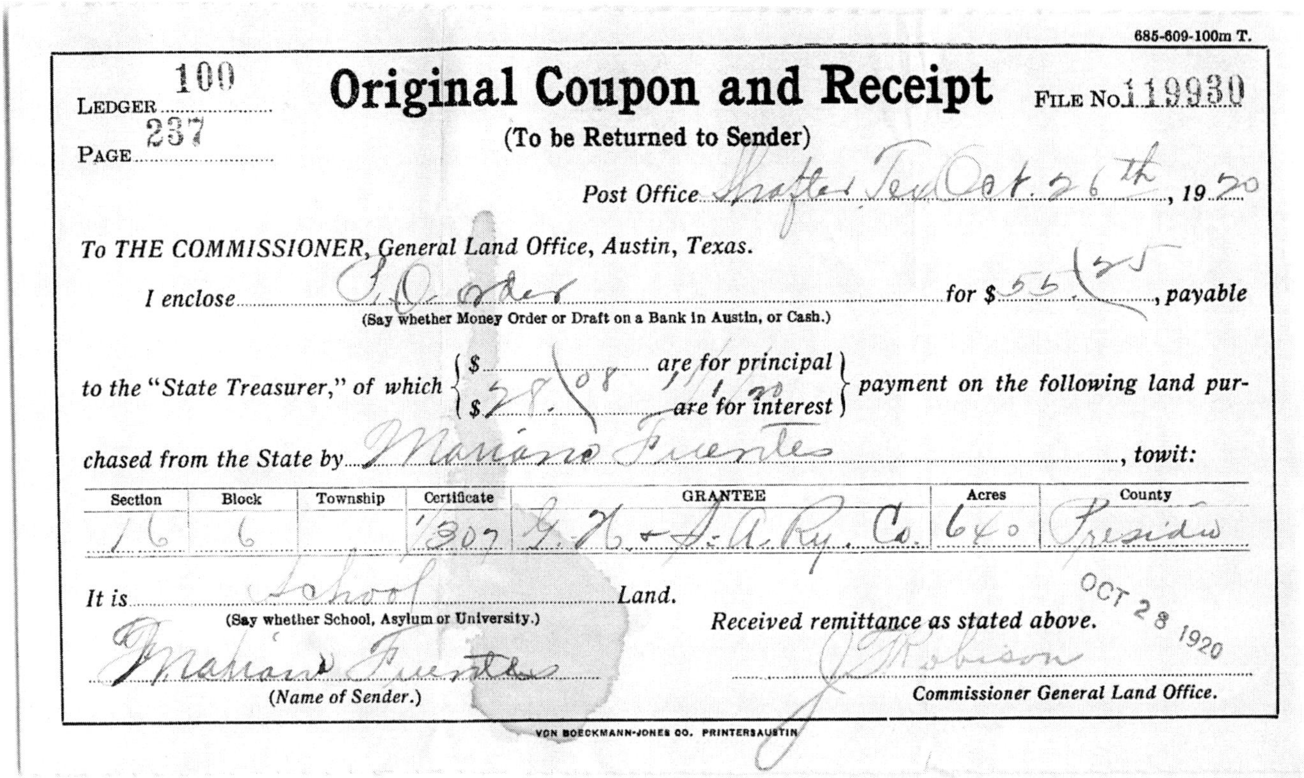

685-609-100m T.

# Original Coupon and Receipt

LEDGER 100
PAGE 237
FILE No. 119930

(To be Returned to Sender)

Post Office Shafter, Tex Oct. 26th, 1920

*To THE COMMISSIONER, General Land Office, Austin, Texas.*

*I enclose* P. O. order *for $* 55.35, *payable*

(Say whether Money Order or Draft on a Bank in Austin, or Cash.)

*to the "State Treasurer," of which* $ ........ *are for principal*, $ 28.08 11/1/20 *are for interest* *payment on the following land purchased from the State by* Mariano Fuentes, *towit:*

| Section | Block | Township | Certificate | GRANTEE | Acres | County |
|---|---|---|---|---|---|---|
| 16 | 6 | | 1/307 | G. H. & S. A. Ry. Co. | 640 | Presidio |

*It is* School *Land.*

(Say whether School, Asylum or University.)

*Received remittance as stated above.* OCT 28 1920

Mariano Fuentes
*(Name of Sender.)*

J. T. Robison
*Commissioner General Land Office.*

VON BOECKMANN-JONES CO. PRINTERS AUSTIN

**Figure 74. Receipt, Purchase of School, Asylum and University Lands, Presidio County, 1920. Even after the General Land Office declared the Texas public domain exhausted, new homesteaders continued to purchase small farms from state agencies. Lands previously patented for the benefit of schools, universities and asylums was priced to qualifying farmers and small ranchers at around $2.50 per acre through the twentieth century. Finances could extend forty years, bearing 5 percent interest. It was not uncommon for large ranch owners to register their ranch hands to vote; afterward, each of the hired hands would purchase a quarter or half-section of school, university or asylum lands. Such schemes were in violation of the intent of the law because the rancher would take an assignment of the property. The extended term at favorable interest contributed to the creation of several ranching empires. The section was originally granted to the Galveston Harrisburg & San Antonio Railway Company but had lapsed back to the public domain, held for the benefit of the School Fund.**

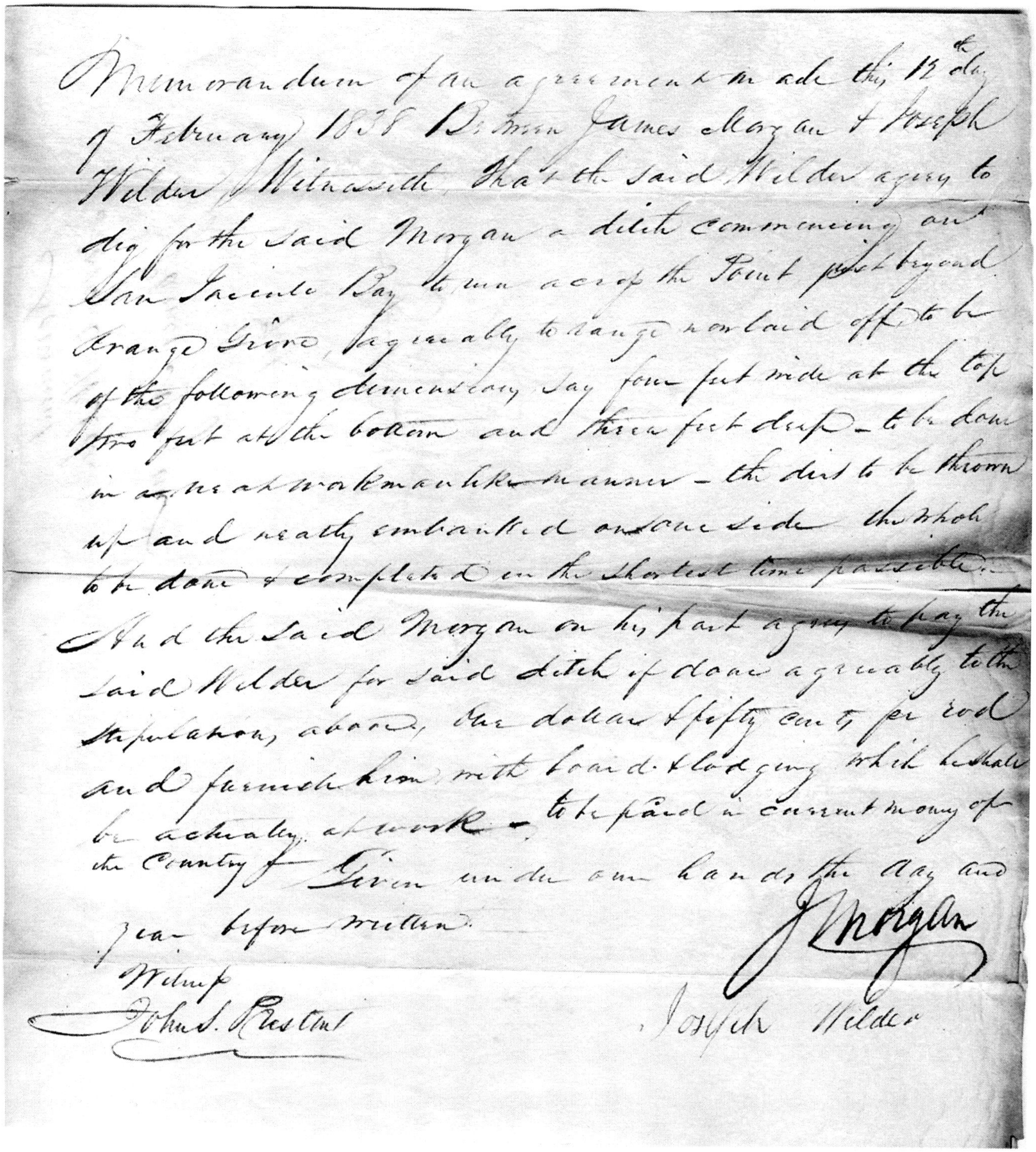

Memorandum of an agreement made this 12th day of February 1838 Between James Morgan & Joseph Wilder Witnesseth That the said Wilder agrees to dig for the said Morgan a ditch commencing on San Jacinto Bay to run across the Point just beyond Orange Grove, agreeably to a range now laid off to be of the following dimensions say four feet wide at the top two feet at the bottom and three feet deep — to be done in a neat workmanlike manner — the dirt to be thrown up and neatly embanked on one side the whole to be done & completed in the shortest time possible —

And the said Morgan on his part agrees to pay the said Wilder for said ditch if done agreeably to the stipulations above, One dollar & fifty cents per rod and furnish him with board & lodging while he shall be actually at work — to be paid in current money of the Country — Given under our hands the day and year before written.

J Morgan

Witness
John S. Preston

Joseph Wilder

**Figure 75. Drainage Ditch Contract, Morgan's Point, San Jacinto Bay, City of New Washington, 1838. Texas had a long tradition of supporting public works projects such as roads, canals and irrigation ditches. During the Mexican period, blocks around the town plaza were reserved for churches, a jail, market and assembly hall. Privately developed town sites had to provide similar facilities but at the promoter's expense. In 1838 the three organizers of the town of New Washington, at Morgan's Point, contracted with Joseph Wilder to construct a ditch between the San Jacinto River and Galveston Bay. The canal was to be four feet wide and three feet deep. Wilder earned $1.50 per rod dug, plus provisions for the work gang. Proceeds from lot sales probably funded the canal project.**

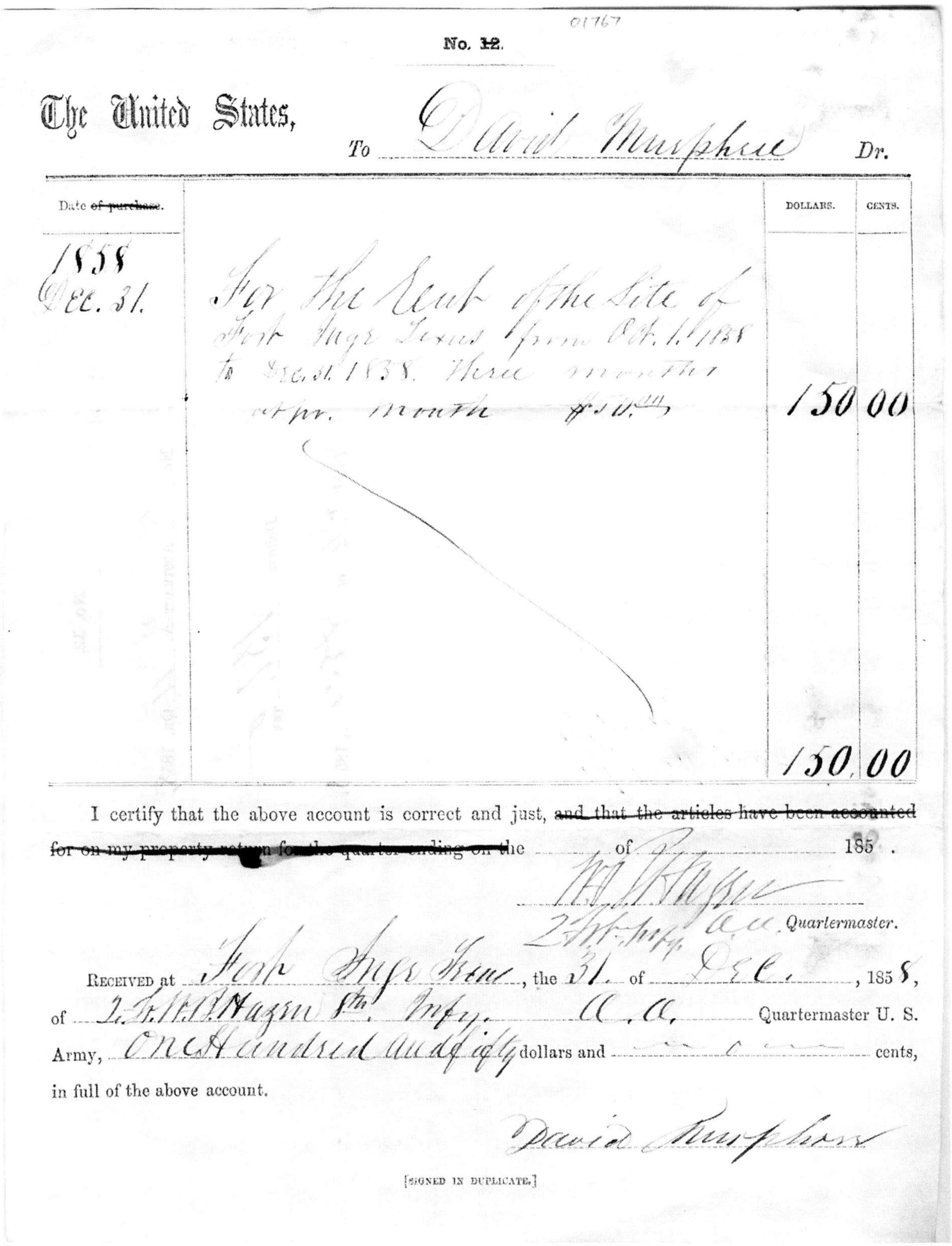
01767

No. 12.

The United States, To David Murphee Dr.

| Date ~~of purchase~~. | | DOLLARS. | CENTS. |
|---|---|---|---|
| 1858 Dec. 31. | For the Rent of the Site of Fort Inge Texas from Oct. 1st 1858 to Dec. 31. 1858. Three months at pr. month $50.00 | 150 | 00 |
| | | 150 | 00 |

I certify that the above account is correct and just, ~~and that the articles have been accounted for on my property return for the quarter ending on the~~ [redacted] ~~for the quarter ending on the~~ ....... of ....... 185 .

W B Hazen
2 Lt. Infy. A.Q.M. Quartermaster.

Received at Fort Inge Texas, the 31. of Dec., 1858, of 2. Lt. W. B. Hazen 8th Infy. A. Q. Quartermaster U. S. Army, One Hundred and fifty dollars and — — cents, in full of the above account.

David Murphee

[Signed in duplicate.]

**Figure 76. U.S. Army Receipt for Lease of Fort Inge for Three Months, Uvalde, 1858. Unlike the other forty-nine states, Texas retained its public domain upon annexation. Federal facilities like courts, custom offices and forts had to either be leased or purchased from the private owners or state. Fort Inge, in Uvalde County, grew out of Camp Leona, which was perched atop a volcanic plug. The post was part of a defensive line across the frontier, strategically placed to provide rest, supplies and protection for travelers and the mail. The United States leased the site in Uvalde from Daniel Murphee of San Antonio for $600.00 annually, payable by the post quartermaster. After the fort was abandoned, the property reverted back to the land owner.**

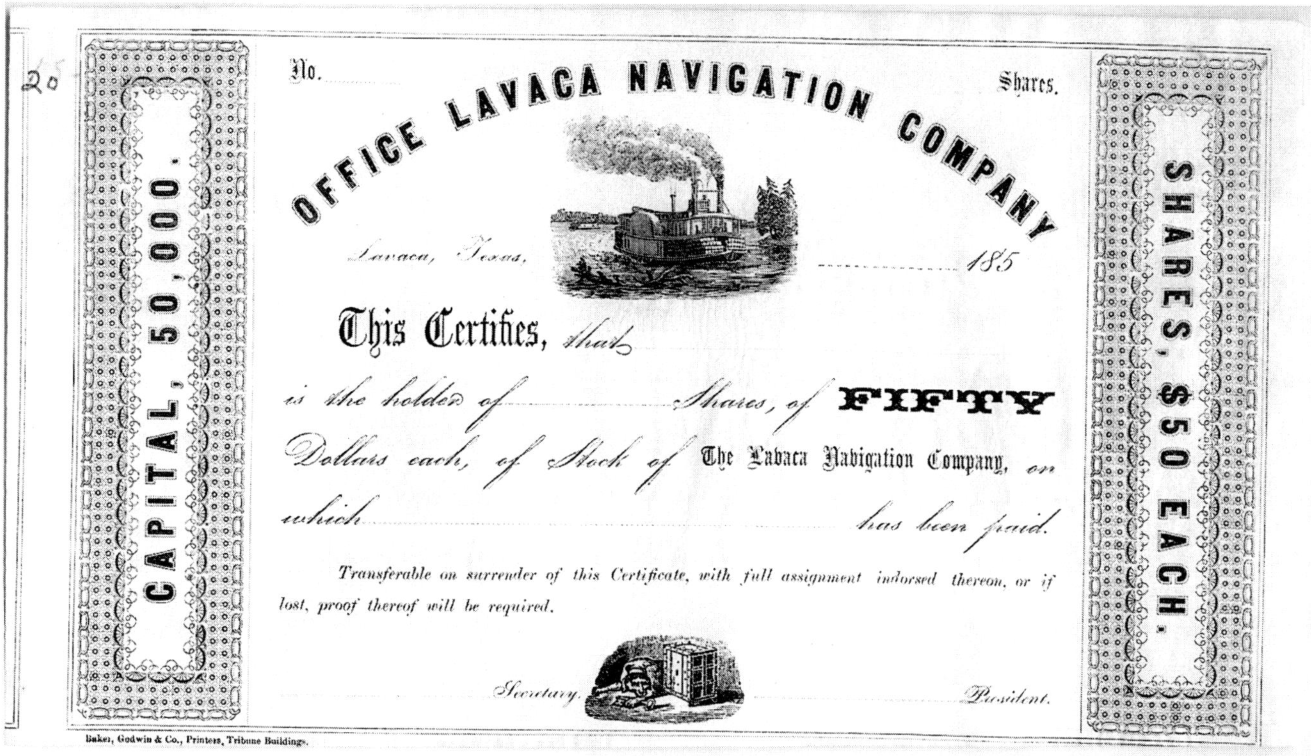


**Figure 77. $50 Stock Certificate [Blank], Lavaca Navigation Company, [185_]. Essential to the growth of early Texas was safe access to steamer ports located along the Gulf Coast. A canal between Matagorda and the Colorado River was a high priority. In 1852 the legislature chartered the Lavaca Navigation Company for that purpose. The State offered land scrip if certified by the State engineer. Lavaca ultimately received forty-eight sections of land for the internal improvements. In 1853 the legislature reserved $300,000 for other canal and river improvements. Work along the Sabine River earned two thousand acres. Navigation companies, after patenting their land, could not retain the property for more than twenty-four years. Baker, Godwin and Co. of New York printed the Lavaca stock certificate.**

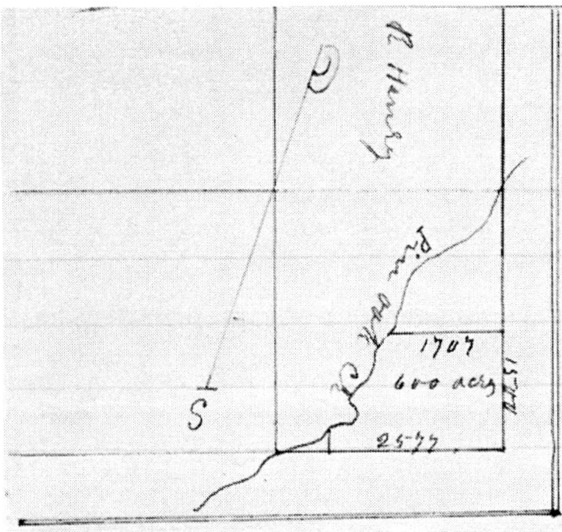


Field notes of a Survey
of Land made for the Brazos
Manufacturing Company
Beginning at the
S E Corner of Robt Henry
H R League Survey at a Stake
from which a Black Jack 12 in Di bears North
4 vrs Thence running N 30 w with Said Henry
East Line 1500 vrs Set a Stake from wh a
Poast Oak 15 in Di brs N 30 w 10 vrs & a P O
8 in Di brs S 5 E 6 vrs Thence S 60 w 1707
vrs to Pinoak Creek Set a Stake in the Chanl
from wh a Pin Oak 7 in Di brs N 19 E 5½ vrs
& an Elm 6 in brs S 57 E 5 vrs Thence down
the Said Creek with its Channel S & west
for a frunt of 1500 vrs Set a Stake from which an
Elm 8 in brs S 21 E 5 vrs another Elm 6 in brs
S 88 E 3½ vrs Thence S 30 E 123 vrs to the South
boundry Line of the Said Henry League planted a
Rock for Corner from wh a Poast Oak 17 in Di
brs S 60 w 9 vrs & a P O 15 in brs N 42 E 10 vrs
Thence N 60 E with the S Line of Said Henry
2577 vrs to the place of Beginning Containing
by Estimation 600 acres of Land
Surveyed May the 11th 1864 B D Grant
Surveyor

**Figure 78. Survey, Brazos Manufacturing Company, Texas Military Board, Brazos County, 1864. When Texas entered the Civil War it was completely free of bonded debt, had a small budget, and endowed schools, universities and asylums. The Confederate Texas legislature was forced to return to land scrip to pay contractors of the Military Board. The Brazos Manufacturing Company of Robertson County was funded with bales of cotton contributed by the organizers. In return for building a wool and flour mill, the Texas Military Board offered scrip to the company upon completion of the factory. Brazos Manufacturing prepared a survey with field notes for the Pine Creek property. Delays of machinery and equipment being shipped from Europe doomed the venture. No scrip was earned, and the May 12, 1864, survey was for naught.**

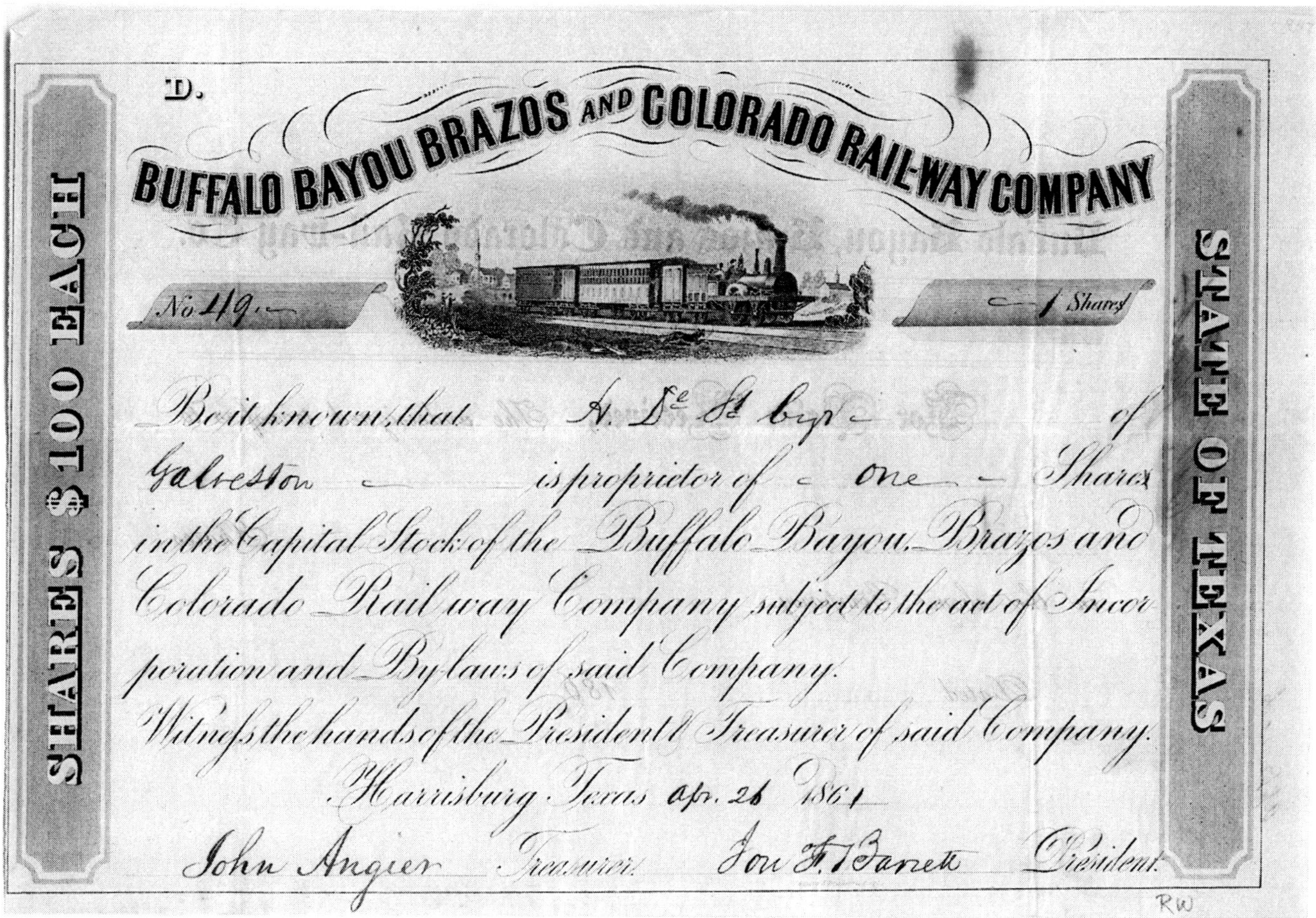
D.

BUFFALO BAYOU BRAZOS AND COLORADO RAIL-WAY COMPANY

No 49 — 1 Shares

SHARES $100 EACH

STATE OF TEXAS

Be it known, that H. De St. Cyr of Galveston is proprietor of one Shares in the Capital Stock of the Buffalo Bayou, Brazos and Colorado Rail way Company subject to the act of Incorporation and By laws of said Company.

Witness the hands of the President & Treasurer of said Company.

Harrisburg, Texas Apr. 26 1861

John Angier Treasurer. Jon F. Barrett President.

RW

**Figure 79. $100 Stock Certificate for Buffalo Bayou, Brazos and Colorado Rail Way Company, Harrisburg, 1861. The 1840 chartered Buffalo Bayou, Brazos and Colorado Rail-Way Company was the first Texas railroad to successfully complete a track, earning eight sections of land for each mile opened after certification by the government engineer. Rail companies had only twelve years to dispose of their lands after receiving a patent. The line was primarily backed by Massachusetts investors. After making it to Harrisburg, the line was dormant during the Civil War, and operations were not resumed for the benefit of creditors until 1867. Management was led by Jonathan Bonnett, president of the line. In 1870 the company merged and became the Galveston, Harrisburg and San Antonio Rail-way. That company received lands in the Panhandle and West Texas.**

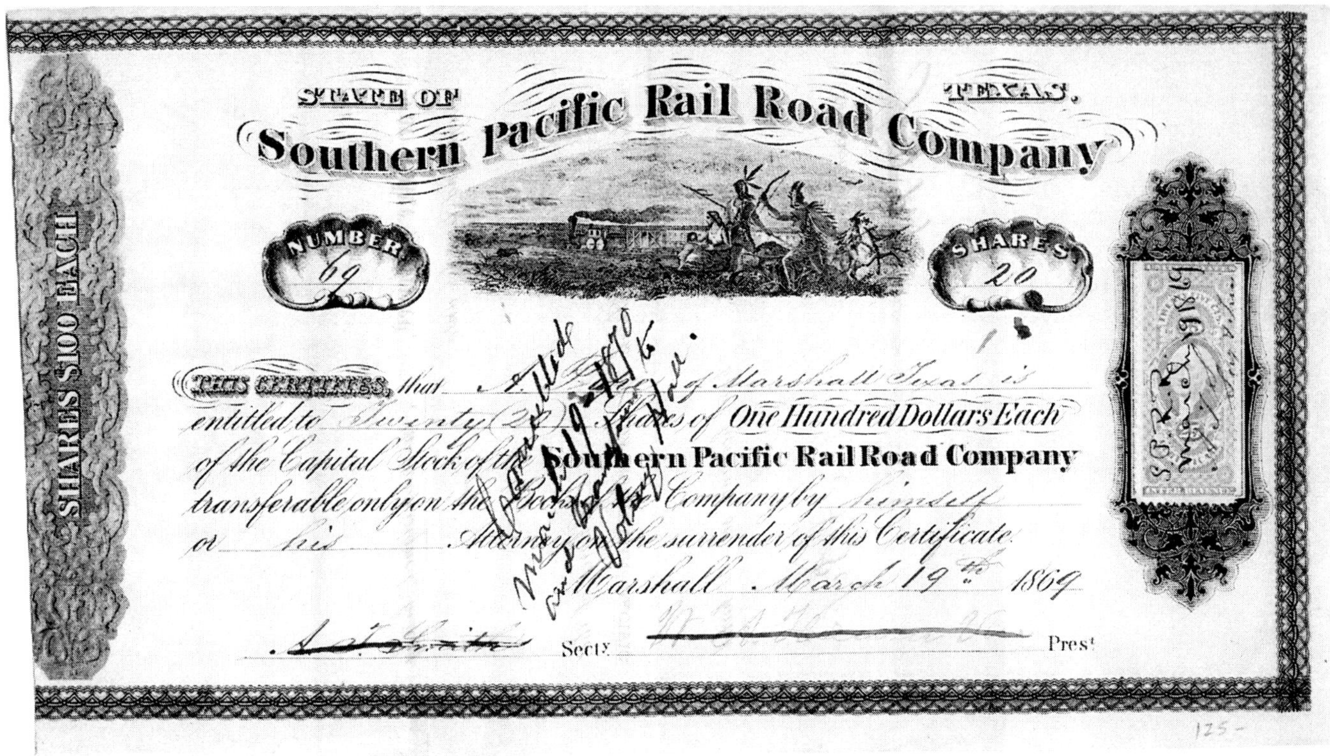


Figure 80. $100 Stock Certificate for Southern Pacific Rail Road Company, Marshall, 1869. From the time of independence, Texas officials and men of commerce dreamed of a Trans-Texas railroad. A number of lines were organized with that purpose in mind. The Southern Pacific Railroad was a survivor of the Texas Western charter of February 16, 1852. Western intended to build a rail from Vicksburg to El Paso and connect to the Pacific Ocean. Before the Civil War a small segment of track from Marshall had been completed. Soon after the war, a connector to Shreveport was finished by the Southern Pacific, the successor. The Texas and Pacific Railroad Company acquired assets of the Southern Pacific and operated as the Southern Trans-Continental Railway Company. Shareholder A. Pope, of Marshall, Texas, upon the merger of the Southern Pacific, received 20 shares in exchange for his old stock.

Scrip Stock

No. 30 — 5 Shares.

OF THE

Southern Trans-Continental

RAILWAY COMPANY.

Par Value of Full Paid Shares, $100.

This Certifies, That the "Southern Trans-Continental Railway Company" has received from J. W. Forney the sum of Five Dollars per share upon each of Five shares, and that the said J. W. Forney or his assigns, will be entitled to Five shares of the capital stock of said Company upon the further payment of Ninety five dollars upon each share, in such amounts and at such times as the same may be called for by the Board of Directors of said Company.

The return of this Certificate will be required upon the payment of any future instalments, when a new Certificate will be issued in the place thereof, and the shares hereby represented shall be transferred only upon the books of the Company, at its office, by the above-named holder or his Attorney, upon the surrender of this Certificate.

No shares can be transferred on which any instalment called for remains unpaid.

The holder of this Certificate, or assigns, accepts the same under the express condition that any failure to pay any instalment, as the same may be called for by the Board of Directors of the said "Southern Trans-Continental Railway Company," shall cause an absolute forfeiture of the shares mentioned in this Certificate to the use of said Company.

In Witness Whereof, the said Company has caused this Certificate to be signed by the President and Secretary, the 22nd day of June 1871

E. N. B. Hart
Secretary.

Henry G. Gibbons
Vice President.

Philp & Solomons, Printers, Washington, D. C.

**Figure 81. $100 Scrip Certificate for the Southern Trans-Continental Railway Company, 1871. The federally chartered Southern Trans-Continental Railway Company, survivor of the Southern Pacific, was the creation of wealthy speculators and Eastern politicians. Favorable court rulings and legislation were essential to both its creation and survival. The "Scrip Stock" certificate representing a claim to land was unique in Texas. Common stock for the Southern Trans-Continental was sold by subscription, which allowed shareholders to pay for the stock in installments. The illustrated "Scrip Stock" of five shares was in return for a $5.00 down payment on the $100.00 par value stock made by subscriber J. W. Forney on June 22, 1871. As other payments followed, Forney was entitled to more scrip. Forney assigned and transferred his "scrip stock" for a quick return of capital. The offering was not made available to the general public.**

Figure 82. Scrip Certificate Representing 1,000 Acres, New York & Texas Land and Emigration Association, New York, 1847. James Phalen, in 1846, as president, John Paine, treasurer, and William H. Paine, secretary, all of New York City, were engaged by J. R. Reynolds of Texas to purchase headrights after receiving a legal opinion from Judge John C. Watrous confirming the legality of the transaction. Judge Watrous, Reynolds and J. G. Miner owned half of the venture. Initially, the company acquired 440 headrights, representing 2,026,200 acres. The requirement that rail companies dispose of patented lands proved too great an economic loss during a soft real estate market. More than empresarios and canal companies, railroads, with the help of their Eastern lawyers, devised ways to sidestep the Texas statute. The Illinois and Great Northern "sold" their scrip land to the New York and Texas Land and Emigration Association. The Texas & Pacific used a similar land trust. The New York and Texas Land Company was organized in Texas by federal judge John C. Watrous, a true land speculator. Each share of the real estate trust represented one thousand acres of land. James D. Wilson received shares September 17, 1847, from the New York company home office.

# TEXAS,

AND

## HER INDUCEMENTS FOR NORTHERN EMIGRATION.

The undersigned would hereby call the attention of the people of the North and West to a few facts concerning the advantages of Texas over the other States and Territories, its present and future.

FIRST. It has a fertility and depth of soil unsurpassed by that of any State or Territory. Its river bottoms and valley lands are of a rich alluvial soil, very productive and easily worked. Its uplands are undulating, rich, and can—as can the bottom lands—invariably be cultivated with improved agricultural implements, while the bottom lands produce one bale of five hundred pounds cotton, and sixty bushels corn per acre, the prairie lands will produce three-fourths of a bale of cotton, and fifty bushels corn.

SECOND. A single hand can cultivate ten acres of cotton, and fifteen of corn; with improved implements much more; not uncommonly making from his own labor upwards of one thousand dollars in gold, the average being from five to eight hundred dollars per year per hand.

THIRD. Our climate is salubrious, with a temperature mild and uniform, not subject to extreme heat or cold. Cases of sun-stroke are hardly ever known. Snow and ice are rarely ever seen. Farming operations are carried on in every month of the year. Corn is usually planted in February; cotton in March.

FOURTH. The growing season in Texas is about twice as long as in the North, crops maturing about two months earlier. The wheat growing section—central and northern counties—are superior to any in the country, unless perhaps lower California. Besides, we have the advantage of the early market. Two crops are often made from the same ground, while vegetables are raised the year round. The soil, climate and seasons are equally well suited to the growing of sugar, rice, the small grains, and all the most valuable staples. Living here is remarkably cheap.

FIFTH. The crops on any of these lands are extremely profitable, always amounting to a sum much greater than the price asked for the land, which ranges from three to fifteen dollars per acre, and which is the result of a surplus of land and a scarcity of labor. Teams and tools are often leased with the lands. Provisions are frequently furnished, when lands are worked upon shares.

SIXTH. Wood and timber generally abundant and of good quality, except for fencing, for which hedge—*Bois d'Arc*—is being successfully substituted. Water is abundant, except in portions of the extreme western part of the State, and is almost invariably good.

SEVENTH. Stock-raising and wool-growing is a source of immense profit in Texas, it only being necessary to brand the stock; neither feeding or salting required, there being salt-licks and good grass perenniel. Beef packing is proving to be extremely profitable. A stock of cattle can be purchased at from $2 to $6 per head. Thousands of cattle are being slaughtered for their hides and tallow only. Hogs require little or no care, subsisting and fattening throughout the year upon mast.

EIGHTH. Sheep do as well in Texas as in New York or New England, with no feed except the sweet mesquite grass, and with not one fourth the care given them in the North. With one half the attention paid in the North, the most improved merinos do equally well, and yield as much wool. Sheep sell here at from $1 to $3 per head—wool according to the quality. Western Texas is particularly adapted to stock-raising and wool growing. Pasturage in Texas is free to all.

NINTH. City and town property, although low, is looking up.

TENTH. The result of the activity in the railroad interests in the State will materially enhance the value of all classes of property. Houston is destined to become a great railroad centre, which, together with her ship channel completed, ensures for this city a bright future.

ELEVENTH. All that remains to be done to make Texas the most desirable State in the Union, is reconstruction and admission, which will undoubtedly be the result of the late election. Once reconstructed, she will make rapid strides on the march of prosperity. Now is the time to come to Texas, to enjoy with her her prosperity.—Emigrants are coming into Galveston harbor at an average of one thousend per week; emigration into the Northern part of the State equally great.

TWELFTH. Property of all kinds can be bought or leased, upon terms and in quantities which cannot fail to be acceptable.

The undersigned, after four years residence, with a knowledge of nearly every county in the State, unhesitatingly invite an investigat on of the above facts on the part of the people of New England, the North and the West, with a view to settling among us, or making investments, which cannot fail to be alike remunerative and safe. Having control of much of the property mentioned above, we are prepared to pay special attention to the purchase, sale, leasing and location of Lands, (with every facility for the investigation of titles, both here and at the General Land Office), and the payment of taxes throughout the State.

☞ Any Information concerning the above furnished upon application to

**GEO. W. SMITH & CO.,**
General Real Estate Agents, Houston, Texas.

### REFERENCES:

| | |
|---|---|
| HON. A. H. CRAGIN, U. S. Senate, N. H. | LIEUT. GOV. GEORGE HENDEE, Vermont. |
| GEN. E. J. DAVIS, Texas. | JUDGE WM. ALEXANDER, U. S. Dist. Attorney, Texas. |
| HON. WM. T. CLARK, Member of Congress, Texas. | KILBORN & LATTA, Real Est. Ag'ts, Washington, D. C. |
| CAPT. NATHAN RANDLETT, Mail Agent, N. H. | H. L. SLAYTON, Real Estate Agent, Chicago, Illinois. |

T. W. HOUSE, Houston, Texas.

**Figure 83. "Texas, and Her Inducement for Northern Emigration," 1869 Broadside (reprinted 1981), Yale Collection of Western Americana. George Washington Smith, of Kentucky, came to Texas in 1847 and lived in Columbus, Colorado County. He was a commissioner of the town's railroad. He opposed secession but remained in Texas serving as the judge of the First District Court through 1866. That year he became an Associate Justice of the Texas Supreme Court. After leaving that court in 1867 he entered the real estate business. Among his associates were northern senators, congressmen and governors. All were listed as references in his promotional broadside, distributed in the 1870s, that boasted the advantages of relocating to Texas. Abundance of timber, water and fertile farm lands were a few of the benefits awaiting northern emigrants. Smith said he "controlled" much of the better properties and offered to assist newcomers in their selection of the ideal property. He offered to investigate titles at the General Land Office.**

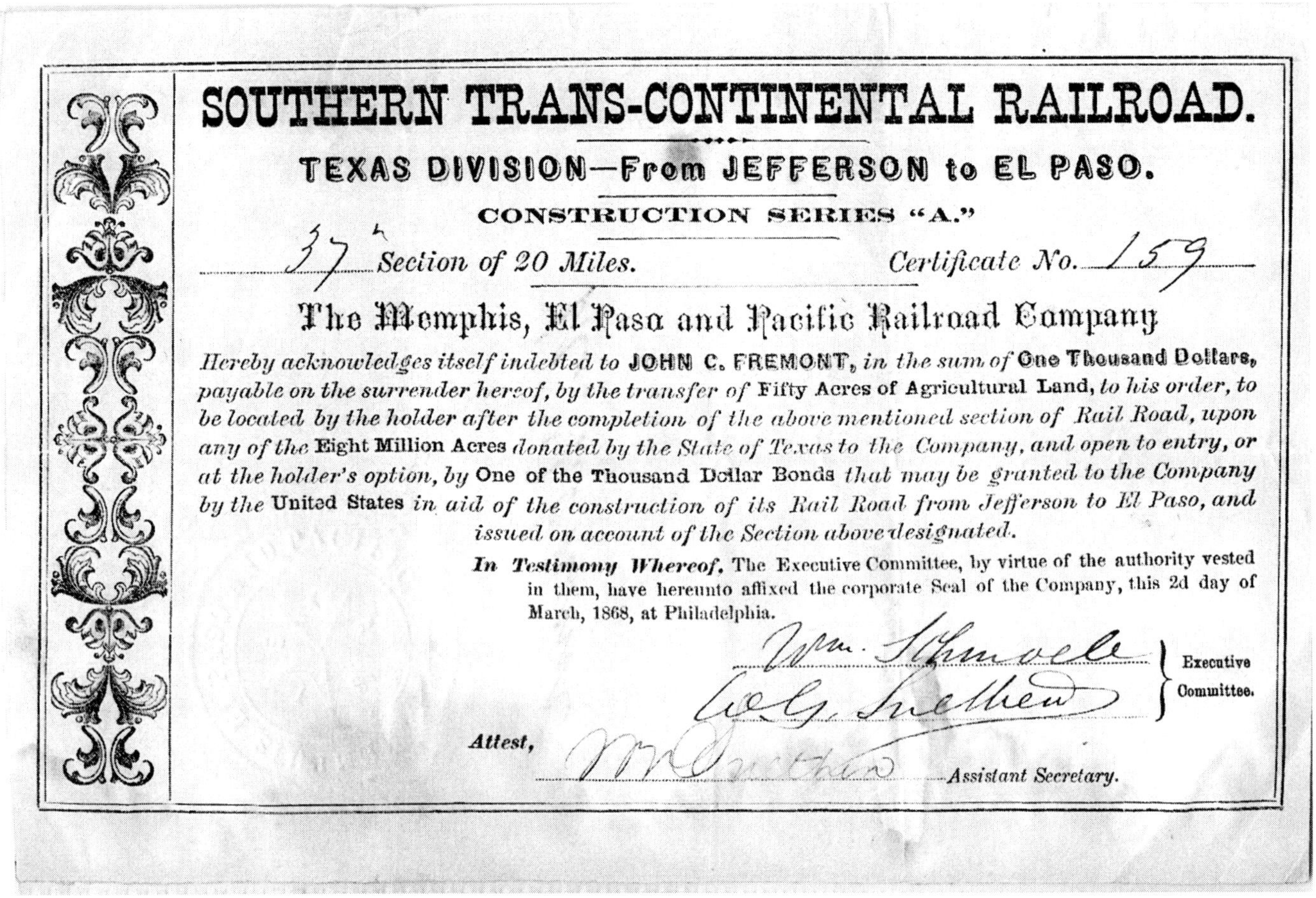

# SOUTHERN TRANS-CONTINENTAL RAILROAD.

## TEXAS DIVISION—From JEFFERSON to EL PASO.

CONSTRUCTION SERIES "A."

37th *Section of 20 Miles.* *Certificate No.* 159

**The Memphis, El Paso and Pacific Railroad Company**

*Hereby acknowledges itself indebted to* **JOHN C. FREMONT**, *in the sum of* **One Thousand Dollars,** *payable on the surrender hereof, by the transfer of* Fifty Acres of Agricultural Land, *to his order, to be located by the holder after the completion of the above mentioned section of Rail Road, upon any of the* Eight Million Acres *donated by the State of Texas to the Company, and open to entry, or at the holder's option, by* One of the Thousand Dollar Bonds *that may be granted to the Company by the* United States *in aid of the construction of its Rail Road from Jefferson to El Paso, and issued on account of the Section above designated.*

*In Testimony Whereof,* The Executive Committee, by virtue of the authority vested in them, have hereunto affixed the corporate Seal of the Company, this 2d day of March, 1868, at Philadelphia.

Executive Committee.

*Attest,* *Assistant Secretary.*

**Figure 84. Scrip Certificate and Bond To John C. Frémont for $1,000, Southern Trans-Continental Railroad, Texas Division, Jefferson to El Paso, Philadelphia, 1868. The Texas legislature at one time offered fifty acres for each twenty miles completed by a Trans-Texas railroad. John C. Frémont controlled the debts of the Southern Trans-Continental Railroad. Security was eight million acres of land scrip donated by the State of Texas. The debt represented by the Construction series "A" $1,000.00 bond could be satisfied with the assignment of fifty acres of agricultural land. Frémont was trustee for debt by authority granted to him by the Executive Committee of the Company on March 2, 1868, in Philadelphia. Similar scrip was used to found the Frémont-inspired Franco-Texan Land Company, an 1876 real estate holding company.**

Figure 85. Share Certificate, Franco-Texan Land Company, Dallas, 1876. The dual-language (French and English) stock certificate of the 1876 Franco-Texan Land Company represented over a half-million acres along with accompanying French bonds of the real estate interest of the Southern Trans-Continental Railroad. The vast holdings were spread over ten counties: Parker, Palo Pinto, Stephens, Callahan, Shackelford, Mitchell, Taylor, Nolan, Jones and Fisher. The bonds had originally been sold by Frémont in the Paris Bourse, raising as much as $5,000,000 that went to his investors rather than the railroad. French bondholders were forced to accept shares representing thirteen acres in exchange for each $100.00 bond they held. To make the real estate holding company appear solvent, the real estate was valued at least five times market value. Ultimately the Frenchmen received only thirteen cents on the dollar. A few appeared in Weatherford, Texas, home office of the Company, to claim their land in exchange for the almost worthless bonds.

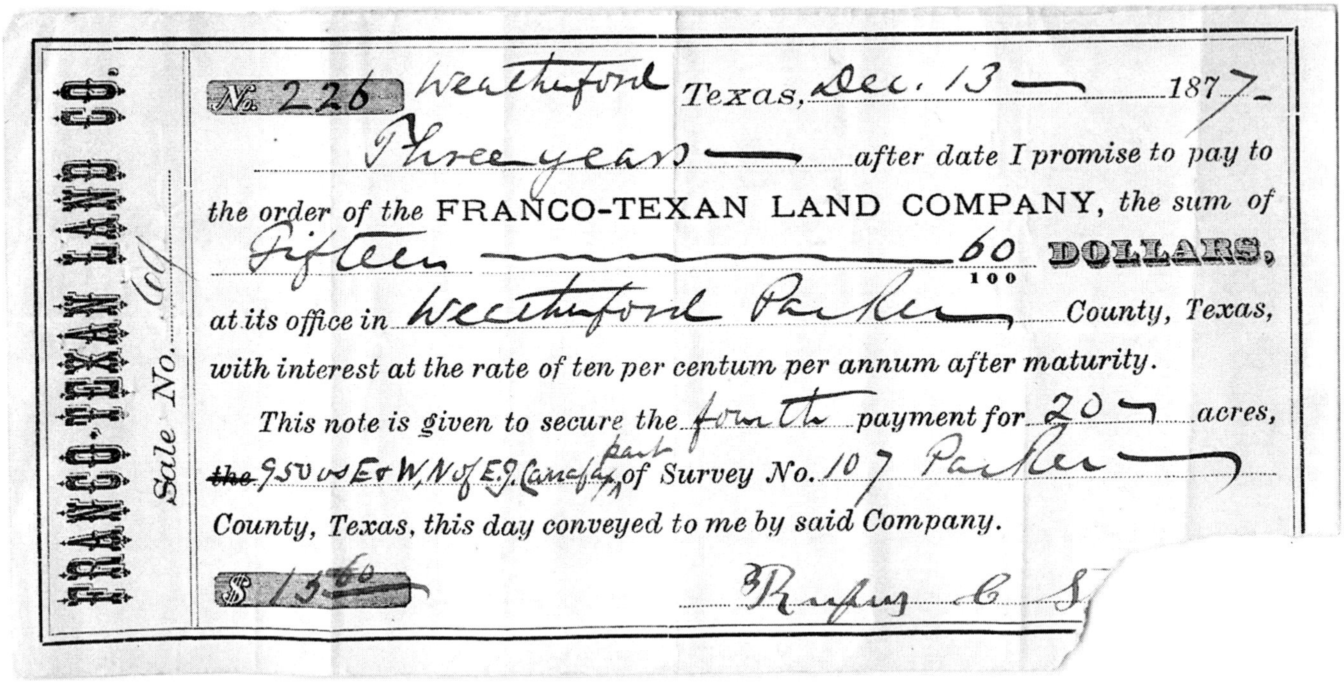

FRANCO-TEXAN LAND CO.

Sale No. 61

No. 226 Weatherford Texas, Dec. 13 — 1877

Three years — after date I promise to pay to the order of the FRANCO-TEXAN LAND COMPANY, the sum of Fifteen — 60/100 DOLLARS, at its office in Weatherford Parker County, Texas, with interest at the rate of ten per centum per annum after maturity.

This note is given to secure the fourth payment for 20 acres, ~~the~~ 950 vs E & W, N of E.J. Canefax part of Survey No. 107 Parker County, Texas, this day conveyed to me by said Company.

$ 15.60

Rufus C. S

**Figure 86. Promissory Note, Franco-Texian Land Company, 20 Acres Parker County, Weatherford, 1879. Surprising to the management of the Franco-Texian Company, a few Frenchmen turned up at their offices in Weatherford, Texas, demanding their promised thirteen acres for every bond held. The Company was marketing the property to third parties. Although proceeds of sale were promised to the shareholders, company directors and agents absorbed 90 percent of the sales proceeds. The illustrated sale to a third party was for twenty acres in Parker County. The buyer singed a promissory note at the Company's office in Weatherford on December 13, 1877. The note carried 10 percent interest. On its reverse the note is marked paid as recorded by the Company's vice treasurer.**

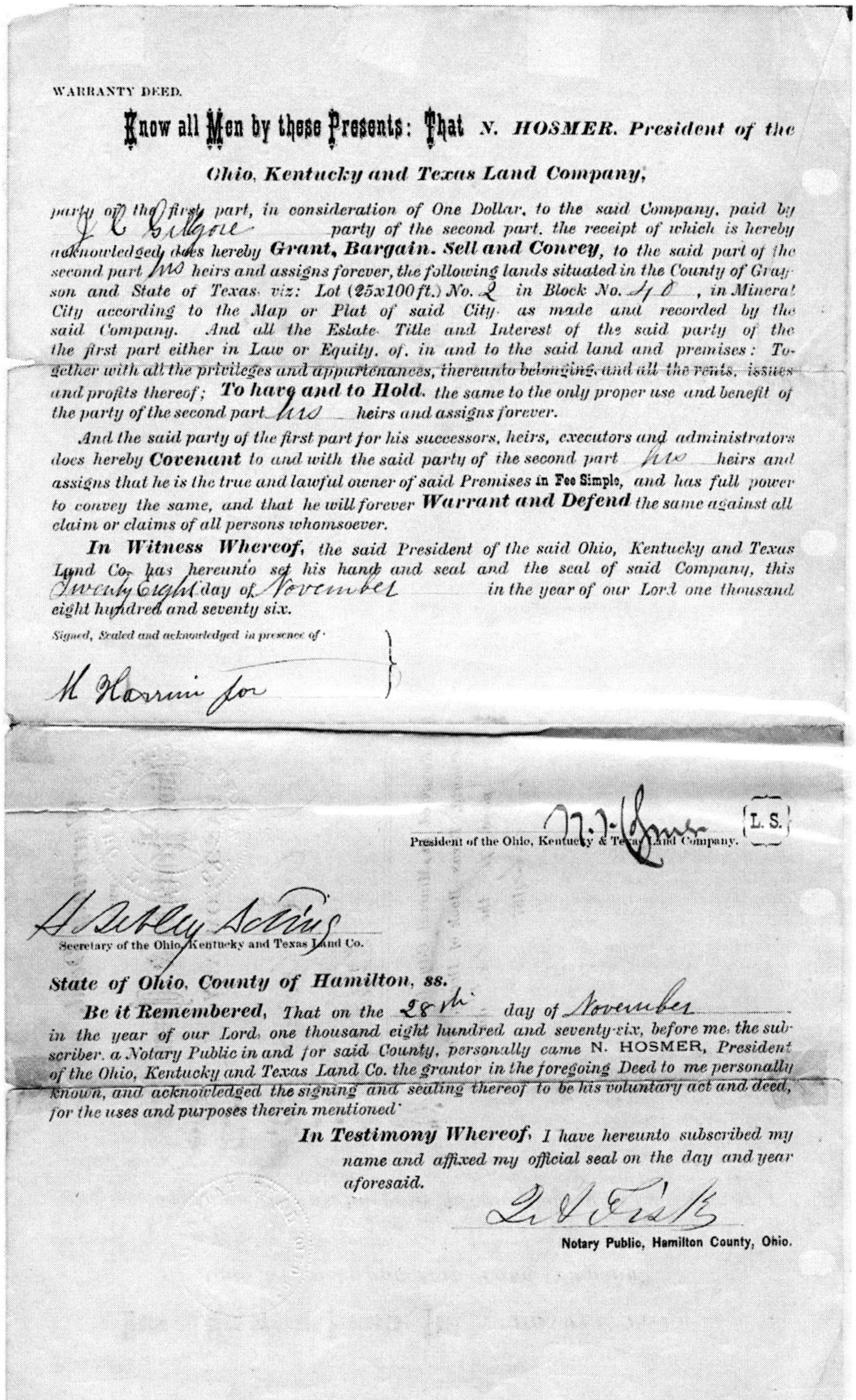

WARRANTY DEED.

**Know all Men by these Presents: That** ***N. HOSMER. President of the***

***Ohio, Kentucky and Texas Land Company,***

*party of the first part, in consideration of One Dollar, to the said Company, paid by* J C Gilgore *party of the second part, the receipt of which is hereby acknowledged, does hereby* **Grant, Bargain, Sell and Convey,** *to the said part of the second part* his *heirs and assigns forever, the following lands situated in the County of Grayson and State of Texas, viz: Lot (25x100 ft.) No.* 2 *in Block No.* 48 *, in Mineral City according to the Map or Plat of said City, as made and recorded by the said Company. And all the Estate, Title and Interest of the said party of the the first part either in Law or Equity, of, in and to the said land and premises: Together with all the privileges and appurtenances, thereunto belonging, and all the rents, issues and profits thereof;* **To have and to Hold,** *the same to the only proper use and benefit of the party of the second part* his *heirs and assigns forever.*

*And the said party of the first part for his successors, heirs, executors and administrators does hereby* **Covenant** *to and with the said party of the second part* his *heirs and assigns that he is the true and lawful owner of said Premises* in Fee Simple, *and has full power to convey the same, and that he will forever* **Warrant and Defend** *the same against all claim or claims of all persons whomsoever.*

**In Witness Whereof,** *the said President of the said Ohio, Kentucky and Texas Land Co. has hereunto set his hand and seal and the seal of said Company, this* Twenty Eight *day of* November *in the year of our Lord one thousand eight hundred and seventy six.*

*Signed, Sealed and acknowledged in presence of*

H Harrison for

N. J. Hosmer [L. S.]

President of the Ohio, Kentucky & Texas Land Company.

S. Ashley Adams

Secretary of the Ohio, Kentucky and Texas Land Co.

***State of Ohio, County of Hamilton, ss.***

**Be it Remembered,** *That on the* 28th *day of* November *in the year of our Lord, one thousand eight hundred and seventy-six, before me, the subscriber, a Notary Public in and for said County, personally came* N. HOSMER, *President of the Ohio, Kentucky and Texas Land Co. the grantor in the foregoing Deed to me personally known, and acknowledged the signing and sealing thereof to be his voluntary act and deed, for the uses and purposes therein mentioned.*

**In Testimony Whereof,** *I have hereunto subscribed my name and affixed my official seal on the day and year aforesaid.*

L. A. Fisk

Notary Public, Hamilton County, Ohio.

**Figure 87. Warranty Deed from Ohio, Kentucky and Texas Land Company, $1.00 Lot in Mineral City, Grayson County, Hamilton County, Ohio, 1876. Throughout the history of Texas, sharpies and swindlers taking advantage of unsophisticated trusting real estate buyers. Most common were forged headrights and bounty lands, followed by questionable titles. Least common were purely bogus deeds. One bogus offering was marketed to unsuspecting emigrants as they boarded excursion trains in Ohio and Kentucky bound for Texas. The Ohio, Kentucky and Texas Land Company promoted 2,500-foot town lots in the fictional town of "Mineral City" in Grayson County. Denison, Texas, the first train stop into Texas from the Ohio Valley. Warranty deeds were available for a dollar per lot. J. C. Gilgore bought a 25 × 100 foot lot November 28, 1876, from the company president, N. Hosme. It was recorded in the Mineral City book of deeds, but not in the County Clerk's office. As may be the case with resort property today, the buyer never saw his lot or even came to Texas.**

# All Aboard For Texas!

## Grand Texas EXCURSION!

UNDER THE MANAGEMENT OF

HENRY H. HANNAN,

## Land Emigration Agent,

SWAN CREEK, OHIO.

LEAVES POMEROY AND GALLIPOLIS, O.,

Stopping at all way points, via Steamer Telegraph, and Ohio & Mississippi, St. Louis, Iron Mountain & Southern, Texas Pacific & Houston, and Texas Central Railways. This Excursion is especially arranged for the benefit of

## Emigrants and Land Buyers

Who wish to make a first-class investment and secure desirable homes at the least possible expense, as well as those seeking recreation, the pleasure of hunting, &c.

In low rates of fare, and other advantages, this is the most desirable opportunity ever offered to those desirous of visiting or seeking

HOMES IN TEXAS!

Single rate excursion and round trip excursion tickets (good for forty days from Cincinnati, O.,) will be furnished at greatly reduced rates on boat, to Arkansas and Texas points, as parties may desire.

Two hundred pounds of baggage allowed with each ticket free. BAGGAGE CHECKED THROUGH AND TRANSFERS FREE. Parties may get on boat at any regular landing by giving due notice thereof.

**All parties wishing to participate in this excursion must give due notice, that suitable arrangements may be made.**

**For further information, rates of fare, &c., address the Manager,**

**HENRY H. HANNAN,**
**Swan Creek, Ohio.**

"THE BULLETIN" PRINT, GALLIPOLIS, OHIO.

**Figure 88. Broadside "All Aboard Texas," Land Emigration Agent, Swan Creek, Ohio, 1878. Emigrant trains were run by most railroads hauling passengers to Texas. Railroad agents and real estate salesmen were present at rail stations where Texas land buyers boarded. The 1878 Gallipolis, Ohio, broadside "All Aboard for Texas" was seen by hundreds at the Texas & Pacific and Texas Central stations. Railroad marketing departments stressed the advantage of purchasing their land instead of the pre-emption tracts offered by the State. Usually the rail companies held land in the more populated parts of the State. In a decade the public domain would be exhausted, raising values of all railroad lands. The broadside was printed by the *Bulletin* for Henry H. Hammon, Land Emigration Agent, Swan Creek, Ohio.**

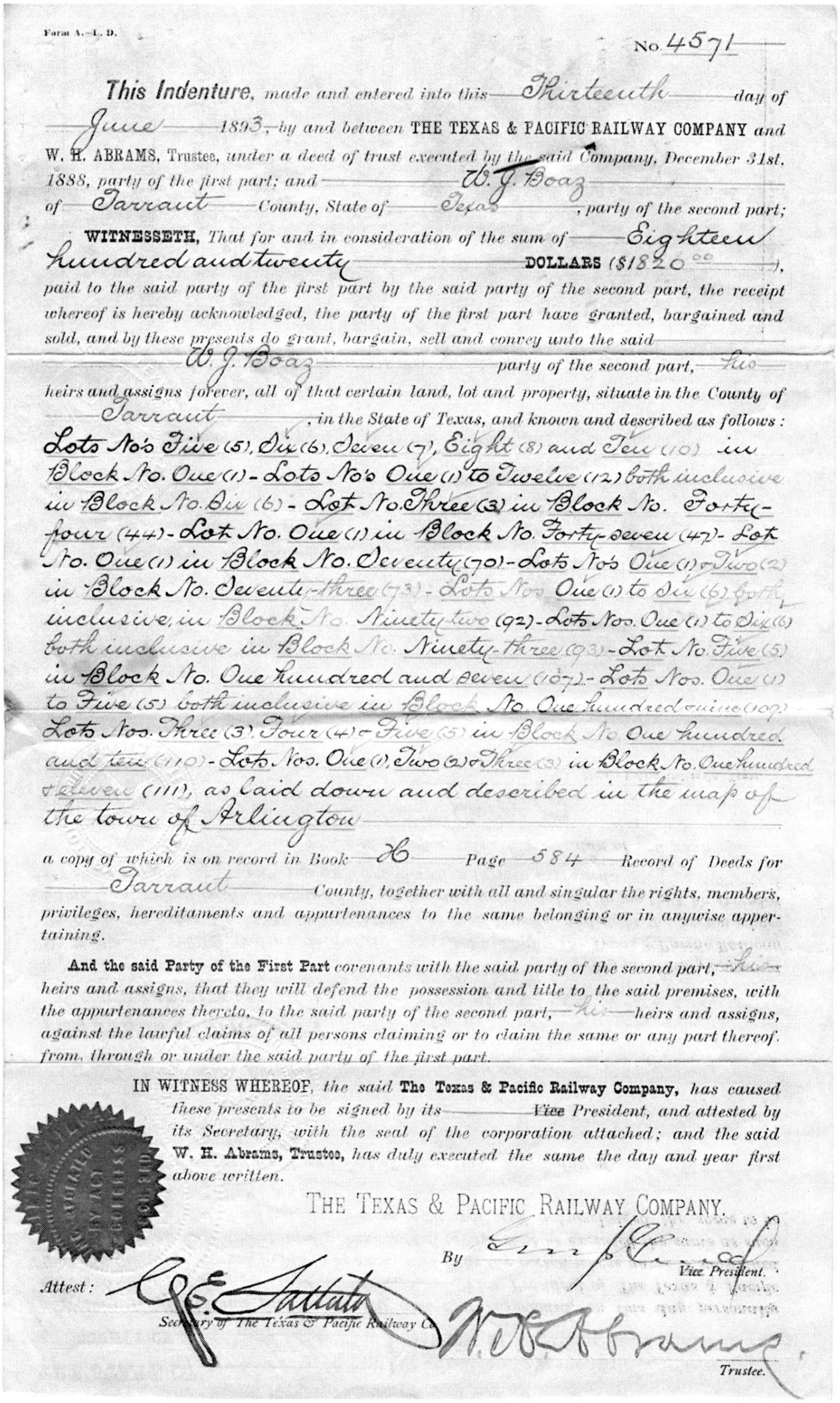
Form A.—L. D.

No. 4571

**This Indenture,** *made and entered into this* Thirteenth *day of* June *1893, by and between* THE TEXAS & PACIFIC RAILWAY COMPANY *and* W. H. ABRAMS, Trustee, *under a deed of trust executed by the said Company, December 31st, 1888, party of the first part; and* W. J. Boaz *of* Tarrant *County, State of* Texas*, party of the second part;*

**WITNESSETH,** *That for and in consideration of the sum of* Eighteen hundred and twenty **DOLLARS** ($1820.00), *paid to the said party of the first part by the said party of the second part, the receipt whereof is hereby acknowledged, the party of the first part have granted, bargained and sold, and by these presents do grant, bargain, sell and convey unto the said* W. J. Boaz *party of the second part,* his *heirs and assigns forever, all of that certain land, lot and property, situate in the County of* Tarrant*, in the State of Texas, and known and described as follows:*

Lots No's Five (5), Six (6), Seven (7), Eight (8) and Ten (10) in Block No. One (1) - Lots No's One (1) to Twelve (12) both inclusive in Block No. Six (6) - Lot No. Three (3) in Block No. Forty-four (44) - Lot No. One (1) in Block No. Forty-seven (47) - Lot No. One (1) in Block No. Seventy (70) - Lots No's One (1) & Two (2) in Block No. Seventy-three (73) - Lots Nos One (1) to Six (6) both inclusive, in Block No. Ninety-two (92) - Lots Nos. One (1) to Six (6) both inclusive in Block No. Ninety-three (93) - Lot No. Five (5) in Block No. One hundred and seven (107) - Lots Nos. One (1) to Five (5) both inclusive in Block No. One hundred nine (109) Lots Nos. Three (3), Four (4) & Five (5) in Block No. One hundred and ten (110) - Lots Nos. One (1), Two (2) & Three (3) in Block No. One hundred & eleven (111), as laid down and described in the map of the town of Arlington

*a copy of which is on record in Book* H *Page* 584 *Record of Deeds for* Tarrant *County, together with all and singular the rights, members, privileges, hereditaments and appurtenances to the same belonging or in anywise appertaining.*

**And the said Party of the First Part** *covenants with the said party of the second part,* his *heirs and assigns, that they will defend the possession and title to the said premises, with the appurtenances thereto, to the said party of the second part,* his *heirs and assigns, against the lawful claims of all persons claiming or to claim the same or any part thereof, from, through or under the said party of the first part.*

IN WITNESS WHEREOF, *the said* **The Texas & Pacific Railway Company,** *has caused these presents to be signed by its* Vice *President, and attested by its Secretary, with the seal of the corporation attached; and the said* **W. H. Abrams, Trustee,** *has duly executed the same the day and year first above written.*

THE TEXAS & PACIFIC RAILWAY COMPANY,

*By* Geo J Gould *Vice President.*

*Attest:* C. E. Satterlee *Secretary of The Texas & Pacific Railway Co.*

W. H. Abrams *Trustee.*

**Figure 89. Deed from Texas & Pacific Railway to W. J. Boaz, Arlington Heights, Tarrant County, 1893. Many North and West Texas towns owe their existence to railroad land departments. One was Arlington, Texas, promoted by the Texas & Pacific Land Trust in 1884. The head of the real estate company was Dallas attorney W. H. Abrams, Trustee. T & P sold blocks of land to developers beginning in 1888. William Jesse Boaz, Fort Worth merchant and North Texas real estate developer, purchased at least thirty lots from Abrams in 1892. The deed was signed by Jay Gould's son, George J. Gould of Lakewood, New Jersey. Lots cost about $50.00.**

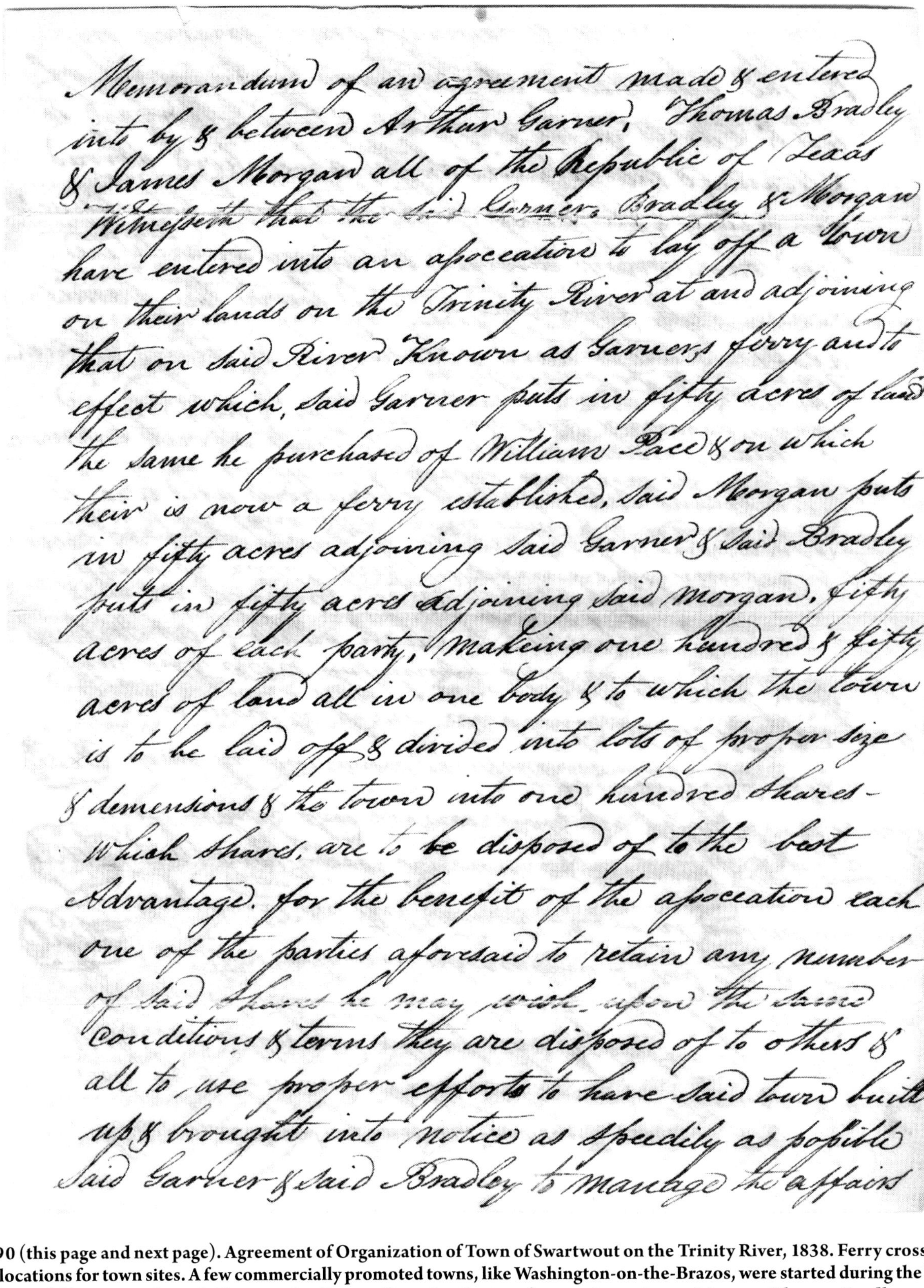

Memorandum of an agreement made & entered
into by & between Arthur Garner, Thomas Bradley
& James Morgan all of the Republic of Texas
Witnesseth that the said Garner, Bradley & Morgan
have entered into an association to lay off a Town
on their lands on the Trinity River at and adjoining
that on said River Known as Garners ferry and to
effect which, said Garner puts in fifty acres of land
the same he purchased of William Pace & on which
their is now a ferry established, said Morgan puts
in fifty acres adjoining said Garner & said Bradley
puts in fifty acres adjoining said Morgan, fifty
acres of each party, makeing one hundred & fifty
acres of land all in one body & to which the town
is to be laid off & divided into lots of proper size
& demensions & the town into one hundred shares -
which shares, are to be disposed of to the best
Advantage, for the benefit of the association each
one of the parties aforesaid to retain any number
of said shares he may wish, upon the same
conditions & terms they are disposed of to others &
all to, use proper efforts to have said town built
up & brought into notice as speedily as possible
Said Garner & said Bradley to manage the affairs

**Figure 90 (this page and next page). Agreement of Organization of Town of Swartwout on the Trinity River, 1838. Ferry crossings were natural locations for town sites. A few commercially promoted towns, like Washington-on-the-Brazos, were started during the Republic. The village of "Swartwout" was laid out at the Garner Ferry by the town's organizers, James Morgan, Thomas Bradley and Arthur Garner, in 1838. Each contributed 150 acres to form the venture, named in honor of New York speculator Samuel Swartwout. The site was purchased from Austin "300" colonist Nicholas Clopper in 1832. The town eventually became the county seat of Polk County. Initially the people relied upon river traffic for their economy, but the coming of the railroad darkened the future when it bypassed the river. Morgan was familiar with the Texas real estate market, having served as Zavala's agent responsible for his empresario grant. "The Memorandum of Agreement" is one of the earliest commercial real estate documents in Texas.**

of the association at the town by disposing of
lots & Shares in the town &c & said Morgan to
Manage the affairs of the association abroad
by Selling & disposing of Shares & lots Advertising &c
and each one to use his influence towards Getting the
County seat established at said town the parties
aforesaid are to have occasional meetings at such
times & at such places as may be agreed on
to make further arrangements about carrying
their plans into further operation and are to
Correspond & give notice to each other of their
proceedings as they may progress in the
business entrusted to each other, as Witness
our hands & seals this 1st day of November
A.D. 1838 -

(Seal)

in Presence of

P. M. Maxwell

Thos. Bradley (Seal)

J. Morgan (Seal)

Wm. A. Bardin

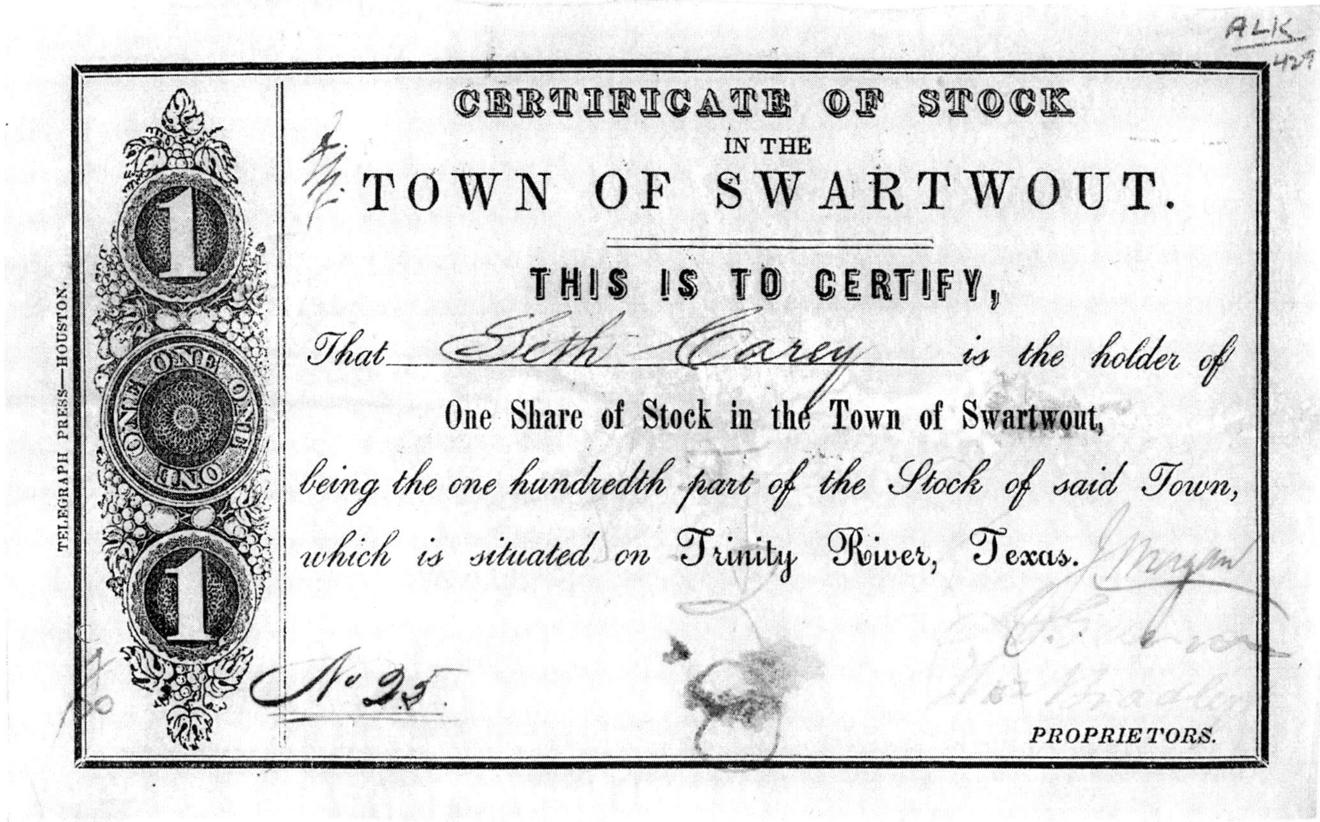
CERTIFICATE OF STOCK
IN THE
TOWN OF SWARTWOUT.
THIS IS TO CERTIFY,
That Seth Carey is the holder of
One Share of Stock in the Town of Swartwout,
being the one hundredth part of the Stock of said Town,
which is situated on Trinity River, Texas.
No 25
PROPRIETORS.
TELEGRAPH PRESS—HOUSTON.

Figure 91. Stock Certificate, Town of Swartwout, 1/100 of 150 Acre Townsite [ca. 1838]. Ownership in the town of Swartwout was represented by a Certificate of Stock in the Association. Shareholders were entitled to 1 percent of the Trinity River land and other assets of the company. The 150 acres contributed by each organizer was divided into 86 blocks measuring 60 × 120 feet. The town was platted in the typical Spanish model with a plaza, with public and religious parcels reserved. The imprint was the product of Telegraph Press of Houston. Both Sam Houston and Albert Sidney Johnston owned shares. Certificate holder Seth Corey had already received donation land for his service during the Siege of Bexar.

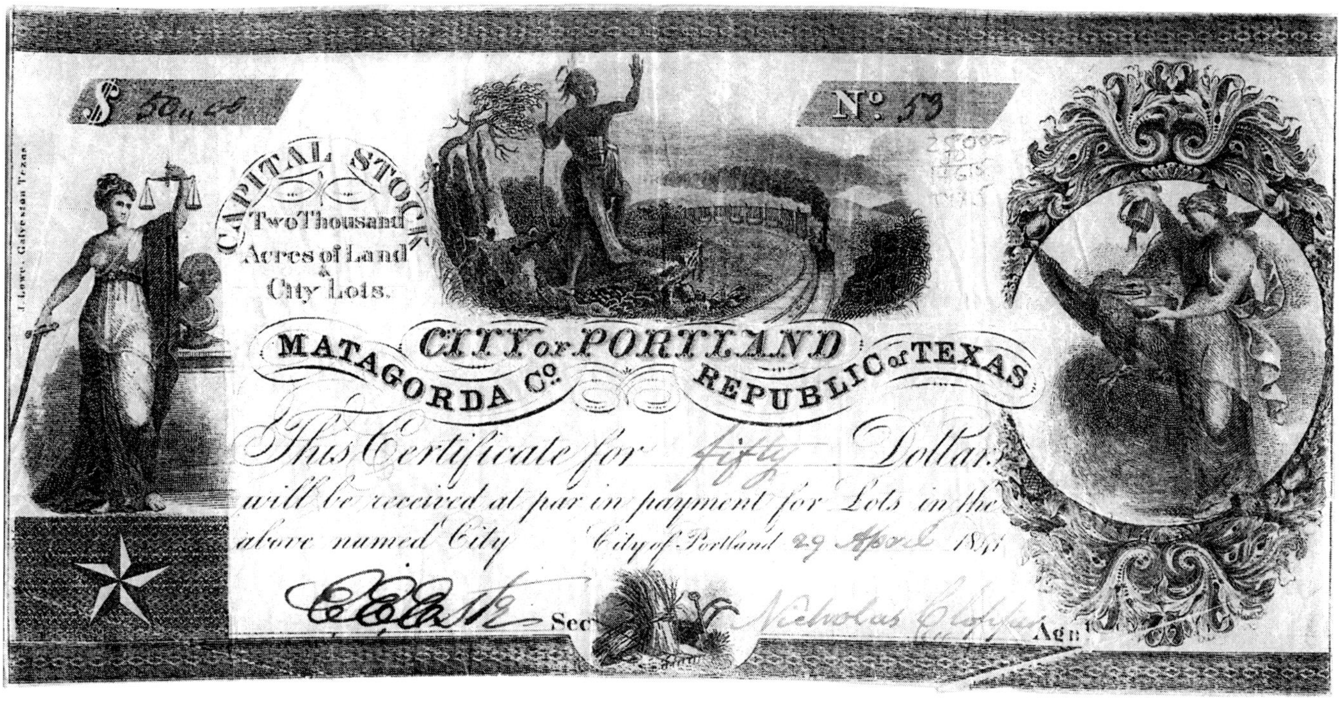


Figure 92. Stock Certificate, City of Portland, Matagorda County, 2,000 Acre Townsite, 1841. Nicholas Clopper of Ohio, with the help of his sons, operated a mercantile business at Clopper's Point before it became Swartwout. After selling out to the organizers of Swartwout, Clopper turned his attention to a site on the Colorado River between Tres Palacios Bay and Matagorda Bay. In 1841 the Cloppers founded the city of Portland. The planned community contained 2,000 acres. The economic incentive for that city was a railroad between Portland and Port Austin on the Bay and Tres Palacios Bay. The engraved stock certificate, the first such printing in Texas, permitted shareholders to exchange at par their stock for town lots.

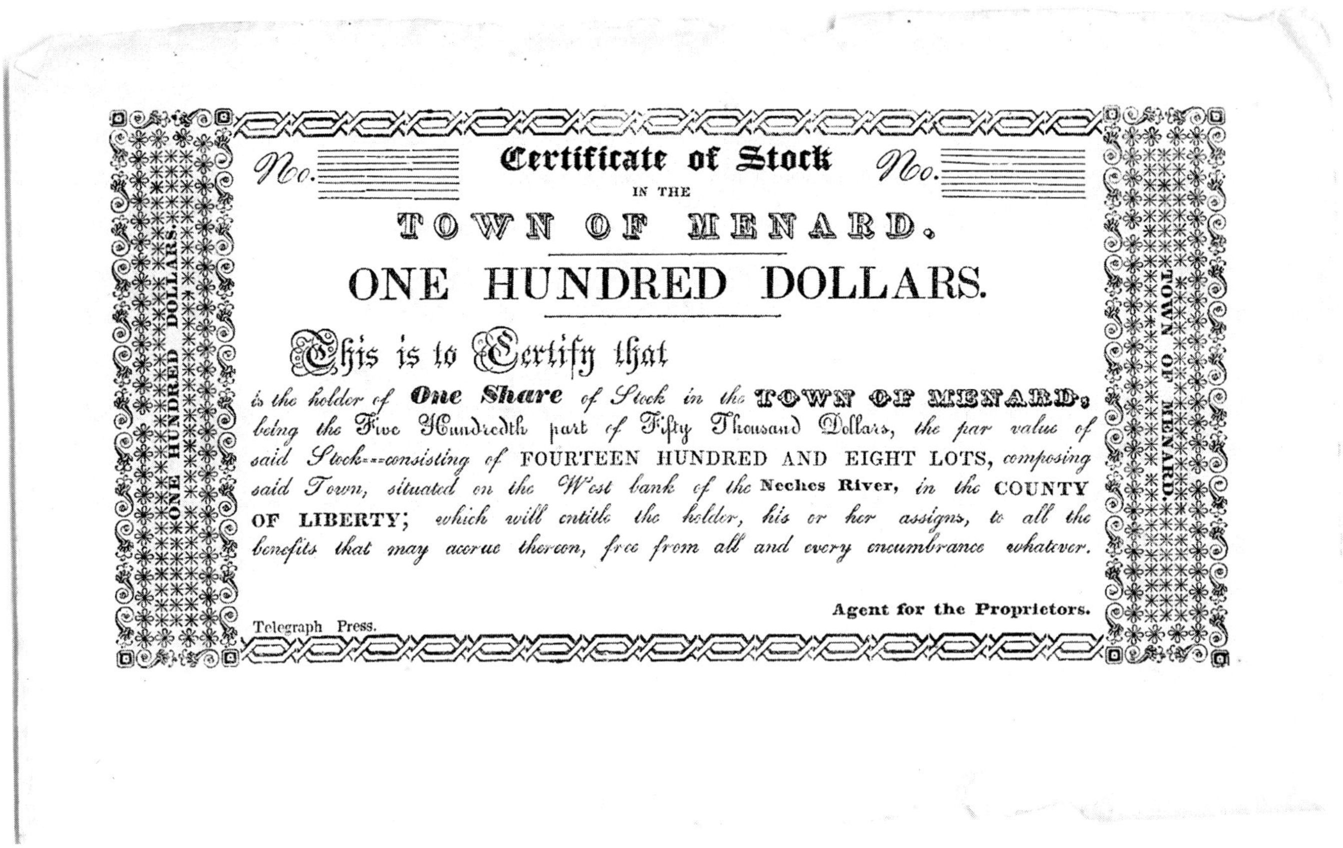
ONE HUNDRED DOLLARS.

No. **Certificate of Stock** No.

IN THE

TOWN OF MENARD.

ONE HUNDRED DOLLARS.

This is to Certify that

is the holder of **One Share** of Stock in the TOWN OF MENARD, being the Five Hundredth part of Fifty Thousand Dollars, the par value of said Stock---consisting of FOURTEEN HUNDRED AND EIGHT LOTS, composing said Town, situated on the West bank of the Neches River, in the COUNTY OF LIBERTY; which will entitle the holder, his or her assigns, to all the benefits that may accrue thereon, free from all and every encumbrance whatever.

Agent for the Proprietors.

Telegraph Press.

TOWN OF MENARD.

**Figure 93. Stock Certificate [Blank], Town of Menard, West Bank of the Neches River, Liberty County, 1,408 Lots [ca. 1838]. Peter J. Menard and his brother Michael Menard, both of Quebec, joined with William & McKinney to organize the town of Menard in 1838. Located on the Neches River in Liberty County, the East Texas site was surveyed into 1408 lots. Agent Stephen H. Everett of Bevilport marketed the shares. Shareholders had the right to exchange stock for lots. Each share represented 2/10 of 1 percent of the land comprising the town. The Menard brothers originally owned two leagues in the Vehlein Colony, which they acquired in 1835.**

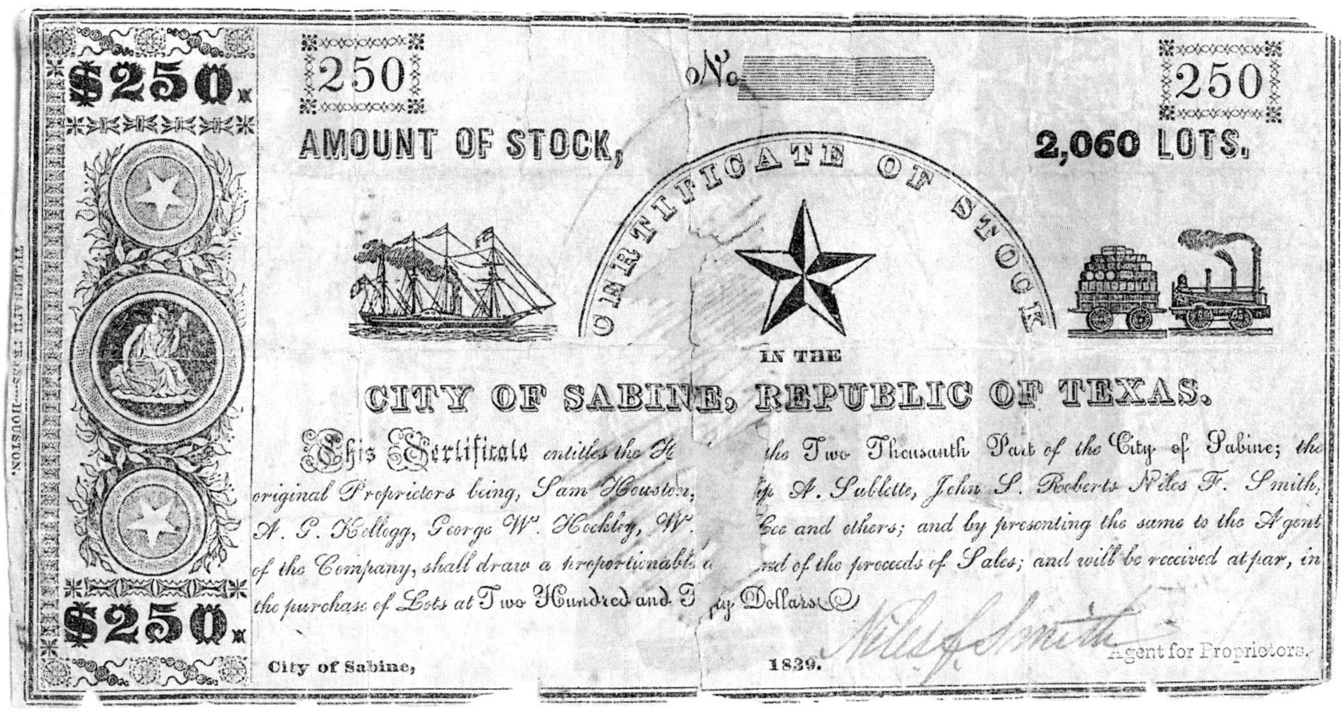


**Figure 94. Stock Certificate, City of Sabine, Receivable for Lots (2,060 Total), ca. 1839. Sam Houston and former Secretary of War Sidney Albert Johnston invested in a number of speculative town sites. They joined with several others to form the city of Sabine on the border of Louisiana. The platted town had 2,060 individual lots. The town proprietors conducted drawings to determine the distribution of the lots to owners of stock. An owner of a $250.00 certificate could redeem his share against the purchase price of the drawn lot. Niles F. Smith of New York was the company's resident agent. He helped design the city, which drew interest from commercial investors. Smith was an engineer and developer. Eventually he was appointed customs collector for the city of Sabine, a port on the Gulf.**

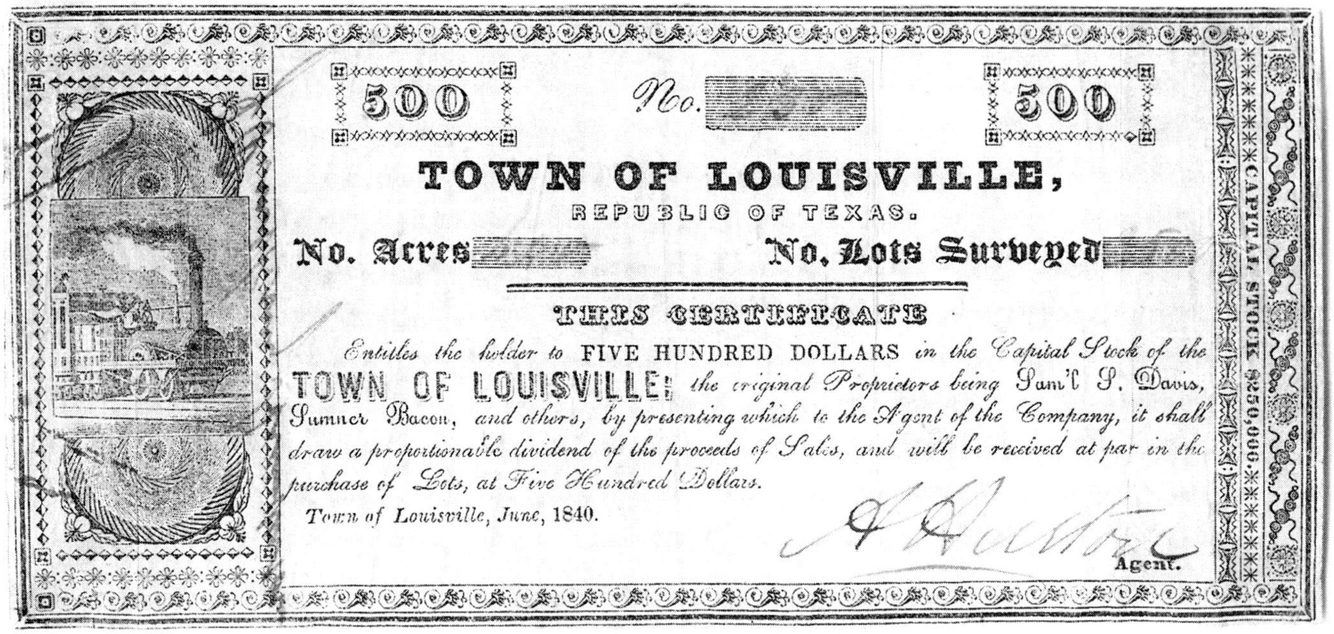


**Figure 95. Stock Certificate, Town of Louisville, Receivable in Lots 640 Acre Townsite of 2,500 Lots, 1840. The town of Louisville, formed in 1840 in Nacogdoches County, was created out of a grant dated 1836 in the Zavala Colony, located between the Neches and Trinity Rivers. The founder, Samuel Davis from Georgia, represented San Augustine in the Texas Congress when the town was organized. Almanzon Huston, who had participated in both the Fredonia and Texas Revolution as Quartermaster General, was the company's resident agent. Huston owned a league in Zavala's Grant located near present day Jefferson. Self-taught Presbyterian minister Samuel Bacon, of Massachusetts, represented the American Bible Society in Texas, and was Sam Davis's partner. Stockholders had the option of exchanging their $500.00 or $250.00 par value shares for town lots. A few hundred shares were sold. The illustrated certificate was owned and endorsed by J. Pinckney Henderson, Attorney General and Secretary of State in 1836.**

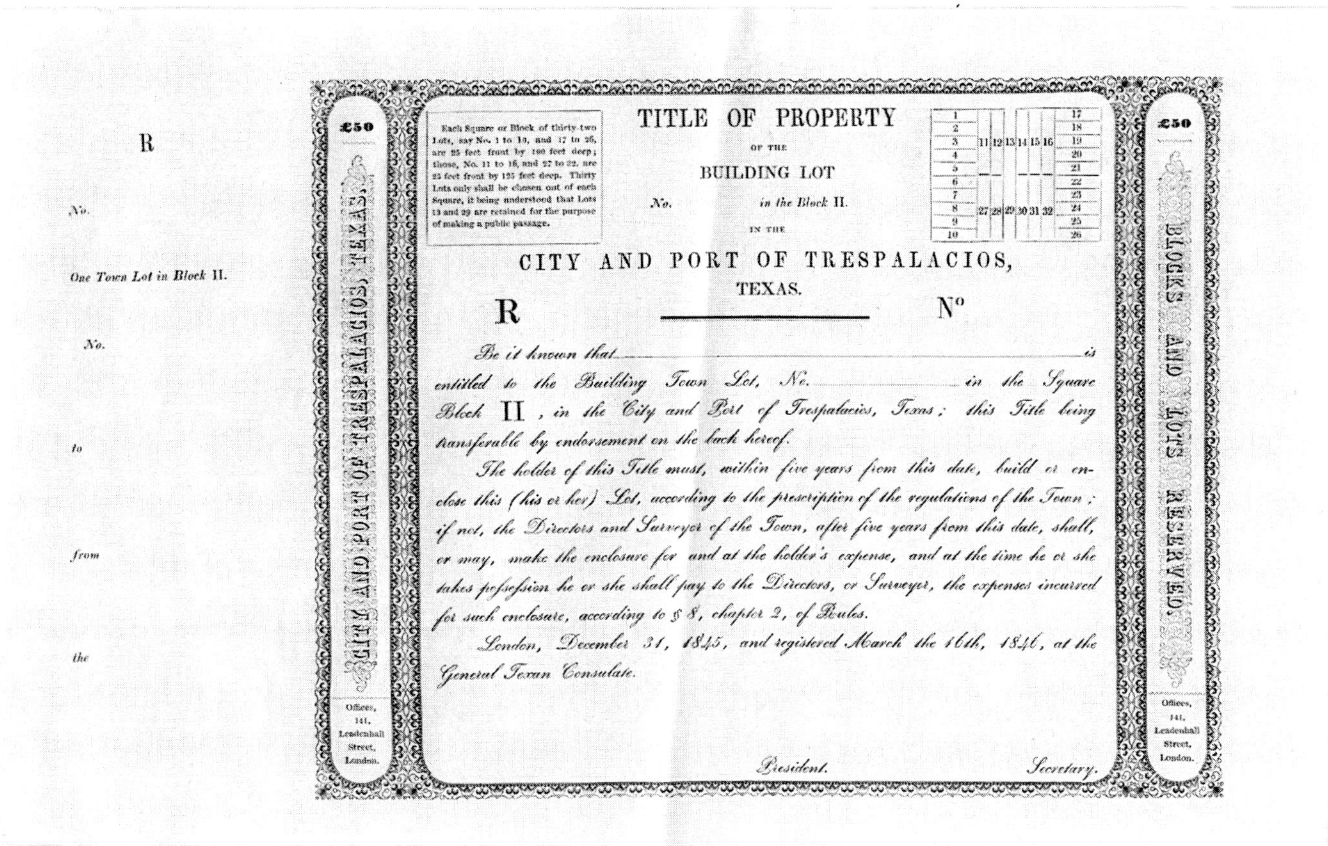

R

No.

One Town Lot in Block II.

No.

to

from

the

£50

CITY AND PORT OF TRESPALACIOS, TEXAS.

Offices, 141, Leadenhall Street, London.

Each Square or Block of thirty-two Lots, say No. 1 to 10, and 17 to 26, are 25 feet front by 100 feet deep; those, No. 11 to 16, and 27 to 32, are 25 feet front by 125 feet deep. Thirty Lots only shall be chosen out of each Square, it being understood that Lots 13 and 29 are retained for the purpose of making a public passage.

TITLE OF PROPERTY

OF THE

BUILDING LOT

No. in the Block II.

IN THE

CITY AND PORT OF TRESPALACIOS,

TEXAS.

R N°

Be it known that is entitled to the Building Town Lot, No. in the Square Block II, in the City and Port of Trespalacios, Texas; this Title being transferable by endorsement on the back hereof.

The holder of this Title must, within five years from this date, build or enclose this (his or her) Lot, according to the prescription of the regulations of the Town; if not, the Directors and Surveyor of the Town, after five years from this date, shall, or may, make the enclosure for and at the holder's expense, and at the time he or she takes possession he or she shall pay to the Directors, or Surveyor, the expenses incurred for such enclosure, according to § 8, chapter 2, of Rules.

London, December 31, 1845, and registered March the 16th, 1846, at the General Texan Consulate.

President. Secretary.

£50

BLOCKS AND LOTS RESERVED.

Offices, 141, Leadenhall Street, London.

**Figure 96. Title Lot [Blank], City and Port of Trespalacios, London, England, 1845. Originally named Tidehaven, the proposed steamer port of Trespalacios was a speculative town founded in 1845 by Pumphrey Burnett, in London, England, for sale in the European market. Purchasers of the Matagorda County town lots received conditional titles for their price of £50.00 per share of stock. The lots, either 2,500 or 3,125 square feet, had to be improved by the owner before title to the land would be deeded. The town grew out of a league in Austin's Colony originally granted to Pumphrey Burnett and Albert Lloyd Sojourner. The Texas Consulate in London registered and executed the foreign certificate in 1846.**

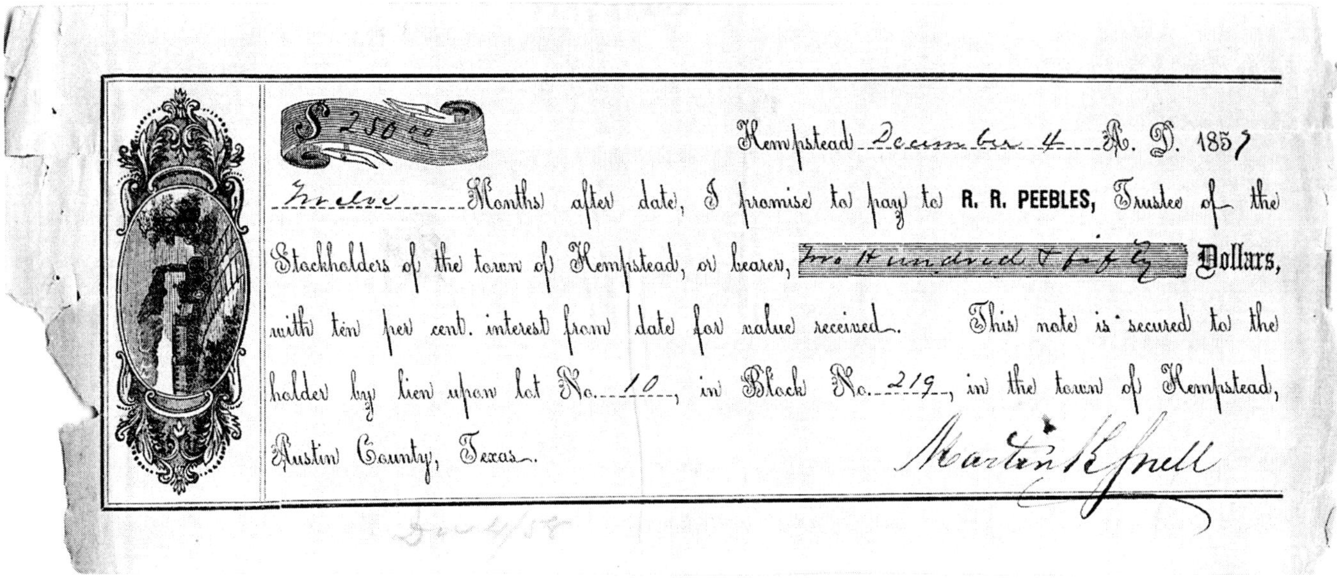

$250.00

Hempstead December 4 A. D. 1857

Twelve Months after date, I promise to pay to R. R. PEEBLES, Trustee of the Stockholders of the town of Hempstead, or bearer, Two Hundred & fifty Dollars, with ten per cent. interest from date for value received. This note is secured to the holder by lien upon lot No. 10, in Block No. 219, in the town of Hempstead, Austin County, Texas.

Martin K Snell

**Figure 97. Promissory Note, Town of Hempstead, Austin County, 1857. Dr. Richard Rodgers Peebles of Ohio settled at Washington-on-the-Brazos prior to the Revolution. He and John Shackelford founded J. Shackelford and Company, merchants in Houston and Galveston. Dr. Peebles' wife, the widow of Jared E. Groce, donated 2,000 acres of right-of-way to the Houston and Central Railroad. In 1858 the line was completed to the town of Hempstead. Peebles had formed the Hempstead Town Association in 1857, to capitalize on the new rail terminal. Residential lots sold for about $250. Buyers could finance over three years at 10 percent interest. Martin K. Snell signed his promissory note for $250.00 December 4, 1857, for lot 10 in Block 219 in Austin County. He paid in full June 10, 1859, and filed for a deed.**

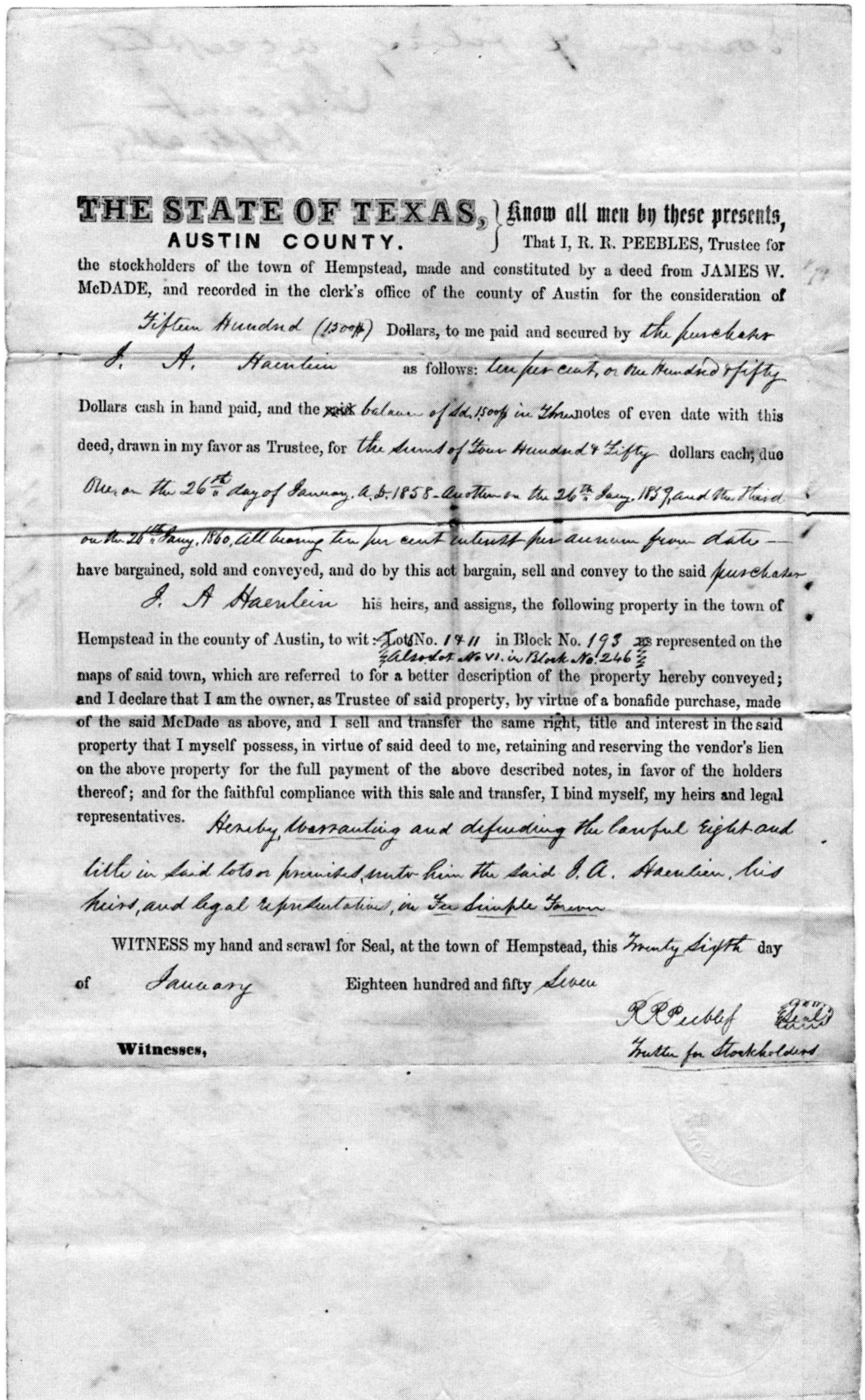

**THE STATE OF TEXAS,** } Know all men by these presents,
**AUSTIN COUNTY.** } That I, R. R. PEEBLES, Trustee for the stockholders of the town of Hempstead, made and constituted by a deed from JAMES W. McDADE, and recorded in the clerk's office of the county of Austin for the consideration of Fifteen Hundred (1500$) Dollars, to me paid and secured by the purchaser J. A. Haenlein as follows: ten per cent, or One Hundred & fifty Dollars cash in hand paid, and the ~~said~~ balance of sd. 1500$ in Three notes of even date with this deed, drawn in my favor as Trustee, for the Sum of Four Hundred & Fifty dollars each; due One, on the 26th day of January A.D. 1858 - Another on the 26th Jany. 1859, and the third on the 26th Jany. 1860, all bearing ten per cent interest per annum from date — have bargained, sold and conveyed, and do by this act bargain, sell and convey to the said purchaser J. A Haenlein his heirs, and assigns, the following property in the town of Hempstead in the county of Austin, to wit: ½ Lots No. 1 & 11 in Block No. 193 as represented on the ½ Also Lot No 21. in Block No. 246 ½ maps of said town, which are referred to for a better description of the property hereby conveyed; and I declare that I am the owner, as Trustee of said property, by virtue of a bonafide purchase, made of the said McDade as above, and I sell and transfer the same right, title and interest in the said property that I myself possess, in virtue of said deed to me, retaining and reserving the vendor's lien on the above property for the full payment of the above described notes, in favor of the holders thereof; and for the faithful compliance with this sale and transfer, I bind myself, my heirs and legal representatives. Hereby Warranting and defending the lawful right and title in said lots or premises, unto him the said J. A. Haenlein, his heirs, and legal representatives, in Fee Simple Forever

WITNESS my hand and scrawl for Seal, at the town of Hempstead, this Twenty Sixth day of January Eighteen hundred and fifty Seven

**Witnesses,**

R R Peebles [Seal]
Trustee for Stockholders

Figure 98. Warranty Deed Lots, Town of Hempstead, Austin County, 1857. J. A. Hawkins purchased commercial lots in the town of Hempstead for $1,500 and paid $150.00 down and financed the balance. He bought lots 1 and 11 in Block 193 and lot 21 in Block 246 on January 26, 1857. Hawkins received his warranty deed in January 1858. The lots were referenced on the town map filed in the county seat. Dr. Peebles personally promised to defend the warranty deed and all the lawful rights and title to which Hawkins was entitled, as a fee simple owner. Peebles signed as Trustee for the stockholder of the town of Hempstead. Peebles held security interest in the lots through a vendor lien.

No. ______ Shares.

Dallas Bridge Company.

This is to Certify

That ______ is entitled to ______

Share upon which the full amount of One Hundred Dollars in Gold each has been paid, in the Capital Stock of the Dallas Bridge Company, incorporated by the State of Texas, which Share ______ transferable only at the office of the Company in person or by attorney, and upon surrender of this Certificate.

Dallas, Texas, ______ 187__

Secretary. President.



Figure 99. "Gold" Stock Certificate for Dallas Bridge Company, Dallas, 1881. Roads, canals and bridges were crucial to the commercial growth of early Texas. After the Houston and Texas Central Railroad reached Dallas in 1872, the regional commercial center experienced a rapid period of expansion. The rail line ran to the Indian Territory north of the Red River. Trinity River ferryman Alexander Cockrell chartered the Dallas Bridge Company in 1860. Sarah Horton Cockrell carried the project to completion after her husband's death. The bridge was completed in 1872 as a connecter between East and West Texas. Mrs. Cockrell sold the bridge to the city of Dallas in 1878. The illustrated certificate, dated 1881, was to her son and business partner Frank Cockrell. At that time, the company had evolved into a real estate investment entity, although it retained the "Bridge Company" corporate form.

• CAPITAL, $65,000.00 •

No. 37

5 Shares.

The East-Side Building and Loan Company,

INCORPORATED UNDER THE LAWS OF THE STATE OF TEXAS.

OF DENISON, TEXAS.

This Certifies That Wm. A. Holmes is the owner of five Shares of the Capital Stock of the

EAST-SIDE BUILDING AND LOAN COMPANY, OF DENISON, TEXAS,

*fully paid, Transferable only at the office of the Company on return of this Certificate.*

In Witness Whereof, *The President and Secretary have hereunto subscribed their names and caused the Seal of the Company to be affixed, at*

*Denison, Texas,* Second *day of* April *A.D. 18*90

J. W. Perry *President.*

Wm. A. Holmes *Secretary.*

• SHARES, $100.00 EACH •

**Figure 100. Stock Certificate, East Side Building and Loan Company, Dennison, Texas, 1890. Both banks and thrift institutions were outlawed in Texas before the Civil War. Finance was through factors, merchants and private unregulated banks. Savings banks began after Reconstruction. Thrift institutions were often formed by real estate departments of railroads to foster sales of their land. The 1890 Dennison, Texas, East Side Building and Loan Company was one of the first in North Texas. It grew as a result of the rail terminal, the first in Texas for emigrants from the Indian Territory and Ohio Valley. The thrift had stated capital of $65,000.00. Wm. A. Holmes' five shares had a par value of $500.00. The company's primary market was home loans, as pictured on the stock certificate.**

**Figure 101. Stock Certificate [Blank], Anáhuac Townsite Company, Chambers County, 190_. Anáhuac has a history that traces back to the European discovery of Texas. The French encountered the Atakapon Indians at that location in the eighteenth century. By 1831 the Mexicans had built a military post and General Manuel de Mier y Terán named it Anáhuac, in honor of the Aztecs. Between 1832 and 1835 the area was the scene of several civil disturbances that preceded the Texas Revolution. After the war, Thomas Jefferson Chambers competed with other developers for control of the town. As a result, he was murdered. The town was dormant until 1907 when incorporators founded the Anáhuac Townsite Company, with stated capital of $40,000. One of the founders may have been a relative of the unindicted killer of Chambers. The discovery of oil brought prosperity to the region.**

# Chapter Notes

## Chapter I

1. Miller, Thomas Lloyd, *The Public Lands of Texas, 1519–1920* (Norman: University of Oklahoma Press, 1922) 8–9; see Seed, Patricia, *Ceremonies of Possession in Europe's Conquest of the New World, 1492–1640* (New York: Cambridge University Press, 1995); Almaraz, Jr., Félix D. & Almaraz, *The San Antonio Missions and Their System of Land Tenure* (Austin: University of Texas Press, 1989) 8–10; Scott, Florence Johnson, *Royal Land Grants of the Rio Grande, 1777–1821* (Rio Grande City: Texas Press, 1969) 14; Texas Title Company *Abstract of Title No. 76041*, vol. G-1, San Antonio; Bexar County Deed Records 515.

2. Bolton, Herbert E., and Thomas M. Marshall, *The Colonization of North America, 1492–1783* (New York: Macmillan, 1920) 26; for a more current interpretation see Chipman, Donald E., *Texas Through Time and Evolving Interpretations* (College Station: Texas A&M University Press, 1991) 102–103, 117–118; in general see Weber, Daniel J., *The Mexican Frontier, 1821–1846: The American Southwestern Under Mexico* (Albuquerque: University of New Mexico Press, 1982); Almaraz, *The San Antonio Missions* 8–9.

3. Castañeda, Carlos, *Our Catholic Heritage in Texas*, vol. 1 (Austin: Von Boeckmann Jones, 1936–1958) 352; Bishop, Curtis, *Lots of Land* (Austin: The Steck Company, 1949) 3–6.

4. Hughes, Anne E., *The Beginning of Spanish Settlements in the El Paso District.* (Berkeley: University of California Press, "Publications in History" vol. 1, no. 3, 1914) 311, 327, 330–334.

5. Chipman, Donald E., and Harriet Denise Joseph, *Spanish Texas 1519–1821* (Austin: University of Texas Press, 1992/2010) 112–113, 118; Almaraz, *The San Antonio Missions* 3–5, 9–15; Taylor, Virginia H., *The Spanish Archives of the General Land Office of Texas* (Austin: The Lone Star Press, 1955) 26–27.

6. *American State Papers, Public Lands*, vol. V, Jan. 4, 1828–Jan. 21, 1834 (Washington: Duff Green, 1834) 226, 229, 245, 254–256; Scott, Florence Johnson, *Royal Land Grants North of the Rio Grande 1777–1821* (Rio Grande City: Texas Press, 1969) 1–8.

7. Taylor, Virginia H., *The Spanish Archives of the GLO* 27–29.

8. Scott, *Royal Land Grants* 9–14.

9. *Ibid.*, 14–15.

10. Chipman and Joseph, *Spanish Texas* 164–165; 174–184; Miller, *The Public Lands of Texas* 6–7.

11. Wallace, Ernest, David M. Vigness and George B. Ward, *Documents in Texas History*, 2nd ed. (Austin: State House Press, 1994) 28.

12. Almaraz, *The San Antonio Missions* 13.

13. *Ibid.*, 17–18.

14. *Ibid.*

15. Simmons, Marc, *Spanish Government in New Mexico* (Santa Fe: University of New Mexico Press, 1968) 78–79, 179–180; Thornhoff, Robert H., "The First Ranch in Texas," *West Texas Historical Association Yearbook*, vol. 40 (Oct. 1964) 90–97.

16. Scott, *Royal Land Grants* 21–78.

17. Vigness, David M., "Nuevo Santander in 1795: A Provisional Inspection by Félix Calleja," *Southwestern Historical Quarterly*, vol. 75 (Apr. 1972) 462–463, 475, 477.

18. Chipman and Joseph, *Spanish Texas* 122, 188, 191, 197, 265; Taylor, *The Spanish Archives of the GLO* 15–16, 21.

19. Streeter, Thomas W., *Bibliography of Texas 1795–1845*, 5 vols. (Cambridge: Harvard University Press, 1955) No. 673.

20. Streeter, *Bibliography* Nos., 1056, 1056A.

21. Henderson, Harry McCamy, "The Magee-Gutiérrez Expedition," *Southwestern Historical Quarterly*, vol. 55 (Jul. 1951).

22. Streeter, *Bibliography* No. 1081.

23. Chipman, Donald E., *Spanish Texas, 1519–1821* (Austin: University of Texas Press, 1992).

24. Taylor, *The Spanish Archives of the GLO* 24–26; Bowden, J.J., *Spanish and Mexican Land Grants in the Chihuahua Acquisition* (El Paso: Texas Western Press, 1971) 182, 208.

## Chapter II

1. Bishop, *Lots of Land* 27; Streeter, *Bibliography* No. 683; Timmons, Wilbert H., *Tadeo Ortiz: Mexican Colonizer and Reformer* (El Paso: Texas Western Press, 1974) 15–16.

2. Gammel, Hans Peter Nielson, *Laws of Texas, 1822–1897*, 10 vols. (Austin: Gammel, 1898) I, 31–32, 38–40, 132–133; in general see Cantrell, Gregg, *Stephen F. Austin: Empresario of Texas* (New Haven, Conn.: Yale University Press, 1999).

3. Gammel, *Laws of Texas* I, 95; Taylor, *The Spanish Archives of the GLO* 60–62; Bishop, *Lots of Land* 30–31; Yokum, *History of Texas* I, 211.

4. Gammel, *Laws of Texas* I, 29; Yokum, *History of Texas* I, 211.

5. Gammel, *Laws of Texas* I, 125, 32; Yokum, *History of Texas* I, 229.

6. Barker, Eugene C., "The Government of Austin's Colony," *Southwestern Historical Quarterly*, vol. 21. (Jan. 1918); Taylor, *The Spanish Archives of the GLO* 37–38.

7. Bishop, *Lots of Land* 34–35; Miller, *The Public Lands of Texas, 1519–1920* 15–17.

8. Gammell, *Laws of Texas* I, 119, 125, 207, 216.

9. Taylor, *The Spanish Archives of the GLO* 41, 50.

10. Streeter, *Bibliography* No. 690.

11. Gammell, *Laws of Texas* I. 22, 384; Taylor, *The Spanish Archives of the GLO* 44–45.

12. Taylor, *The Spanish Archives of the GLO* 52–53; Rather, Ethel Ziwley, "Dewitt's Colony," *Quarterly of the Texas State Historical Association*, vol. 8 (1904–1905).

13. Gammell, *Laws of Texas* I, 109; Taylor, *The Spanish Archives of the GLO* 54–55; Bishop, *Lots of Land* 41–51.

14. Greaser, Galen D., *Catalogue of the Spanish Collection of the Texas General Land Office* (Austin: Texas GLO, 2003) Nos. 54, 55, 56, 1096; Yokum, *History of Texas* I, 277.

15. Greaser, *Catalogue of the Spanish Collection of the GLO* Nos. 451, 452, 458, 1091, 1092, 1078, 1080.

16. Gammel, *Laws of Texas* I, 223, 340; Taylor, *The Spanish Archives of the GLO* 51–52.

17. Gammel, *Laws of Texas* I, 180.

18. Gammell, *Laws of Texas* I, 384; Taylor, *The Spanish Archives of the GLO* 52.

19. Bishop, *Lots of Land* 76–77, 81–82; Taylor, *The Spanish Archives of the GLO* 53.

20. Streeter, *Bibliography* Nos. 1099, 1105; Bishop, *Lots of Land* 77, 80; Taylor, *The Spanish Archives of the GLO* 47–48.

21. Streeter, *Bibliography* No. 114; Garver, Lois, "Benjamin Rush Milam," *Southwestern Historical Quarterly*, vol. 38 (Oct. 1934), 112–115; Bishop, *Lots of Land* 78.

22. Gammel, *Laws of Texas* I, 305; Taylor, *The Spanish Archives of the GLO* 49; Bishop, *Lots of Land* 63–64.

23. Gammell, *Laws of Texas* I, 208, 224, 305; Taylor, *The Spanish Archives of the GLO* 49; Bishop, *Lots of Land* 63–64.

24. Taylor, *The Spanish Archives of the GLO* 49–50, 63; Bishop, *Lots of Land* 63–65.

25. Gammel, *Laws of Texas* I, 23; Taylor, *The Spanish Archives of the GLO* 45.

26. Streeter, *Bibliography* Nos. 9, 10, 11.

27. Greaser, *Catalogue of the Spanish Collection of the GLO* Nos. 522, 525, 526, 528, 530, 535, 542.

28. Taylor, *The Spanish Archives of the GLO* 63; Bishop, *Lots of Land* 88–89; Gammel, *Laws of Texas* I, 272, 336.

29. Taylor, *The Spanish Archives of the GLO* 56; Streeter, *Bibliography* Nos. 1102, 1110; Herrera, José María, "Vision of a Utopian Texas: Robert Owen's Colonization Scheme," *Southwestern Historical Quarterly*, vol. 116 (Apr. 2013) 343–356.

30. Taylor, *The Spanish Archives of the GLO* 56; Streeter, *Bibliography* Nos. 1121, 1120, 1196.

31. Henderson, Mary Virginia, "Minor Empresario Contracts for the Colonization of Texas, 1825–1834," *Southwestern Historical Quarterly*, vols. 31, 32 (Apr., Jun. 1928); Taylor, *The Spanish Archives of the GLO* 55–56; Bishop, *Lots of Land* 86–88; Streeter, *Bibliography* No. 1154.

## Chapter III

1. Bishop, *Lots of Land* 57–61; Gammel, *Laws of Texas* I, 256.

2. Manning, William R., "Poinsett's Mission to Mexico: A Discussion of His Interference in International Affairs," *American Journal of International Law* (New York, 1913); for an updated discussion see Parton, Dorothy Martha, *The Diplomatic Career of Joel Roberts Poinsett* (Washington D.C.: Catholic University of America Press, 1934).

3. Streeter, *Bibliography* No. 225, 761, 773, 794, 795, 814, 819; Graf, LeRoy P., "Colonizing Projects in Texas South of the Nueces 1820–1845," *Southwestern Historical Quarterly*, vol. 50 (Apr. 1947) 431–448.

4. Streeter, *Bibliography* Nos. 1168, 1169, 1176, 1230; Graf, "Colonizing Projects in Texas South of the Nueces 1820–1845" 437–444.

5. Greaser, *Catalogue of Spanish Collection* No. 1297; Gammel, *Laws of Texas* I, 291; Yokum, *History of Texas* I, 237.

6. Gammel, *Laws of Texas* I, 355, 387.

7. Greaser, *Catalogue of Spanish Collection* Nos. 1083, 1084, 458, 461, 462, 463, 1103, 1096; Gammel, *Laws of Texas* I, 410.

8. Greaser, *Catalogue of Spanish Collection* Nos. 1086, 1087, 1089, 718, 719, 721, 1082, 1083; *The Texas Almanac for 1857* 39.

9. Gammel, *Laws of Texas* I, 256.

10. "Instructions" of April 25, 1830; Kimball, M. D., *Laws and Decrees of the State of Coahuila and Texas...* (Houston: Telegraph Press, 1839) 70–74.

11. Henderson, "Minor Empresario Contracts for the Colonization of Texas, 1825–1834," vols. 31, 32; Taylor, *The Spanish Archives of the GLO* 56–57.

12. Gammell, *Laws of Texas* I, 277, 357; Taylor, *The Spanish Archives of the GLO* 59.

13. Gammel, *Laws of Texas* I, 299; Henson, Margaret Swett, *Samuel May Williams: Early Texas Entrepreneur* (College Station: Texas A&M University Press, 1976) 45–48, 54, 57.

14. Gammel, *Laws of Texas* I, 189; Taylor, *The Spanish Archives of the GLO* 61–62.

15. Greaser, *Catalogue of the Spanish Collection of the GLO* I, 3–4; Timmons, *Tadeo Ortiz: Mexican Colonizer and Reformer*, 70–74.

16. Taylor, *Spanish Archives of the GLO* 63–65; Streeter, *Bibliography* No. 790. Greaser, *Catalogue of the Spanish Collection of the GLO* I, 4; Gammel, *Laws of Texas* I, 357.

17. Birster, Louis E., *John Charles Beales Rio Grande Colony* (Austin: State Historical Association, 2009) 102, 110–111, 133–136, 247–248; Taylor, *The Spanish Archives of the GLO* 56–57; Bishop, *Lots of Land* 82–84.

18. Streeter, *Bibliography* Nos. 1119, 1138; Bishop, *Lots of Land* 82, 85.

19. Streeter, *Bibliography* Nos. 1146, 1147, 1151, 1152, 1153; Bishop, *Lots of Land* 82–86; Taylor, *The Spanish Archives of the GLO* 56.

20. Streeter, *Bibliography* Nos. 1157, 1158, 1159, 1160; Bishop, *Lots of Land* 84–85.

21. Williams, *The Animating Pursuit of Speculation* 19–20; Bishop, *Lots of Land* 63–68.

22. Streeter, *Bibliography* No. 1117; Taylor, *The Spanish Archives of the GLO* 49; Bishop, *Lots of Land* 65–68.

23. Streeter, *Bibliography* No. 1133; Webster, Daniel, *Claims of the Union Land Company* (New York, 1949); Greaser, *Catalogue of Spanish Collection* Nos. 1481, 1576.

24. Bishop, *Lots of Land* 68–73; Taylor, *The Spanish Archives of the GLO* 45–47.

25. Taylor, *The Spanish Archives of the GLO* 46–47; Gammel, *Laws of Texas* I, 385; Bishop, *Lots of Land* 68–76.

26. *The Texas Almanac for 1857...* (Galveston: Richardson and Co. at the News Office, 1856) 39–46; Rowland, Kate Mason, "General John Thompson Mason," *Quarterly of the Texas State Historical Association*, vol. 11 (Jan. 1908).

27. Gammel, *Laws of Texas* I, 380, 389, 391, 397; Bishop, *Lots of Land* 98–101; Taylor, *The Spanish Archives of the GLO* 57; Greaser, *Catalogue of the Spanish Collection of the GLO* I, 142, 143, 179, 173; Lack, Paul, *The Diary of William Fairfax Gray: From Virginia to Texas, 1835–1837* (Dallas: Southwest Studies SMU, 1997) 105–106; Attorney Mussina, letter to the editor, "Judge John C. Watrous and the New York Land Company" (*Civilian and Gazette*, New York, June 6, 1859).

28. Gammel, *Laws of Texas* I, 391, 357; Taylor, *The Spanish Archives of the GLO* 58; Greaser, *Catalogue of the Spanish Collection* I, 52, 28; Lack, *The Diary of William Fairfax Gray* 90–91.

29. Gammel, *Laws of Texas* I, 389, 394, 393, 272; Taylor, *Spanish Archives of the GLO* 57–58; Greaser, *Catalogue of the Spanish Collection of the GLO* I, 171, 58; Hogan, William Ransom, *The Texas Republic. a Social and Economic History* (Norman: University of Oklahoma Press, 1946).

30. Gammel, *Laws of Texas* I, 407, 413; Lang, *Financial History of the Public Lands of Texas* 30–31.

31. Thrall, A. M., *A History of Texas* (New York: University Publishing, 1876) 84–85; Yokum, *History of Texas* I, 352–353, II, 65.

32. Gammel, *Laws of Texas* I, 352, 419.

## Chapter IV

1. Gammel, *Laws of Texas* I, 541, 1081.

2. Gammel, *Laws of Texas* I, 737, 747; Streeter, *Bibliography* No. 189.

3. Gammel, *Laws of Texas* I, 411, 420, 541, 1081.

4. Streeter, *Bibliography* No. 140; Miller, *The Public Lands of Texas, 1519–1920* 23–24.

5. Gammel, *Laws of Texas* I, 397, 1018, 1036.

6. *The Texas Almanac of 1857* 47; Yokum, *History of Texas* II, 229; Lack, *The Diary of William Fairfax Gray* 86.

7. Gammel, *Laws of Texas* I, 593.

8. Gammel, *Laws of Texas* I, 948, 956, 960.

9. Gammel, *Laws of Texas* I, 972, 1029; Williams, *The Animating Pursuit of Speculation* 69, 84, 92–93.

10. Gammel, *Laws of Texas* I, 1128, 1133; Brown, Alma Howell, "The Counselor Service of the Republic of Texas," *Southwestern Historical Quarterly*, vol. 33 (Jan., Apr. 1930).

11. Lang, Aldon Socrates, *Financial History of the Public Lands of Texas* (New York: Arno Press, 1979) 38.

12. McKitrick, Reuben, *The Public Land System of Texas, 1823–1910* (New York: Arno Press, 1918/1979) 79–83; Streeter, *Bibliography* No. 1222.

13. Gouge, W. M., *The Fiscal History of Texas* (Philadelphia: Lippincott, Grambo, 1852) 53; Lang, *Financial History of the Public Lands of Texas* 38–39.

14. Gammel, *Laws of Texas* I, 1289, 1488, 1498, 1507.

15. Gammel, *Laws of Texas* I, 1092.

16. Gammel, *Laws of Texas* I, 1136, 1311, 1400, 1309; Item #176, "Vermont Texas Land Company, One Share, One Hundred Dollars!" Wm. Reese Co., Catalogue #309, *Western Americana* [Jan. 2014].

17. Gammel, *Laws of Texas* I, 1136; Williams, *Animating Pursuit of Speculation* 80–82, 94.

18. Gammel, *Laws of Texas* I, 1484; Miller, *Financial History of Texas* 60; Gauge, *Fiscal History of Texas* 280–281; Williams, *Animating Pursuit of Speculation* 82–85.

19. Miller, *Financial History of Texas* 60–62; Williams, *Animating Pursuit of Speculation* 100–104, 117, 125.

20. Gammel, *Laws of Texas* II, 624.

21. Gammel, *Laws of Texas* V, 663, 683; Miller, *Financial History of Texas* 150.

## Chapter V

1. Gammel, *Laws of Texas* I, 525.
2. Gammel, *Laws of Texas* I, 538, 925, 951, 982, 1094; Lang, *Financial History of the Public Lands of Texas* 92–94; Miller, *The Public Lands of Texas, 1519–1920* 45–46.
3. Miller, *The Public Lands of Texas, 1519–1920* 34, 36; Gammel, *Laws of Texas* I, 1134, 1094, 1324, 1367, 1368, 1414.
4. Gammel, *Laws of Texas* I, 50, III, 52; Miller, *The Public Lands of Texas, 1519–1920* 49–50.
5. Miller, *The Public Lands of Texas, 1519–1920* 56.
6. Gammel, *Laws of Texas* II, 15, 17, 688; Miller, *The Public Lands of Texas, 1519–1920* 46–47.
7. Miller, *The Public Lands of Texas, 1519–1920* 47; Gammel, *Laws of Texas* VI, 45, VII, 423.
8. Miller, Thomas E., "Texas Land Grants to Veterans," *The Southwestern Historical Quarterly*, vol. 64 (Jan. 1961) 342, 347; Gammel, *Laws of Texas* VIII, 1334, 1475.
9. Gammel, *Laws of Texas* VII, 423, IX, 214, 319; Miller, Thomas L., "Texas Land Grants to Confederate Veterans and Widows," *The Southwestern Historical Quarterly*, vol. 69 (Jul. 1965) 59–65.
10. McKitrick, *The Pubic Land System of Texas*, 76–78; Gammell, *Laws of Texas*, V, 220.
11. Miller, Thomas Lloyd, *Bounty and Donation Land Grants of Texas, 1835–1888* (Austin: University of Texas Press, 1967) 55; Gammel, *Laws of Texas* I, 1404.
12. Gammel, *Laws of Texas* I, 1069.
13. McKitrick, *The Public Land System of Texas* 42; Gammel, *Laws of Texas* I. 1069.
14. Gammel, *Laws of Texas* I, 1324; Bishop, *Lots of Land* 119.
15. Gammel, *Laws of Texas* I, 1407; Bishop, *Lots of Land* 115–118, 124.
16. Miller, *The Public Lands of Texas, 1519–1920* 32; Gammel, *Laws of Texas* II, 591; Lang, *Financial History of the Public Lands of Texas* 95; Yokum, *History of Texas* II, 283–284.
17. Gammel, *Laws of Texas* II, 554, 777; Miller, *The Public Lands of Texas, 1519–1920* 34.

## Chapter VI

1. Streeter, *Bibliography* No. 137.
2. Gammel, *Laws of Texas* I, 1404, 1323, 1276.
3. Streeter, *Bibliography* No. 1313.
4. Lang, *Financial History of the Public Lands of Texas* 37.
5. Streeter, *Bibliography* Nos. 698, 700, 705; Henson, Margaret Swett, *Samuel May Williams* (College Station: Texas A&M University Press, 1976) 90–91, 94–96; Gammel, *Laws of Texas* I, 1289, 1130, 1136.
6. Streeter, *Bibliography* Nos. 272, 357, 443.
7. Gammel, *Laws of Texas* I, 1327, II, 61; Lang, *Financial History of the Public Lands of Texas* 49–51.
8. Streeter, *Bibliography* No. 1352; Gammel, *Laws of Texas* II, 161, 377.
9. Gammel, *Laws of Texas* III, 790, 1539, V, 619; Lang, *Financial History of the Public Lands of Texas* 52–53; Bishop, *Lots of Land* 183–185.
10. Texas Christian University, Center for Texas Studies, Sul Ross State University, and Museum of the Big Bend, *Going to Texas. Five Centuries of Texas Maps* (Fort Worth: TCU Press, 2007) 106.
11. Streeter, *Bibliography* No. 320.
12. Streeter, *Bibliography* Nos. 428, 1429.
13. Miller, *Financial History of Texas* 145.
14. Gouge, William M., *The Fiscal History of Texas* (Philadelphia: Lippincott, Grambo, 1852) 272, 286.

## Chapter VII

1. Morgenthaler, Jefferson, *Promised Land: Solms, Castro & Sam Houston's Colonization Contracts* (College Station: Texas A&M University Press, 2009) VIII, 68.
2. Morgenthaler, *Promised Land* 20–21.
3. Vigness, David M., "Relations of the Republic of Texas and the Republic of the Rio Grande," *Southwestern Historical Quarterly*, vol. 57 (Jan. 1954); Yokum, *History of Texas* II, 289–298.
4. Gammel, *Laws of Texas* III, 1219, 1220, IV, 626.
5. Gammel, *Laws of Texas* I, 264, II, 35, 554, 785; McKitrick, *The Public Land System of Texas* 46–47; Yokum, *History of Texas* II, 309; Winchester, Robert Glenn, *James Pinckney Henderson: Texas' First Governor* (San Antonio: Naylor, 1971) 42–44.
6. Morgenthaler, *Promised Land* 14–16; Gammel, *Laws of Texas* II, 542; Bishop, *Lots of Land* 84–85.
7. Streeter, *Bibliography* No. 982.
8. Morgenthaler, *Promised Land* 20–21, 25–29.
9. Chase, Mary Katherine, *Négociations de la République du Texas en Europe, 1837–1845* (Paris: Librairie Ancienne Honoré Champion, 1932) "Corte Ii." 114–115; Streeter, *Bibliography* No. 1452.
10. Gammel, *Laws of Texas* II, 785; Morgenthaler, *Promised Land* 19–21, 24, 151; Adams, Ephraim Douglass, *British Interests and Activities in Texas, 1838–1846* (Baltimore: Johns Hopkins Press, 1910) 51, 74–75.
11. McKitrick, *Public Land System of Texas* 45–46; Miller, *The Public Lands of 1519–1970* 36–37.
12. Bishop, *Lots of Land* 139–142; Gammel, *Laws of Texas* II, 554, 786, 851.
13. Connor, Seymour V., "The Peters' Colony of Texas" (Austin: Texas State Historical Association, 1959) 42; Streeter, *Bibliography* Nos. 1462, 1463.
14. Streeter, *Bibliography* No. 1461; Connor, "The Peters' Colony of Texas" 91–92, 99; *Map of Clay County*. Austin, February 1880. Lithographer, August Gast and Co. New Press, St. Louis.
15. Connors, "The Peters' Colony of Texas" 163–164.
16. Connor, "The Peters' Colony of Texas" 52, 61–65, 81; Gammel, *Laws of Texas* II, 958, 1154; Eagleton, Nancy E., "The Mercer Colony of Texas, 1844–1883," *Southwestern Historical Quarterly*, vol. 39 (Apr. 1938) 275–291.
17. Streeter, *Bibliography* Nos. 1520, 1594, 1596, 1597, 1598, 1599; Bishop, *Lots of Land* 142–143.
18. Bishop, *Lots of Land* 140, 145–146; Eagleton, "The Mercer Colony in Texas, 1844–1883," vol. 39 (Apr. 1938) 275–291.
19. Morgenthaler, *Promised Land* 20–21.
20. Bishop, *Lots of Land* 166–170; Crook, Cornella English, *Henry Castro: A Study of Early Colonization in Texas* (San Antonio: St. Mary's Christianity Press, 1988) 187–195.
21. Crook, *Henry Castro* 141–146, 217–224, 161–164, 169–172.
22. Biesele, Rudolph, *History of the German Settlements in Texas, 1831–1861* (Austin: Eakin Press, 1931/1987) 25–27, 46–47, 64–65, 71–76, 66–69; Reed, S. G., *A History of the Texas Railroad* (Houston: St. Clair Publishing, 1941) 114.
23. Gammel, *Laws of Texas* II, 954, 958; Bishop, *Lots of Land* 159–165;

Roemer, *Texas with Particular Reference to German Immigration and the Physical Appearance of the Land* 15–18.

24. Gammel, *Laws of Texas* III, 146, 492, 1469, 1471, 1479, IV, 1440, V, 478, VIII, 565; Biesele, *German Settlement in Texas* 77–82.
25. Bishop, *Lots of Land* 165; *The Texas Almanac of 1857* 37.

## Chapter VIII

1. Gammel. *Laws of Texas* I, 1193; Bancroft, Hubert Howe, *History of Arizona and New Mexico, 1530–1888* (Albuquerque: Horn & Wallace, 1962) 194–195, 647–649, 756–764.
2. "Memorial for the Establishment of a Territorial Government," February 27, 1850; *Constitution of the State of West Texas* (Austin, 1869) sections I, IX, X; Winkler, Ernest William, ed., "Platforms of Political Parties in Texas," *Bulletin of the University of Texas*, no. 51 (Austin: University of Texas Press, 1916) 122–123.
3. Bishop, *Lots of Land* 180–181; Gammel, *Laws of Texas* I, 324; Scott, Florence Johnson, *Royal Land Grants North of the Rio Grande, 1777–1821* (Rio Grande City: Texian Press, 1969) 105–107.
4. Gammel, *Laws of Texas* III, 1533, IV, 1027; Scott, *Royal Land Grants of the Rio Grande* 105–107; Bowden, J. J., *Spanish and Mexican Land Grants in the Chihuahua Acquisition* (El Paso: Texas Western Press, 1971) 96–97, 106; Gammel, *Laws of Texas* III, 1533, IV, 1027; Scott,

*Royal Land Grants of the Rio Grande* 105–107; Bowden, *Spanish and Mexican Land Grants in the Chihuahua Acquisition* 96–97, 106.

5. Greaser, Galen D. and Jesús F. de la Teja, "Initiating Title to Spanish and Mexican Land Grants in the Trans-Nueces," *Southwestern Historical Quarterly*, vol. 95 (Apr. 1992); Taylor, *The Spanish Archives of the GLO* 132–136; *The Texas Almanac for 1857* 36.

6. Gammel, *Laws of Texas* IX, 1371, X, 234; Bowden, *Spanish and Mexican Land Grants in the Chihuahua Acquisition* 151–154.

7. Bowden, *Spanish and Mexican Land Grants in the Chihuahua Acquisition* 110–112, 129–134, 178–182, 175–176, 184–192.

8. Rubio, Abel S., *Stolen Heritage: A Mexican American's Rediscovery of His Family's Lost Land Grant* (Austin: Eakin Press, 1986) viii; Grant, Ulysses S., *The Personal Memoirs*, 2 vols. (New York: Charles L. Webster, 1886) 544.

9. Streeter, *Bibliography* Nos. 243, 286, 288, 290; Yokum, *The History of Texas* I, 328, II, 265–271.

10. Gammel, *Laws of Texas* I, 410, 546.

11. Streeter, *Bibliography* Nos. 261, 604; Gammel, *Laws of Texas* I, 1001, II, 814, 946, III, 812.

12. Gammel, *Laws of Texas* III, 1019, 1495, VIII, 376.

13. Gammel, *Laws of Texas* IV, 503, 1154, V, 991, 1086; Wright, Bill, *The Tiguas: Pueblo Indians of Texas* (El Paso: Texas Western Press, 1985) 15–27; Wright, Bill, and E. John Gesick, Jr., *The Texas Kickapoo: Keeper of Tradition* (El Paso: Texas Western Press, 1996) 20–25.

## Chapter IX

1. Gammel, *Laws of Texas* II, 125, 1294; McKitrick, *Public Land System of Texas* 49–51.

2. Gammel, *Laws of Texas* II, 16, 668.

3. McKitrick, *Public Land System of Texas* 47–52; Gammel, *Laws of Texas* II, 1073.

4. Gammel, *Laws of Texas* II, 1073, III, 1317, 1550, IV, 474, 1017; "Decreto Imperial de 5 Septiembre de Para Fomentar La Inmigración" (Mexico: Imprenta de Mariano Villanueva, 1866).

5. Gammel, *Laws of Texas* V, 1121.

6. Gould, Florence C., and Patricia N. Pando, *Claiming Their Land: Women Homesteaders in Texas* (El Paso: Texas Western Press, 1991) 2–5, Appendix "A" and "B," 53–98.

7. Rozek, Barbara J., *Come to Texas: Enticing Immigrants, 1865–1915* (College Station: Texas A&M University Press, 2009) 12–15, 18–20.

8. Gammel, *Laws of Texas* V, 1375, VII, 152.

9. Rozek, *Come to Texas* 89.

10. Gammel, *Laws of Texas* VI, 242.

11. *Proceedings of the Democratic State Convention* (Austin: State Gazette Job Office, 1871) 8; Rozek, *Come to Texas* 18; Gammel, *Laws of Texas* VII, 420, VI, 1031.

12. Rozek, *Come to Texas* 25–27, 33–35; *Texas: The Home for the Emigrant, from Everywhere* (Houston: A.C. Gray, State Printer, 1873).

13. Gammel, *Laws of Texas* VII, 201, 211, 285.

14. Gammel, *Laws of Texas* VII, 1049, 1124, 1505.

15. Rozek, *Come to Texas* 105–106, 111, 120.

16. Gammel, *Laws of Texas* VIII, 823.

17. *Hogue V Baker*, 92 Texas 58, 1898; Gammel, *Laws of Texas* VIII, 144, IX, 55, 211, 296, 881; Bishop, *Lots of Land* 292–293.

18. Bishop, *Lots of Land* 289–290; Miller, *The Public Lands of Texas, 1519–1920* 108–110; McKitrick, *The Public Land System of Texas* 92–93; Gammel, *Laws of Texas* I, 333, 86, II, 134, 320, III, 195, 475.

19. *The Texas Almanac of 1857* 35–37.

20. *The Texas Almanac of 1857* 35; Bishop, *Lots of Land* 280–293; Gammel, *Laws of Texas* II, 135, IV, 1020, 489, VIII, 74, 812, 911, 1052.

21. Gammel, *Laws of Texas* IV, 489.

22. Gammel, *Laws of Texas* III, 1461, V, 504, 1126, VI, 53, 242, VII, 419, 467.

23. Gammel, *Laws of Texas* IV, 494, VIII, 811, IX, 633.

24. Gammel, *Laws of Texas* XI, 653, 970; *Statistics and Information Concerning the State of Texas*, General Passenger Department of the Missouri and Pacific Railroad Co. (Woodman & Dicerman Printing, St. Louis, 1889) 21–22.

## Chapter X

1. Taylor, *Spanish Archives of the GLO* 208–209; Gammel, *Laws of Texas* I, 1256.

2. In general see Ray Miller, *Texas Forts* (Houston: Concobran Press, 1995).

3. Gammel, *Laws of Texas* I, 1217, 191, 1523, II, 193, 952, 499, III, 360.

4. Gammel, *Laws of Texas* II, 15, 1013, 1169; Bishop, *Lots of Land* 252–253.

5. Gammel, *Laws of Texas* VIII, 482; Reed, A. *History of Texas Railroads* 164.

6. Gammel, *Laws of Texas* I, 1188, 1371, II, 1173, 1237, 1305.

7. Gammel, Laws of Texas IV, 31, 464, 653, V, 162.

8. Miller, *The Public Lands of Texas, 1519–1920* 72–74, 287–289; Gammel, *Laws of Texas* VIII, 331.

9. Gammel, *Laws of Texas* III, 1478; Miller, *The Public Lands of Texas, 1519–1920* 85–87.

10. Gammel, *Laws of Texas* IV, 956; Miller, *The Public Land of Texas, 1519–1920* 90–91; Yokum, *History of Texas* I, 259.

11. Gammel, *Laws of Texas* V, 485, 749.

12. Gammel, *Laws of Texas* V, 676; Miller, *The Public Lands of Texas, 1519–1920* 91–94.

13. Miller, *The Public Lands of Texas, 1519–1920* 93; Nance, Joseph Milton, "The Early History of Bryan: Hoods Brigade" (N.p.: Bryan Centennial Committee, June 1862); Gammel, *Laws of Texas* V, 737.

14. Gammel, *Laws of Texas* VIII, 630.

15. Gammel, *Laws of Texas* VI, 1621, VII, 80, 316, 714.

16. Gammel, *Laws of Texas* VIII, 310, 449.

17. Gammel, *Laws of Texas* VIII, 449, 1089, IX, 263; Miller, *The Public Lands of Texas, 1519–1920* 74, 83.

18. Miller, *The Public Lands of Texas, 1519–1920* 291–293.

19. Reed, *A History of Railroads in Texas* 123, 141–149; Bishop, *Lots of Land* 256–258; Gammel, *Laws of Texas* III, 1145, 1178, 1184, 1190, 1208, 1214, 1231, 1245, 1253, 1268.

20. Reed, *A History of Texas Railroads* 99–103; Bishop, *Lots of Land* 259–262; Gammel, *Laws of Texas* III, 1245, IV, 7.

21. Reed, *A History of Texas Railroads* 137; Gammel, *Laws of Texas* IV, 449.

22. Reed, *A History of the Texas Railroads* 150–157, 170–171; Miller, *The Public Lands of Texas, 1519–1920* 100–105; Bishop, *Lots of Land* 262–266; Gammel, *Laws of Texas* VII, 676, IX, 263.

23. Bishop, *Lots of Land* 267–269; Reed, *A History of Texas Railroads* 172, 185; Gammel, *Laws of Texas* X, 84, 370.

24. Gammel, *Laws of Texas* IX, 1202, 263, XI, 660, XII, 967.

## Chapter XI

1. Van Zant, Lee, *Early Economic Policies of the Government of Texas* (El Paso: Texas Western Press, 1966) 9–13.

2. Gammel, *Laws of Texas* X, 84, 370.

3. Gammel, *Laws of Land* IX, 80; McKitrick, *The Public Lands of Texas, 1519–1920* 86–87; Bishop, *Lots of Land* 196–199.

4. Haley, J. Evetts, *XIT Ranch of Texas* (Austin: University of Texas Press, 1953/1967) 51–55, 71–73.

5. Haley, *XIT Ranch* 208–211, 225.

6. Bishop, *Lots of Land* 203–204, 212, 224–229.

7. Clarke, Mary Whatley, *The Swenson Saga and the SMS Ranches* (Austin: Jenkins Publishing, 1976) 5.

8. Shelly, Lester Fields, *The Francklyn Land and Cattle Company: A Panhandle Enterprise 1882–1957* (Austin: University of Texas Press, 1963) 5–6.

9. Taylor, Virginia H., *The Franco-Texas Land Company* (Austin: University of Texas Press, 1969) 111–116, 121, 139–141, 278.

10. Taylor, *The Franco-Texas Land Company* 290–293; Map of Texas Showing Route the "Houston and Texas Central" (ca. 1880) De Córdova, Wither and Company, Austin. Author's collection.

## Chapter XII

1. Barker, E. C., "Land Speculation as a Cause of the Texas Revolution," *Quarterly of the Texas Historical Association*, vol. 10 (1906–1907) 86.

2. Williams, *Animating Pursuit of Speculation* 138–139.

3. Sterling, Susanne, *Land Is the Cry: Warren Angus Ferris, Pioneer Texas Surveyor and*

*Founder of Dallas County* (Austin: State Historical Commission, 1998) 99–107, 124.

4. Streeter, *Bibliography* No. 1324.

5. Streeter, *Bibliography* Nos. 450, 1389, 1390, 328.

6. Streeter, *Bibliography* No. 236.

7. Streeter, *Bibliography* No. 1640.

8. Streeter, *Bibliography* No. 312.

9. Hogan, *The Texas Republic: A Social and Economic History* 87–93; Streeter, *Bibliography* No. 311.

10. Moore, Francis, Jr., *Maps and Descriptions of Texas...* (Philadelphia: H. Tanner, 1840) 28–29; Bonnell, George W., *Topographical Description of Texas to Which Is Added an Account of Indian Tribes* (Austin: Clark, Wing and Brown, 1840) 119, 120, 150.

11. Fisher, Orceneth, *Sketches of Texas in 1840* (Springfield, Ill.: Walters and Weber, Printers, 1841) 12, 20–41; Hunt, Richard S., and Jesse F. Randel, *A New Guide to Texas...* (New York: Sherman & Smith, 1845).

12. Spinder, Frank M., "The History of Hempstead and the Formation of Waller County," *Southwestern Historical Quarterly*, vol. 63 (Jan. 1960) 404–406.

13. Davidson, Rondel V., "Victor Considerant and the Failure of La Réunion," *Southwestern Historical Quarterly*, vol. 76 (Jan. 1973) 272–296; Cabet, Étienne, "Supplement Al Almanach Icarcen Pour 1848...." (Paris: de E. B. Delenchy, 1847); Bishop, *Lots of Land* 148–149; Kagay, Donald J., "Icaria: An Aborted Utopia on the Texas Frontier," *Southwestern Historical Quarterly*, vol. 116 (Apr. 2013) 359–385.

14. Bishop, *Lots of Land* 232–234, 269–270, 269, 271–275.

## Conclusion

1. Conger, Roger N., "The Tomás De La Vega Eleven League Grant on the Brazos," *Southwestern Historical Quarterly*, vol. 61 (Jan. 1958) 371–382.

# Bibliography


Adams, Ephraim Douglas. *British Interests and Activities in Texas, 1838–1846*. Baltimore: Johns Hopkins University Press, 1910.

Alcorn, Bill. *History of Texas Land*. Austin: General Land Office, 1958.

Almaraz, Félix D., Jr. *The San Antonio Missions and Their System of Land Tenure*. Austin: University of Texas Press, 1989.

Almaraz, Felix D,. Jr., editor. *Inventory of the Rio Grande Missions 1772, San Juan Bautista and San Bernardo*. San Antonio: Center of Archaeological Research. University of Texas at San Antonio, 1980.

*American State Papers, Public Lands: Documents, Legislative and Executive of the Congress of the United States in Relation to Public Lands*. Volume V, January 4, 1828 to January 21, 1834. Washington: Printed by Duff Green, 1834.

Bancroft, Hubert Howe. *History of Arizona and New Mexico, 1530–1888*. Albuquerque: Horn and Wallace, 1889 (1962).

Barker, Eugene C. "The Government of Austin's Colony." *Southwestern Historical Quarterly*. Vol. 21 (Jan. 1918).

______. "Land Speculation as a Cause of the Texas Revolution." *Quarterly of the Texas Historical Association*. Vol. 10 (1906–1907).

______. *Mexico and Texas, 1821–1835*. Dallas: P.L. Turner, 1928.

Bass, Feris A., Jr., and B.R. Brunson, editors. *Fragile Empires: The Texas Correspondence of Samuel Swartwout and James Morgan*. Austin: Shoal Creek Publishers, 1978.

Beers, Henry Putney. *Spanish and Mexican Records of the American Southwest*. Tucson: University of Arizona Press, 1979.

Biesele, Rudolph. *History of the German Settlements in Texas, 1831–1861*. Austin: Eakins Press, 1930/1987.

Bishop, Curtis, and Bascom Giles. *Lots of Land*. Austin: The Steck Company, 1949.

Bowden, J.J. *Spanish and Mexican Land Grants in the Chihuahuan Acquisition*. El Paso: Texas Western Press, 1971.

Brister, Louis E., editor. *John Charles Beales's Rio Grande Colony*. Austin: Texas State Historical Association, 2008.

Brown, Alma Howell. "The Counselor Service of the Republic of Texas." *Southwestern Historical Quarterly*. Vol. 33 (Jan.–Apr. 1930).

Cabet, Étienne. "Supplément à l'Almanach Icarien pour 1848...." Paris: de E.B. Delenchy, 1847.

Cantrell, Gregg. *Stephen F. Austin: Empresario of Texas*. New Haven, Conn.: Yale University Press, 1999.

Castañeda, Carlos. *Our Catholic Heritage in Texas*. 7 Vols. Austin: Von Boeckman Jones, 1936–1950.

Chase, Mary Katherine. *Négociations de la République du Texas en Europe, 1837–1845*. Paris: Libraire Ancienne Honoré Champion, 1932.

Chipman, Donald E. *Texas Through Time: Evading Interpretation*. College Station: Texas A&M University Press, 1991.

______, and Harriet Denise Joseph. *Notable Men and Women of Spanish Texas*. Austin: University of Texas Press, 1999.

______, and ______. *Spanish Texas, 1519–1821* (Revised). Austin: University of Texas Press, 1992/2010.

*Circular No. 26. from the General Land Office showing The Manner of Proceeding to Obtain Title to Public Lands By Purchase, By Location with Warrants or Agricultural College Scrip, By Pre-Emption and Homestead*. Department of the Interior, General Land Office. Washington, D.C., March 10, 1869.

*Circular No. 32, Soldiers and Sailors Homestead Rights*. Department of the Interior, General Land Office. Washington, D.C., May 26, 1922.

*Circular No. 523, Stock-Raising Homestead Act of December 29, 1916 (Instructions)*. Department of the Interior, General Land Office. Washington, D.C., December 4, 1922.

*Circular No. 541, Suggestions to Homesteaders and Persons Desiring to Make Homestead Entries*. Department of the Interior, General Land Office. Washington, D.C., Revised January 16, 1922.

*Circular No. 837, Vacant Public Lands on July 1, 1922*. Department of the Interior, General Land Office. Washington, D.C., July 1, 1922.

Conger, Roger N. "The Tomás de la Vega Eleven League Grant on the Brazos." *Southwestern Historical Quarterly*. Vol. 61 (Jan. 1958).

Connor, Seymour V. *The Peters Colony in Texas*. Austin: Texas State Historical Association, 1959.

*Constitution of the State of West Texas*. Austin: 1869.

Crook, Conella English. *Henry Castro: A Study of Early Colonization in Texas*. San Antonio: St. Mary's University Press, 1988.

Darden, Stephen H. *Abstract of Land Titles of Texas Comprising the Titled, Patented and Located Lands*. Galveston: Shaw and Blaylock, 1878 (2 vols.).

Davidson, Rondel V. "Victor Considérant and the Failure of La Réunion." *Southwestern Historical Quarterly*. Vol. 76 (Jan. 1973).

Davis, John Martin and Others. *Going to Texas. Five Centuries of Texas Maps*. Fort Worth: TCU Press, 2007.

"Decreto Imperial de 5 Septiembre de Para Fomentar La Inmigración 1865." Mexico: Imprenta de Marcano Villanueva, 1866.

Eagleton, Nancy C. "The Mercer Colony of Texas, 1844–1883." *Southwestern Historical Quarterly*. Vol. 39 (Apr. 1938).

Fisher, Ernest G. *Marists and Utopias in Texas: The Lone Star State's Flirtation with Socialism and Communism*. Burnet, Texas: Eakin Press, 1980.

Fisher, Orceneth. *Sketches of Texas in 1840*. Springfield, IL: Walters and Weber Printers, 1841.

Frantz, Joe Bertram. *Lure of the Land: Texas County Maps and the History of Settlement*. College Station: Texas A&M University Press, 1988.

Gammel, Ham Peter Nielsen, compiler. *Laws of Texas, 1822–1897* (10 Volumes). Austin: Gammel, 1898.

Garrison, George P., editor. *Texas Diplomatic Correspondence* (3 Volumes). Washington, D.C.: American Historical Association, G.P.O. 1908/1911.

Garver, Lois. "Benjamin Rush Milam." *Southwestern Historical Quarterly*. Vol. 38 (Oct. 1934).

Giles, Bascom. *History and Disposition of Texas Public Domain*. Austin: Texas General Land Office, 1942.

Gouge, William M. *The Fiscal History of Texas*. Lippincott: Grembo, 1852.

Gould, Florence C. and Patricia M. Pando. *Claiming Their Land: Women Homesteaders in Texas*. El Paso: Texas Western Press. "Southwestern Studies No. 93," 1991.

Graf, Leroy P. "Colonizing Projects in Texas South of the Nueces, 1820–1845." *Southwestern Historical Quarterly*. Vol. 50 (Apr. 1947).

Greaser, Galen D. *Catalogue of the Spanish Collection of the Texas General Land Office*. (2

Volumes). Austin: Texas General Land Office, 2003.
______, and Jesús F. de la Teja. "Instituting Title to Spanish and Mexican Land Grants in the Trans-Nueces." *Southwestern Historical Quarterly.* Vol. 95 (Apr. 1992).
Hammett, A.B.J. *The Empresario Don Martín de León.* Waco: Texian Press, 1973.
Hébert, Rachel Bluntzer. *The Forgotten Colony: San Patricio de Hibernia.* Burnet, Texas: Eakin Press, 1981.
Henderson, Harry McCamey. "The Magee-Gutiérrez Expedition." *Southwestern Historical Quarterly.* Vol. 55 (Jul. 1951).
Henderson, Mary Virginia. "Minor Empresario Contracts for the Colonization of Texas, 1825–1834." *Southwestern Historical Quarterly.* Vols. 31; 32 (Apr., Jun. 1928).
Henson, Margaret Scott. *Samuel May Williams: Early Texas Entrepreneur.* College Station: Texas A&M University Press, 1976.
Herrera, José María. "Visions of a Utopian Texas: Robert Owen's Colonization Scheme." *Southwestern Historical Quarterly.* Vol. 116 (Apr. 2003), 343–356.
Hinojosa, Gilberto Miguel. *A Borderland Town In Transition: Laredo, 1755–1870.* College Station: Texas A&M University Press, 1983.
Hogan, William Ranson. *The Texas Republic: A Societal and Economic History.* Norman: University of Oklahoma Press, 1946.
Hughes, Anne E. *The Beginnings of Spanish Settlement in the El Paso District.* Berkeley: University of California Press, 1914.
Hunt, Richard S., and Jesse F. Randel. *A New Guide to Texas.* New York: Sherman and Smith, 1845.
Kagay, Donald J. "Icaria: An Aborted Utopia on the Texas Frontier." *Southwestern Historical Quarterly.* Vol. 116 (Apr. 2003), 359–385.
Kennedy, William. *Texas: The Rise, Progress and Prospect of the Republic of Texas.* London: R. Hastings, 1841.
Kimball, M.D., translator. *Laws and Decrees of the State of Coahuila and Texas, in Spanish and English*... Houston: Telegraph Power Press, 1839.
Lack, Paul, editor. *The Diary of William Fairfax Gray: From Virginia to Texas, 1835–1837.* Dallas: Southwest Studies, Southern Methodist University, 1997.
Lang, Aldon Socrates. *Financial History of the Public Lands in Texas.* New York: Arno Press, 1932/1979.
Lawler, Ruth Curry. *The Story of Castroville.* Castroville: N.p., 1936.
Livermore, Shaw. *Early American Land Companies: Their Influence on Corporate Development.* New York: The Commonwealth Fund, Columbia University School of Law, 1939.
Luken, Edward Albert. *DeWitt Colony in Texas.* Austin: Jenkins Publishing, 1976.
Manning, William R. "Poinsett's Mission to Mexico: A Discussion of His Interference in International Affairs." *American Journal of International Law.* New York: 1913.
Mauro, Gary. *Land: A History of the Texas General Land Office.* Austin: Texas General Land Office, 1992.
McKitrick, Reuben. *The Public Land System of Texas, 1823–1910.* New York: Arco Press, 1918/1979.
McLean, Malcolm D., editor. *Papers Concerning Robertson's Colony in Texas* (19 Volumes). Fort Worth: Texas Christian University Press (1974–1976). Arlington: University of Texas at Arlington Press (1977–1992).
Miller, Thomas L. "Texas Land Grants to Confederate Veterans and Widows." *Southwestern Historical Quarterly.* Vol. 69 (Jul. 1965).
______. "Texas Land Grants to Veterans." *Southwestern Historical Quarterly.* Vol. 64 (Jan. 1961).
Miller, Thomas Lloyd. *Bounty and Donation Land Grants of Texas, 1835–1888.* Austin: University of Texas Press, 1967.
______. *The Public Lands of Texas 1519–1970.* Norman: University of Oklahoma Press, 1972.
Moore, Francis, Jr. *Map and Description of Texas*.... New York: Tanner and Disturnell, 1840.
Morgenthaler, Jefferson. *Promised Lands: Solms, Castro & Sam Houston's Colonization Contracts.* College Station: Texas A&M University Press, 2009.
Muir, Andrew Forest, editor. *Texas in 1873: An Anonymous, Contemporary Narrative.* Austin: University of Texas Press, 1958.
Newcomb, W.W., Jr. *The Indians of Texas.* Austin: University of Texas Press, 1961.
Parton, Dorothy Martha. *The Diplomatic Career of Joel Roberts Poinsett.* Washington, D.C.: Catholic University of America Press, 1934.
Oberste, William H. *Texas Irish Empresarios and Their Colonists: Power and Hewetson, McMullen and McGloin.* Austin: Von Boeckmann-Jones, 1953/1973.
*Proceedings of the Democratic State Convention.* Austin: State Gazette Job Office, 1871.
Rather, Ethel Ziwley. "DeWitt's Colony." *Quarterly of the Texas State Historical Association.* Vol. 8 (1904–1905).
Reed, S.G. *A History of the Texas Railroad.* Houston: St. Clair Publishing, 1941.
Rock, James L., and W.L. Smith. *Southern and Western Texas Guide for 1878.* St. Louis: A.H. Granger, 1878.
Roemer, Ferdinand. *Texas with Particular Reference to German Immigration and the Physical Appearance of the Country.* San Antonio: Standard Printing, 1935.
Rowland, Kate Mason. "General John Thompson Mason." *Quarterly of the Texas State Historical Association.* Vol. II (Jan. 1908).
Rozek, Barbara J. *Come to Texas: Enticing Immigrants, 1865–1915.* College Station: Texas A&M University Press, 2003.
Rubio, Abel G. *Stolen Heritage: A Mexican-American's Rediscovery of His Family's Lost Land Grant.* Austin: Eakins Press, 1986.
Seed, Patricia. *Ceremonies of Possession in Europe's Conquest of the New World, 1492–1640.* New York: Cambridge University Press, 1995.
Scott, Florence Johnson. *Royal Land Grants North of the Rio Grande, 1777–1821.* Rio Grande City: Texian Press, 1969.
Simmons, Marc. *Spanish Government in New Mexico.* Santa Fe: University of New Mexico Press, 1968.
Smith, George Otis, et al. *Bulletin No. 537, The Classification of the Public Lands.* Department of the Interior, General Land Office, U.S. Geological Survey. Washington, D.C.: General Printing Office, 1913.
Spinder, Frank M. "The History of Hempstead and the Formation of Waller County." *Southwestern Historical Quarterly.* Vol. 63 (Jan. 1960).
*Statistics and Information Concerning the State of Texas.* General Passenger Department of The Missouri and Pacific Railway Co. Woodward and Dicerman Printing Co., St. Louis, 1889.
Steinert, Wilhelm. *North America, Particularly Texas in the Year 1849: A Travel Account.* Dallas: Southwest Studies, Southern Methodist University, 1999.
Sterling, Susanne. *Land Is The Cry: Warren Angus Ferris, Pioneer Surveyor and Founder of Dallas County.* Austin: Texas State Historical Association, 1998.
Streeter, Thomas W. *Bibliography of Texas: 1795–1845.* (5 Volumes). Cambridge: Harvard University Press, 1955.
Taylor, Virginia H. *The Spanish Archives of the General Land Office of Texas.* Austin: The Lone Star Press, 1955.
*Texas Almanac for 1857 with Statistics etc. Relating to Texas.* Galveston: Richardson and Co., 1856.
*Texas State Library, Governor's Message, Coke to Ross, 1874–1891.* Austin: A.C. Baldwin and Sons Printers, 1916.
*Texas Title Guaranty Company. Abstract of Title, No. 76041, By Spanish Government to Antonio Rivas, 1765.* San Antonio (N.D.).
Thornhoff, Robert H. "The Ranch in Texas." *West Texas Historical Association Yearbook.* Vol. 40 (Oct. 1864).
Timmons, Wilbert H. *Tadeo Ortiz: Mexican Colonizer and Reformer.* (Southwestern Studies Monograph No. 43). El Paso: Texas Western Press, 1974.
Triplett, Robert and William F. Gray. *Memorial of the Texian Loan Contractors to the Congress of Texas.* New Orleans: 1837.
Tyler, Ron, Douglas E. Barnett, and Roy R. Barkley, editors. *The New Handbook of Texas.* (6 Volumes). Austin: Texas State Historical Association, 1996.
Van Zant, Lee. *Early Economic Policies of the Government of Texas.* (Southwestern Studies Monograph No. 14). El Paso: Texas Western Press, 1966.
Vigness, David M. "Relations to the Republic of Texas and the Republic of the Rio Grande." *Southwestern Historical Quarterly.* Vol. 39 (Jan. 1954).
______. "Nueva Santander in 1975: A Provisional Inspection by Félix Calleja." *South-*

*western Historical Quarterly* Vol. 75 (Apr. 1972).

Wallace, Ernest, David M. Vigness, and George B. Ward. *Documents of Texas History* (2nd Edition). Austin: State House Press, 1994.

Watkins, Sue, editor. *One League to Each Wind: Accounts of Early Surveying in Texas.* Austin: Von-Boeckmann Printers, 1964.

Weaver, Bobby D. *Castro's Colony: Empresario Development in Texas, 1842–1865.* College Station: Texas A&M University Press, 1985.

Weber, David J. *The Spanish Frontier in North America.* New Haven: Yale University Press, 1992.

White, Gifford. *Character Certificates in the General Land Office.* Baltimore: Genealogical Publishing, 1985.

William, Elgin. *The Animating Pursuit of Speculation: Land Traffic in the Annexation of Texas.* New York: Columbia University Press, 1949.

Winchester, Robert Glenn. *James Pinckney Henderson: Texas' First Governor.* San Antonio: Naylor, 1971.

Wright, Bill. *The Tiguas: Pueblo Indians of Texas.* El Paso: Texas Western Press, 1985.

______, and E. John Gesick, Jr. *The Texas Kickapoo: Keeper of Tradition.* El Paso: Texas Western Press, 1996.

Yoakum, H. *History of Texas: From Its First Settlement in 1685 to Its Annexation to the United States in 1846* (2 Volumes). New York: Redfield, 1855.

# Index

Page numbers in bold italics indicate pages with illustrations.